What's the Use of Race?

DATE DUE

What's the Use of Race?

Modern Governance and the Biology of Difference

edited by Ian Whitmarsh and David S. Jones

The MIT Press
Cambridge, Massachusetts
London, England

For information about special quantity discounts, please email special_sales@mitpress.mit.edu

This book was set in Stone Sans and Stone Serif by Toppan Best-set Premedia Limited. Printed and bound in the United States of America.

Library of Congress Cataloging-in-Publication Data

What's the use of race? : modern governance and the biology of difference / edited by Ian Whitmarsh and David S. Jones.
     p.   cm.
Includes bibliographical references and index.
ISBN 978-0-262-51424-8 (pbk. : alk. paper)
1. Genetics—Social aspects. 2. Racism. I. Whitmarsh, Ian, 1975– II. Jones, David S. (David Shumway), 1970–
QH438.7.W53   2010
323.11—dc22
                                                                                2009037118

10 9 8 7 6 5 4 3 2 1

Contents

Caring

Looking Forward

Acknowledgments

This book is the final product of a series of conversations begun at a conference hosted by the Center for the Study of Diversity in Science, Technology, and Medicine (CSD) in April 2008. The CSD was founded at the Massachusetts Institute of Technology (MIT) in June 2000 by a generous grant from The Andrew W. Mellon Foundation. Professor Evelynn M. Hammonds envisioned a center that would pursue two primary goals. Scholars would examine the impact of diversity on the theory and practice of science, medicine, and technology, as well as the contributions of racial and ethnic minorities to those fields.

Starting in 2006, the CSD organized a series of three conferences that explored questions of race and technology. The first, "Race, Pharmaceuticals, and Medical Technology," focused on BiDil, the first (and still only) medication approved by the Food and Drug Administration for use in a specific racial or ethnic group, people who self-identify as black. Many of the papers from this conference were published as a special symposium in the *Journal of Law, Medicine & Ethics* in the fall of 2008. Generalizing beyond pharmaceuticals, the 2007 conference, "The Business of Race and Science," examined how the modern sciences of race have been used to justify a series of race-specific products and policies, from cosmetics, vitamins, and jogging shoes to tests of genetic ancestry. The final conference, "What's the Use of Race," broadened the conversation still further, asking how race has been, and should be, used in governance, with examples drawn from law, science and medicine. A subset of the papers presented were expanded into full length essays and then revised substantially to produce the essays found in this volume.

The conference and this resulting volume would not have been possible without the assistance of many people. Rosalind Williams and David Mindell, the chairs of the Program in Science, Technology, and Society (STS) at MIT, and Philip Khoury and Deborah Fitzgerald, the deans of the School of Humanities, Arts, and Social Sciences, provided an institutional home and much needed support for the CSD. Debbie Meinbres, who orchestrated public programs for STS, handled most of the planning and logistical details that made each of the three conferences a seemingly effortless success.

The conferences themselves would not have been possible without the thoughtful contributions of all of the speakers, as well as the active participation of a surprisingly dynamic and challenging audience. Many of our colleagues at MIT, especially Stefan Helmreich, Erica James, Heather Paxson, Susan Silbey, Mike Fischer, David Kaiser, Beth Coleman, Melissa Nobles, and Abha Sur provided useful advice as well. Evelynn Hammonds, despite her new roles at Harvard University, always remained a valuable source of wisdom.

At MIT Press, Marguerite Avery has been an exceedingly encouraging and productive editor. Erin Shoudy, Marcy Ross, and Deborah Cantor-Adams guided us through the maze of details of the publishing process. Continued support from The Andrew W. Mellon Foundation allowed us to see this project through to completion.

None of these essays are expected to provide the last word on these subjects. We hope, however, that they will stimulate on-going dialog on these vital issues for science and society.

1 Governance and the Uses of Race

Ian Whitmarsh and David S. Jones

Race in America at the start of the twenty-first century remains in a turbulent ferment. The erosion of segregation in schools, workplaces, marriages, and politics—an erosion symbolized by the election of the first black president—is accompanied by, and masks, persistent racial inequalities and injustices. Although some crises, such as Hurricane Katrina or the state of American prisons, have brought continuing racial injustice into the public eye and led to calls for remediation, legislatures and courts in the United States have retreated from affirmative action and other traditional policies that sought to compensate for the history of racial inequality. Yet even as the government backs away from race-based social welfare policies, it has established the importance of race in medical research and practice: federally funded research must now examine racial difference, and both the Patent and Trademark Office (PTO) and the Food and Drug Administration (FDA) have sanctioned the concept of race-specific pharmaceuticals.

Such government action on race is in line with broad interest in addressing racial disparities through technological means. The marketplace is now flush with products advertised as solutions for racial injustice. Race-specific vitamins offer to rescue dark-skinned peoples from the vitamin deficiencies they suffer as a result of having moved— or been moved by slavery—from the sunny tropics to temperate climates. Race-specific genetic tests can recover the ancestral histories of African Americans whose heritage had been erased by the slave trade. Nike has even marketed race-specific jogging shoes, designed specifically for the supposedly thicker feet of American Indians, to combat the epidemic of obesity and diabetes on impoverished reservations.

The current tumult in race commerce and governance can be traced, in part, to recent and surprising developments in the science of genetics and race (Koenig, Lee, and Richardson 2008). Coming out of the civil rights era, many scientists and scholars joined a consensus that found race to be nothing more than an arbitrary social construction. They hoped that policies would be enacted to address the existing social injustices that had been created by past false beliefs about race and racial hierarchies. Once this remediation work was done, race would be able to disappear, taking its place among history's other misguided and unnecessary concepts. Such social reforms never came to fruition: race continues to be a powerful social force in America, shaping the distribution of health, wealth, and power in this country. The failure of reform and the persistence of racial inequality are not a surprise. What is unexpected, however, is the way in which the relevance of race as a social, legal, and medical category has been reinvigorated by science, especially genetics.

The persistence and revival of race science calls for critical reflection. New knowledge, practices, and products have elicited excitement and curiosity alongside the concern and confusion of social analysts. This book seeks to intervene on this conundrum. Generations of scholars have turned their analytical talents to the uses and misuses of race. What can be said about those areas in which some use of race is considered still warranted amid this critique? What can we make of the appeal of race in spheres in which some attention to difference is an ethical necessity? The essays in this collection look to areas in which difference must be addressed—in medicine, law, and science—to ask how we can most appropriately understand and use race in our era of genomics. Taken as a whole, this collection complements existing work on genomics and race (Koenig, Lee, and Richardson 2008) by focusing on the promise and dangers of genetics, race, and governance.

Genetics has been promised to be, for the twenty-first century, what physics was for the twentieth century. It has captured the public imagination and offers solutions to an astonishing range of problems. Genetic research hopes to unlock the secrets of disease, yielding improved diagnosis and treatment. Genetics will decipher the mysteries of evolution, improving our knowledge of the history of life on earth and of the human race. Genetics can restore justice to those falsely convicted, with many incarcerated inmates having now been set free on the basis of new genetic analyses. Genetics even offers the ultimate in consumer indulgence for the hyperrich: full sequencing of your genome.

This rise of genetics, in terms of both its science and public profile, has had an enormous and unexpected impact on race (Koenig, Lee, and Richardson 2008). Until quite recently, many scientists and politicians had hoped and thought that genetics would show once and for all that race had no basis in science. When Bill Clinton, Tony Blair, Craig Venter, and Francis Collins shared a stage in June 2000 to celebrate the completion of the Human Genome Project, they focused on the finding of human sameness: with all humans sharing 99.9 percent of their genetic code, theories of racial difference or hierarchy could not possibly have any basis in genetics. As Clinton stated so eloquently, "I believe one of the great truths to emerge from this triumphant expedition inside the human genome is that in genetic terms, all human beings, regardless of race, are more than 99.9 percent the same. . . . The most important fact of life on this Earth is our common humanity" (Clinton 2000, paras. 17–18). Within only a few years, however, scientists began to argue that the degree of variation was actually larger than this, and that this variation maps naturally onto conventional categories of race.

These developments draw on the long history of changing meanings of race and biology. Human plurality—bodily, culturally, physiologically—has long been a seductive object of study going back to classical history. The Mediterranean basin, for instance, collected a diverse enough group of people into a small region that early Greek writers, such as Herodotus and the authors of the Hippocratic Corpus, often commented on the existence and consequences of the differences. Difference here did not connote fixed racial types. Ancient Greek medicine, for instance, focused on environmental malleability and attributed the plurality of appearances, susceptibilities, and customs to the influence of climate, foods, and modes of living (see Stepan 1982). This focus on malleability persisted into the early modern period. The early colonists of Europe's age of exploration and conquest worried about the ways in which they, and especially their children, might be transformed by their move to exotic environments (Harrison 1996; Chaplin 2001). The eighteenth century saw a transition in thinking about difference, as naturalists attempted to create systematic classifications of human variability that were complete (see Augstein 1999; Banton 2000; Stepan 1982). In 1781 Blumenbach used skull formations to classify all humans into five varieties: Caucasian, Ethiopian, Malay, Mongol, and American. By the nineteenth century, such classifications were taken to describe radically distinct groups with internal physiological logics, as in Cuvier's hierarchies of intelligence, moral aptitude, and body (see Banton 2000; Graves 2001; Stepan 1982). Historian Nancy Stepan (1982, 18) notes the significance of these attempts at total classification: "differences that Blumenbach had treated as relatively superficial racial markers, such as head or nose shapes, were now treated as signs of deeper differences in biological organization." This transition inverted the pre-nineteenth-century relationship of environmental malleability and human variation: the variable contexts and experiences that had shaped bodies and physical attributes were now a background, revealing the rigidity of the internal processes that shaped the progress of each race. This approach—by which visible physical characteristics are quantitatively measured to indicate the abilities, character, and history of peoples—became foundational to nineteenth-century uses of race. The shift toward the intrinsic character of living beings contributed to the formation of what has been called the *epistemic space* of heredity (Müller-Wille and Rheinberger 2007). By the mid-nineteenth century, notions of heredity and race were firmly entrenched among the elites of western Europe and North America.

The mode of classification was more stable than the content. Stepan (1982) shows that the science of race in the nineteenth century created hierarchies of, variably, Africans, Mediterraneans, Jews, Caucasians, Asiatics, Gypsies, and other groups. Racial theories were also used to constitute political legitimacy of nation-states, as western

Europe was divided into the racial types of Celts and Anglo-Saxons, Gauls and Franks, Germans and Slavs (Augstein 1999). This relational character of racial classification—its ability to integrate divergent, sometimes contradictory contents—has been foundational to its extensive scientific and medical use (Ernst 1999). But this radically variable content did not preclude extraordinarily precise attempts to measure it. Technological measurements were critical to the nineteenth-century science of race; for example, skull measurements were used to give exact numbers on intellect, moral worth, capacity for civilization, level of spirituality, cultural complexity, technological sophistication, and so on. The result was a science that examines visibly physical characteristics as constituting historical trajectories of biologically distinguishable populations (Hammonds and Herzig 2009).

Blood was central to this nineteenth-century science of race. Taboos of mixing and the association with disease in perspectives on immigrants, populations in the colonies, and those considered black in the United States revealed an obsessive interest in race being carried in the blood (see Banton 2000; Foucault 1997/2003; Jacobson 1998; Stoler 1995). In the twentieth-century United States, this scientific link between blood, race, and disease came under the purview of the new science of genetics. In the 1920s and 1930s, the genetics of race was mutually constituted with the genetics of disease (Kevles 1985/1995). Racially mixed populations were valued as genetically variable, taking the (conceptual) place of hybrids made in controlled experiments. This mixing relied on the idea of pure groups, whether as abstract ideal populations or as in existence somewhere (i.e., the races prior to or unaffected by hybridization). The scientific interest in the genetics of racial subgroups helped generate the emerging human genetics (e.g., in blood group research). Such analyses of race reframed former meanings, geneticizing blood-race links, pure races, and the associations of disease and race. In the United States, sickle-cell anemia exemplified the new ties made between blood, race, disease, and genetics in the early twentieth century. Keith Wailoo (1997, 134–161) shows the ways in which Mendelian genetics was used in the 1920s to shape the meaning of sickle-cell anemia as a "potential disease" within "negro blood." Such links between diseases, races, blood, and heredity were implicated in brutal practices toward particular populations, as Wailoo, Kevles, and others have documented, including immigrant sterilization and other eugenics programs (Kevles 1985/1995, 2004), faith in the eventual extinction of American Indians (Jones 2004), medical discrimination (Wailoo 1997), and the Tuskegee study on syphilis (see Brandt 1978; Jones 1981; Reverby 2009).

The increasingly authoritarian interventions of eugenics began to trigger a backlash in the 1930s. Skeptics worried that eugenic science had overreached and that policies simply implemented long-standing race and class biases. The links between race science and Nazism had a decisive impact on the sciences of race and eugenics in the United States in the 1940s and 1950s. In her historical analysis of race in twentieth-century science, Reardon (2005) shows that new moral and political stances were taken in opposition to the association of racial distinctions with moral and mental hierarchies. Population geneticists distinguished their work from political implications that were no longer tenable in the climate of the United States. Reardon points out that these shifts did not include a widespread rejection of a biological basis for racial distinctions; instead, geneticists and anthropologists attempted to delineate more precisely the biological meaning of race. The genetic links of blood, race, and disease became explicit objects of evaluation in this process. This reanalysis led some postwar anthropologists to argue that the biological concept of race was a myth (Livingstone 1962; Montagu 1942/1997). They worked to shift focus, instead, onto ethnicity, a cultural category, in place of race, a biological category.

Intensive study of ethnicity did not resolve long-standing dilemmas. First, race persisted as a relevant category of analysis. Second, these studies revealed that both race and ethnicity functioned as radically relational categories. Focus on the Americas alone reveals this plurality. In Trinidad the category "mixed" (Afro-Trinidadian and Indo-Trinidadian) unsettles U.S. strict divisions. A similar vexation of American racial binaries is also found in countries such as Jamaica and Brazil, where fine distinctions of skin tone are paramount, making for multiple categories within what would be one category of black in the United States. In Canada, as in much of Latin America, markers of indigeneity make racial divisions that do not map onto American ones. And these are only the official uses of race. Anthropologists have shown that ethnic identities are contradictory and multiple in ways not reducible to racial classifications throughout the world. Racial and ethnic categorizations interweave unpredictably with gender, class, and religion in discourses distinguishing others (see, e.g., Avruch 2002; Gabbert 2004; Hartigan 1999; James 1999; Khan 2004; Lesser 1999; Warren 2001; Whitmarsh 2008). Some biologists and population geneticists joined in this effort to delegitimize race. Most famously, Richard Lewontin (1972) argued that the very structure of human variability—with most variation existing within populations and very little variation distinguishing between populations—undermined the scientific credibility of race (see also Bolnick 2008; Dupré 2008; Marks 2008).

This emerging anthropological, historical, and biological critique of the concept of race as a biological category, however, never managed to contain the ideas and practices of race. Despite now long-standing critiques of the concept, race continues to thrive as a category of analysis among scholars and pundits and in conventional wisdom. Researchers routinely collect data about racial and ethnic subpopulations in their studies. Journals in fields as diverse as genetics, public health, and sociology report data on race and ethnicity and use these variables as significant factors in their analyses. This pursuit of race has produced overwhelming documentation of racial disparities, from birthrates to education, income, crime, punishment, disease, medical treatment, and life expectancy. As a result, genetic research on race is often framed in terms of social justice (Lee 2008). Meanwhile, courts use racial analyses to interpret DNA tests and predict the appearance of perpetrators, and the FDA allows the marketing of race-based pharmaceuticals. These ongoing practices have found new legitimacy in recent reanalyses of human genetic variation that seem to reverse Lewontin's claims. The completion of the Human Genome Project has facilitated large-scale genomic analysis of human populations, much of which uses "ancestry" to map genetics onto traditional racial categories (see Bolnick et al. 2007; Dupré 2008; Nelson 2008). This all contributes to what Troy Duster (2005) has identified as the molecular reinscription of race.

With genetics fueling old ideas about race and race difference, it is important to analyze and understand the ways in which race is being used today. At one level, this is a descriptive pursuit: exactly how is race used by the government (e.g., U.S. Bureau of the Census, PTO, FDA, National Institutes of Health [NIH]), by researchers (e.g., NIH Revitalization Act, reporting data by racial groups), in courts (e.g., DNA fingerprinting), in health care (e.g., studies of health disparities, efforts against them), or by businesses (e.g., GenSpec, Nike)? Cataloging these uses of race is crucial to making visible and drawing attention to an important development that has gone largely unnoticed. One recent book makes a substantial contribution to this endeavor (Koenig, Lee, and Richardson 2008), offering the first interdisciplinary discussion of the use of race in the advent of genomic research and tests. The authors explore the uses of race in science, markets, and media, with specific analyses of population genomics, ancestry tests, and medical research. The editors emphasize the need for continuing and deeper interdisciplinary dialogue about these issues.

We hope to build on this start by exploring what happens when the descriptive question becomes a normative question. *What's the Use of Race* asks both how race *is* being used and how race *should* be used. Should the concept of race be invoked to further the goals of science or social justice? Do racial and ethnic distinctions produce natural categories for scholarly or political analysis? Do the benefits of including diverse populations in research outweigh the potential harm caused by reifying racial and ethnic distinctions? Will efforts to improve the precision of these categories with subtler distinctions based on ancestry or genetic markers increase the utility of the resulting data? What role do funding agencies (whether governmental or philanthropic) have as gatekeepers for the appropriate use of racial and ethnic categories? What hopes and conflicts are embedded in analyses of race as a scientific, medical, or social category? This book probes these quandaries by bringing together researchers in medicine, science, law, and social science to explore the competing interests that make studies of race both feared and desired.

The history of BiDil illustrates this well (Jones, Dorr, and Pollock 2008). In the 1980s, medical researchers proposed that a combination of two existing medicines, hydralazine and isosorbide dinitrate, both of which affect nitric oxide metabolism, would have synergistic effects for the treatment of heart failure. Although initial clinical data were disappointing, retrospective analyses were used to suggest that the combination might actually have benefited the few African American patients in the trial. Obtaining a patent on the use of this combination specifically in this one group of patients, the researchers consequently conducted a new clinical trial that only enrolled patients who self-identified as black. This trial found that BiDil substantially reduced mortality from heart failure. Supported by the National Medical Association, the Association of Black Cardiologists, the National Association for the Advancement of Colored People, and the Congressional Black Caucus, BiDil won approval from the FDA in 2005. This was the first and, so far, only time that the FDA has approved a medication specifically for use in a specifically described racial or ethnic group. Although the FDA has vigorously defended its decision (Temple and Stockbridge 2007; Ellison et al. 2008), the approval of BiDil has received scathing criticisms from a range of scholars, who have argued that it represents a cynical exploitation of loopholes in U.S. patent regulation (Kahn 2004) or a naive effort to redress social injustice through pharmaceuticals (Roberts 2008).

Similar tensions run through the broader literature on health disparities. Even as medical outcomes are routinely differentiated by race, their causes remain open to interpretation: differences in genetics, physiology, socioeconomic status, and access to medical care are noted as potential causes of disease disparities. Genetic uses of race in medicine show similarly troubling reconfigurations of older notions of essential differences (see Tate and Goldstein 2008). Ethnographies have shown that the strange contradictions and ambiguities of race also extend to the science of genetics (Dingel and Koenig 2008; Fullwiley 2007; Montoya 2007; Reardon 2008; Whitmarsh 2008).

Similar critiques can be made of the other commercial ventures inspired by the new sciences of race. Genetic tests of ancestry stand accused of radically overextending claims about what they actually deliver (Bolnick et al. 2007; Dupré 2008; Nelson 2008), with California going so far as to issue a cease-and-desist order to several prominent companies. New attention to people with "skin of color" from dermatologists and Nike's assertions of race-specific jogging shoes have more to do with identity marketing than with any credible claim of addressing substantial biological differences in an effort to alleviate inequalities. This commerce in racialized products has a certain fervor: there is a mania to the use of racial and ethnic categories to sell shoes, skin products, and ancestry tests. In the United States, such commercialism is supposed to have a certain excess: marketers are expected to make a pitch, which the customer knows is exaggerated. Americans have long associated commerce with hucksterism, and the claims of marketing are seen as having, at best, a dubious truth to them.

But if the market in racialized products is expected to have a certain mania, what of governance, those practices by which the nation-state studies and acts on its population? The claims of the absurdity of race in commerce often imply the existence of contrasting and appropriate uses of race in the arenas of law, medicine, and science. Arguments about race from these institutions often carry an authority not given to marketplace claims. What happens as these arenas employ biological meanings of race?

Racial and ethnic designations have been integral to the nation-state since its inception (see Bhabha 1994; Comaroff and Comaroff 1991; Fanon 1963; Foucault 1997/2003; Prakash 1999; Stoler 1995). As Frantz Fanon (1963) showed, the colonial state tied bodily health, population health, and eradication of disease intimately to moral worth, religious conversion, and proper and civil behavior. Michel Foucault (1978) called such a set of governing techniques around the body *biopolitics*: state governance was constituted in an increasing array of rules and interventions around sex, health, and illness. Biopolitics was dispersed in state institutions such as the army, schools, and medicine. A proliferation of economic, military, and medical analyses and practices around the population were produced to maximize economic and social productivity. This configuration of knowledge and techniques tied together the social body and the subject's body. Anthropologists, historians, and sociologists have since taken up Foucault's concept of biopolitics to interrogate the way populations are categorized and acted on, ranging from public health ventures and biotechnological endeavors to military interventions and penal systems. For example, the configuration of commercial, governmental, and nongovernmental organizations (NGOs) around AIDS in Africa and South America has been explored by anthropologists looking at how populations are defined for treatment and what groups and health interventions are excluded (see Biehl 2007; Fassin 2007; Nguyen 2005). Such literature has explored the set of techniques, policies, and practices that govern sexuality, health, and bodies in different locales: the ways that new techniques, forms of power, and ethics take shape around life itself (see also Rabinow 1992; Rose 2007; Sunder Rajan 2006; Whitmarsh 2009).

Through biopolitics and the idioms of race, the state has revealed its contradictory impulses. It acknowledges the importance of privacy, while maintaining an obsession with watching and documenting, routinely focused on immigrants and poorer urban communities. The heralding of individual freedom allows constraints on sexuality to be imposed, from laws banning miscegenation to eugenic sterilization programs that target poor minorities. Acting for the sanctity of life and public safety entails a police system marked by brutality and a death penalty whose burden has fallen heavily on minorities. Caring for the ill includes categorizing those unfit to be cared for, and racialized populations have been alternately left outside the system and exposed to the most regressive aspects of state power, at times in the name of "public health." And amid the rhetoric welcoming others to join our inclusive and tolerant polity, the state repeatedly cordons off its borders through racially selective immigration policies.

At the center of changes in the governance of race is technology. As forensics, medical practice, and regulations of scientific research increasingly attempt to address difference, they all rely on genetic technologies as the foundation of authority for claims around race. Genetic technology promises to make explicit what had once only been assumed. Traditional racial categorization relied on physical appearance, especially skin color and hair color and texture; but as has been well known, looks can be deceiving. Genetics now offers a seemingly more fundamental method of differentiation: the analysis of genetic sequences. To the extent that we are products of our genes, the sequence contains fundamental information about individual identity and can, in theory, serve as a fundamental measure of difference. This has made genetics irresistibly appealing to those interested in difference, fueling the questions this book addresses.

Biopolitics, governance, and race all raise fundamental questions about how we define ourselves, both biologically and socially. How do we understand our biological relationships to people beyond our families? How do we situate ourselves in society, and what obligations do we feel toward others? What are the intersections of biology and citizenship? It often seems counterintuitive to think about citizenship and biology. After all, citizenship is traditionally seen as a phenomenon of civic behavior (e.g., obeying laws, voting, etc.). But increasingly biological, especially medical, concerns come under the domain of citizenship, from government concern about health behaviors (e.g., smoking, diet) to citizens' concerns about access to and quality of health care. In these domains, individuals, families, and communities make use of scientific designations to identify themselves for recognition by the state and NGOs. Central to all of these issues are questions of difference. How is difference defined? How is it relevant? This book explores areas in which the state is obligated to address difference, and especially racial difference, in forensics, medicine, and scientific research.

Amid the talk of a future of personalized medicine and individualized identification, these chapters analyze the ways race becomes part of new scientific, medical, and legal techniques. How does the precision of genetic technologies give credence to racial categories and associations in forensics? What problematic connections of race, blood, and illness persist in biomedical techniques attempting to address race and disease disparities? How do concepts of ethnicity, diversity, and inclusion undermine or instantiate older concepts of race in the science of genomics and biobanking? In exploring these issues, the collection addresses how these legal, medical, and scientific institutions might think about race without reification amid the increasing use of genomic technologies. The authors draw on extensive ethnographic, historical, and epidemiological research to show the problems and possibilities found in addressing difference in governance in an era of genomic technologies.

We have organized the chapters into three sections—"Ruling" (law and regulation), "Knowing" (science), and "Caring" (medicine)—in an attempt to reflect the three spheres of governance. Analyses of governance from Weber to Foucault have shown that these domains are mutually constitutive: that knowing is a kind of ruling, caring is a kind of regulating, and ruling is framed in how a population is known. Each of these sections explores this interplay in the modern governance of race.

These explorations begin with analyses of the legal and regulatory uses of the new genetics of race. The first section focuses on the areas of research regulation and forensics to see how genetic techniques of determining race are being integrated into the courtroom, law enforcement, and scientific oversight. In chapter 2, Jonathan Kahn discusses the use of race in presenting DNA evidence in criminal cases. When DNA fingerprinting was introduced in the 1980s, only a few genetic loci could be tested; probabilities were calculated within racial categories to increase their significance. Whatever utility this practice had, Kahn shows that the precision of genotyping technology today, based on an increasing number of loci, makes this use of race with DNA evidence entirely superfluous—yet this use persists, creating strange but common statistics in the courtroom, such as one in two billion African Americans versus one in three billion Caucasians. Kahn argues that "the only thing that race adds to the presentation of such DNA evidence is race itself." Race is added ostensibly to refine the evidence but, in fact, functions to associate the defendant with the crime through long-standing racial associations with violence. Kahn draws attention to the precision of DNA techniques to show the imprecision of racial designations: he finds a lack of attention to the technical complexities of using race among forensic DNA experts, which contrasts with the attention given to the technical sophistication of genetic technologies. Self-identification or visual ascertainment by police officers is uncritically accepted in generating racialized databases. Kahn argues that such unexamined means of identification would be disallowed for other types of data and evidence. In Kahn's analysis, the continued use of race in the courtroom to generate bizarre numbers is a flawed practice created out of the inertia of racial categories imprecisely used in racial databases and courtroom evidence. The law looks to the authority of scientific databases to justify such use, creating a self-perpetuating system of racialized evidence that has long been obviated by the same scientific technologies that supposedly underpin it.

In chapter 3, Pamela Sankar explores a new kind of racial profiling, forensic DNA phenotyping (FDP), which is poised to emerge into law enforcement practice. FDP is designed to provide law enforcement with a verbal portrait on which to base a search for suspects. Sankar notes the radical break of FDP from the use of racial identification and DNA in the courtroom that Kahn discusses. Rather than being used to confirm a suspect's identification, FDP is used to predict it. Sankar argues that this shift from genotypes associated with populations to individual profiles can create spurious searches that play into existing stereotypes of racial profiling. She explores how the authority accorded DNA gives new importance to racial designations: there is an acknowledgment that police either eyeballing or asking about racial identity is fallible, unscientific, and open to misuse—but who would dispute DNA? In this account, the authority attributed to DNA takes on a life of its own. Sankar shows that as DNA enters new arenas of law enforcement, it interacts with an older calculus of racial identification and assumptions, giving new authority to designations long problematized.

Steven Epstein closes this section with an analysis of how the research regulatory system in the United States has attempted to address race. With the 1993 NIH Revitalization Act, federally funded researchers faced a mandate to include diverse populations—by race, gender, and ethnicity—in their research. Epstein explores how interacting interests and institutions converged on this policy as a solution to the problem of race and health inequalities in the United States. He then describes the ways in which implementation of this policy has proven more complicated than anticipated, concluding with a discussion of possible alternative ways of addressing difference in biomedical research.

The second section of this collection turns from law to science, from the work of ruling to the work of knowing. These authors explore large-scale biological research projects to learn how race implicitly or explicitly becomes part of the genomic science that attempts to address human diversity. In chapter 5, Simon M. Outram and George T. H. Ellison set the stage by providing a taxonomy of the criticisms that have been leveled at the use of race as a biological characteristic in genetics and biomedicine. These critiques include social, genetic, and ethical misgivings: the lack of genetically distinct populations along racial lines; the reification of what are fluid and relational categories into biological and stable ones; the instability in the measurement techniques of changing categories over time and between countries; and the stigmatization and preclusion of attention to social causes of health disparities potentially entailed. Outram and Ellison depict a give-and-take between the use of race as biological and the critique of race as a social construct. As they show, human genetics research addressing race is an attempt to address health disparities, carrying a social justice argument that also undergirds the critiques of the biological notion of race. One of the consequences of this integration of the social critique into biomedical and genetic approaches has been that the term "ethnicity" has replaced "race" in medical research. In the process, while ostensibly drawing attention to a contingent identity, ethnicity is frequently reified as a given and immutable characteristic, according to Outram and Ellison. In their view, this uneven inclusion of criticisms into genetic and biomedical approaches constitutes a "selective engagement." As a result, the ambiguity of racial categorization is employed to give credence to an underlying biological reality that only genetics or other biological research can determine. In this analysis, the creation of biological knowledge about populations is incorporating an interpretation of racial categories as politicized, ambiguous, and sociopolitical but leaves a biological reality to race intact.

In chapter 6, Richard Tutton, Andrew Smart, Richard Ashcroft, Paul Martin, and George T. H. Ellison take up how scientists themselves see this ambiguity in racial categorization. If, as Dorothy Roberts argues in chapter 12 of this volume, a genetic concept of race is central to the emerging concept of biocitizenship, muting attention to older ideas of race, Tutton and colleagues explore the point where these two forms of identification most explicitly interact. They explore the use of self-identification to establish racial and ethnic categories in large-scale, population-based biobanks, focusing on the British government's UK Biobank. Self-identification is the established technique in the United States and United Kingdom wherever governance addresses difference, including census, hospitals, prisons, and research. The authors draw on interviews with medical researchers studying common diseases and responses to medications to see how they envision the troubled shift from self-identification to biomedical or biological categories of race. The researchers interviewed depict self-identification as problematic for biomedical results, particularly framed in terms of a lack of standardization of categories and incorrect responses. Actual race or ethnicity is considered a real aspect of an individual that self-identification or other sociocultural forms of determining are flawed (but practical) tools for revealing. This actual race or ethnicity is, by turns, considered "genetic ethnicity," or "ancestry," or population history. As a result, practice often differs from explicit policy in such genetic research, and those administering questionnaires use physical observation to determine ethnicity or race. In large-scale genomics research like UK Biobank, the idea of race as a social, historical construct creates an uneasy perspective on the means by which the government generates a science of population and biology among its practitioners.

In chapter 7, Amy Hinterberger examines what happens when the creation of genomic knowledge about race, ethnicity, and populations becomes a national enterprise. The Canadian government has launched a federal endeavor, Genome Canada, to fund and manage genomics research. In looking at two sites of genomics-related research, the chapter traces national genealogies of citizenship and identity to demonstrate how racialized histories have come to shape the politics of inclusion in contemporary population genomics projects in Canada. Hinterberger draws on ethnographic work among Canadian researchers and bioethicists to show that the concepts of multiculturalism and diversity in genomics research, at times, transform social distinctions into stabilized biological ones, as the government grapples with how to include indigenous populations. She argues that the mapping of race, ethnicity, and population by genomics, like other cartographies, carries political and social histories. In her reading, there are continuities between the biopolitical practices found in colonial history and the government's current interest in including aboriginal populations, and other population groups, as a genetically unique group to be researched. Indeed, the meaning of diversity is at stake in the new genomics. As genomics projects recruit aboriginal groups and the founding populations of Quebec as genetically distinct populations, multicultural science comes to mean the inclusion of what are considered biologically distinct peoples. In turn, such groups can use life science institutionalization to make claims on the nation-state. Hinterberger and Tutton and colleagues join other ethnographers in revealing that the rhetoric of globalization can mask the fact that the nation-state is at the heart of the new genomics (see Pálsson and Rabinow 1999; Sunder Rajan 2006). In light of the growing number of national genomics strategies and the global aspects of major population genomic research projects, Hinterberger argues that the task should be not only to consider how race may be used in these projects, but to attend to the diverse histories and multiple meanings of race and ethnicity that compose *biosocialities*.

In chapter 8, Joan H. Fujimura, Ramya Rajagopalan, Pilar N. Ossorio, and Kjell A. Doksum use a sociomaterial approach to explore variations in concepts and technologies used in human genetic variation studies as they examine how race does, and does not, get used in new genomic studies of human disease. Somewhat in response to recent debates about and arguments against the use of race in biomedical genetics research, some geneticists have attempted to construct technologies for finding disease-related genetic markers without employing notions of race or ethnicity. Through ethnographic methods, Fujimura and colleagues investigate these attempts and focus, in particular, on the work of medical and population geneticists who emphasize that they are *accounting for* population differences due to different "ancestries," rather than *assessing* differences among racial groups. The authors examine the relationships between the notions of ancestry and race by examining the theories and practices that geneticists use to construct ancestry measures. Although one could regard ancestry as a concept produced using population genetics tools and race as a sociocultural set of understandings, the two are not so clearly separated in scientific or popular cultural deployments. By comparing the construction of ancestry in genome-wide association studies (GWAS) versus admixture mapping studies, they show that just as race is a socially constructed set of categories, so ancestry is also a constructed concept. They conclude that the relationship between race and ancestry is intricate and difficult to disentangle, which helps to explain the difficulties of separating the reading practices of consumers from the production practices of scientists. Nevertheless, they argue that with caution and care, GWAS technologies can provide alternative means to conduct searches for genetic markers associated with complex diseases, without relying on race or ethnic categories.

Although its implementation has proven problematic, the NIH Revitalization Act addressed a serious problem in the United States. The science of race and disease has produced a wealth of literature correlating race with disparities in disease prevalence, diagnosis, treatment, and mortality and morbidity rates (Good et al. 2002; Graves 2001; Smedley, Stith, and Nelson 2002). For instance, African Americans have higher mortality rates for tuberculosis, diabetes, pneumonia, ulcers, and heart disease (Graves

2001). Researchers have shown disparities in health insurance, health care delivery and availability, and exposure to hazardous waste and environmental toxins (Graves 2001, Smedley, Stith, and Nelson 2002). African Americans and Hispanic populations have been found to have higher rates of asthma in the United States, with considerably higher morbidity and mortality rates (National Center for Health Statistics n.d.; Nsieh-Jefferson 2003). As biomedicine addresses these disparities, race is integrated into attempts to interpret, treat, and diagnose patients. The final section explores what happens to race in the clinic, medical education, and medical research, as race is used to understand inequities of health and illness.

In chapter 9, Jay S. Kaufman and Richard S. Cooper examine the use of racial categories in the clinic to make diagnostic and treatment decisions. They show that "significant differences" detected in research at the population level are often mistranslated by clinicians into decisions at the individual level. As the authors point out, the new genomic medicine, while promising a "post-racial" approach, continues to draw on outmoded concepts of race. Kaufman and Cooper argue that the use of race to make medical decisions, like other clinical practices, should be subject to evidentiary assessment. Toward this end, they recommend a model for analyzing the utility of employing race in making clinical decisions in the case of any given condition. They show that currently used techniques of evidentiary assessment in medicine, when applied to current diseases thought to be racially specific, usually reveal that the current use of race to make medical decisions is not a rational practice. They begin with the example of sickle-cell anemia, often considered the paradigmatic racially specific disease, to show that despite the fact that African Americans are six times more likely to have the condition than Caucasian Americans, the amount of information gained by using race in deciding who should be diagnosed is minimal, and any benefit is offset by the tendency to exaggerate the association. They then turn to the example of response to antihypertensives, an area in which many believe that race must be considered to make an informed medical decision. Once again, the authors show that there is little benefit from employing racial categories. Finally, they discuss chlamydia as a case in which race might be appropriately used in the clinic, demonstrating that social and political concepts of race have a utility in the clinic where biological meanings do not. In biomedicine, the racial identity of the patient is expected to reveal a biological history that confers the likelihood of an illness as well as the best way to intervene. Kaufman and Cooper show that in medical practice, this search generates a wealth of speculation: medical researchers and practitioners frequently posit strange connections between illnesses and imagined cultural histories, as older links of blood and race are integrated into the new medicine.

In chapter 10, Angela C. Jenks looks to what is happening with medicine and race in the daily work of practitioners. The interest in addressing racial disparities has given rise to the movement of "culturally competent" healthcare: training of medical personnel in what are conceived as the traditions, behaviors, and other practices of the populations being served. Because of a long history of inconsistent distinctions between race, ethnicity, and culture, cultural competence inevitably incorporates old traditions of racial thinking and stereotyping. Specifically, based on ethnographic work with cultural competency advocates, Jenks explores the ways "culture" is conceptualized as a cause of observed racial disparities in health status, and as a means to ending them. She argues that the attempt to address diversity has in some areas essentialized culture as a stable characteristic of a patient population, drawing attention away from structural inequalities organized along racial lines. Jenks finds an individualization of the concept in cultural competency programs, such that culture is considered to be what makes each patient unique, precluding attention to what communities who experience inequalities share. Culture is recast as a set of personality traits, rather than social positions and relationships between groups. Cultural competency thereby inscribes what Jenks calls "decontextualized difference," obviating attention to the power dynamics that create inequalities. In this reading, culture, like race, can become reified in the individualization of patients amid the rhetoric of diversity.

In chapter 11, Nancy Krieger argues that despite these varied critiques of race, the concept has a definite purpose. While she accepts the argument that race is not a valid biological entity in medicine, she does not think that use of the category should be discontinued. On the contrary, for Krieger, the continued use of race in state approaches to health and inequality is morally urgent and indispensable. Krieger draws on her study of preterm deliveries to argue that racial inequalities in health can only be understood by collecting data both on people's self-reported experiences of discrimination (implicit as well as explicit) and on racial/ethnic disparities in health outcomes and deleterious exposures. In this sense, race/ethnicity continues to be a critical marker to be studied. She points out that removing race from the census and other forms of state identification would only make invisible the extreme disparities in health and other experiences in the United States caused by racism and discrimination. Why is race still an important issue? Krieger makes a compelling argument based on studies of the biological consequences of racism. The experience of racism and other forms of discrimination becomes embodied in individuals, shaping their health outcomes in many ways. Studying racism, and its effects, is therefore essential to understanding health. Only once the effects of racism have been ended will it be safe to dispense with studies of the health effects of racism and race. In the meantime, it is essential that legislation continues to consider both racism and race. In her epidemiological studies on U.S. census data, Krieger shows that legislation is an effective means of reducing inequities, as disparities in the United States decreased in the 1970s, during the "war on poverty," and increased after 1980, with Reagan-era legislation. Krieger's essay offers an ecosocial model, in which disparities in exposure to economic and social deprivation, toxic substances, pathogens and hazardous conditions, social trauma, harmful commodities, and medical care create bodily differences in illness. Krieger forcefully calls for studies that analyze the mutual interaction of class, race, gender, and other forms of discrimination in determining our biological, psychological, and social health.

The analyses in this book are guided by the work of sociologists and anthropologists who, over the past two decades, have explored the genetic and cultural significance of genetic technologies. Inspired by Foucault's notion of biopolitics, Paul Rabinow (1992) coined the term *biosociality* in the early 1990s to describe the potential for social groups and identities to form around genetic information. Several anthropologists have explored the ways in which genetics takes on cultural significance, changing ideas of illness (e.g., Konrad 2005; Lock 2001/2002), kinship (Strathern 1999), and parenthood (Rapp 2000). As biological ideas of health have become increasingly salient in patient identities, public health ventures, and medicine, social scientists have observed the emergence of a new form of citizenship: a *biological citizenship* (Rose and Novas 2005). The state increasingly defines citizens by their biology, through prenatal testing, newborn screening, and government use of biometrics to determine medical access. Governance here is a mix of commerce and civic institutions acting on an individualized subject. Families, in turn, use biological meanings to affect policy, medicine, and science, through patient organizations, interactions with their doctors, and amassing biomedical information (Heath, Rapp, and Taussig 2004; Petryna 2002). What does this concept of biocitizenship teach us about the new science and medicine of race, and reciprocally, what do we learn about biocitizenship from the changes happening as the state takes up genetic technologies to understand racial differences?

Dorothy Roberts addresses these queries in chapter 12, arguing that race is fundamental to the emerging category of biological citizenship. In ancestry testing, pharmaceutical patenting, genetic testing, and assisted reproduction, the neoliberal logic of biocitizenship includes the racialized subject as a target for commercial and state interventions. If biocitizenship offers new ways of participating, creating novel forms of being a citizen, Roberts inquires over the obligations entailed. She argues that the use of cutting-edge genetic technologies to address race amid the disparities in health and incarceration reveals a biocitizenship based on the preclusion of other rights. As biomedicine and biotechnology focus on race, the concept loses salience in government social policy. As she puts it, "It is as if straining their eyes to see race at the molecular level blinds people to the continuing impact of race in society." In Roberts's analysis, the use of genetics to determine race offers a kind of citizenship in which high-technology expertise subsumes other forms of group membership: what does the use of genetics to understand identity do to religious, civic, and community ties? Where genetic technologies are used to determine historical kinship, the meanings of *race* and *family* are reconfigured (see Palmié 2007). As anthropologists, sociologists, and bioethicists have examined biotechnologies and bioscientific knowledge, they have tended to focus on the new, emerging perspectives on kinship, disorders, and patient identity that have been facilitated by the flood of technologies and data around "life itself." Roberts's dual lens, which juxtaposes social policies around people of color alongside the new technologies, broadens this perspective. By following the policy and science constituted around a racialized citizenship, Roberts is able to see biocitizenship not as a radically new set of possibilities and rights, but rather, as a nexus of policy, desire, and exclusion, as fraught with power as other approaches to race have been, are, and likely will be.

The essays in this collection pose a number of difficult questions for scholarship and policy. Although clear answers are rarely forthcoming, the essays do indicate a series of specific places where pauses are prescribed. The multiplicity of ethnic identifications requires further interrogation of facile adjudications of the biological and social dimensions of race. In descriptions of race for medical, scientific, and legal use, we need to attend to what is considered "the sociocultural" and "the biological." Often the sociocultural aspects of race are operationalized as factors that impinge on the biological, when biomedical and genetic researchers discuss changing categories across governments and historical periods. Rather than revealing a foundational ambiguity in racial or ethnic categorizations, the socially determined race is taken to be a poor approximation for a stable apolitical characteristic underlying this social confusion. This approach precludes the radically relational character of ethnicity/race, which shifts across geographic and historical spaces, and the contradictions that inhere in the multiplicity of ethnic designations. A more self-critical analytics opens up attention to the ways any adjudication on race is fraught with contradictions, as has been the case since the inception of the concept. These essays suggest that in the use of race for governance, recognition of this contradictory status is critical. Such recognition might institutionalize some doubt and humility about using race as a biological reality. This perspective might also enhance exploration of the criteria being used to categorize race by race. In current research, regulation, and care, the basis for racial designation is usually kept obscure. A focus on its contradictory character brings to view which criteria—appearance, genetic loci, self-identification on a form—are considered appropriate for the task at hand.

The motives for using genetic technologies of race are multiple: to market products, to redress racial disparities, to be an inclusive means of addressing ignored heterogeneity, to fine-tune law enforcement, and to increase health. As genetic technologies enter new arenas of governance, race is increasingly given an authority as a biological reality underlying the social identity. Discovering this reality is considered urgent where the nation-state addresses difference: in law, medicine, and science. This enterprise creates a new mix of the commercial and the ethical: the claims of addressing disparities are conjoined with increasing commercialization, particularly in securing investment for the biotechnological breakthroughs to come. Biocitizenship here pegs desire to responsibility. For the racialized biocitizen, this includes medical, legal, and scientific knowledge of the subject as an urgent need, responsibility, and potential. In this endeavor, new genotyping technologies and techniques are intimately tied to traditional ways of knowing populations. The essays collected here remind us that for abstraction of nucleotides to enter governance (or anything else social), they must be tethered to older means of judgment. The state works its techniques through statistics and the sciences of identity and difference. These inevitably incorporate ethics, histories, aversions, and enticements—these associations grant them significance in the daily operations of governance, whether in judging, penalizing, protecting, healing, warring, or knowing. In North America and Great Britain, this drama has always carried race. It is this mix of convoluted desires and taboos through which the hyperspecific, authoritative, and arcane DNA enters governance. The result is rarely predictable. One finds judges using the existence of scientific databases to give authority to DNA, databases that designate race from identifications made by law enforcement officers; medical texts excluding diagnoses based on hypothesizing over the blood of the presumed race of the patient; and researchers drawing on speculative racial histories of "culture and biology" to depict purities in some distant past to map out current hybridities. This reliance on older judgments throws into doubt the futuristic image of high-technology tools and methods bringing a new way of being, divorced from the past. The convoluted uses of race by the state to address difference—relying on emerging genetic technologies—constitute new (but somehow familiar) forms of biopolitics and citizenship.

References

Augstein, H. F. 1999. From the land of the Bible to the Caucasus and beyond: The shifting ideas of the geographical origin of humankind. In *Race, science, and medicine, 1700–1960*, ed. Waltraud Ernst and Bernard Harris. New York: Routledge, 58–79.

Avruch, K. 2002. Culture and ethnic conflict in the new world disorder. In *Race and ethnicity: Comparative and theoretical approaches*, ed. John Stone and Rutledge Dennis. Oxford: Blackwell, 72–82.

Banton, M. 2000. The idiom of race: A critique of presentism. In *Theories of race and racism*, ed. Les Back and John Solomos. New York: Routledge, 51–63.

Bhabha, H. K. 1994. Race, time and the revision of modernity. In *The location of culture*. New York: Routledge, 338–367.

Biehl, J. 2007. *Will to live: AIDS therapies and the politics of survival*. Princeton, NJ: Princeton University Press.

Bolnick, D. A. 2008. Individual ancestry inference and the reification of race as a biological phenomenon. In *Revisiting race in a genomic age*, ed. Barbara A. Koenig, Sandra Soo-Jin Lee, and Sarah S. Richardson. Piscataway, NJ: Rutgers University Press, 70–85.

Bolnick, D. A., D. Fullwiley, T. Duster, R. S. Cooper, J. H. Fujimura, J. Kahn, J. S. Kaufman, et al. 2007. The science and business of genetic ancestry testing. *Science* 318:399–400.

Brandt, A. M. 1978. Racism and research: The case of the Tuskegee Syphilis Study. *Hastings Center Report* 8:21–29.

Chaplin, J. E. 2001. *Subject matter: Technology, the body, and science on the Anglo-American frontier, 1500–1676*. Cambridge, MA: Harvard University Press.

Clinton, W. J. 2000. Remarks on the completion of the first survey of the entire Human Genome Project. National Archives and Records Administration. http://clinton5.nara.gov/WH/New/html/genome-20000626.html.

Comaroff, J., and J. L. Comaroff. 1991. *Of revelation and revolution*. Vol. 1. Chicago: University of Chicago Press.

Dingel, M. J., and B. A. Koenig. 2008. Tracking race in addiction research. In *Revisiting race in a genomic age*, ed. Barbara A. Koenig, Sandra Soo-Jin Lee, and Sarah S. Richardson. Piscataway, NJ: Rutgers University Press, 172–197.

Dupré, J. 2008. What genes are and why there are no genes for race. In *Revisiting race in a genomic age*, ed. Barbara A. Koenig, Sandra Soo-Jin Lee, and Sarah S. Richardson. Piscataway, NJ: Rutgers University Press, 39–55.

Duster, Troy. 2005. Buried alive: The concept of race in science. In *Genetic nature/culture: Anthropology and science beyond the two culture divide*, ed. Alan H. Goodman, Deborah Heath, and M. Susan Lindee. Berkeley: University of California Press, 258–277.

Ellison, G. T., J. S. Kaufman, R. F. Head, P. A. Martin, and J. D. Kahn. 2008. Flaws in the U.S. Food and Drug Administration's rationale for supporting the development and approval of BiDil as a treatment for heart failure only in black patients. *Journal of Law, Medicine & Ethics* 36:449–457.

Ernst, W. 1999. Introduction: Historical and contemporary perspectives on race, science and medicine. In *Race, science, and medicine, 1700–1960*, ed. Waltraud Ernst and Bernard Harris. New York: Routledge, 1–28.

Fanon, F. 1963. *The wretched of the earth*. New York: Grove Press.

Fassin, Didier. 2007. *When bodies remember: Experiences and politics of AIDS in South Africa*. Berkeley: University of California Press.

Foucault, M. 1978. *History of sexuality*. New York: Vintage Books.

Foucault, M. 1997/2003. *"Society must be defended": Lectures at the College de France 1975–1976*. ed. Mauro Bertani and Alessandro Fontana. Trans. David Macey. New York: Picador.

Fullwiley, D. 2007. The molecularization of race: Institutionalizing human difference in pharmacogenetics practice. *Science as Culture* 16:1–30.

Gabbert, W. 2004. Of friends and foes: The caste war and ethnicity in Yucatan. *Journal of Latin American Anthropology* 9(1):90–118.

Good, M.-J. DelVecchio, C. James, Byron Good, and A. Becker. 2002. The culture of medicine and racial, ethnic and class disparities in health care. In *Unequal treatment: Confronting racial and ethnic disparities in health care*, ed. Brian D. Smedley, Adrienne Y. Stith, and Alan E. Nelson. Washington, DC: National Academies Press, 594–625.

Graves, J. L. 2001. *The emperor's new clothes*. Piscataway, NJ: Rutgers University Press.

Hammonds, E. M., and R. M. Herzig. 2009. *The nature of difference: Sciences of race in the United States from Jefferson to genomics*. Cambridge, MA: MIT Press.

Harrison, M. 1996. 'The tender frame of man': Disease, climate, and racial difference in India and the West Indies, 1760–1860. *Bulletin of the History of Medicine* 70:68–93.

Hartigan, J. 1999. *Racial situations: Class predicaments of whiteness in Detroit*. Princeton, NJ: Princeton University Press.

Heath, D., R. Rapp, and K.-S. Taussig. 2004. Genetic citizenship. In *A companion to the anthropology of politics*, ed. David Nugent and Joan Vincent. Camden, MA: Blackwell, 153–167.

Jacobson, M. F. 1998. *Whiteness of a different color: European immigrants and the alchemy of race*. Cambridge, MA: Harvard University Press.

James, D. 1999. Bagagešu (Those of My Home): Women migrants, ethnicity, and performance in South Africa. *American Ethnologist* 26:69–89.

Jones, D. S. 2004. *Rationalizing epidemics: Meanings and uses of American Indian mortality since 1600*. Cambridge, MA: Harvard University Press.

Jones, D. S., G. M. Dorr, and A. Pollock. 2008. Symposium: Race, pharmaceuticals, and medical technology. *Journal of Law, Medicine & Ethics* 36:443–535.

Jones, J. H. 1981/1993. *Bad Blood: The Tuskegee Syphilis Experiment*. New York: The Free Press.

Kahn, J. 2004. How a drug becomes 'ethnic': Law, commerce, and the production of racial categories in medicine. *Yale Journal of Health Policy, Law, and Ethics* 4:1–46.

Kevles, D. J. 1985/1995. *In the name of eugenics: Genetics and the uses of human heredity*. Cambridge, MA: Harvard University Press.

Kevles, D. J. 2004. International eugenics. In *Deadly medicine: Creating the master race*. Chapel Hill: University North Carolina, 41–59.

Khan, A. 2004. *Callaloo nation: Metaphors of race and religious identity among South Asians in Trinidad*. Durham, NC: Duke University Press.

Koenig, B. A., S. S.-J. Lee, and S. S. Richardson. 2008. *Revisiting race in a genomic age*. Piscataway, NJ: Rutgers University Press.

Konrad, M. 2005. *Narrating the new predictive genetics: Ethics, ethnography, and science*. Cambridge: Cambridge University Press.

Lee, S. S.-J. 2008. Racial realism and the discourse of responsibility for health disparities in a genomic age. In *Revisiting race in a genomic age*, ed. Barbara A. Koenig, Sandra Soo-Jin Lee, and Sarah S. Richardson. Piscataway, NJ: Rutgers University Press, 342–358.

Lesser, J. 1999. *Negotiating national identity: Immigrants, minorities, and the struggle for ethnicity in Brazil*. Durham, NC: Duke University Press.

Lewontin, R. C. 1972. The apportionment of human diversity. *Evolutionary Biology* 6: 381–398.

Livingstone, F. B. 1962. On the non-existence of human races. *Current Anthropology* 3:279–281.

Lock, M. 2001/2002. The alienation of body tissue and the biopolitics of immortalized cell lines. In *Commodifying bodies*, ed. Nancy Scheper-Hughes and Loïc Wacquant. Thousand Oaks, CA: Sage, 63–92.

Marks, J. 2008. Race: Past, present, and future. In *Revisiting race in a genomic age*, ed. Barbara A. Koenig, Sandra Soo-Jin Lee, and Sarah S. Richardson. Piscataway, NJ: Rutgers University Press, 21–28.

Montagu, A. 1942/1997. *Man's most dangerous myth: The fallacy of race*. New York: Altamira Press.

Montoya, M. J. 2007. Bioethnic conscription: Genes, race, and Mexicana ethnicity in diabetes research. *Cultural Anthropology* 22:94–128.

Müller-Wille, S., and H.-J. Rheinberger, eds. 2007. *Heredity produced: At the crossroads of biology, politics, and culture 1500–1879*. Cambridge, MA: MIT Press.

National Center for Health Statistics. N.d. Asthma prevalence, health care use and mortality, 2000–2001. The Centers for Disease Control and Prevention. http://www.cdc.gov/nchs/products/pubs/pubd/hestats/asthma/asthma.htm.

Nelson, A. 2008. The factness of diaspora: The social sources of genetic genealogy. In *Revisiting Race in a Genomic Age*, ed. Barbara A. Koenig, Sandra Soo-Jin Lee, and Sarah S. Richardson. Piscataway, NJ: Rutgers University Press, 253–268.

Nguyen, V.-K. 2005. Antiretroviral globalism, biopolitics, and therapeutic citizenship. In *Global assemblages: Technology, politics, and ethics as anthropological problems*, ed. Aihwa Ong and Stephen J. Collier. Malden, MA: Blackwell, 124–144.

Nsieh-Jefferson, L. 2003. Pharmacogenomics: Considerations for communities of color. In *Pharmacogenomics: Social, ethical and clinical dimensions*, ed. Mark A. Rothstein. Hoboken, NJ: John Wiley, 267–290.

Palmié, S. 2007. Genomics, divination, "racecraft." *American Ethnologist* 34:205–222.

Pálsson, G., and P. Rabinow. 1999. Iceland: The case of a national human genome project. *Anthropology Today* 15(2):14–18.

Petryna, A. 2002. *Life exposed: Biological citizens after Chernobyl.* Princeton, NJ: Princeton University Press.

Prakash, G. 1999. *Another reason: Science and the imagination of modern India.* Princeton, NJ: Princeton University Press.

Rabinow, P. 1992. Artificiality and enlightenment: From sociobiology to biosociality. In *Incorporations, Zone 6*, ed. J. Crary and S. Kwinter. Cambridge, MA: MIT Press, 234–252.

Rapp, R. 2000. Extra chromosomes and blue tulips: Medico-familial interpretations. In *Living and working with the new medical technologies: Intersections of inquiry*, ed. Margaret Lock, Allan Young, and Alberto Cambrosio. Cambridge: Cambridge University Press, 184–208.

Reardon, J. 2005. *Race to the finish: Identity and governance in an age of genomics.* Princeton, NJ: Princeton University Press.

Reardon, J. 2008. Race without salvation: Beyond the science/society divide in genomic studies of human diversity. In *Revisiting Race in a Genomic Age*, ed. Barbara A. Koenig, Sandra Soo-Jin Lee, and Sarah S. Richardson. Piscataway, NJ: Rutgers University Press, 304–319.

Reverby, S. M. 2009. *Examining Tuskegee: The infamous syphilis study and its legacy.* Charlotte: University of North Carolina Press.

Roberts, D. E. 2008. Is race-based medicine good for us? African American approaches to race, biomedicine, and equality. *Journal of Law, Medicine & Ethics* 36:537–545.

Rose, N. 2007. *The politics of life itself: Biomedicine, power, and subjectivity in the twenty-first century.* Princeton, NJ: Princeton University Press.

Rose, N., and C. Novas. 2005. Biological citizenship. In *Global assemblages: Technology, politics, and ethics as anthropological problems*, ed. Aihwa Ong and Stephen J. Collier. Malden, MA: Blackwell, 439–463.

Smedley, B. D., A. Y. Stith, and A. E. Nels*on, eds. 2002. *Unequal treatment: Confronting racial and ethnic disparities in health care.* Washington, DC: National Academies Press.

Stepan, N. 1982. *The idea of race in science.* Hamden, CT: Archon Books.

Stoler, A. L. 1995. *Race and the education of desire: Foucault's history of sexuality and the colonial order of things.* Durham, NC: Duke University Press.

Strathern, M. 1999. Regulation, substitution and possibility. In *Technologies of procreation: Kinship in the age of assisted conception*, 2nd ed., ed. Jeanette Edwards, Sarah Franklin, Eric Hirsch, Frances Price, and Marilyn Strathern. New York: Routledge, 132–161.

Sunder Rajan, K. 2006. *Biocapital: The constitution of postgenomic life.* Durham, NC: Duke University Press.

Tate, S. K., and D. B. Goldstein. 2008. Will tomorrow's medicines work for everyone? In *Revisiting race in a genomic age*, ed. Barbara A. Koenig, Sandra Soo-Jin Lee, and Sarah S. Richardson. Piscataway, NJ: Rutgers University Press, 102–128.

Temple, R., and N. L. Stockbridge. 2007. BiDil for heart failure in black patients: The U.S. Food and Drug Administration perspective. *Annals of Internal Medicine* 146:57–62.

Wailoo, K. 1997. *Drawing blood: Technology and disease identity in twentieth-century America*. Baltimore: Johns Hopkins University Press.

Warren, K. B. 2001. Introduction: Rethinking bi-polar constructions of ethnicity. *Journal of Latin American Anthropology* 6(2):90–105.

Whitmarsh, I. 2008. *Biomedical ambiguity: Race, asthma, and the contested meaning of genetic research in the Caribbean*. Ithaca, NY: Cornell University Press.

Whitmarsh, I. 2009. Hyperdiagnostics: Postcolonial utopics of race-based biomedicine. *Medical Anthropology* 28(3):285–315.

Ruling

2 What's the Use of Race in Presenting Forensic DNA Evidence in Court?

Jonathan Kahn

Race, Genes, and Justice

How and when, if at all, is it appropriate to use race[1] in presenting forensic DNA evidence in a court of law? In October 2002, a California jury convicted William Curtis Wilson of first degree murder with use of a dangerous weapon during commission of an attempted rape and a lewd act on a child. The court sentenced him to a term of life in prison without possibility of parole (*People v. Wilson* 2004, 106). DNA evidence played a central role in obtaining the conviction. This, in itself, is neither extraordinary nor unusual, given the broad acceptance of the use of DNA evidence in courts across the country and, indeed, around the world. The case is noteworthy, however, for its discussion of the appropriate use of racially identified forensic DNA databases in calculating the odds that DNA left at the scene of the crime by the perpetrator might be that of the defendant. The crime scene DNA was found to match the defendant Wilson's DNA at nine distinct loci, or specific points on the genome. The question, then, became, what were the odds that someone else might share the defendant's same genetic profile? In calculating the odds, Nicola Shea, a criminalist with the California Department of Justice's Sacramento laboratory, found that Wilson's genetic profile would be expected to occur in 1 of 96 billion Caucasians, 1 of 180 billion Hispanics, and 1 of 340 billion African Americans (*People v. Wilson* 2004, 76). Shea noted that these profiles were extremely rare; after all, the world contains only about six and a half to seven billion human beings (*People v. Wilson* 2004, 76). On appeal, Wilson's attorneys strenuously contested this use of race-specific DNA databases to calculate odds to assist the trier of fact in reaching a verdict. Invoking the 2003 California Supreme Court decision in *People v. Pizarro* (2003, 530), they argued that the presentation of such race-specific odds was permissible *only* when the race of the *perpetrator* was known. Otherwise, they contended, the use of such evidence lacked sufficient evidentiary foundation because it was based on the improper assumption that the defendant was, in fact, the perpetrator (*California v. Wilson* 2005, 26). In July 2006, the California Supreme Court rejected this argument, finding that the introduction of evidence of the odds of a DNA match calculated using race-specific databases from major racial/ethnic groups represented in the local population was acceptable—thereby effectively overturning its recent ruling in *Pizarro*.

Paired together, the holdings in *Pizarro* and *Wilson* provide a relatively bounded and focused site for the examination of debates relating to the use of racialized databases in forensic DNA analysis. *Pizarro* involved an appeal from a case originally tried in 1990, when forensic DNA testing was still in its infancy. At the original trial, the forensic expert for the state testified that the odds of the defendant's genetic profile occurring in other population groups ranged from 1 in 250,000 of "Hispanics" up to 1 in 10 million "Caucasians" (frequencies in other racial populations were not presented to the jury; *People v. Pizarro* 2003, 631). Here the difference produced by using racially marked databases may be significant—not only statistically, but also as a legal matter. The lower denominators in this situation may be understood in large part as a function of the more rudimentary techniques for DNA analysis in use at the end of the 1980s. Race seemed relevant because it appeared to refine the results of a newly developing and still relatively crude technology. Hence race became instantiated at the outset of forensic DNA analysis as a basic framework for presenting data. By the time of Wilson's case, however, the technology had developed to such an extent that it was regularly capable of producing odds ratios on the order of one in hundreds of billions (Butler 2005, 8–10; Budowle et al. 2000). With such odds, the practical utility of race disappears, and yet it has remained ingrained in the framework of the production and interpretation of forensic DNA evidence.

This chapter questions the underlying assumption of the utility of race itself in forensic DNA analysis. It examines what race adds as a practical matter to ability of the finder of fact to make fair and accurate decisions and weighs this against the potential dangers of bias created by introducing issues of race as genetic into the context of what is usually a violent crime. It argues, given current technology, that the only thing race adds to forensic DNA analysis is race itself—presenting unnecessary dangers of conflating race, genes, and violent crime. Specifically, DNA evidence is usually presented in cases of violent crime, often of the most heinous variety (Prottas and Noble 2007, 310). In such contexts, there is significant danger of creating stigmatizing racial stereotypes by conflating race, violence, and genes that should be deemed to outweigh any minimal probative value provided by race-specific random match probabilities (RMPs) (Rothenberg and Wang 2004, 343; Ossorio and Duster 2005, 115, 117–118). In most cases, therefore, race-specific RMPs should be excluded by judges as irrelevant, or if deemed relevant, they should be held inadmissible because the dangers of infecting the proceedings with racial prejudice outweigh any possible benefit that introducing the race-based statistics could provide.

Whatever justifications originally proffered for the use of race-specific RMPs in forensic contexts have long since been superseded by basic technological developments that allow for the calculation of extremely powerful RMPs without reference to race. There is no legal or practical justification for the continued presentation of forensic DNA evidence in terms of race. The practice can and should be replaced with the use of nonracial general population databases to generate RMPs. Following this recommendation will fundamentally alter the way in which forensic DNA evidence is generated and presented in court. Ironically, it will not materially impede the ability of law enforcement to obtain convictions using DNA evidence, nor will it affect a defendant's ability to challenge such evidence. Forensic experts will still be able to generate regularly astronomically low RMPs using a general reference population. Taking race out of the equation, however, does have the potential to affect larger issues of how science and the criminal justice system are implicated in constructing, perpetuating, or deepening broader racialized understandings of the relations among race, genetics, and violent crime. By eliminating at least one powerful site for the improper use of genetics as a prism through which to view race and crime, this recommendation aims to take a step toward developing a more appropriate understanding of the complex relations among race, genes, and justice.

Presenting Race and Forensic DNA in Court

DNA is made up sequences of four nucleotides: adenine, cytosine, guanine, and thymine, commonly represented as A, C, G, and T, respectively. Each nucleotide base is paired through a process known as hybridization: A is always paired with T; C is always paired with G. There are approximately three billion of these base pairs in the human genome (Butler 2000, 18–20). There are two major steps in using DNA for purposes of forensic identification. First, a sample left at the crime scene by the perpetrator is compared to a sample from a suspect. Second, if there is a "match," then statistics must be used to calculate the frequency of that DNA profile in an appropriate reference population (Kaye 1993, 101, 104). This latter step is required because although every person's DNA is unique, it is impractical to compare the full three billion nucleotide base pairs between two samples for forensic purposes. Therefore two samples will be compared only with a limited set (usually between four and thirteen) of loci, or specific parts of the genome. For this practice to be effective, it is necessary to find loci that are highly variable between individuals and test only for them. Humans, however, are essentially identical in about 99.5 percent of their DNA (Weiss 2007). Finding the specific points of variation among individuals, therefore, can be difficult.

In 1985, English geneticist Alec Jeffreys first described a method for developing a DNA profile for a person in a manner that might be used for purposes of forensic identification (Butler 2005, 2–3; National Institute of Justice 2000, 14–15). Jeffreys's innovation consisted in observing that in particular regions of the human genome, short segments of DNA—the ACGT nucleotide sequence—are repeated between twenty and one hundred times (Butler 2005, 2–3; Lewontin and Hartl 1991, 1745). These repeat regions became known as variable number of tandem repeats (VNTRs). Different VNTR alleles—or variations—are composed of different numbers of repeats. To examine and visualize the VNTRs, Jeffreys employed a technique known as restriction fragment length polymorphism (RFLP), which uses a restriction enzyme to cut the regions of DNA surrounding the VNTR (Butler 2005, 2–3). By looking at VNTRs from several distinct loci on the genome, it is possible to calculate the probability that a particular genetic profile comprising distinct sets of VNTRs will appear in one or more individuals in a particular population.

Jeffreys's innovation was first used in a forensic setting in England in 1986 (Butler 2005, 3). Forensic DNA testing was first used in the United States in 1987 (Maclin 2006, 165). Soon thereafter, some commercial laboratories made use of this fingerprinting procedure, and in 1988, the U.S. Federal Bureau of Investigation (FBI) implemented forensic DNA techniques (National Institute of Justice 2000, 14–15). A standard way to estimate the frequency of a particular profile is to count occurrences in a random sample of an appropriate reference population and then use classical statistical formulas to place upper and lower confidence limits on the evidence (Committee on DNA Technology in Forensic Science 1992, 10). The resulting conclusion of identity or nonidentity between two samples is therefore necessarily probabilistic (Lewontin and Hartl 1991, 1745–1746; Cho and Sankar 2004, S8–S9). In conducting the comparison, investigators came to adopt the product rule[2] for determining the RMP—the probability of finding the same DNA profile identified in the crime scene sample in a randomly selected, unrelated individual (Lempert 1993; Butler 2005, 481, 486; Lewontin and Hartl 1991, 1746).[3] Any given VNTR may be calculated to occur at a certain frequency in a random population. By the early 1990s, the standard was to test for VNTRs at four independent loci on the genome. The product rule allows for multiplying each independent genotype frequency together to produce an overall probability of a match at all four loci (Lewontin and Hartl 1991, 1746).

To calculate RMPs, one must have an appropriate reference population. Generally speaking, the more related a person is to a particular population group, the higher the odds are of finding shared alleles. Siblings would likely share more DNA than cousins; cousins would share more than others in the same isolated village; members of the same isolated village would share more than others in the same region; and so forth. Higher odds favor a suspect or defendant because they indicate a greater likelihood that some other person may have left the DNA sample found at a particular crime scene. The choice of reference population, therefore, can play a critical role in shaping the weight and authority of DNA evidence. The choice, however, is not always straightforward. Indeed, some of the earliest and most contentious controversies involving the use of DNA technology in forensic science involved choosing the appropriate population against which a suspect's DNA should be compared and defining just how the suspect may be related to this population (Butler 2005, 455–517).

In 1991, in the pages of the journal *Science*, two pairs of eminent geneticists squared off on this question (Lewontin and Hartl 1991, 1745, 1747; Chakraborty and Kidd 1991, 1735), prompting a debate that fundamentally shaped the development and application of racial data in DNA profiling in criminal law. On one side were professors Richard Lewontin of Harvard University and Daniel Hartl of the University of Washington. On the other side were Ranajit Chakraborty of the University of Texas and Kenneth Kidd of Yale University. Their dispute did not revolve around the question of *whether* to use race, but rather, *how much* race to use in constructing reference population databases from which to calculate match probabilities (Aronson 2007, 120–146).

Lewontin and Hartl questioned the then current practice of calculating allele frequencies in the broad racial categories used in the census, such as "Caucasian," "Black," and "Hispanic," to provide the basis for calculating RMPs. They argued that such groupings were too broad and that substantial "genetic substructuring" occurred *within* the broad racial groupings that should be taken into account in calculating match probabilities. Using the broader racial groupings could produce RMPs with substantially lower odds than those that might be produced using more fine-grained ethnically identified subpopulations (Lewontin and Hartl 1991, 1745–1747). These concerns grew logically out of Lewontin's earlier pathbreaking work showing how genetic variation *within* socially identified racial groupings was actually greater than variation observed *between* such groups (Lewontin 1972, 381). This work laid the foundations for understanding that race was incoherent as a genetic concept or, at best, an overly crude surrogate for genetic variation that improperly tended to reify race as genetic (Duster 2005, 1050–1051). Lewontin and Hartl (1991, 1745, 1747) noted that problems were even greater for the "heterogeneous assemblage" known as Hispanic, which, they asserted, was perhaps "the worst case for calculating reliable probabilities." Consequently, they concluded that using reference databases organized by the broad racial groupings "Caucasian," "black," and "Hispanic" was "unjustified" (Lewontin and Hartl 1991, 1747).

Chakraborty and Kidd argued that Lewontin and Hartl exaggerated both the extent of ethnic substructuring in America and its significance for calculating match probabilities. While conceding that some substructuring existed, they argued that its effects on frequency estimates generated by using the broader racial databases were "trivial." Chakraborty and Kidd did not deny that using finer-grained ethnic reference populations might produce more precise allele frequency estimates; rather, their point was that such an approach was unnecessary—and unnecessarily burdensome. Present technology and understandings of population genetics, they asserted, justified the use of broad racial and ethnic categories, which were, additionally, far more practical and currently available (Chakraborty and Kidd 1991, 1735). Race, then, was at the center of this early debate. But for these eminent scientists, it was not a question of *whether* to use race, but *how*, or more specifically, *how much* (i.e., how fine grained) race to use.

In 1996, the National Research Council (NRC) issued a report titled "The Evaluation of Forensic DNA Evidence" (Committee on DNA Technology in Forensic Science 1996), which largely adopted the view of Chakraborty and Kidd (1991). Ever since, race-specific reference population databases have been used to generate RMPs for presentation as evidence before juries in criminal trials. Ironically, by the end of the 1990s, forensic DNA technology developed new methods that have since come to supplant the need for using race at all. At the time of the debates in the early 1990s, forensic DNA experts generally used RFLP techniques to identify up to four VNTR loci. The limitations of this technique prompted the focus on using racial databases to try to provide more refined RMPs than would be available using a general reference population. By the end of the 1990s, this technique was supplanted by the use of polymerase chain reaction to type up to as many as thirteen short tandem repeat (STR) loci. This technique is regularly capable of generating astronomically low RMPs, with denominators in the hundreds of billions, or even trillions.

As early as 2000, when discussing the possibility of moving beyond race in forensic DNA analysis, the National Commission on the Future of DNA Evidence mentioned that a general population database "may appeal to those who would like to emphasize individual differences and ignore group differences" (National Institute of Justice 2000, 27). Today, however, the question presented by technological advances in forensic DNA analysis is not, do we want to ignore group difference? Rather, it is, what justification is there to continue to present DNA evidence in terms of race? It is to this question that we now turn by looking at how race is currently used in presenting forensic DNA evidence in courts of law, focusing, in particular, on the California cases of *Pizarro* and *Wilson*.

From *Pizarro* to *Wilson*: Race in Flux

The 2003 case of *People v. Pizarro* (2003) represented a major shift in the presentation and use of racially marked forensic DNA evidence in court. Michael Pizarro was convicted of murder and rape in 1990 (*People v. Pizarro* 2003, 540). He appealed the case in 1992, arguing that RFLP testing of DNA evidence was not, at that time, generally accepted in the scientific community (*People v. Pizarro* 2003, 540). The case was remanded for a thorough evidentiary hearing, which occurred in 1998 (by which time, such issues as the legitimacy of RFLP testing were largely resolved in the scientific community), and the court ruled that the evidence was admissible and reentered the judgment (*People v. Pizarro* 2003, 540).

In his second appeal of 2003, Pizarro contended that there was a basic error in the presentation of the DNA evidence when the prosecution informed the jury that the DNA profile frequency was the probability of finding a matching profile in the *Hispanic* population (*People v. Pizarro* 2003, 622). Pizarro himself was identified as Hispanic, but the ethnic identity of the perpetrator was not known independently (e.g., through eyewitness testimony). The court ruled in Pizarro's favor, finding that the use of the Hispanic database presumed that the perpetrator was, in fact, Hispanic, when there was no sufficient evidentiary foundation to establish that fact (*People v. Pizarro* 2003, 622–623). It concluded that "recurring thematically throughout the issues in this case are evidentiary violations founded on the improper assumption that *defendant was in fact the perpetrator* and that defendant's traits therefore could be relied upon to provide or clarify those traits of the perpetrator forming the basis of the DNA evidence" (*People v. Pizarro* 2003, 540). The court argued that "in the absence of sufficient evidence of the perpetrator's ethnicity, *any* particular ethnic frequency is irrelevant" (*People v. Pizarro* 2003, 631) and found that "the improper mention of ethnicity unfairly and unjustifiably encourages the jurors to focus on ethnicity and race—specifically the ethnicity and race of the defendant, the only suspect before them" (*People v. Pizarro* 2003, 540).

In a footnote (*People v. Pizarro* 2003, 633n85), the court ultimately presented three options for presenting profile frequencies:

(1) establish that the perpetrator more likely than not belongs to a particular ethnic population, then present only the frequency in that particular ethnic population;

(2) present only the most conservative frequency, without mention of ethnicity; or

(3) present the frequency in the general, nonethnic population. These options promote the goals of admitting only relevant evidence and eliminating unjustifiable and potentially prejudicial references to ethnicity and race.

The court here seemed to be acutely sensitive to the dangers of improperly injecting race into the presentation of DNA evidence. Significantly, it broached the possibility of moving beyond race in the presentation of frequencies. Nonetheless, it remained primarily concerned with the proper management of racial references and did not go on specifically to question the underlying utility (or lack thereof) of race itself as an analytic category in the presentation of DNA evidence.

In the course of reaching this conclusion, the court's opinion presents some revealing discussions of the meaning and significance of race in forensic DNA analysis. For example, the state argued that any reference to race was harmless in part because "frequencies do not vary greatly by ethnicity" (*People v. Pizarro* 2003, 631). This, of course, raises the issue of why we should use ethnicity (or race) at all if the differences are so insignificant? Indeed, here it becomes clear that under such circumstances, the only thing that race adds to the presentation of such DNA evidence is *race itself*—not simply as a marker of the suspect, but as a conceptual framework for constructing a relationship among violent crime, genetics, and race.

The court's 2003 opinion was premised on its reading of evidence originally adduced at the first 1990 trial. At that trial, the sole scientific witness testified that "the likelihood of finding another unrelated Hispanic individual with a similar profile as Mr. Pizarro is approximately one in 250,000" (*People v. Pizarro* 2003, 624). Such odds of a match are far higher than the one in hundreds of millions presented in the *Wilson* trial. In the interest of protecting the rights of the defendant, using different racial databases may seem justified in this case. It turns out, however, that Pizarro was actually identified as "half Hispanic and half Caucasian" (*People v. Pizarro* 2003, 624). When asked how he could calculate RMPs in such a situation, the expert in the original trial stated that "there is nothing we can do other than to compare them to the two populations and we would use only the smaller one of the two in our report . . . [because it] is less detrimental to the defendant" (*People v. Pizarro* 2003, 624–625). Pizarro's "mixed race" presented a problem for the witness. Analytically, the expert literally *segregates* Pizarro's racial identities, producing separate RMPs with reference to distinct white and Hispanic databases. His conceptual framework cannot encompass the concept of mixed race; rather, it is premised on, and indeed demands, racial purity. Ironically, one might ask how it is possible to conceive of the category "Hispanic" as anything other than "mixed." As Lewontin and Hartl (1991, 1749) noted, "the census designation 'Hispanic' is a biological hodgepodge. It includes people of Mexican, Puerto Rican, Guatemalan, Cuban, Spanish and other ancestries."

In the aftermath of *Pizarro*, David Kaye (2004), of the Arizona State University School of Law, wrote a powerful and influential critique of the court's reasoning regarding the use of ethnic reference populations in calculating RMPs. Kaye (2004, 214) essentially agreed with the *Pizarro* court that "if the perpetrator could have come from any of several racial groups, looking into only one racial group for a random match probability could be misleading." He expressed grave concern, however, over the court's conclusion that giving a range of frequencies for the major racial or ethnic groups in the United States was therefore unacceptable. Kaye (2004, 214) noted that

since providing statistics from several racial groups is the standard way of assessing the significance of a match in cases in which the racial and ethnic status of the perpetrator of the crime initially is unknown, the opinion [in *Pizarro*] casts doubt on the outcome in innumerable cases.

Kaye (2004, 215) disputed what he sees as the court's presentation of an "unbridgeable gap between scientific and legal reasoning in this situation," asserting that

the scientific reasoning that the court questioned is nothing less than the kind of hypothesis testing—considering the principal alternatives and examining the probability of certain outcomes under each of these alternative hypotheses—that dominates modern statistical thinking.

In this instance, the DNA expert simply testifies to how surprising the match would be if some major alternatives to the hypothesis that the defendant is the source of the biological samples were true.

Thus, he concluded, "When it comes to deciding what evidence is logically relevant, however, it is difficult to conceive of any substantive difference between legal and scientific reasoning" (Kaye 2004, 215). In the abstract, there is much merit to Kaye's argument. But in declaring no difference between scientific and legal *reasoning*, he obscures the distinction between scientific and legal *relevance*.

When noting that a perpetrator may "share the defendant's race or ethnicity," Kaye (2004, 212) conflates race and genetics referring to a defendant's "genetic heritage." The concept of sharing is very peculiar and particular here. *Pizarro* involved someone who Kaye and the court define as half Hispanic and half Caucasian—implicitly making these two categories mutually exclusive. Yet in social practice, this makes no sense and reinforces the idea of genetically distinct and bounded races, rather than continuums of variable mixes. Michael Pizarro could not be allowed to be a Hispanic Caucasian because the databases were not constructed that way. Two suspects may share the same race, but that race itself must be singular and unmixed; it must not be shared with other races, but rather, be capable of being broken down into parts "half *x*" and "half *y*." In short, the entire model of using race to improve probability estimates depends on keeping genetic databases segregated by race—and the segregation produces segregated statistical probability estimates.

Kaye correctly notes that there is no necessary presumption made about a perpetrator's identity if the suspect's DNA is compared to an array of racial databases of populations to which the perpetrator *might* belong. He therefore adequately addresses and effectively undermines two of the *Pizarro* court's three permissible options for the presentation of profile frequencies: "(1) establish that the perpetrator more likely than not belongs to a particular ethnic population, then present only the frequency in that particular ethnic population; (2) present only the most conservative frequency, without mention of ethnicity" (*People v. Pizarro* 2003, 633n85). Kaye's logic, however, is based on a presumption that race itself remains relevant in the calculation of RMPs. Thus it fails to address the third option: to "present the frequency in the general, nonethnic population" (*People v. Pizarro* 2003, 633n85).

In the case of *People v. Wilson* (2006, 1243–1245), the California Supreme Court embraced Kaye's arguments to disapprove of the reasoning in *Pizarro* and revalidate the calculation of RMPs using race-specific databases, even when the race of perpetrator is not otherwise known. In reaching its conclusions, the court (*People v. Wilson* 2006, 1239–1240) asserted that

the question here revolves around exactly what is the relevant population. The question is complicated by the fact that the odds vary with different racial and ethnic groups. Because of this variation, separate databases are maintained for different population groups, and the odds for each group are calculated separately.

The court (*People v. Wilson* 2006, 1239–1240) then agreed with the lower court's finding that

when the perpetrator's race is unknown, the frequencies with which the matched profile occurs in various racial groups to which the perpetrator *might* belong are relevant for the purpose of ascertaining the rarity of the profile.

This effectively overturned *Pizarro* and reinstantiated the practice of using racially marked databases to generate profile frequencies.

Race, Genes, and Relevance

In the case of *Daubert v. Merrell Dow Pharmaceuticals, Inc.* (1993, 597), the U.S. Supreme Court notably articulated a gatekeeping role for the trial court judge in considering the admissibility of scientific evidence. Central to the holding in *Daubert* was the Court's articulation of a requirement that the trial judge ensure that "an expert's testimony both rests on a reliable foundation and is relevant to the task at hand" (*Daubert v. Merrell Dow* 1993, 597). The *Federal Rules of Evidence* (FRE) were subsequently revised in 2000 in response to *Daubert*. In particular, FRE 702 now reads as follows:

If scientific, technical, or other specialized knowledge will assist the trier of fact to understand the evidence or to determine a fact in issue, a witness qualified as an expert by knowledge, skill, experience, training, or education, may testify thereto in the form of an opinion or otherwise, if (1) the testimony is based upon sufficient facts or data, (2) the testimony is the product of reliable principles and methods, and (3) the witness has applied the principles and methods reliably to the facts of the case.

Considered in light of the preceding discussion, it now seems clear that the use of race in generating RMPs for forensic DNA matches should be deemed inadmissible by courts as neither relevant nor reliable.

When Race Is Not Relevant

FRE 401 states that " 'relevant evidence' means evidence having any tendency to make the existence of any fact that is of consequence to the determination of the action more probable or less probable than it would be without the evidence." Clearly forensic DNA evidence is often relevant to a criminal proceeding. RMPs generated through reference to a population database are therefore also often relevant. A central argument of this chapter, however, is that in the presentation of such RMPs, race is *not* relevant. It does not add information that has "any tendency to make the existence of any fact that is of consequence to the determination of the action more probable or less probable than it would be without the evidence."

Taking the *Wilson* case as a paradigmatic example of how race is used in the presentation of forensic DNA evidence, we can see that central to the court's decision were its concept of relevance and the assumptions it brought to bear regarding the relevance of race in producing DNA evidence. Following its assertion that data from racial groups to which the perpetrator might belong were relevant, the court made the relatively straightforward assertion that "relevant evidence is evidence 'having any tendency in reason to prove or disprove any disputed fact that is of consequence to the determination of the action'" (*People v. Wilson* 2006 1247). The court went on to note that "the test of relevance is whether the evidence tends, 'logically, naturally, and by reasonable inference' to establish material facts such as identity, intent, or motive" (*People v. Wilson* 2006 1247). These are basic rules of evidence. The court, however, obscured a very basic issue by framing the question of relevance in terms of "what is the relevant population," rather than considering whether differentiation among populations itself provides any *legally* relevant data. In Wilson's case, and in most cases using current techniques of forensic DNA analysis, the answer to this latter question should simply be no.

The RMPs at issue in *Wilson* ranged from 1 in 96 billion Caucasians, 1 in 180 billion Hispanics, to 1 in 340 billion African Americans (*People v. Wilson* 2006, 1241). The court accepted this racially marked data as relevant because forensic scientists had identified statistical variation in frequencies when using different racial reference populations to generate RMPs (*People v. Wilson* 2006 1239–1240). The court went on to quote approvingly Professor Kaye's assertion that "contrary to the *Pizarro* court's assertions, in a 'general population case'—one in which the investigation cannot be limited to a particular racial group—the statistics for a range of groups surely are relevant" (*People v. Wilson* 2006 1245). Kaye made the apparently reasonable point that having more data about RMPs for a range of populations would "surely" aid a jury in establishing a material fact such as identity. And indeed, the court concluded that "it is relevant for the jury to know that most persons of at least major portions of the general population could not have left the evidence samples" (*People v. Wilson* 2006, 1245).

But forensic (and other) scientists have also repeatedly made the point that once a particular odds threshold is passed, any difference among profile frequencies is of little or no practical significance. As Yale geneticist Kenneth Kidd noted in the California case of *People v. Soto* (1999, 534), "any difference in estimates over one in a million was pragmatically meaningless." Moreover, in *People v. Wilson* (2006, 1241) itself, state criminologist Nicola Shea testified that when nine genetic markers are used (as in Wilson's) case, "the result would be a 'pretty discriminating number' no matter what population data base was used." Yet at no point does the court consider the logical implication of Shea's statement—that under such circumstances, using racially marked databases to generate RMPs adds nothing to the ability of the jury to make determination of guilt or innocence. The difference between 1 in 96 billion and 1 in 340 billion simply does not "hav[e] any tendency in reason to prove or disprove any disputed fact that is of consequence to the determination of the action" (*People v. Wilson* 2006, 1245). Such information provides nothing of use to the finder of fact that would not already be available using a nonracially marked RMP generated by reference to a general, undifferentiated reference population. In other words, where experts can generate such astronomically low RMPs, race simply is *irrelevant* and should not play a role in the presentation of DNA evidence.

Several other statements by prominent forensic DNA experts further highlight the glaring irrelevance of race to presenting DNA evidence given the power of current technology. Arguing in 1996 for the adequacy of using broad racial databases to generate RMPs, the FBI's own Bruce Budowle and Keith Monson (1996) noted that "a profile would be considered rare whether it had an estimated frequency of 1/5,000,000 or 1/500,000,000. Obviously the difference in the rarity of such estimates would have little consequence in a forensic context." More to the point, Lander and Budowle (1994 738), in their highly influential 1994 *Nature* article on forensic DNA technology, argued that a distinction in population frequency between "10^{-5} or 10^{-7}" was "irrelevant for courtroom use."

Ironically, the issue prompting these observations was the original dispute with Lewontin and Hartl over whether reference populations needed to be *more* racially specific, reflecting finer-grained genetic structuring in ethnic subgroups. Kidd, Budowle, Monson, and Lander all were arguing that using the *less* racially specific, broader general census categories of race to organize reference population databases produced more than adequate RMPs for the purposes of courtroom use. They never considered the possibility or implications of taking the additional step of eliminating race-specific reference populations altogether, in favor of a general population database, for the simple reason that such a move was never at issue.

The distinction in population frequencies across the diverse, race-specific RMPs generated in *Wilson* (roughly between 10^{-11} and 3.4×10^{-11}) was far smaller than that cited by Budowle and Lander (1996) as irrelevant. Given that current techniques regularly generate RMPs in the range of 10^{-11} (one in one hundred billion) across diverse racial databases, any distinction among race-specific RMPs must be understood as similarly "of little consequence in a forensic context" and hence "irrelevant for courtroom use" (Butler 2000, 95; Budowle et al. 2000). In short, in forensic contexts, the only thing that race adds to RMPs is race itself. It provides no additional information that is relevant to aiding the finder of fact to resolve any material issue at trial.

When Race Is Not Reliable

The requirement that scientific evidence be "reliable" is typically discussed in terms of the following factors set forth in *Daubert v. Merrell Dow* (1993, 593–594): (1) whether the technique or theory underlying the evidence has been tested; (2) whether it has been subject to peer review and publication; (3) the known or potential rate of error of the technique or theory when applied; (4) the existence and maintenance of standards or controls; and (5) whether the technique or theory has been generally accepted in the scientific community.

When looking at these factors in relation to the generation and presentation of race-specific RMPs for DNA evidence, it is immediately clear that factors 1, 2, and 5 have been met. Over the years, numerous studies have been published in peer-reviewed journals testing and evaluating the use of race-specific databases to generate RMPs. Thus, since the inception of forensic DNA evidence, the use of race has been standard and generally accepted practice. Such general acceptance, however, is no longer the sole determining factor in assessing the reliability of scientific evidence. When scientific practices concerning the use of race in relation to forensic DNA are examined more closely, it becomes clear that they fail to meet factors 3 and 4: there has been little or no consideration of potential rates of error regarding the definition of race and its assignment to particular DNA samples, nor have any standards or controls for the definition and assignment of racial categories to DNA samples been applied. Such lack of basic scientific rigor calls into question the reliability of RMPs generated using racial categories.

Specifically, in the context of forensic DNA research, we see that the scientists who have developed racialized databases have, in effect, let the concept of self-identification supplant the need for any scientifically rigorous or coherent rationale for classifying genetic data by race. This is apparent in the article written by Budowle et al. (2001), which has become a primary reference in calculating race-specific RMPs.[4] Titled "CODIS STR loci data from 41 sample populations," the Budowle et al. (2001, 453) article purports to present "STR allele distribution data on 12 or 13 of the CODIS core STR loci in several sampled populations from each of the following major population groups: African American, U.S. Caucasian, Hispanics, Far East Asians, and Native Americans." These distribution data were derived samples provided by twenty laboratories distributed widely across the United States, Canada, the Caribbean, and Mexico (Budowle et al. 2001, 453).

Budowle et al. (2001) take care to specify the technical laboratory instruments and practices used to analyze the samples. But with regard to race, Budowle et al. provide absolutely no information on how or by whom racial identity was ascribed to these samples. Most of the samples came from law enforcement agencies. Self-identification may have been used, but it is also quite likely that law enforcement authorities themselves ascribed racial identities to the samples.

In an article on the ethical, legal, and social implications of forensic DNA analysis, Cho and Sankar (2004, S10) discuss at length a British study by Lowe et al. showing that external ascriptions of racial identity by law enforcement authorities correspond very poorly with underlying patterns of genetic variation. They note that the British study reported

"a method for inferring the ethnic origin of a DNA sample profiled using the SGM [second generation multiplex]" in five British populations (classified as Caucasian, Afro-Caribbean, Indian sub-continental, Southeast Asian, and Middle Eastern). In an attempt "to discriminate between the ethnic groups in the suspect population . . . a set of 10,000 profiles was simulated from each of the five ethnic groups considered here, using allele distributions estimated from the data. For every profile in a set, its probability within each ethnic group was estimated."

Cho and Sankar (2004, S10) go on to note that "classifications into the five 'ethnic' groups were assigned by police officers by visual characteristics," based on perceptions of outward appearance, rather than on knowledge of individual ancestry. The actual correspondence of these external ascriptions to the true ancestry of the individuals ranged from 30 percent for the Middle Eastern category up to 67 percent for Afro-Caribbeans, with Caucasians falling in between, at 56 percent (Cho and Sankar 2004, S10 citing Lowe et al. 2001). In other words, if the samples providing the basis for the Budowle et al. (2001) article were classified based on external ascriptions of race by law enforcement authorities, it would not be unreasonable to suppose that somewhere around 50 percent of the classifications were inaccurate in terms of their relation to genetically based ancestral origins. If this is the case, it calls into question the legitimacy of any RMPs derived from these reference populations.

Perhaps the samples provided to Budowle et al. were classified by self-identification. This, however, would not solve the problem. Self-identification is a *social* practice, not a *genetic* one. Some studies argue that there is often a reasonable correlation between self-identification and genetic ancestry (Tang et al. 2005, 2006; Risch 2006), but such studies do not consider, for example, that as a social practice, self-identification certainly may fail to correspond to underlying genetic variation in the same manner as the external ascription of race by law enforcement officials. Moreover, as Cho and Sankar (2004, S9) note, "individual self-classification is not stable. For example, one U.S. study found that one-third of people change their own self-identified race or ethnicity in two consecutive years" (Cho and Sankar 2004, S9). Complicating matters still further, a recent study by Condit et al. (2003, 385) found that people often have very incomplete knowledge of their biological ancestry. Of a sample of 224 subjects interviewed for a study on attitudes toward race-based pharmacogenomics (the tailoring of drugs to genetic profiles), Condit et al. found that 39.6 percent did not know all four of their biological grandparents. In such situations, self-declared race may fail to capture significant variation in biological ancestry.

In short, the Budowle et al. (2001) article failed to consider or elaborate adequately how particular racial identities were ascribed to the samples it analyzed. It further failed to consider how those racial identities might correspond (or not) to the diverse allele frequencies uncovered. As a result, the legitimacy of the allele frequencies presented in the article must be called into question, as must the race-specific RMPs generated by using the data presented in the article. This is due to a basic failure by the authors to take the same care in handling concepts of race as they took in handling samples of DNA.

This lack of care for the meaning and attribution of race in a genetic context contrasts markedly with the obvious scientific rigor applied to the elaboration of the more technical aspects concerning the extraction, amplification, and analysis of forensic DNA samples. Clearly the general practice of using forensic DNA to help identify criminal suspects meets all the *Daubert* standards of reliability. It is only with respect to the handling of race that the reliability of particular RMPs should be called into question. The use of a general reference population to generate RMPs without regard to race would directly overcome this lack of reliability.

Race, Genes, and Prejudice

Ironically, it was often defense attorneys who advocated the use of race in framing the presentation of DNA evidence to juries. The hope was that using more fine-grained racial databases would produce RMPs more favorable to defendants (Aronson 2007, 120–145). Yet today, the use of race-specific RMPs typically adds nothing other than race itself to the charged context of genetic evidence in violent crimes. Thus, even if race-specific RMPs were to be deemed somehow relevant and reliable, they should still be excluded as prejudicial. FRE 403 states that

although relevant, evidence may be excluded if its probative value is substantially outweighed by the danger of unfair prejudice, confusion of the issues, or misleading the jury, or by considerations of undue delay, waste of time, or needless presentation of cumulative evidence.

The probative value of race-specific RMPs must be evaluated in relation to the alternative probative value of non-race-specific RMPs. When current technology can use nonracial general reference populations to generate RMPs in excess of one in five million, then the probative value of any refinement of the odds pr)ovided by the addition of race-specific RMPs, even if relevant, should be deemed of minimal import.

What concerns for prejudice should then be balanced in the scales against this minimal relevance? As Eberhardt et al. (2004, 876) have noted, "the stereotype of Black Americans as violent and criminal has been documented by social psychologists for almost 60 years. . . . Not only is the association between Blacks and crime strong (i.e., consistent and frequent), it also appears to be automatic (i.e., not subject to intentional control)." The dangers of racial bias tainting the evaluation of forensic evidence are paramount in this context. DNA evidence is overwhelmingly presented in cases of violent crimes, often of the most heinous variety (Prottas and Noble 2007). Where race is gratuitously injected into the context of violent crime, and genetics is added to the mix, the danger of conflating race, violence, and genes should be deemed to outweigh any minimal probative value provided by the addition of race-specific RMPs over general RMPs.

Concern to ensure that racial prejudice does not infect the justice system must be primary in any evaluation of the admissibility of forensic DNA evidence. As the U.S. Supreme Court noted in *McCleskey v. Kemp* (1987, 309), "because of the risk that the factor of race may enter the criminal justice process, we have engaged in 'unceasing efforts' to eradicate racial prejudice from our criminal justice system." Thus, for example, the prosecution may not challenge a juror on the basis of race (*Batson v. Kentucky* 1986, 85); a change of venue may be constitutionally required as a result of widespread racial bias in a community (*Irwin v. Dowd* 1961, 728); and the prosecution is barred from appealing to racial prejudice in its argument to the jury (*People v. Cudjo* 1993, 625).

In their treatise on federal practice and procedure, Wright and Graham (2007, 237n11)note that "any reference to race by prosecutor must be justified by compelling state interest." They caution, in particular, that "while many jurors would reject crude appeals to prejudice, more sophisticated forms of this technique may not be recognized as such. *Today the appeal to prejudice is apt to be disguised as some form of science*" (Wright and Graham 2007, 162–163) With specific reference to FRE 403, Wright and Graham (2007, 163) conclude that

fairness in adjudication does not consist entirely in the accuracy of the factual determinations but may require some sacrifice of accuracy to avoid the suspicion that the decision rests on prejudice disguised as science. Therefore, the party who asserts a major premise based on one of the suspect classifications must expect that his premise will be more rigorously scrutinized than is typical in rulings on relevance.

Thus far, the use of race in the presentation of forensic DNA evidence has received virtually no scrutiny from courts in terms of the value or lack thereof that race adds to the accuracy of the RMPs thus generated. Wright and Graham allow that some measure of accuracy may need to be sacrificed to avoid the suspicion of racial prejudice. In the case of presenting RMPs without regard to race, such a sacrifice would be minimal.

Wright and Graham's reference to the distinctive power of science to disguise appeals to prejudice is especially apt in the context of forensic DNA evidence. In discussing generally the psychological power of framing RMPs in the presentation of DNA evidence, Jonathan Koehler (2001, 1277) notes that in a study of mock jurors, he found that "the way in which DNA match statistics are framed and presented to legal fact finders may affect how they think about and use the DNA evidence." Koehler's study looked only at different probabilistic frames for presenting the same statistic, but it is important to consider that similar subtle psychological dynamics may be at work in framing RMPs in terms of race.

Sheri Lynn Johnson (1993) has argued that the use of negative racial stereotypes pervades the presentation of criminal cases to juries. She argues that "if the entire body of relevant data is surveyed, the inference that race influences many white jurors' determinations of guilt is unavoidable" (Johnson 1993, 1804). In their recent article "Implicit Bias: Scientific Foundations," Greenwald and Hamilton Krieger (2006, 945) discuss the science of implicit cognition, which "suggests that actors do not always have conscious, intentional control over the processes of social perception, impression formation, and judgment that motivate their actions." They define *implicit biases* as "discriminatory biases based on implicit attitudes or implicit stereotypes" (Greenwald and Hamilton Krieger 2006, 951). Being implicit, such biases are not conscious—yet they are significant. Greenwald and Hamilton Krieger (2006, 951) note that

implicit biases are especially intriguing, and also especially problematic, because they can produce behavior that diverges from a person's avowed or endorsed beliefs or principles. The very existence of implicit bias poses a challenge to legal theory and practice, because discrimination doctrine is premised on the assumption that, barring insanity or mental incompetence, human actors are guided by their avowed (explicit) beliefs, attitudes, and intentions.

Greenwald and Hamilton Krieger (2006) go on to review data from the Implicit Attitude Test, which is widely used to assess implicit attitudes toward African Americans relative to European Americans. They observe that researchers have consistently found what they describe as "implicit attitudinal preference" for European Americans over African Americans (Greenwald and Hamilton Krieger 2006, 952). They conclude that "a substantial and actively accumulating body of research establishes that implicit race bias is pervasive and is associated with discrimination against African Americans" (Greenwald and Hamilton Krieger 2006, 952). To the extent that such implicit race bias might already be present among average jurors, the danger that injecting race into the presentation of forensic DNA evidence will taint the proceedings is significant.

This danger is heightened by the pervasive association of race and violent crime in the public mind. For example, Hurwitz and Peffley (2005) argue that since the infamous "Willie Horton" ad run by the National Security Political Action Committee (NSPAC) against Democrat Michael Dukakis during the 1988 presidential campaign, subtly associating race and crime has been a staple of modern politics. In that spot, "the narrator notes that Willie Horton, a convicted murderer, received multiple weekend furlough passes from prison, during the last of which, the narrator informs us, he 'fled, kidnapping a young couple, stabbing the man and repeatedly raping his girlfriend.' While the ad could have conveyed exactly the same information without graphics, NSPAC elected to superimpose the most menacing possible picture of Horton, an African American, over the narrative" (Hurwitz and Peffley 2005, 100). Hurwitz and Peffley (2005, 100–101) go on to note that the ad was particularly effective because of its "implicitness," which allows white Americans to internalize the association of African Americans and violent crime, without directly challenging their conscious commitments to norms of racial equality.

Taken together, the presence of racial imagery in criminal trials, the psychological dynamics of implicit prejudice, and the prominent association of race and violent crime in the public mind counsel strongly against the unnecessary introduction of race into the presentation of forensic DNA evidence. Professor of theology Ted Peters (2003, 73) further cautions that "if we identify crime with genes and then genes with race, then we may inadvertently provide a biological support for prejudice and discrimination." More specifically, the dangers they present of infecting criminal proceedings with racial bias clearly outweigh the minimal probative value provided by the use of race-specific RMPs. Thus, even if relevant evidence, race-specific RMPs should be excluded as prejudicial.

Conclusion

Race has been present in forensic DNA evidence since its inception. Over the past twenty years, the use of race-specific RMPs has become a normative, routine, and largely unquestioned practice. Whatever justifications may have originally been proffered for this practice have long since been superseded by basic technological developments that allow for the calculation of extremely powerful RMPs without reference to race. In relation to the presentation of forensic DNA evidence to juries, race is simply a concept whose time has passed. Race-specific RMPs provide little or no relevant information to finders of fact. They present a significant danger of prejudicing deliberations through the gratuitous association of race with genetics and violent crime. Ending the practice of generating race-specific RMPs will not materially impede the ability of law enforcement to obtain convictions using DNA evidence. Forensic experts will still be able to generate regularly astronomically low RMPs (often with denominators far in excess of the world's population) using a nondifferentiated general reference population. There is no legal or practical justification for the continued presentation of forensic DNA evidence in terms of race. The practice can and should be ended. It should be replaced with the use of nonracial general population databases to generate RMPs. Indeed, David Kaye (2008), an influential member of the NRC committee that issued the 1996 report arguing for the legitimacy of race-specific databases, has recently noted that such an approach, while statistically more complex than using the current racially differentiated databases, is certainly technically feasible.

Given the current technical ability to generate minuscule RMPs, even using a general population database, these recommendations may not change the specific outcomes of individual cases. They will, however, affect larger issues of how the criminal justice system is implicated in constructing, perpetuating, or deepening broader racialized understandings of the relations among race, genetics, and violent crime. By eliminating at least one powerful site for the improper use of genetics as a prism through which to view race and crime, these recommendations aim to take a step toward developing a more appropriate understanding of the complex relations among genes, race, and justice.

Notes

Work on this chapter was supported in part by the Ethical, Legal, and Social Implications Research Program, National Human Genome Research Institute (grant R03-HG004034-02).

1. I do not attempt to provide a set definition of *race* in this chapter; rather, I focus primarily on how actors in specific legal and scientific contexts have used the term. In the interests of economy and manageable syntax, in the remainder of this chapter, I will often refer only to race when speaking generally of racial and ethnic categories. I am assuming both to be socially constructed categories that nonetheless have come to have biological implications as they play out in real-world biomedical and forensic contexts. I will use the terms *race* and/or *ethnic* when referring to specifically marked groups. Thus, for example, the U.S. census codes "White" and "Asian" as racial categories and "Hispanic" and "Latino" as ethnic categories. In the context of forensic practice, Hispanic is also sometimes referred to as a racial group. Ethnic groups are often also discussed as subgroups within races. For example, Italian or Irish might be understood as ethnic subgroups within the racial category of Caucasian.

2. Richard Lempert (1993, 1n3) defines the product rule as follows:

According to the product rule, the probability of two independent events equals the probability of the first event times the probability of the second; with *n* independent events the separate probabilities of each of the *n* events are multiplied together to give the probability of their joint occurrence. Thus if the probability that a person had allele A = 1/10 and the probability that he had allele B = 1/10 and the probability that he had allele C = 1/10, and if the probability that the person had one of these alleles was not affected by whether or not he had either or both of the others, the probability that the person would have alleles A, B, and C would be 1/10 × 1/10 × 1/10, or 1/1000.

3. That the individual be unrelated is significant because related individuals will have a higher likelihood of sharing a greater percentage of DNA, hence altering the probabilities of a random match (Lempert 1993; Butler 2005, 481, 486; Lewontin and Hartl 1991).

4. Bruce Butler, pers. email comm., April 26, 2007.

References

Aronson, Jay. 2007. *Genetic witness*. Piscataway, NJ: Rutgers University Press.

Batson v. Kentucky. 1986. 476 U.S. 79.

Budowle, Bruce, George Carmody, Ranajit Chakraborty, and Keith Monson. 2000. Source attribution of a forensic DNA profile. *Forensic Science Communications* 2(3). http://www.fbi.gov/hq/lab/fsc/backissu/july2000/source.htm#Introduction.

Budowle, Bruce, and Keith Monson. 1996. Accepted practices by the forensic DNA community supported by NRC II report. In *Genetic Identity Conference proceedings: Seventh International Symposium on Human Identification—1996.* http://www.promega.com/geneticidproc/ussymp7proc/0703.html.

Budowle, Bruce, Brendan Shea, Stephen Niezgoda, and Ranjit Chakraborty. 2001. CODIS STR loci data from 41 sample populations. *Journal of Forensic Sciences* 46:453–459.

Butler, John. 2005. *Forensic DNA typing: Biology, technology, and genetics of STR markers.* 2nd ed. Burlington, MA: Elsevier.

California v. Wilson. 2005. Appellant's Opening Brief on the Merits. Cal.4th S130156.

Chakraborty, Ranajit, and Kenneth Kidd. 1991. The utility of DNA typing in forensic work. *Science* 254:1735–1745.

Cho, Mildred, and Pamela Sankar. 2004. Forensic genetics and ethical, legal and social implications beyond the clinic. *Nature Genetics* 36:S8–S10.

Committee on DNA Technology in Forensic Science. 1992. *DNA technology in forensic science.* Washington, DC: National Research Council.

Committee on DNA Technology in Forensic Science. 1996. *The Evaluation of Forensic DNA Evidence.* Washington, DC: National Research Council.

Condit, Celeste, Alan Templeton, Benjamin Bates, Jennifer Bevan, and Tina Harris. 2003. Attitudinal barriers to delivery of race-targeted pharmacogenomics among informed lay persons. *Genetics in Medicine* 5:385–392.

Daubert v. Merrell Dow Pharmaceuticals, Inc. 1993. 509 U.S. 579.

Duster, Troy. 2005. Race and reification in science. *Science* 307:1050–1051.

Eberhardt, Jennifer, Philip Goth, Valerie Purdy, and Paul Davies. 2004. Seeing black: Race, crime and visual processing. *Journal of Personality and Social Psychology* 87:876–893.

Fed. Rul. Evid. 401.

Fed. Rul. Evid. 702 (as amended April 17, 2000, effective December 1, 2000).

Greenwald, Anthony, and Linda Hamilton Krieger. 2006. Implicit bias: Scientific foundations. *California Law Review* 94:945–986.

Hurwitz, Jon, and Mark Peffley. 2005. Playing the race card in the post–Willie Horton era. *Public Opinion Quarterly* 69:99–101.

Irwin v. Dowd. 1961. 366 U.S. 717:728.

Johnson, Sheri Lynn. 1993. Racial imagery in criminal cases. *Tulane Law Review* 67:1739-1805.

Kaye, David. 1993. DNA evidence: Probability, population genetics and the courts. *Harvard Journal of Law and Technology* 7:101–138.

Kaye, David. 2004. Logical relevance: Problems with the reference populations and DNA mixtures in *People v. Pizarro*. *Law Probability and Risk* 3:211–245.

Kaye, David. 2008. The role of race in DNA statistics: What experts say, what California courts allow. *Southwestern University Law Review* 37:304–322.

Koehler, Jonathan. 2001. The psychology of number in the courtroom: How to make DNA-match statistics seem impressive or insufficient. *Southern California Law Review* 74:1275–1328.

Lander, Eric, and Bruce Budowle. 1994. DNA fingerprinting dispute laid to rest. *Nature* 371: 734–736.

Lempert, Richard. 1993. The suspect population and DNA identification. *Jurimetrics* 34:1–8.

Lewontin, Richard. 1972. The apportionment of human diversity. *Evolutionary Biology* 6:381–398.

Lewontin, Richard, and Daniel Hartl. 1991. Population genetics in forensic DNA typing. *Science* 254:1745–1749.

Maclin, Tracey. 2006. Is obtaining an arrestee's DNA a valid special needs search under the Fourth Amendment? *Journal of Law, Medicine & Ethics* 34:165–174.

McCleskey v. Kemp. 1987. 48 U.S. 279:309.

National Institute of Justice. 2000. The future of forensic DNA testing: Predictions on the Research and Development Working Group. National Commission on the Future of DNA Evidence. http://www.ncjrs.gov/pdffiles1/nij/183697.pdf.

Ossorio, P., and T. Duster. 2005. Race and genetics: Controversies in biomedical, behavioral and forensic sciences. *American Psychologist* 60:115–121.

People v. Cudjo. 1993. 6 Cal.4th 585.

People v. Pizarro. 2003. 100 Cal.App.4th 530.

People v. Soto. 1999. 21 Cal.4th 512.

People v. Wilson. 2004. 21 Cal.Rptr.3d 102.

People v. Wilson. 2006. 38 Cal.4th 1237.

Peters, Ted. 2003. *Playing God? Genetic Determinism and Human Freedom*. 2nd ed. New York: Routledge.

Prottas, Jeffrey, and Alice Noble. 2007. Use of forensic DNA evidence in prosecutors' offices. *Journal of Law, Medicine & Ethics* 35:310–315.

Risch, N. 2006. Dissecting racial and ethnic differences. *New England Journal of Medicine* 354:408–411.

Rothenberg, K., and A. Wang. 2004. The scarlet genes: Behavioral genetics, criminal law and racial and ethnic stigma. *SPG Law and Contemporary Problems* 69:343–397.

Tang, H., Tom Quertermous, Beatriz Rodriguez, Sharon L. R. Kardia, Xiaofeng Zhu, Andrew Brown, James S. Pankow, et al. 2005. Genetic structure, self-identified race/ethnicity, and confounding in case-control association studies. *American Journal of Human Genetics* 76:268–275.

Tang, H., Marc Coram, Pei Wang, Xiaofeng Zhu, and Neil Risch. 2006. Reconstructing genetic ancestry blocks in admixed individuals. *American Journal of Human Genetics* 79:1–8.

Weiss, Rick. 2007. Mom's genes or Dad's? Map can tell. *Washington Post*, September 4, A1. http://www.washingtonpost.com/wp-dyn/content/article/2007/09/03/AR2007090301106.html.

Wright, Charles, and Kenneth Graham. 2007. Federal Practice and Procedure § 5179:22.

3   Forensic DNA Phenotyping: Reinforcing Race in Law Enforcement

Pamela Sankar

Criminal identification practices have evolved over the past two hundred years from improvised, vague descriptions noting a person's birthplace or demeanor (Sankar 1992, 81–82) to automated, scientific biometric and genetic technologies capable of reliably and predictably distinguishing one individual from among millions. Facial recognition software can pick out a deadbeat dad from crowded stands at a sporting event (Woodward 2001; Trigaux 2001), and DNA typing can identify a murderer from the saliva left behind from licking closed an envelope (Gillespie 2003). Still, as impressive as this progress has been, one limit unites the new with the old. Identifying a wrongdoer—whether by birthplace or genetics—requires already knowing him or her. In all identification technologies that rely on matching unknown against known, there must already have been an encounter that generated a record against which the information produced in a subsequent encounter can be compared. The dad in the stands is identified as deadbeat because the database against which the new images are compared has already stored and labeled his image as such. The saliva on the stamp provides damning evidence because its analysis matches a DNA-typing profile police already have on file. But there is a new technology, forensic DNA phenotyping (FDP)—also sometimes referred to as ancestry profiling or phenotypic profiling (Cho and Sankar 2004; Ossorio 2006)—that promises to get past this limit and produce an identity sui generis. By any name, its potential utility to police is clear; however, its reliance on race to predict identity also makes it controversial (Newsome 2007).

Forensic DNA Phenotyping (FDP)

FDP analyzes DNA left at a crime scene to locate genotypes linked to ancestry and physical appearance, such as eye or skin color, and uses these genotypes to assign race and predict appearance. Researchers anticipate being able to add features for outwardly apparent behaviors, such as gait or a predisposition to smoking, or, according to one account, "physical features such as the space between the eyes, the shape of a jaw—all the things a sketch artist might want to know" (Spagnoli 2007). Imagine the advantages to police of being armed not only with the clues that a crime scene routinely provides, such as the crime's location, timing, and method, but also with the knowledge, as the senior official in charge of Great Britain's National DNA Database (Staley 2005, 31) suggested, that they are looking for "a 6 ft 3 in man with red hair and a tendency to obesity." The chief scientific officer of a company that specializes in FDP predicted an even greater potential for the technology when he forecast, "A few years from now, we're going to have figured out so many traits that a criminal might as well leave his driver's license at the scene of the crime" (Sachs 2004). Traditionally eyewitnesses have been relied on to provide critical details about suspects' appearance, but ample research has shown that they are often wrong (Cutler and Penrod 1995). Not only might FDP descriptions provide more detail than most eyewitnesses, but, restricted as it would be to analysis of DNA associated directly with the crime, FDP also would overcome the limits of eyewitnesses and not confuse a hapless (and innocent) deliveryman with the murderer.

Similar to DNA typing, FDP relies on genetic analysis, but in other important respects, the two technologies differ. In contrast to DNA typing (and to other matching technologies), FDP's objective is to predict, rather than only confirm, the identity of a wrongdoer. FDP's moment occurs during the investigation or arrest, when police are trying to locate the perpetrator. Once the perpetrator is in custody, DNA typing takes over. Its job is to convince the court that the defendant is the same person who left DNA at the crime scene. Also in contrast to DNA typing, FDP does not seek to demonstrate unique identity—it does not seek to determine precisely whether the perpetrator is *this* tall, red-haired man or *that* one; rather, FDP seeks to distinguish who might be the wrongdoer from who is not. Told that the perpetrator is a tall, red-haired, white male, the police can ignore all of the women and most of the men, or at least all those who appear not to be white or to have red hair.

In theory, FDP could move from this kind of group level sorting to unique identification, for example, identifying a specific tall, red-haired man. Doing so would require adding more and more features to a description until, as with fingerprints or DNA typing, the likelihood of the description matching more than one person would drop so infinitesimally low as to be judged impossible. Conducting the research that would support such an application would require enormous effort and methodological innovation. But whether FDP predicts a set of features or a unique description is less the point than that FDP predicts, rather than confirms, identity, a capability unmatched by other technologies.

Although one can see why this technology might appeal to law enforcement, it raises serious social and ethical questions. For now, at least, the primary, if not sole, feature on which its descriptions rely is race. While researchers hope to develop the capacity to predict other features, such as gait, voice, age, or facial morphology (Shriver 2007), they have yet to declare success on these fronts. With the exception of information about gender from the X and Y chromosomes, FDP analysis focuses on a set of genotypes linked to *biogeographical ancestry* (BGA), a term proponents have defined as "the heritable component of race" (Sachs 2004). From this "heritable component of race," FDP purportedly predicts the perpetrator's personal appearance. For example, in one case, analysts reported that a DNA sample revealed that its owner's biogeographical ancestry was 85 percent sub-Saharan African and 15 percent Native American, and thus predicted that the perpetrator was an African American "of average skin tone" (Noel 2003).

FDP's emphasis on race follows from an established interest in race in population genetics research, on which FDP is based. Thirty to forty years ago, population geneticists interested in questions such as how to estimate the rate of mutation among different human populations (Neel 1973, 1974) or how to estimate the degree of admixture among different populations (Reed 1969b, 1973) began to identify mutations that appeared to be present in one population but not in others, and they named these "private biochemical variants" (Neel 1974). Following established conventions, they described these variants, or alleles, as belonging to different races, as in the article title "Caucasian Genes in American Negroes," which appeared in *Science* (Reed 1969a). Research in the intervening decades reported many more such alleles and built up an extensive body of work. In the 1990s, researchers interested in forensic applications of genetics turned to this work and incorporated its reliance on race into their own research.

Most of the work developing FDP has been done in the United States by the company DNAPrint Genomics, which developed a computer program, DNAWitness, for this purpose. (Unable to secure funding in the recent poor economy, DNAPrint ceased operating in March 2009. Plans for the company's return to operations are currently unclear [Anonymous 2009]). But they are not alone in the field. The governments of Great Britain and the Netherlands conduct FDP analyses using their own procedures; Japan has announced plans to develop a genetic database for tracking ethnic minorities in that country (Cyranoski 2004); and the U.S. government recently funded a lab in Iowa to develop DNA tests to infer "population of origin" from forensic samples (Miller 2007). Only limited information about each program and its methods is available. DNAPrint reports using nearly two hundred genotypes to make its determinations, which probably qualifies it as conducting the most comprehensive analysis (Frudakis 2007). Nonetheless, what unites these programs is the assumption that geographic origins or ancestry can be inferred from genes and the information used to assign race and predict appearance.

Ancestry Informative Markers (AIMs)

The basis for this set of assumptions lies, in part, in science that developed from Neel's research on "private biochemical variants," which are roughly analogous to what are now called ancestry informative markers (AIMs) (Shriver et al. 2003). As with private biochemical variants, AIMS are also genetic markers, or alleles, whose frequencies have been shown to vary globally among human populations.

The distinctive distribution of these alleles results from the history of human population migration. As human populations grew and fanned out over the globe from Africa thirty thousand to forty thousand years ago, populations dispersed and settled farther and farther away from one another (Bamshad et al. 2004). At the same time, genetic changes occurred, such as those resulting from spontaneous mutation, that could be passed down from generation to generation. Depending on how close populations lived to one another, they were more or less likely to share these alleles. For example, they might be more likely to spread among people living on the same continent than among those from different continents. Thus the distribution of a small number of human genotypes varies geographically in a way that roughly reflects something of the history of human population migration. As a result, they can provide information about human ancestry, hence the name "ancestry informative markers."

AIMs provide, however, only an estimate of ancestry. There is no one-to-one correspondence between the geographic region in which a population lives and AIMs that are common to it. AIMs that appear more frequently in one population also appear in others. For example, analysis of populations with ancestry in China would reveal certain AIMs that occur at a higher rate than they do among a population tracing its ancestry to Sweden, but any single member of either population might or might not have a particular AIM associated with that population, might have an AIM more frequently associated with the other population, or might exhibit none of the identified AIMs at all. AIMs are associated probabilistically with a population, not predictably with an individual. Applying population-level data to an individual, referred to as the ecological fallacy, is a common mistake in another venue of similar DNA testing conducted by commercial labs for people seeking to learn more about their families' origins. Furthermore, not all genotypes, or alleles, that appear to be AIMs actually are. Alleles that vary across geographic regions might also have developed in relation to similar environmental exposures, for example, as have some alleles related to malaria resistance. As a result, a shared allele might reflect similar environmental exposures, rather than shared ancestry (Bolnick et al. 2007, 2008).

From AIMs to Appearance

The research relating population migration and AIMs is widely accepted. However, some uses of AIMs, such as claims about using AIMs to predict a person's appearance, are highly controversial (Bolnick 2008). One concern is the oversimplification of the relationship between genotype and phenotype on which such claims rest. As critics stress (McCabe and McCabe 2006), the relationship between genotype and phenotype is complex. It is well understood only in exceptional cases, such as single gene diseases like Huntington's disease or cystic fibrosis, where the presence of a specific, single, changed gene predicts the disease, virtually without exception. Historically, scientists assumed that more conditions would mirror the single gene model and that scientific advances would proceed by identifying a limited set of disease genes with treatments targeted at the associated phenotypes. But these assumptions are increasingly being proved wrong. Instead, researchers are discovering complex, highly contingent relationships between genotype and phenotype that challenge ready explanation. Some are associated with epigenetic events, which are heritable changes in phenotype or gene expression that result from influences external to changes in the underlying DNA (Riddihough and Pennisi 2001). Others remain unexplained, and in many fields, understanding of the genotype-phenotype relationship seems to recede, rather than advance, despite intensive study (Gaedigk et al. 2005; McCabe and McCabe 2006).

The fact that gene expression depends on complex interactions with the environment, broadly construed, means that the potential for similar phenotypic expression based on shared alleles is not always realized. Thus, for example, people who share AIMs, even AIMs proven to influence physical appearance, do not necessarily look the same. And, just as significant, to the extent that such a similarity is realized, insufficient research exists to provide a basis for accurate prediction of physical appearance based on genotype. Another concern about using AIMs to predict appearance lies with how race is implicated in predicting phenotype from genotype.

In FDP, specifically as formulated by DNAWitness, the move from AIMs to appearance starts with demarcating AIMs into groups that parallel "major continents of Europe, Asia, Africa and the Americas," which proponents justify based on the claim that statistical analysis of AIMs produced this "4-population parental model" as the most parsimonious (Gabriel, Frudakis, and Thomas 2008, para. [0002]). Globally distributed AIMs thus become continental groups, and in turn, these continental groups provide the basis for assigning BGA, defined as "the heritable component or race." Thus, through these steps, the broad diversity and subtle differences among groups— what some might consider a hallmark of relative youth of the human species—is reduced to four categories. At times, supporters of FDP argue that these categories are not the same as races (Gabriel 2005), but defining BGA as "the heritable component or race" seems to contradict this claim, as does using BGA as the link from AIMs to appearance.

In any case, BGA provides the link to appearance in the sense that analysis moves from BGA labels, such as European or African, to popular race categories, such as white or black. Some descriptions stop here, as in one provided for a suspect in a Boulder, Colorado, murder case, in which FDP predicted that the perpetrator would exhibit "features common to Hispanics or Native Americans" (Frudakis 2007, 607). Others add details about the value or shade of skin color, as in the description "light skinned black male" (Johnston 2006). For the most part, however, a person's description is conveyed implicitly through the race label.

This approach to predicting identity is troublesome for many reasons, one of which is that it does not take into account a widely recognized feature of race, which is that the meaning of race labels varies across time and place. For example, people labeled in the 1980s in Great Britain as white were, by the mid-1990s, labeled Middle Eastern (Aspinall 1998; Forensic Science Service 2005), a shift that suggests that labels are transitory expressions of political relationships, rather than enduring biological categories. In admixed populations, which are populations that result from relatively recent mixing of previously distinct populations, such as Africans and Europeans might have been prior to the enslavement and transfer to the New World of Africans by Europeans, the problem of predicting appearance based on genotype is compounded and the chances of useful prediction even more diminished. Thus, although AIMs that influence physical appearance are well documented and their geographic distribution roughly parallels population migration mapped for the reasons outlined here, their capacity to predict appearance is limited.

Nonetheless, it is also important to grasp that this capacity is not entirely illusory and to understand what makes this so. Under the following conditions, FDP can work. *To the extent* that continental ancestry and popular race categories overlap, and *to the extent* that the person to be identified physically conforms to local racial stereotypes, which, *in turn*, need to overlap with established BGA groupings, an FDP description can predict a suspect's identity. Similarly, say you want a rose but know only how to ask for a red flower. In certain instances, you will get a rose. This does not mean that all roses are red or that all red flowers are roses, only that some red flowers are roses (and vice versa), and thus, in certain settings (ones in which the only red flowers happen to be roses), the two appear equivalent.

FDP can work in an analogous way. If FDP provides a description that coincides sufficiently with the popular race categories held by the people looking for a suspect and with the population to be scrutinized for suspects, a description such as "light-skinned black man" might point toward the right person. This does not mean that it will always, usually, or, importantly, predictably do so. It could just as well be the case that a DNA sample described by analysts as belonging to someone who is Hispanic, or black, or white leads nowhere because the person in question does not appear Hispanic, or black, or white to the people who are looking for him. But the fact that it is likely to fail often does not mean it cannot sometimes succeed, and this is important to understand should debate over FDP become a public issue. In other words, a categorical claim that FDP cannot work is inaccurate. A stronger position highlights, instead, that it does not work predictably and that, as discussed later, it relies on stereotyping to apply results.

FDP Cases

The use of FDP has generated scant public information, but details about a few cases are available. The most fully described case, and the first official police use of FDP in the United States, involved a Louisiana man, Derrick Todd Lee. A series of murders in southeastern Louisiana reported over the late 1990s to early 2000s demanded police attention when, in 2002, four murders in a row occurred that seemed to be attributable to the same man. A multiagency homicide task force was formed, and scores of officers enlisted in the effort to locate the perpetrator. Despite spending over $500,000 in overtime, however, the police had no luck arresting a suspect (Mustafa, Clayton, and Israel 2006, 111, 151).

Eyewitness accounts from women who thought they might have been attacked by the same man but who managed to escape, or by people who had been in the area when confirmed murders had occurred, led police to believe that they were looking for a white man, perhaps driving a white van. Federal Bureau of Investigation profiling confirmed that the murderer was likely to be white. These leads failed to turn up a viable suspect. Frustrated by the continuing murders and pressured by the growing expenses of the task force, police decided, in early 2003, to consult DNA-Print. Police submitted twenty-one samples to the company: one from the killer's crime scenes and twenty additional samples from people known to the police (Mustafa, Clayton, and Israel 2006). This selection would allow them to use the accuracy of reports on known samples to judge the accuracy of the one report they cared about. The results came back ten days later. The twenty known samples were all accompanied by descriptions judged to be accurate, which implied that the twenty-first would be, as well. A spokesperson for the company reported that the ancestry of the person represented in the twenty-first sample was "85% sub-Saharan African and 15% Native American" and that the man "could be Afro-Caribbean or African American but there is no chance that this is a Caucasian" (Newsome 2007). Skeptical, police asked the analyst if he was sure, to which he replied, "I'm positive. You're wasting your time dragnetting Caucasians; your killer is African American" (Simons 2003).

Police finally accepted the description and used it to reorient their search. Less than two months later, they had identified Derrick Lee Todd as their man and taken a DNA sample from him to compare to those collected from the murder victims (Mustafa, Clayton, and Israel 2006). Todd had been known to police as a sexual predator and had been previously arrested and jailed, but for a variety of reasons, including his race, police had dismissed him as a suspect in these murders. On the basis of a DNA-typing match, Todd was arrested. Subsequently, he was tried and convicted for two of the seven murders possibly attributable to him. He is currently in jail, appealing his 2004 death sentence.

A second FDP case is more difficult to trace in full and is still not resolved, but is interesting nonetheless for its broader implications. The case is a rape and murder of a sixteen-year-old girl who had lived near Kollum, a small town north of Amsterdam, in the Netherlands. On the way to a dance in summer 1999, the teenager was dragged from her bike, raped, and her throat slashed (Reijnders 2005). The incident occurred near a hostel for asylum seekers, many of whom were from the Middle East or north Africa. Some in the town were quick to suspect a resident of the hostel, and the incident rapidly took on political overtones. A visit by a controversial Dutch television personality led to the development among townspeople of what one account described as a "lynching mentality" (Reijnders 2005, 636), and another commented that the response was in danger of becoming a "witch hunt against asylum seekers" (Fekete and Hoppe 2000). Officials at town meetings convened to discuss the issues were pelted with eggs. The event triggered what became a national movement in the Netherlands to change the government's policy of dispersing asylum seekers throughout the country, including in less urban areas accustomed to a homogenous society populated by northern European Dutch (Fekete and Hoppe 2000).

The police pursued hundreds of leads in the case, but few turned up that linked the crime to the asylum seekers. A 2000 report stated, "Not one [lead] mentioned a dark-skinned person near the scene of the crime" (Fekete and Hoppe 2000). Four residents from the hostel were brought in for standard DNA typing, but no matches were produced. As of early 2009, no arrests have been made.

There are no detailed accounts of how circumstances moved along after the failed DNA typing, perhaps because what happened next appears to have been illegal. One article states that the attorney general of the province in which the crime occurred decided to seek information about the perpetrator's possible ethnic identity through DNA analysis (M'Charek 2008, 400), while another suggests that the director of a forensic laboratory at a nearby university independently contacted authorities to obtain a sample for ethnic origins analysis (Hoekstra 2007, 10). In any case, the results indicated that the presumed perpetrator was of western European parentage, a finding that pointed away from the asylum-seeking population and toward a native Dutchman. Once made public, this information helped to deflect attacks against the asylum seekers. Eventually the incident moved the Dutch government to request that its justice department draft an amendment to the Dutch DNA law allowing FDP. The law, which passed in May 2003, remains the only statute of its kind in Europe.

Previously, in line with other European countries, Dutch law expressly prohibited forensic DNA analysis linked to personal characteristics and permitted only standard DNA typing (Koops and Schellekens 2006). The new law permits FDP analysis restricted to features that have been visible since birth, including gender (*geslacht*), race (*ras*), and population or community (*bevolkingsgroep*) (Korthals 2001–2002). The restriction to visible features is meant to limit the possibility of revealing genetic information to the suspect of which he or she is not aware such as a predisposition to some illness. The law also stipulates that such phenotyping is permitted only "if all other investigative tools have failed to lead to a suspect" (van der Beek 2004, 293).

Whether the Dutch case will offer the same proof of principle that the Lee case offered remains to be seen, when and if the perpetrator is caught. Nonetheless, it is significant that absent such proof, the case still led the government to amend DNA law. In light of the fact that the perpetrator has not been caught, this testifies strongly to a belief that one can infer racial or ethnic identity from genetics.

Conclusion

FDP helped to catch a brutal serial murderer in Louisiana and to defuse the threat of ethnic violence in the Netherlands. This sounds useful, so what downsides offset these potential benefits? They fall into two groups. First are the technical and logical limits to the reliability of FDP predictions and thus the utility of the technology. As discussed, the presence or absence of a particular allele or set of alleles in a person's DNA in itself cannot infallibly reveal a person's ancestry. While research has repeatedly demonstrated that certain alleles are more common in certain populations, it provides no basis on which to predict whether any particular individual in that population will or will not have a certain allele. Furthermore, advancing research in fields such as epigenetics suggests that predicting appearance (phenotype) based on genotype (AIMs) is a risky endeavor.

The second set of drawbacks concerns the practical implementation of FDP and the role of racial stereotyping in law enforcement. Considering that FDP descriptions are rather vague, for example, "light-skinned black man" or "Hispanic," they could be used to target and detain any of a very large number of people. It seems possible that instead of making suspect searches more exact, the vagueness of FDP descriptions might make them more vulnerable to stereotyping. Of course, the same might be said of most descriptions the police are handed. Other descriptions, however, are not based on genetics. This is where the cultural legacy of DNA typing as the "truth machine" comes into play (Lynch et al. 2009). It is not hard to imagine that the illusion of certainty that surrounds the use of genetics in law enforcement, created by DNA typing, could confer legitimacy on FDP, as well. FDP proponents dismiss this problem. If the suspect's DNA does not match the crime scene DNA that generated the description, proponents point out, the person will be released from custody (Schneider 2007). While logically this is true, it is scarcely reassuring, especially to members of racial and ethnic minorities in the United States, who, research has shown, are "approximately five times more likely than White suspects, per capita, to die at the hands of a police officer" (Correll et al. 2007, 1006). In the U.S. context, at least, it is easy to see how FDP might only reinforce bias and increase the dangers of racial discrimination.

In light of these concerns, it is important to consider further details about the forensic uses of DNA in the Netherlands. The original Dutch forensic DNA-typing law from the early 1990s had been written to fend off possible future innovations in DNA analysis that might permit ethnic profiling because such a practice seemed unacceptably reminiscent of the Nazi-era obsession with racial purity. The willingness to change the law less than a decade later likely speaks to the dramatic changes that the Netherlands experienced over that time as a result of the repeated waves of asylum seekers moving north from impoverished and war-torn states to settle in a more prosperous and generally safer country. The Netherlands, as much of Europe, is accustomed to stable, homogeneous populations and has struggled greatly with how to accommodate and integrate new settlers with substantially different beliefs and appearances seeking to put down roots (King et al. 2008; Monar 2008). Progress has been made overall in devising strategies to better integrate immigrants and asylum seekers, but the apparent interest in genetics as a way to grapple with an influx of strangers seems to be a step backward. Recent talk of eliminating the word *ras* (race) in the Dutch law and emphasizing, instead, geographic origins suggests an awareness of these problems. However, it is not clear how much difference this will make (Koops and Schellekens 2006). The current paradigm for FDP, originating in the United States, already claims to originate in geography, starting, as it does, with a framework based on the "major continents of Europe, Asia, Africa and the Americas" (Gabriel, Frudakis, and Thomas 2008, para. [0002]). This provenance, however, does not stop it from moving immediately to race. In other words, simply declaring a technology not to be about race does not make it so. The meaning or character of a technology emerges through its history and use. To wit, FDP is a technology firmly anchored in race—both through its connection to the population genetic research and through the racial nature of social deviance, law enforcement, and political authority in both Europe and the United States today. As such, its use will likely contribute to racialism. Arguably, this is potentially true of any technology, at least until such a future time when race has become socially, politically, and culturally meaningless. Nonetheless, this particular technology is so evidently troublesome that its rejection should be immediate and strong.

References

Anonymous. 2009. DNAPrint Genomics goes bust. GenomeWeb Daily News. http://www .genomeweb.com/node/912684?emc:e1&m:325264&1-1&v:e993a10706.

Aspinall, P. J. 1998. Describing the "white" ethnic group and its composition in medical research. *Social Science and Medicine* 47:1797–1808.

Bamshad, M., S. Wooding, B. Salisbury, and J. Stephens. 2004. Deconstructing the relationship between genetics and race. *Nature Reviews Genetics* 5:598–609.

Bolnick, Deborah A. 2008. Individual ancestry inference and the reification of race as a biological phenomenon. In *Revisiting race in a genomic age*, ed. B. A. Koenig, S. S.-J. Lee, and S. S. Richardson. New Brunswick, NJ: Rutgers University Press, 70–85.

Bolnick, D. A., D. Fullwiley, T. Duster, R. S. Cooper, J. H. Fujimura, J. Kahn, J. S. Kaufman, et al. 2007. Genetics: The science and business of genetic ancestry testing. *Science* 318:399–400.

Bolnick, D. A., D. Fullwiley, J. Marks, S. M. Reverby, J. Kahn, K. TallBear, J. Reardon, et al. 2008. The legitimacy of genetic ancestry tests: Response. *Science* 319:1039–1040.

Cho, M. K., and P. Sankar. 2004. Forensic genetics and ethical, legal and social implications beyond the clinic. *Nature Genetics* 36(Suppl):S8–S12.

Correll, J., B. Park, C. M. Judd, B. Wittenbrink, M. S. Sadler, and T. Keesee. 2007. Across the thin blue line: Police officers and racial bias in the decision to shoot. *Journal of Personality and Social Psychology* 92:1006–1023.

Cutler, Brian L., and Steven D. Penrod. 1995. *Mistaken identification: The eyewitness, psychology and the law*. New York: Cambridge University Press.

Cyranoski, D. 2004. Japan's ethnic crime database sparks fears over human rights. *Nature* 427:383.

Fekete, Liz, and Mieke Hoppe. 2000. Populist anti-asylum movement born at Kollum. Independent Race and Refugee News Network. http://www.irr.org.uk/europebulletin/netherlands/asylum_seekers_refugees/2000/ak000016.html.

Forensic Science Service. 2005. *Annual report and accounts 2004–2005*. Birmingham, UK: Forensic Science Service.

Frudakis, Tony. 2007. *Molecular photofitting: Predicting ancestry and phenotype using DNA*. Burlington, MA: Academic Press.

Gabriel, Richard. 2005. Company interview: DNAPrint Genomics, Inc. The Wall Street Transcript. April 25. http://www.twst.com/ceos/ABN618.htm.

Gabriel, Richard, Tony N. Frudakis, and Matthew J. Thomas. 2008. Systems and methods for identifying and tracking individuals. World Intellectual Property Organization Patent Application WO/2008.005309, filed June 29, 2007, and published Jan. 10, 2008. http://www.freepatentsonline.com/WO2008005309.html.

Gaedigk, A., A. Bhathena, L. Ndjountché, R. E. Pearce, S. M. Abdel-Rahman, S. W. Alander, L. DiAnne Bradford, and J. Steven Leeder. 2005. Identification and characterization of novel sequence variations in the cytochrome P4502D6 (CYP2D6) gene in African Americans. *Pharmacogenomics Journal* 5:173–182.

Gillespie, Elizabeth M. 2003. New trick by cops closes old case. CBS News. http://www.cbsnews.com/stories/2003/05/30/national/main556194.shtml.

Hoekstra, Wiel. 2007. Barcode van het DNA [Of the DNA barcode]. *De Academische Boekengids* 61 (March): 10–11.

Johnston, Dave. 2006. The use of DNA in Operation Minstead: Metropolitan Police Authority. September 7. http://www.mpa.gov.uk/committees/x-eodb/2006/060907/10.

King, R., M. Thomson, N. Mai, and J. Y. Keles. 2008. 'Turks' in the UK: Problems of definition and the partial relevance of policy. *Journal of Immigrant and Refugee Studies* 6:423–434.

Koops, Bert-Jaap, and Maurice Schellekens. 2006. Forensic DNA phenotyping: Regulatory issues. Working Paper 002/2006, TILT Law and Technology.

Korthals, A. H. 2001–2002, Revision of the rules governing DNA analysis in criminal matters in connection with setting by observable characteristics. Presented at the Meeting of the Second Chamber, Netherlands, 2001–2002, 28 072, no. 3.

Lynch, Michael, Simon A. Cole, Ruth McNally, and Kathleen Jordan. 2009. *Truth machine: The contentious history of DNA fingerprinting.* Chicago: University of Chicago Press.

McCabe, Linda L., and Edward R. B. McCabe. 2006. Complexity in genetic diseases: How patients inform the science by ignoring the dogma. *American Journal of Medical Genetics* 140A:160–161.

M'charek, Amade. 2008. Contrasts and comparison: Three practices of forensic investigation. *Comparative Sociology* 7:387–412.

Miller, Raymond. 2007. Testing DNA samples for population of origin: Quarterly report. Quarter 2 Progress Report. Midwest Forensics Resource Center. http://snp.wustl.edu/snp-research/forensics/MFRC-Report-Miller-070815.pdf.

Monar, Jörg. 2008. Justice and home affairs. *Journal of Common Market Studies* 46(Suppl 1):109–126.

Mustafa, Susan D., Tony Clayton, and Sue Israel. 2006. *I've been watching you: The south Louisiana serial killer.* Bloomington, IN: AuthorHouse.

Neel, J. V. 1973. "Private" genetic variants and the frequency of mutation among South American Indians. *Proceedings of the National Academy of Sciences of the United States of America* 70:3311–3315.

Neel, J. V. 1974. Developments in monitoring human populations for mutation rates. *Mutation Research* 26:319–328.

Newsome, Melba. 2007. A new DNA test can ID a suspect's race, but police won't touch it. *Wired Magazine,* December 20. http://www.wired.com/politics/law/magazine/16-01/ps_dna.

Noel, Josh. 2003. Florida lab pointed to race: Serial killer search changed course. *Baton Rouge Advocate*, June 4. http://www.uic.edu/orgs/uicsymrg/uicsymrg/Florida%20Lab%20Pointed%20to%20Race.pdf.

Ossorio, Pilar N. 2006. About face: Forensic genetic testing for race and visible traits. *Journal of Law, Medicine, & Ethics* 34:277–292.

Reed, T. E. 1969a. Caucasian genes in American Negroes. *Science* 165:762–768.

Reed, T. E. 1969b. Critical tests of hypotheses for race mixture using Gm data on American Caucasians and Negroes. *American Journal of Human Genetics* 21:71–83.

Reed, T. E. 1973. Number of gene loci required for accurate estimation of ancestral population proportions in individual human hybrids. *Nature* 244:575–576.

Reijnders, Stijn. 2005. The people's detective: True crime in Dutch folklore and popular television. *Media, Culture, and Society* 27:635–651.

Riddihough, Guy, and Elizabeth Pennisi. 2001. The evolution of epigenetics. *Science* 293:1063.

Sachs, Jessica Snyder. 2003. DNA and a new kind of racial profiling. *Popular Science.* http://www .popsci.com/scitech/article/2004-06/dna-and-new-kind-racial-profiling.

Sankar, Pamela. 1992. *State power and record-keeping: The history of individualized surveillance in the United States, 1790–1935.* PhD diss., University of Pennsylvania.

Schneider, Peter M. 2007. DNA-based prediction of physical traits: A new dimension for forensic genetics, or a first step towards violation of privacy leading to genetic discrimination? Paper presented at the 22nd Congress of the International Association for Forensic Genetics, Copenhagen.

Shriver, M. 2007. Complex physical traits. Paper presented at the 22nd Congress of the International Association for Forensic Genetics, Copenhagen.

Shriver, M. D., E. J. Parra, S. Dios, C. Bonilla, H. Norton, C. Jovel, C. Pfaff, et al. 2003. Skin pigmentation, biogeographical ancestry and admixture mapping. *Human Genetics* 112:387–399.

Simons, Dana Hawkins. 2003. Getting DNA to bear witness. U.S. News and World Report, June. http://www.usnews.com/usnews/culture/articles/030623/23dna.htm.

Spagnoli, Linda. 2007. Beyond CODIS: The changing face of forensic DNA analysis. *Law Enforcement Technology,* http://www.officer.com/print/Law-Enforcement%20Technology/Beyond-CODIS/1$37894.

Staley, Kristina. 2005. *The police national DNA database: Balancing crime detection, human rights and privacy.* Glossop, UK: GeneWatch UK.

Trigaux, Robert. 2001. Cameras scanned fans for criminals. *St. Petersburg Times,* January 31. http://www.sptimes.com/News/013101/TampaBay/Cameras_scanned_fans_.shtml.

van der Beek, C. P. 2004. Evolution of the Dutch DNA-law. *Der Kriminalist.* http://www .dnasporen.nl/docs/literatuur/The-Dutch-DNA-law-final-version.doc/.

Woodward, John D. 2001. *Super Bowl surveillance: Facing up to biometrics.* Santa Monica, CA: RAND Corporation / Arroyo Center.

4 Beyond Inclusion, Beyond Difference: The Biopolitics of Health

Steven Epstein

In recent years, scholars have devoted significant energy to understanding the ways in which physicians, biomedical scientists, and medical institutions adopt and use racial identifiers. Conversely, and perhaps more importantly, these analysts have called attention to the prominent role of biomedical actors within the broader cultural processes by which concepts of race are given meaning in society—and in particular, the processes by which race becomes treated as a meaningful construct at the level of biology (Marks 1995; Haraway 1997, chap. 6; Graves 2001; Lee, Mountain, and Koenig 2001; Sankar and Cho 2002; Cooper, Kaufman, and Ward 2003; Duster 2003, 2005; Templeton 2003; Wailoo 2003; Fausto-Sterling 2004, 2008; Kahn 2004; Reardon 2005; Shields et al. 2005; Shim 2005; Montoya 2007; Fujimura, Duster, and Rajagopalan 2008; Fullwiley 2008; Nelson 2008; Pollock 2008; Whitmarsh 2008). The goal of this chapter is to argue that, at least with reference to the United States, we should view these developments—what we might call the biomedical remaking of race, or the racial remaking of biomedicine—against the backdrop of a sweeping set of changes at the level of biomedical research policy and practice. This broad wave of reform, which combines new ways of understanding human differences with new emphases on social, political, and medical inclusion, has concerned the politics of race, but it does not concern race alone. In particular, studying the effects of reform helps to pinpoint the intersecting (and also divergent) trajectories of race and sex[1] as objects of biomedical and political attention and helps reveal the commonalities in how they are frequently naturalized and reified.

A New Regime

In the early to mid-1980s, in the United States, an eclectic group began to demand new ways of attending to identity and difference in the domain of biomedical research. Reform was promoted by an assortment of health advocates, politicians, biomedical researchers, drug company scientists, and federal health officials; this effort encompassed women's health and minority health advocacy groups, AIDS and breast cancer activists, mainstream political organizations such as the Congressional Caucus for Women's Issues, and professional groups such as the American Academy of Pediatrics, among others.[2] Reformers championed the goal of equity in biomedical research, insisting that every group in society is deserving of biomedical attention. At the same time, reformers declared war on the biomedical "standard human." They argued that while this standard human was being used as a stand-in for all humanity, in practice, he was typically white, male, and middle-aged. And they insisted that a variety of social differences are medically meaningful—that it is simply not appropriate to take findings derived from the study of one sort of person and extrapolate them to other sorts.

In fact, the claim that medical researchers were only studying middle-aged white males and had never focused on others was an exaggeration, and in some respects, it was importantly wrong (Epstein 2007, chap. 2). It left out the long history of researchers taking advantage of those people with less power in society (a practice that has continued to some degree in recent decades), and it overestimated the extent to which groups, such as men, actually were predominant in research populations. But the critique did capture something about standard operating procedures in certain domains of medical research and pharmaceutical drug development—for example, cardiovascular disease, where women were significantly underrepresented. Moreover, this charge quickly became the conventional wisdom that united a diverse group of proponents of social and biomedical change. As Bernadine Healy, the first female director of the National Institutes of Health (NIH), recalled of the status quo ante, when looking backward from the perspective of the year 2003 (Office of Research on Women's Health 2003),

the orthodoxy of sameness and the orthodoxy of the mean, which has dominated much of the thinking in medical science . . . often impaired our attitude toward clinical research in those days—we tended to want to reduce the human to that 60 kilogram white male, 35 years of age, and make that the normative standard—and have everything extrapolated from that tidy, neat mean, "the average American male."

Critics suggested that this narrow conception of the standard human had thoroughly penetrated medical theory, practice, education, and training, and that its signs ranged from the composition of clinical trials, to the anatomical images used in medical textbooks, to the presumptions about which sorts of people could best work as doctors or scientists.

Reformers opposed this false universalism and argued for the inclusion of more women, people of color, children, and the elderly as research subjects. These were the categories of political mobilization, but these were also the categories deemed to hold biological relevance. Drawing, in particular, on scientific findings of differential responses to medications according to sex, race, or age, advocates of measuring differences portrayed social groups as bodily distinct and medically incommensurable:

they suggested that knowledge simply failed to travel across these categories. Thus reformers joined together ethical and political arguments about equity and inclusion with scientific arguments about embodied difference. The presumption—one which merits scrutiny—was that the relevant categories of identity politics were also the relevant categories of medical differentiation. On the basis of this presumption, reformers called for the measurement of medical differences by categorical identity.

At the broadest level, the result in the United States has been a distinctive fusion of biomedical and governmental goals, terminology, and procedures that I call the *inclusion-and-difference paradigm*. The name is meant to reference the dual mandate of this new approach. First, advocates have demanded that various groups considered to be underrepresented in medical research—in particular, women, racial and ethnic minorities, children, and the elderly—be included in greater numbers in clinical studies and in pharmaceutical drug development. Second, they have insisted that researchers test for differences across these populations, rather than assuming that findings from any one group, such as adult white men, can be extrapolated to others.

In the United States, this paradigm takes particular forms. First, it includes a political and scientific process of determining which categories are going to matter—or, in the policy lingo used within federal health agencies, who is going to count as a "special population." And in the policies, guidelines, and laws that I track, the categories that have most explicitly been made to matter are sex and gender, race or ethnicity, and age (at both extremes—pediatric and geriatric). Second, we can perceive the outlines of the paradigm in the new expectations codified in a series of federal laws, policies, and guidelines issued between 1986 and the present that require or encourage research inclusiveness and the measurement of difference. For example, the NIH Revitalization Act, signed into law by President Clinton in 1993, requires not only that women and minorities be included in NIH-funded clinical research, but also that clinical trials be "designed and carried out in a manner sufficient to provide for a valid analysis of whether the variables being studied in the trial affect women or members of minority groups, as the case may be, differently than other subjects in the trial" (National Institutes of Health Revitalization Act 1993). The NIH Revitalization Act of 1993 has received attention from scholars because of its specifications about sexual and racial/ethnic inclusion, but in fact, it is only one of many such policies. Finally, the paradigm takes visible form in the creation of bureaucratic offices within the U.S. Department of Health and Human Services (DHHS) and within its component agencies such as the NIH, the Food and Drug Administration (FDA), and the Centers for Disease Control and Prevention (CDC). These particularly include offices of women's health and offices of minority health.

Looking farther downstream, the paradigm institutionalizes new standard operating procedures for biomedical research and pharmaceutical drug development (Epstein

2007, chap. 6). For example, researchers with federal funding and drug companies seeking marketing approval are obliged to document the numbers of people from various social groups who participate in studies and, in some cases, to describe differences in outcomes between these groups. The NIH standard grant application form, called the "PHS 398," was revised to include a chart on which investigators must enter their study recruitment targets by "sex/gender" and by race and ethnicity. If the proposal is then funded, the investigator is also required to submit annual reports on accrual of subjects, demonstrating that the actual demographics of the study are consistent with the inclusion plan that was proposed originally. The adoption of census categories for this purpose has led to predictable difficulties and a certain measure of force-fitting of bodies to categories—particularly in the growing number of cases in which clinical trial subjects are recruited from outside the United States.[3] The NIH then aggregates these figures in a database and uses the information to prepare reports for Congress. If investigators do not intend to include both women and men, a range of racial and ethnic groups, and children as well as adults in a proposed study, then they must explain the rationale for exclusion as part of their grant application text. When received by the NIH, all applications are coded by peer review panels to indicate whether women, minorities, and children are included, and whether the inclusion or exclusion is considered acceptable or unacceptable. In addition, if the applicant is proposing a large, phase III clinical trial, then reviewers are expected to comment on whether the investigator is planning to conduct subgroup analysis (either a full-fledged analysis capable of showing statistical significance, for those cases in which prior evidence suggests that results may vary by sex/gender, race, ethnicity, or age, or a simpler, "valid analysis of differences," for those cases in which there is no reason to expect variation by subgroup; U.S. Public Health Service 1998; National Institutes of Health 2001).

Similarly, in the late 1980s, the FDA began calling for each "new drug application" to "give the number, age range, and sex distribution of subjects" as part of a table showing all studies conducted on the drug being considered for licensing. In addition to providing figures on clinical trial participants, pharmaceutical companies are required to give specific information by subset for any differences in response to a drug revealed by the clinical trials. The "subsets of interest," the FDA noted, might well vary with the drug and condition being studied, but usually would include sex, race, age, and size, along with such diverse potential factors as the severity of the disease, whether patients suffer from other ("concomitant") illnesses, the patients' histories of therapy with other medications for the condition, and smoking and alcohol use. However, the subsets that pharmaceutical companies are specifically requested to tabulate are what they describe as the major ones of age, sex, and race (U.S. Department of Health and Human Services 1988; see also Epstein 2007, chap. 6).

While some experts, policy makers, and health advocates have embraced these new understandings about bodies, groups, and health as obviously valuable, and others have dismissed them as pernicious or silly, my goal is to do neither of these things. In my book *Inclusion*, where I discuss these developments at length, I seek to understand, first, how a particular way of thinking about medical difference in the United States helped give rise to a strategy to improve medical research by making it more inclusive. Second, I show how this strategy gained supporters, took institutional form, and became converted into common sense. Third, I try to shed light on its various consequences for government agencies, biomedical researchers, and pharmaceutical companies as well as for the social groups targeted by new policies. And finally, by comparing this approach to other ways of imagining the meanings of identities, differences, and inequalities in biomedical contexts, I examine the extent to which the new common sense might lead to better health and a more just society as well as the extent to which I believe it falls short or takes a wrong turn.[4]

In this chapter, my goals are more restricted. I will bypass the story of how the inclusion-and-difference paradigm came into being and will instead consider specific issues relating to the significance of these developments. I argue that the recent debates concerning the scientific meaning of race (and particularly, the biomedical significance of race) ought to be analyzed in relation to these broader biopolitics of inclusion and difference. To make this point, I focus on three topics. First, I emphasize the biopolitical significance of group-specific medical research within present-day practices of governance. Second, I argue for the importance of race, sex, and age as attributes that permit new forms of standardization for political and biomedical purposes. Finally, I draw out what I take to be the important implication that scholars interested in these historical developments should not be studying the race-science-medicine nexus alone, separately from other social categorizations.

Biopolitics

Michel Foucault (1980) used the term *biopolitics* to describe the increasing concern by modern states with managing and measuring human populations as well as the treatment of such populations as a resource and object of administrative rule. Building on this influential concept, I suggest that the inclusion-and-difference paradigm can be understood as an example of a *biopolitical paradigm*, a term meant to suggest how practices of governance and scientific investigation have become interwoven. By *biopolitical paradigm*, I mean a framework of ideas, standards, formal procedures, and unarticulated understandings that specifies how concerns about health, medicine, and the body are made the simultaneous focus of biomedicine and state policy.[5] The inclusion-and-difference paradigm is one such biopolitical paradigm both because it reflects the presumption that health research is an appropriate and important site for state intervention and regulation and because it infuses the life sciences with new political import.

While some might see the inclusion-and-difference paradigm as an example of how biomedicine (for better or for worse) gets politicized, it might just as well be taken as evidence of the converse—how, in the present period, governing gets "biomedicalized." Medical research thereby becomes reconceived as a domain in which a host of political problems can get worked out—the nature of social justice, the limits and possibilities of citizenship, and the meanings of equality and difference at the biological as well as social levels.

The label "inclusion-and-difference paradigm" is my own invention, and no one within the DHHS, the pharmaceutical industry, or the academic world of clinical research uses the term. But this general approach to health research policy can be seen as built into the standard operating procedures, discourse, and organizational structure of the DHHS as well as a wide range of other biomedical contexts. What work is it doing? As a biopolitical paradigm, the inclusion-and-difference approach hybridizes scientific and state policies and categories. Specifically, it takes two different areas of concern—the meaning of biological difference and the status of socially subordinated groups—and weaves them together by articulating a distinctive way of asking and answering questions about the demarcating of subpopulations of patients and citizens.

This is not an outcome that we should simply take for granted. Although the domains of scientific work and governance are constantly and increasingly crisscrossing, it is hard to anticipate the specific ways in which they can become woven together through words and deeds. Who would have expected that technical questions about the methodologies used by medical researchers and political struggles about group rights would come to be seen as inextricably linked? A contingent set of historical circumstances in the United States prompted an eclectic set of reformers to bring these issues into joint focus—and to assume not only that political pressure should be brought to bear to make science function better, but also that clinical research was an appropriate arena in which goals of social equality and social justice could be worked on. Yet the bridging of concerns made cultural sense, given the existing relations among biomedical institutions, state administration, and social movement activism in countries like the United States in recent decades.

The point here is not that the pristine domain of science was invaded by political concerns; rather, the inclusion-and-difference paradigm is biopolitical because it promotes ways of defining, knowing, and governing populations that are derived from, and serve to shape, both governmental and scientific practices simultaneously. Biomedical science is linked to governance, in this case, not simply because the health of the people has become conceived of as a matter of crucial public concern, but because academic medical researchers, pharmaceutical company scientists, federal health bureaucrats, and lay health advocates have collaborated in deciding on the

basic population subunits for biomedical purposes. The effect, as I have already suggested, is to presume that the axes of differentiation and categories of personhood
used in the worlds of political organizing and bureaucratic rule are also the best categories to use for biomedical purposes.

In that sense, the inclusion-and-difference paradigm reflects three broad, long-term,
and convergent historical trends that have been on the rise, particularly over the past
century. First, the agencies of modern democratic states have become increasingly
more involved in naming and singling out subgroups of people for policy purposes,
assigning social rewards (or punishments) according to administrative categories, and
thereby placing phenomena such as race and gender at the heart of the state's maintenance of social order (Omi and Winant 1986; Connell 1990; Brown 1992; Espiritu
1992; Starr 1992, 160–161; Nagel 1995; Porter 1995; Luker 1998; Benhabib 1999;
Goldberg 2002; Skrentny 2002, 85–142; De Zwart 2005). Second, social movements
have become ever more likely both to assert demands on the basis of claimed social
identities and to elaborate new collective identities through their very activism
(Melucci 1989; Morris and Mueller 1992; Johnston, Laraña, and Gusfield 1994). Third,
scientific experts progressively have developed new technologies and understandings
that result in the segmenting or classifying of the human species, with the result of
sometimes shoring up familiar forms of social differentiation, and sometimes (e.g., by
the identification of shared genetic characteristics) creating new demarcations or bases
of solidarity (Rabinow 1996).

The inclusion-and-difference paradigm unites and harmonizes the categorical work
being done in these different worlds of state administration, identity politics, and
biomedical science. The various opponents of the so-called standard human were
adept practitioners of what I term *categorical alignment*. Reformers proceeded as if it
were self-evident that the mobilization categories of identity politics, the biological
categories of medical research, and the social classifications of state bureaucrats were
all one and the same system of categorization. In effect, they assumed that the differences defined *politically* in our society between various haves and have-nots mapped
onto the differences that emerged out of biomedical research—for example, the differences in the distribution of genetic variants of the cytochrome p450 enzymes
responsible for drug metabolism. By bridging manifestly scientific and political arguments, proponents of inclusion were able to *act as if* the social movement identity
labels, the biomedical terms, and the state-sanctioned categories were all one and the
same set of classifications—that is, that the politically salient categories were simultaneously the scientifically relevant categories. It followed from this presumption that
political and biomedical remedies could be pursued simultaneously through a single
project of reform.

The marker of successful categorical alignment work is that it becomes invisible in
hindsight: the superimposition of political classifications with scientific ones seems
natural and inevitable. But it is worth noting that there are many bases by which

claims of inequality could plausibly be put forward in the domain of health research, including by social class and geographic region, or in relation to social practices and social structures, *rather than* categorical membership. And, likewise, there are many ways of representing the dispersion of biological or genetic differences within the human population. So it was not foreordained that medical and political categories would come to be aligned in this case.

Standardization: Beyond the Standard Human

Let me now take up a second question about the significance of these biomedical reforms, one that concerns the way that biomedical researchers and policy makers seek to standardize their practices. Or to put it another way, what has come to replace the much-maligned standard human?

Advocates of the inclusion-and-difference paradigm repudiated one-size-fits-all medicine along with the notion that humanity could be standardized at the level of the species—that is, they rejected the presumption that biomedical knowledge could be derived from the study of, or be broadly applicable to, the standard human. But at the same time, these skeptics of universalism did not veer fully to the opposite extreme of embracing total particularity. Though they frequently invoked the rhetoric of "individualized therapy," their response, in fact, was *not* to insist on the medical uniqueness of each individual; rather, advocates proposed that the working units of biomedical knowledge making could be *social groups*: women, children, the elderly, Asian Americans, and so on. The inclusion-and-difference paradigm therefore enshrines what I call *niche standardization*: a general way of transforming human populations into standardized objects available for scientific scrutiny, political administration, marketing, or other purposes that rejects both universalism and individualism and instead standardizes at the level of the categorical social group—one standard for men, another for women; one standard for blacks, another for whites, another for Asians; one standard for children, another for adults; and so on. In place of a standard human, we find an intersecting set of standard subtypes.

Niche standardization has perhaps not gotten the attention it deserves because many analysts of state bureaucratic practices have emphasized the tendency of modern states to homogenize populations—what Max Weber once called the "leveling of the governed" by the bureaucratic machine (Gerth and Wright Mills 1946, 226). Or alternatively, analysts of practices of governance have considered the contrary tendency to administer through individuation. These analysts have emphasized how states control populations through technologies of identification, such as passports, fingerprints, and biometrics, which seek to precisely distinguish one citizen from another (Torpey 2000; Caplan and Torpey 2001; Cole 2001), or how states make use of the practices, emphasized by Foucault and his followers, of surveillance and comparison of persons against norms (Foucault 1979). What all these discussions share is the presumption of a polar opposition between leveling and individuation, or between universalism and particularity. This binary focus diverts attention from niche standardization: the management (and redefinition) of population subgroups via a specification of standards at the intermediate level of the categorical group.

Within the world of modern biomedicine, as well, niche standardization has been overlooked because of the presumption of a fundamental tension between the universal and the individual. A familiar and continuing debate in biomedicine juxtaposes two ways of conceiving the patient. On one hand, modern medical practice is associated with more or less universal, homogeneous, and standardized approaches to patient care. This standardization reflects a number of historical developments, including the rise of "scientific medicine" in the late nineteenth century and the advent of the randomized clinical trial and modern methods of pharmaceutical drug regulation in the twentieth century. However, it is most often preached by adherents of evidence-based medicine, which prescribes standardized treatment protocols that are well supported by research (Timmermans and Berg 2003). On the other hand, when treating individual patients, physicians frequently reject these standardized formulas (which they sometimes dismiss contemptuously as mere "cookbook medicine") in favor of more particularistic approaches that depend less on data than on experience and seasoned judgment—the art, as opposed to the science, of medicine. New scientific developments like pharmacogenomics that aim, eventually, at so-called personalized medicine through access to the patient's genetic profile represent a different individualizing approach, one that would be particularistic but also scientific. But if these are the usual polar alternatives, then what is missing is the important intermediate solution, targeted at the middle level of the collective actor: medicine that is not personalized, but rather, group-specific.

To be sure, niche standardization is broadly familiar in the domain of consumer production and consumption. If the existence of a single standard human was the presumption of fordism (the old-fashioned system of producing mass commodities as predictably invariant as the Model T, to be sold to a universal consumer), then niche standardization is consistent with postfordist production—the niche marketing of diverse products to well-defined subgroups. It is in this context that we may consider recent and familiar examples of pharmaceutical industry marketing practices in relation to distinct racial or ethnic groups.

In 2005, the compound called BiDil, which treats heart failure, became the first drug ever approved by the FDA for use only in a single ethnic group. The drug had initially failed in tests with a diverse population, but analysis of racial subsets had suggested a reduced mortality for African Americans. A subsequent trial with 1,050 African Americans, conducted by the manufacturer, NitroMed, appeared to bear out the claim of benefit. In this way, niche standardization in medical research went hand in hand with niche marketing by industry (Kahn 2004).

Here is a less familiar example: in 2002, Zelnorm, a drug made by Novartis to treat irritable bowel syndrome, became the first of a few drugs so far approved by the FDA for use only in women for a condition that affects both sexes.[6] The drug's advantages over a placebo in a mixed-sex population could not be demonstrated with statistical significance. In this case, as well, the presumption is that the effects of medications correlate in a more or less standard way with categories of group belonging—that is, niche standardization provides the justification for niche marketing.

It is noteworthy, however, that proponents of niche standardization in medicine often adopt a discourse of individualism, but then develop policies that are aimed at social groups. To give one of many examples, an article by FDA officials published in *Science* in 1995 observes, "Since the early 1980s, [the FDA] has been interested in the individualization of therapy, that is, determining whether and how treatment should be modified for various demographic groups within the population" (Sherman, Temple, and Merkatz 1995, 793). This slippage between referencing individuals and groups is a common feature of discourse surrounding niche standardization; it endows the practice with legitimacy by associating it with individualism, one of the cherished values of U.S. political culture.

One additional biomedical domain where we see niche standardization playing an interesting role is in the renewed attention to group-specific differences at the level of recruitment of subjects into medical experiments. As a consequence of the policies that make up the inclusion-and-difference paradigm, researchers and pharmaceutical companies are now much more attentive to the practical challenges involved in recruiting people from so-called hard-to-recruit populations to participate in clinical research (Epstein 2008). Not only must researchers find willing subjects, and not only must those subjects be diverse, but the groups that researchers now feel pressure to represent include groups, such as children or African Americans, that are routinely considered among the most difficult of all to find and convince to participate.

In fact, I would argue that there has recently emerged a new science—one that has not named itself, but that I call *recruitmentology*—that has sought to develop an empirical body of studies scientifically evaluating the efficacy of various social, psychological, technological, and economic means of locating members of hard-to-recruit populations and convincing them that they want to become human subjects (Epstein 2008). Recruitmentology has promoted hybrid ways of thinking about race via the filtering of social scientific frameworks into the clinical research domain—awkward encounters in which depictions of race as a bounded, quasibiological, medical, and administrative category sit uneasily alongside an evolving interest in understanding racial identities and communities as sociocultural phenomena. In addressing the mandate to recruit racially diverse subject populations, recruitmentologists try to make sense of race, while simultaneously grappling with problems of community mistrust and collective memory of abuse. At the same time, the increasingly transnational character of biomedical research is intensifying the exploitative dimensions of recruitment, while further transforming the racialized character of human experimentation (Petryna 2006).

Connecting Inequalities

A central implication of this analysis is that attempts to study the modern biomedical and bioscientific remaking of race—at least in the United States[7]—should do so in a way that places race in relation to the other forms of difference and inequality that are encompassed within the biopolitical regime that I have been describing. I would like to deepen this argument with some closer attention to the relation between race and sex in debates about biology and health. My goal here is to hang on to two intuitions simultaneously.

On one hand, race differences and sex differences are *different differences*, and they cannot be conflated. They operate according to different logics; they have different histories; they have different groundings in the body and in the body politic. Therefore it is important to question the manner in which the inclusion-and-difference paradigm functions to construct rough equivalences among the various forms of difference that are recognized within it. From the standpoint of DHHS policies and procedures, sex/gender, race/ethnicity, and age are all treated as formally equivalent modes of difference to be handled administratively in similar ways. Because of contingent factors relevant to their histories, the policies and standards that make up the inclusion-and-difference paradigm do vary somewhat from one type of difference to another. (For example, the NIH does not compile statistics on the age distribution of subjects in its research portfolio, for the simple reason that Congress never required it to do so.) There are also some differences between agencies in the definitions of terms. (For example, the NIH considers anyone under the age of twenty-one to be a child for research purposes, while at the FDA, the definition is sixteen years or younger.) Nevertheless, in a more overarching sense, the paradigm tends to flatten differences—to conceptualize sex/gender, race/ethnicity, and age as ways of differing that are all analogous or commensurate from a policy standpoint.[8] Formally, the policies also tend to treat sex/gender, race/ethnicity, and age as discrete characteristics of individuals, rather than as complexly intersecting relational properties of groups (Shim 2000, 180). Hence, out of "different differences," the policies of the inclusion-and-difference paradigm have created a sort of generalized difference. This flattening may facilitate bureaucratic administration, but it also may problematically presume equivalences and analogies across very different sorts of categorizing systems.

But on the other hand, even while asserting the incommensurability of differences, we should also pay careful attention to the broadly *similar* processes by which scientific and political actors seek to naturalize differences *of whatever sort* and to ground them in human biology. In particular, by juxtaposing the question of race differences with that of sex differences, not only can we better understand how race and sex are jointly naturalized within the inclusion-and-difference paradigm, but we can also raise questions about why the naturalization of race has received so much more critical scrutiny than the naturalization of sex.

One of the consequences of the policies and regulations that make up the inclusion-and-difference paradigm is that they have promoted a whole host of findings of apparent race differences and apparent sex differences in drug response, health outcomes, and biological processes. But there is a noteworthy distinction to be drawn between the cases of race differences and sex differences: reports of biological difference by race have sparked a heated medical and public controversy about "racial profiling" (Jamerson 1993, 979; Schwartz 2001; Burchard et al. 2003; Cooper, Kaufman, and Ward 2003; Phimister 2003), but no corresponding debate seems to have arisen as yet with regard to biological differences by sex. For the most part, there has been little public discussion of the merits or risks of sex profiling in medicine—indeed, the phrase does not even exist.

Emphasis on sex differences in medicine is part of a larger trend toward claiming or assuming the overriding significance of biology and genetics in understanding the behavior of males and females, in domains ranging from brain functioning to mating behavior.[9] As with race, arguments about sex differences drawn from genetics can cut both ways, and occasionally, reports of fundamental genetic similarities make their way into public view. For example, in 2001, *The Scientist* magazine reported, "Genetic studies are revealing that men and women are more similar than distinct. So far, of the approximately 31,000 genes in the human genome, men and women differ only in the two sex chromosomes, X and Y, and only a few dozen genes seem to be involved" (Beale 2001, 18). However, the notion that our usual distinction between "pink and blue" might be replaced with "a blurred rainbow of confusion"—as the article's author put it—runs up against the vast wave of commentary that assumes or reports on stark differences between the sexes.

Nowhere is the attention to biological sex differences more pronounced at present than in biomedicine, and the concern with the effects of pharmaceutical drugs is an especially important example. Over the course of the 1990s, a range of reports in the medical literature described differences in drug effects involving both the metabolizing of drugs and their effects on bodily tissues, building on earlier research dating back to the early 1970s. A review in 2001 by pharmacologist Mary Berg noted a wide variety of sex- or gender-related differences, significantly including the effect of oral contraceptives in increasing or decreasing the speed of clearance of drugs such as aspirin, caffeine, and morphine. Berg also described research in "chronopharmacology"—the effect of bodily rhythms, such as the menstrual cycle, on how drugs are processed (Berg 2001). Another review essay—by Monica Gandhi and coauthors, published in 2004—attributed pharmacokinetic differences by sex not only to variation in the cytochrome P450 enzymes, but also to a number of other factors, including body weight and gastric emptying time (Gandhi et al. 2004). Gandhi and coauthors also discussed the burgeoning literature on sex differences in response to pain medications (believed to reflect differences in how men and women actually experience pain) as well as the evidence on differences in the effects and side effects of antipsychotic and antidepressant medications. Antiviral drugs targeting HIV have provided yet another important example: women appear to have more frequent and more severe side effects with several classes of anti-HIV medications, though some research also indicates that such drugs may also be more efficacious for women in terms of keeping the virus in check (Gandhi et al. 2004, 512–513).

"We now know that gender is one of the most important factors that influences and predicts response to all kinds of treatments," FDA commissioner Mark McClellan said in 2003 in a public speech. "The FDA is working to better define the genetic differences between men and women that influence how they are going to respond to a particular medication" (*Sexx Matters* 2003, 1). Indeed, research on these various differences in the effects of medications has been a priority at the various women's health offices, which have organized conferences and developed research agendas. A particular concern has been the issue of adverse drug reactions, estimated by the FDA to affect women at least one and half times as often as men (Anderson 2005, 25). In April 2004, the Agency for Healthcare Research and Quality (a DHHS agency) held a two-day meeting of experts to consider the problem of adverse drug reactions and to focus on the goal of "Improving the Use and Safety of Medications in Women through Sex/ Gender and Race/Ethnicity Analysis" (Correa-de-Araujo 2005, 12).

The growing literature on biological sex differences in medicine extends beyond the important issue of pharmacology to include attention to many other kinds of differences in biological processes with health implications. According to the "statement of editorial purpose" of an electronic journal devoted to women's health research, "it is increasingly evident that sex-based differences exist in a range of conditions, including heart disease, cancer, stroke, depression, HIV/AIDS, autoimmune disorders, neurologic diseases, bone and joint disorders, as well as in reactions to drugs" (Medscape 2003). Heart function and cardiovascular disease provide an excellent example. According to an editorial published in *Cardiovascular Research* in 2004 (titled "A Radical Idea: Men and Women Are Different"), "gender has a pronounced influence on the type and severity of cardiovascular disease that will likely ensue during one's lifetime. Sex differences have been noted in most major cardiovascular diseases including coronary heart disease, stroke, and hypertension" (Bowles 2004, 5). Women also tend to develop heart disease at a later age than do men, and women and men are reported to have different symptoms prior to heart attacks—indeed, the canonical symptom of chest pain "was notably absent or was described differently by the women," according to research reported by Gardner in 2004. Women are more likely than men to have a hidden form of coronary disease (Grady 2006), and women with coronary artery disease and implantable cardioverter-defibrillators also have been reported to develop a form of arrhythmia more often than do men with the device (Medscape 2004). As described in a recent article in *Science* on the "Molecular and Cellular Basis of Cardiovascular Gender Differences," many of these differences may be linked to hormones, and some may be traced to developmental pathways laid down in utero (Mendelsohn and Karas 2005).

On April 25, 2001, the Institute of Medicine (IOM) of the National Academy of Sciences announced the forthcoming publication of a book-length report titled *Exploring the Biological Contributions to Human Health: Does Sex Matter?* This 288-page volume was the product of a lengthy review by a sixteen-member panel of experts, and it was sponsored by a range of government agencies, advocacy groups, and pharmaceutical companies. The report answered the rhetorical question, does sex matter? emphatically in the affirmative: "Sex does matter. It matters in ways that we did not expect. Undoubtedly, it also matters in ways that we have not begun to imagine" (Wizemann and Pardue 2001, x). Calling for medical researchers to study sex differences "from womb to tomb," the panel reviewed the literature on sex differences in the efficacy of pharmaceutical drugs, sex differences in the etiology and pathogenesis of autoimmune conditions, sex differences in the experiencing of pain, sex differences in coronary heart disease, and so on. The panel also offered a raft of recommendations, including the quite radical one that researchers should "determine and disclose the sex of origin of biological research materials" and that "journal editors should encourage researchers . . . to specify the extent to which analyses of the data by sex were included in the study" (Wizemann and Pardue 2001, 178–179).

By coincidence, the announcement of the IOM report preceded by only about a week the publication, in the *New England Journal of Medicine*, of an editorial by a journal editor that blasted the practice of "racial profiling" in medicine (Schwartz 2001). But where reports of medically relevant, biological differences by race provoked controversy, the IOM report seemed almost universally to be praised. For example, in a fifteen-minute segment on *NewsHour with Jim Lehrer*, the story was presented straightforwardly as an episode in the forward march of medical knowledge ("Sex Matters" 2001). Particularly keen to promote the IOM's conclusions was the Society for Women's Health Research (SWHR), one of the groups that had sponsored the report. In the early 1990s, the SWHR had coalesced around the goal of inclusion of women in research and had campaigned for the NIH Revitalization Act. By the late 1990s, the society's raison d'être was the furtherance of research on differences between men and women that bore medical significance. "This report substantiates everything we've been saying for six years," Phyllis Greenberger, the president of SWHR, told the press. "Many scientists see the emphasis on sex and gender differences as a passing fad, reflecting some kind of political agenda. But the Institute of Medicine has validated this as an important field of research" (Pear 2001, A14). Some time later, at a conference sponsored by the NIH's Office of Research on Women's Health, Sherry Marts, the SWHR's scientific director, repeated the rhetorical question in the report's subtitle and suggested that the most pithy executive summary to the report might be the single word *yes*.[10]

The SWHR has been a key proponent of a social movement within biomedicine, on which the IOM report conferred crucial legitimacy. Along with academic medical researchers, NIH scientists, and scientists at pharmaceutical companies invested in women's health, the SWHR has sought to establish a new field of study known as *gender-based biology* or (more recently, in an attempt to clarify their interest in what they understand to be biological, and not social, processes) *sex-based biology*. Others, such as cardiologist Marianne Legato at Columbia University, have used the term *gender-specific medicine*. As distinct from more generic proposals for the development of a women's health specialty in medicine, advocates of sex-based biology emphasize fundamental, thoroughgoing, biological differences between men's and women's bodies, from the heart, to the brain, to the immune system. Those who subscribe to this movement believe that women—and men—deserve separate medical scrutiny because they are biologically different at the level of the cell, the organ, the system, and the organism (Haseltine 1997, 331–336).

To what extent, if any, is the case of biological differences by sex or gender analogous to that of biological differences by race and ethnicity? What does it mean that racial profiling in medicine has become an intellectual battleground, while sex profiling has not? These questions have received little direct discussion. To the very limited extent that analysts (in academia and elsewhere) have addressed the comparison, it has been to contrast the "tricky" case of race with the "easy" case of sex: obviously men and women are biologically different, it is claimed, while racial difference at the biological level—and even the determination of which racial categories to work with, or whether race exists at all—is contested terrain. Thus (the argument goes), while choosing a medication on the basis of the patient's sex may be sensible and commendable, making such determinations according to race is deeply problematic. Even those who differ on the merits of racial profiling, such as the philosophers of science Ian Hacking (2005, 106) and Michael Root (2003, 1181), are in agreement when it comes to this point.

It appears that many critics of racial profiling in medicine have engaged in boundary work, erecting a wall between sex and race to designate the study of sex differences as good science and the study of race differences as bad science. Certainly the biological significance of sex and race are different cases to consider. However, it immediately bears saying that biological sex is *not* an either-or—not at the anatomic, the hormonal, or the chromosomal level. There are no truly dichotomous variables in nature, and as many scholars have shown, there is no precise or fully satisfactory biological means of demarcating all males from all females. Moreover, most sex differences reported in the medical literature, like most race differences, are statistical differences between means, not absolute differences between groups. (Furthermore, many of the published findings of sex differences may be less robust than claimed or may simply be incorrect.[11]) And if so, then the problems associated with profiling—such as the risk of treating individuals improperly on the basis of their group affiliations—may apply to medical research on sex differences, too, and not just to research on differences by race.

It is noteworthy that so many claims in the sex-based biology literature are framed, at least rhetorically, as universal observations about all women and all men. Florence Haseltine (1997, 333) has written that "the female body has more fat and less water"; Marianne Legato and Carol Colman's (1991) book is called *The Female Heart*. Representations of medically relevant sex differences in the popular press likewise use the language of blanket differences. According to *USA Today Magazine* (2003, 8), "women are less active and consume less oxygen than men. Rib cages are smaller in women, resulting in lower lung capacity." Also, "Women say 'ouch!' to pain before men do, but tolerate the pain better." At least at the level of rhetoric, such claims appear to divide the universe of human experience into two utterly separate camps, while thoroughly homogenizing all that which lies within each one. Because of the binary and either-or nature of the discourse on sex differences, such claims seem even more all encompassing and less nuanced than those about racial and ethnic differences in medicine.

Certain sex differences, such as sex-linked traits linked to genes on the X chromosome, may indeed function to demarcate half of humanity from the other half—leaving aside, just for the moment, those individuals whose chromosomal sex is nonstandard. But most of the claims about sex differences are, once again, statements about differences between averages. Clearly it is not the case that all women have smaller rib cages than all men, or that all women say ouch first. Just as the science of statistics has constructed diseases as racial, so statistical processes also result in the sexing of diseases. Stefan Hirschauer and Annemarie Mol (1995, 377) have described how this process works using the example of anemia:

There is nothing inherently sexed about this disease. . . . A normal hemoglobin level differs from one person to the next and has no sex. . . . Statistical practice turns anemia into a sexed disease. Statistical practice builds on the anatomical differentiation between the sexes and clusters hemoglobin levels of hundreds of people identified anatomically as either males or females. Two curves emerge. The median and cut-off point of the first are a little higher than those of the second. Thus "men" have a higher normal hemoglobin level than do "women."

As Hirschauer and Mol (1995, 377) observed, "the sex generated in this way is not one of bodies but is one of populations."

Particularly in the case of the pharmacokinetics and pharmacodynamics of medications, usually the best that can be claimed is a statement about probabilities. Raymond Woosley, a pharmacology expert who has researched the harmful effects of drugs that prolong the "QT interval" in the heartbeat, noted that certain of those drugs affect men and women in strikingly different ways, while with other drugs, "the most sensitive male [is] equal to the average female, so there is considerable overlap; . . . it's a mean difference" (pers. comm., August 9, 2000). Thus sex profiling in the clinic—drawing a decision about treatment based on knowledge of the patient's sex—may function quite reliably in certain circumstances, while in other circumstances, it might raise the familiar problem of taking statistical generalities about a group and applying them to individual cases. In other words, Hacking's claim that "many medical differences between males and females are uniform, but medical differences between races are almost always only statistical" fails to ask the crucial question of just how many medical differences between males and females are statistical as well.

As Judith Lorber (1993) has argued, the overriding mistake of so many "epistemologically spurious" studies of sex differences in both the biological and social sciences is that they begin simply by assuming that "men" and "women" are the relevant groups to compare; they then look for differences between them, and then attribute whatever they find to the underlying sex difference. Lorber (1993, 571) observed, "These designs rarely question the categorization of their subjects into two and only two groups, even though they often find more significant within-group differences than between-group differences."

People and groups differ in an unlimited variety of ways. The problem here—as with race—is when we assume that the ways of differing that are most socially salient and obvious are necessarily the ones that carry the most explanatory weight (Hanson 1997). In the context of clinical care, this becomes dangerous. The unavoidable risk is that some individuals might receive the wrong diagnosis or treatment if they are approached as representative members of their social group. The hard-and-fast language of binary sex difference makes it particularly difficult to catch sight of this limitation, while the reliance on the group stereotype then serves to reinforce that hardness and fastness.

Conclusion

Once again, it is important to insist on the irreducibility of forms of difference and inequality. There can be no simple parallels drawn from the stories of race differences and sex differences in biomedicine. However, as we increasingly recognize the flaws and limits in biological conceptions of racial difference in health, this should lead us to recognize the similar flaws that may exist in notions of sex differences. In both cases, an overeagerness to assume and naturalize difference may actually get in the way of addressing the serious racial and gender disparities in health outcomes.

This recognition itself calls attention to the importance of considering race jointly with the other forms of identity, difference, and disparity that are all handled administratively by the inclusion-and-difference paradigm. (Of course, that includes attending to the *intersections* of these categories.) For each of these categories that have been fully or partially integrated within this same biopolitical framework, we should be asking a common set of questions: What are the consequences of assuming that a category of political mobilization is also, automatically, inevitably, and uniformly, a relevant category for biomedical purposes? When does this work? When does it not? What categories does it leave out? What happens to our ability to address social inequalities when we assume that differential health outcomes are simply a consequence of biological differences between groups? How can we make sure that we are being appropriately attentive to all the health risks that are shaped less immediately by membership in a group than by the practices in which one engages, the networks within which one moves, or the material and social resources one has at one's disposal? These are the critical questions across the board.

Notes

1. The categorical terms used in this article are meant to represent the terms employed by the actors I studied, in all the ambiguity of everyday usage. On the history of the biomedical reliance on age, sex, and race categories, see also Hanson (1997).

2. I analyze these developments at greater length in Epstein (2007).

3. On one hand, NIH investigators are encouraged to collect identifying data from their participants around the globe in ways that allow participants to use meaningful, indigenous identifying terms. On the other hand, investigators nonetheless must take these culturally specific responses and aggregate them into the categories sanctioned by the Office of Management and Budget (the FDA guidance on racial categories takes a similar approach to this question; Food and Drug Administration 2005, 5). Exactly how this aggregating work is to be performed is not explained in NIH guidelines (National Institutes of Health 2000; the instructions changed slightly in 2004; see also Epstein 2007, 148–154).

4. Data for the larger project of which this article is a part were obtained in accordance with a strategy to juxtapose perceptions and trace actions across multiple "social worlds" (Clarke 1990), including those of clinical researchers concerned with recruiting underrepresented groups, pharmaceutical companies, federal health officials promoting the health of so-called special populations, politicians, and health advocacy organizations. Data have been obtained from seventy-two semistructured, in-person interviews in and around Boston, New Haven, New York, Baltimore, Washington, D.C., Atlanta, Ann Arbor, Chicago, Denver, Boulder, San Francisco, Los Angeles, and San Diego. Those interviewed included past and present NIH, FDA, and DHHS officials;

clinical researchers; pharmacology researchers; biostatisticians; medical journal editors; drug company scientists; women's health advocates and activists; bioethicists; members of Congress; congressional aides; lawyers; representatives of pharmaceutical company trade associations; experts in public health; and social scientists. Additional primary data sources included documents and reports from the NIH, the FDA, the CDC, the DHHS, and the U.S. Congress; archival materials from health advocacy organizations; materials from pharmaceutical companies and their trade organizations; articles, letters, editorials, and news reports published in medical, scientific, and public health journals; and articles, editorials, letters, and reports appearing in the mass media.

5. In using the term *paradigm*, my goal is not to resurrect historian and philosopher of science Thomas Kuhn's familiar (but often criticized) account of decisive shifts over time in how communities of scientific practitioners look at the world (Kuhn 1970). I explain my usage in greater detail in Epstein (2007, chap. 1).

6. Subsequently, the drug was withdrawn from the market.

7. On the extent to which aspects of the inclusion-and-difference paradigm can be found in the policies and practices of other countries, see Epstein (2007, 273–276).

8. This construction of equivalences bears similarities to the "commensuration" practices described by Wendy Espeland and Mitchell Stevens (1998, 316), and it serves a similar function: it "offers standardized ways of constructing proxies for uncertain and elusive qualities [and] condenses and reduces the amount of information people have to process, [thereby] simplifying decision-making."

9. For a characteristic example, see Marano (2003). For critiques of biological reductionism in the understanding of male-female differences, see Tavris (1992), Fausto-Sterling (1993, 2000a, 2000b, 2005), van den Wijngaard (1997), Lancaster (2003), and Harding and O'Barr ([1975] 1987).

10. Author's field notes, "Science Meets Reality: Recruitment and Retention of Women in Clinical Studies, and the Clinical Role of Relevance," scientific workshop sponsored by the NIH Office of Research on Women's Health, Washington, D.C., January 6–9, 2003.

11. A telling moment came in August 2007, with the publication of an article in the *Journal of the American Medical Association* reanalyzing reported sex differences in the effects of genes on disease. Nikolaos Patsopoulos et al. (2007) scoured the published literature for articles so certain about having found such differences that the claims appeared in the articles' titles. But when they reviewed 432 sex-difference claims made in seventy-seven articles, these researchers found a vast tendency to overstate or misinterpret. Most of the claims to have found sex differences were poorly documented. Many were spurious due to faulty statistical analyses. Hardly any had been corroborated in later studies. When the researchers reanalyzed the original data from the studies, half of the supposed sex differences were not statistically significant.

References

Anderson, Gail D. 2005. Sex and racial differences in pharmacological response: Where is the evidence? Pharmacogenetics, pharmacokinetics, and pharmacodynamics. *Journal of Women's Health* 14:19–29.

Beale, Bob. 2001. The sexes: New insights into the X and Y chromosomes. *Scientist (Philadelphia, Pa.)* 23:18.

Benhabib, Seyla. 1999. Civil society and the politics of identity and difference in a global context. In *Diversity and its discontents: Cultural conflict and common ground in contemporary American society*, ed. N. J. Smelser and J. C. Alexander. Princeton, NJ: Princeton University Press, 293–312.

Berg, Mary J. 2001. Pharmacological differences between men and women. In *Principles of clinical pharmacology*, ed. A. J. Atkinson, C. E. Daniels, R. L. Dedrick, C. V. Grudzinskas, and S. P. Markey. San Diego, CA: Academic Press, 265–275.

Bowles, Doug. 2004. A radical idea: Men and women are different. *Cardiovascular Research* 61:5–6.

Brown, Wendy. 1992. Finding the man in the state. *Feminist Studies* 18:7–34.

Burchard, Esteban González, Elad Ziv, Natasha Coyle, Scarlett Lin Gomez, Hua Tang, Andrew J. Karter, Joanna L. Mountain, Eliseo J. Pérez-Stable, Dean Sheppard, and Neil Risch. 2003. The importance of race and ethnic background in biomedical research and clinical practice. *New England Journal of Medicine* 348:1170–1175.

Caplan, Jane, and John C. Torpey, eds. 2001. *Documenting individual identity: The development of state practices in the modern world*. Princeton, NJ: Princeton University Press.

Clarke, Adele E. 1990. Controversy and the development of reproductive sciences. *Social Problems* 37 (1):18–37.

Cole, Simon A. 2001. *Suspect identities: A history of fingerprinting and criminal identification*. Cambridge, MA: Harvard University Press.

Connell, R. W. 1990. The state, gender, and sexual politics. *Theory and Society* 19:507–544.

Cooper, Richard S., Jay S. Kaufman, and Ryk Ward. 2003. Race and genomics. *New England Journal of Medicine* 348:1166–1170.

Correa-de-Araujo, Rosaly. 2005. Improving the use and safety of medications in women through sex/gender and race/ethnicity analysis: Introduction. *Journal of Women's Health* 14:12–15.

De Zwart, Frank. 2005. The dilemma of recognition: Administrative categories and cultural diversity. *Theory and Society* 34:137–169.

Duster, Troy. 2003. Buried alive: The concept of race in science. In *Genetic nature/culture: Anthropology and science beyond the two-culture divide*, ed. A. H. Goodman, D. Heath, and M. S. Lindee. Berkeley: University of California Press, 258–277.

Duster, Troy. 2005. Race and reification in science. *Science* 307:1050–1051.

Epstein, Steven. 2007. *Inclusion: The politics of difference in medical research*. Chicago: University of Chicago Press.

Epstein, Steven. 2008. The rise of "recruitmentology": Clinical research, racial knowledge, and the politics of inclusion and difference. *Social Studies of Science* 38:739–770.

Espeland, Wendy Nelson, and Mitchell L. Stevens. 1998. Commensuration as a social process. *Annual Review of Sociology* 24:313–343.

Espiritu, Yen Le. 1992. *Asian American panethnicity: Bridging institutions and identities*. Philadelphia: Temple University Press.

Fausto-Sterling, Anne. 1993. The five sexes: Why male and female are not enough. *Sciences* 33:20–26.

Fausto-Sterling, Anne. 2000a. The five sexes, revisited. *The Sciences* (July–August:): 19–23.

Fausto-Sterling, Anne. 2000b. *Sexing the body: Gender politics and the construction of sexuality*. New York: Basic Books.

Fausto-Sterling, Anne. 2004. Refashioning race: DNA and the politics of health care. Differences: *A Journal of Feminist Cultural Studies* 15:1–37.

Fausto-Sterling, Anne. 2005. The bare bones of sex: Part 1—sex and gender. *Signs* 30: 1491–1527.

Fausto-Sterling, Anne. 2008. The bare bones of race. *Social Studies of Science* 38:657–694.

Food and Drug Administration. 2005. *Guidance for industry: Collection of race and ethnicity data in clinical trials*. Rockville, MD: U.S. Department of Health and Human Services.

Foucault, Michel. 1979. *Discipline and punish: The birth of the prison*. New York: Vintage Books.

Foucault, Michel. 1980. *The History of Sexuality, Volume 1*. Translated by R. Hurley. New York: Vintage Books.

Fujimura, Joan, Troy Duster, and Ramya Rajagopalan. 2008. Introduction: Race, genetics, and disease: Questions of evidence, matters of consequence. *Social Studies of Science* 38:643–656.

Fullwiley, Duana. 2008. The biologistic construction of race: "Admixture" technology and the new genetic medicine. *Social Studies of Science* 38:695–735.

Gandhi, Monica, Francesca Aweeka, Ruth M. Greenblatt, and Terrence F. Blaschke. 2004. Sex differences in pharmacokinetics and pharmacodynamics. *Annual Review of Pharmacology and Toxicology* 44:499–523.

Gardner, Amanda. 2004. The gender differences of heart disease. HealthScout News Service. http://www.healthday.com/printer.cfm?id=516951.

Gerth, H. H., and C. Wright Mills, eds. 1946. *From Max Weber*. New York: Oxford University Press.

Goldberg, David Theo. 2002. *The racial state*. Malden, MA: Blackwell.

Grady, Denise. 2006. Many women face hidden risk of heart disease. *New York Times*, February 1.

Graves, Joseph L. 2001. *The emperor's new clothes: Biological theories of race at the millennium*. Piscataway, NJ: Rutgers University Press.

Hacking, Ian. 2005. Why race still matters. *Daedalus*, Winter, 102–116.

Hanson, Barbara. 1997. *Social assumptions, medical categories*. Greenwich, CT: JAI Press.

Haraway, Donna J. 1997. *Modest_witness@second_millennium. Femaleman_meets oncomouse*. New York: Routledge.

Harding, Sandra, and Jean F. O'Barr, eds. [1975] 1987. *Sex and scientific inquiry*. Chicago: University of Chicago Press.

Haseltine, Florence B. 1997. Conclusion. In *Women's health research: A medical and policy primer*, ed. F. B. Haseltine and B. G. Jacobson. Washington, DC: Health Press International, 331–336.

Hirschauer, Stefan, and Annemarie Mol. 1995. Shifting sexes, moving stories: Feminist/constructivist dialogues. *Science, Technology and Human Values* 20:368–385.

Jamerson, Kenneth A. 1993. Prevalence of complications and response to different treatments of hypertension in African Americans and white Americans in the U.S. *Clinical and Experimental Hypertension* 15:979–995.

Johnston, Hank, Enrique Laraña, and Joseph R. Gusfield. 1994. Identities, grievances, and new social movements. In *New social movements: From ideology to identity*, ed. E. Laraña, H. Johnston, and J. R. Gusfield. Philadelphia: Temple University Press, 3–35.

Kahn, Jonathan. 2004. How a drug becomes "ethnic": Law, commerce, and the production of racial categories in medicine. *Yale Journal of Health Policy, Law, and Ethics* 4:1–46.

Kuhn, Thomas S. 1970. *The structure of scientific revolutions*. 2nd ed. Chicago: University of Chicago Press.

Lancaster, Roger N. 2003. *The trouble with nature: Sex in science and popular culture*. Berkeley: University of California Press.

Lee, Sandra Soo-Jin, Joanna Mountain, and Barbara A. Koenig. 2001. The meanings of "race" in the new genomics: Implications for health disparities research. *Yale Journal of Health Policy, Law, and Ethics* 1:33–75.

Legato, Marianne J., and Carol Colman. 1991. *The female heart: The truth about women and coronary artery disease*. New York: Simon and Schuster.

Lorber, Judith. 1993. Believing is seeing: Biology as ideology. *Gender and Society* 7:568–581.

Luker, Kristin. 1998. Sex, social hygiene, and the state: The double-edged sword of social reform. *Theory and Society* 27:601–634.

Marano, Hara Estroff. 2003. The new sex scorecard. *Psychology Today,* July–August, 38–46.

Marks, Jonathan. 1995. *Human biodiversity: Genes, race, and history.* New York: Aldine de Gruyter.

Medscape. 2003. Instructions for authors. http://www.medscape.com/viewpublication/128 _guideline.

Medscape. 2004. More common, arrhythmias in men than women with implanted defibrillators. http://www.medscape.com/viewarticle/481325.

Melucci, Alberto. 1989. *Nomads of the present: Social movements and individual needs in contemporary society.* Philadelphia: Temple University Press.

Mendelsohn, Michael E., and Richard H. Karas. 2005. Molecular and cellular basis of cardiovascular gender differences. *Science* 308:1583–1587.

Montoya, Michael. 2007. Bioethnic conscription: Genes, race and Mexicana/o ethnicity in diabetes research. *Cultural Anthropology* 22:94–128.

Morris, Aldon D., and Carol McClurg Mueller, eds. 1992. *Frontiers in social movement theory.* New Haven, CT: Yale University Press.

Nagel, Joane. 1995. American Indian ethnic renewal: Politics and the resurgence of identity. *American Sociological Review* 60:947–965.

National Institutes of Health. 2000. *NIH policy on reporting race and ethnicity data: Subjects in clinical research.* Washington, DC: U.S. Department of Health and Human Services.

National Institutes of Health. 2001. *NIH instructions to reviewers for evaluating research involving human subjects in grant and cooperative agreement applications.* Bethesda, MD: National Institutes of Health.

National Institutes of Health Revitalization Act. 1993. Public Law 103-43 [S. 1]. 103rd Congress, 10 June.

Nelson, Alondra. 2008. Bio science: Genetic genealogy testing and the pursuit of African ancestry. *Social Studies of Science* 38:759–783.

Office of Research on Women's Health. 2003. Science meets reality: Recruitment and retention of women in clinical studies and the critical role of relevance. National Institutes of Health. http://www4.od.nih.gov/orwh/smr.html.

Omi, Michael, and Howard Winant. 1986. *Racial formation in the United States: From the 1960's to the 1980's.* New York: Routledge and Kegan Paul.

Patsopoulos, Nikolaos A., Athina Tatsioni, and John P. A. Ionnadis. 2007. Claims of sex differences: An empirical assessment in genetic associations. *Journal of the American Medical Association* 298:880–893.

Pear, Robert. 2001. Sex differences called key in medical studies. *New York Times,* April 25.

Petryna, Adriana. 2006. Globalizing human subjects research. In *Global pharmaceuticals: Ethics, markets, practices,* ed. A. Petryna, A. Lakoff, and A. Kleinman. Durham, NC: Duke University Press, 33–60.

Phimister, Elizabeth G. 2003. Medicine and the racial divide. *New England Journal of Medicine* 348:1081–1082.

Pollock, Anne. 2008. Pharmaceutical meaning-making beyond marketing: Racialized subjects of generic thiazide. *Journal of Law, Medicine and Ethics* 36:530–536.

Porter, Theodore M. 1995. *Trust in numbers: The pursuit of objectivity in science and public life.* Princeton, NJ: Princeton University Press.

Rabinow, Paul. 1996. *Essays on the anthropology of reason.* Princeton, NJ: Princeton University Press.

Reardon, Jennifer. 2005. *Race to the finish: Identity and governance in an age of genomics.* Princeton, NJ: Princeton University Press.

Root, Michael. 2003. The use of race in medicine as a proxy for genetic differences. *Philosophy of Science* 70:1173–1183.

Sankar, Pamela, and Mildred Cho. 2002. Toward a new vocabulary of human genetic variation. *Science* 298:1337–1338.

Schwartz, Robert S. 2001. Racial profiling in medical research (editorial). *New England Journal of Medicine* 344:1392–1393.

Sex matters. 2001. *NewsHour with Jim Lehrer.* April 25, PBS.

Sexx Matters. 2003. FDA Commissioner and SWHR outline critical steps to improve women's health. *Sexx Matters,* Fall, 1.

Sherman, Linda Ann, Robert Temple, and Ruth B. Merkatz. 1995. Women in clinical trials: An FDA perspective. *Science* 269:793–795.

Shields, Alexandra E., Michael Fortun, Evelynn M. Hammonds, Patricia A. King, Caryn Lerman, Rayna Rapp, and Patrick F. Sullivan. 2005. The use of race variables in genetic studies of complex traits and the goal of reducing health disparities: A transdisciplinary perspective. *American Psychologist* 60:77–103.

Shim, Janet K. 2000. Bio-power and racial, class, and gender formation in biomedical knowledge production. *Research in the Sociology of Health Care* 17:173–195.

Shim, Janet K. 2005. Constructing "race" across the science-lay divide: Racial formation in the epidemiology and experience of cardiovascular disease. *Social Studies of Science* 35:405–436.

Skrentny, John David. 2002. *The minority rights revolution.* Cambridge, MA: Harvard University Press.

Starr, Paul. 1992. Social categories and claims in the liberal state. In *How classification works: Nelson Goodman among the social sciences*, ed. M. Douglas and D. Hull. Edinburgh: Edinburgh University Press, 159–174.

Tavris, Carol. 1992. *The mismeasure of woman*. New York: Simon and Schuster.

Templeton, Alan R. 2003. Human races in the context of recent human evolution: A molecular genetic perspective. In *Genetic nature/culture: Anthropology and science beyond the two-culture divide*, ed. A. H. Goodman, D. Heath, and M. S. Lindee. Berkeley: University of California Press, 234–257.

Timmermans, Stefan, and Marc Berg. 2003. *The gold standard: The challenge of evidence-based medicine and standardization in health care*. Philadelphia: Temple University Press.

Torpey, John C. 2000. *The invention of the passport: Surveillance, citizenship, and the state*. Cambridge: Cambridge University Press.

USA Today Magazine. 2003. Men and women are different. April 8.

U.S. Department of Health and Human Services. 1988. *Guideline for the format and content of the clinical and statistical sections of new drug applications*. Rockville, MD: Center for Drug Evaluation and Research, Food and Drug Administration.

U.S. Public Health Service. 1998. Grant application instructions (PHS 398). National Institutes of Health. http://www.nih.gov/grants/funding/phs398/phs398.html.

van den Wijngaard, Marianne. 1997. *Reinventing the sexes: The biomedical construction of femininity and masculinity*. Bloomington: Indiana University Press.

Wailoo, Keith. 2003. Inventing the heterozygote: Molecular biology, racial identity, and the narratives of sickle cell disease, Tay-Sachs, and cystic fibrosis. In *Race, Nature, and the Politics of Difference*, ed. D. D. Moore, J. Kosek, and A. Pandian. Durham, NC: Duke University Press, 235–253.

Whitmarsh, Ian. 2008. *Biomedical ambiguity: Race, asthma, and the contested meaning of genetic research in the Caribbean*. Ithaca, NY: Cornell University Press.

Wizemann, Theresa M., and Mary-Lou Pardue, eds. 2001. *Exploring the biological contributions to human health: Does sex matter?* Washington, DC: National Academies Press.

Knowing

5 Arguments against the Use of Racialized Categories as Genetic Variables in Biomedical Research: What Are They, and Why Are They Being Ignored?

Simon M. Outram and George T. H. Ellison

This chapter provides a detailed analysis of published criticisms and concerns surrounding the use of racialized categories as (if they were) markers of genetic variation in genetics and related biomedical research. Using a systematic citation-based literature search, we identified 335 articles containing such criticisms and concerns and subjected these to in-depth thematic analysis. Two broad groups of arguments were observed: those relating to the use of racialized categories as (if they were) genetic variables, and those exploring their use as such within biomedical research. Five specific groups of arguments against the use of racialized categories as (if they were) markers of genetic variation emerged from these articles. These drew on concerns that most genetic variation is found within all racialized groups; only a modest amount of genetic variation loosely clusters around racialized groups (but does not result in distinct packages of genetic traits that are unique to each racialized group); genetically "pure" racialized populations do not exist (and have never existed); variation in phenotypic traits among racialized groups cannot be assumed to reflect variation in genotypic traits; and using racialized categories as (if they were) markers of genetic variation tends to reify these categories as essential qualities of the individuals and groups concerned (rather than as context-specific and fluid forms of sociocultural identity). Six related themes emerged concerning the use of racialized categories as (if they were) genetic variables in biomedical research, drawing on concerns about the lack of consensus regarding the definition of racialized categories; the limited reliability and external validity of racialized categories; the limited internal validity of racialized categories; the way in which using racialized categories as (as if they were) markers of genetic variation tends to encourage their widespread use to (erroneously) infer genetic causality for disparities in health among racialized groups; the way in which research emphasizing differences in health risk and health care need among racialized groups can lead to the development of inappropriately targeted services for different racialized groups; and how the use of racialized categories to explore disparities in health (and particularly the possible genetic basis for these) can lead to stigmatization and stereotyping. We discuss how these arguments are not simply overlooked, ignored, rejected, or circumvented by contemporary geneticists and biomedical scientists within the context of contemporary genetics and biomedical science, but are selectively engaged with to generate a largely self-referential case for the continued use of racialized categories as (if they were) markers for genetic variation between populations by the researchers involved. As such, while the criticisms and concerns reviewed in this chapter provide powerful arguments for removing the use of racialized categories as (if they were) genetic variables from most genetic (and related biomedical) research, selective engagement with these arguments, together with the self-referential interpretation of findings from analyses using racialized categories as (if they were) genetic variables, continues to make their use as such appear useful to geneticists and biomedical researchers alike.

Introduction

While the creation of racialized categories dates from late-eighteenth-century European science, today, these same categories (albeit with some modification in taxonomy and nomenclature) continue to be associated with the contemporary science of genetics and with biomedical studies of social disparities in health. The principal argument against using these categories within genetics and biomedical research is not simply that by using the term *race* (or related racialized categories such as ethnicity, nationality, or, more recently, biogeographical ancestry), scientists are likely to repeat the abuses of the past. Instead, it seems clear that the political climate has shifted, as has the scientific rationale for using these categories. With the benefit of new scientific knowledge concerning the nature and extent of variation across the human genome, arguments over the use of racialized categories in genetics and biomedical research increasingly focus on their utility as markers for genetic variation (and their related applicability to whatever innovations in clinical practice may emerge from new developments in genetic technology). Indeed, mainstream genetic research does *not* appear to be especially preoccupied with looking for alleles capable of differentiating between racialized groups (Cavalli-Sforza et al. 1991), but instead focuses on exploring whether a better understanding of the extent and nature of genetic variation within and between racialized groups might benefit these groups and/or the population as a whole. Much of this work seeks to examine whether the persistence of disparities in health among racialized groups can be accounted for by genetic variation between them. Given the exponential growth in gene-disease association studies, alongside the continued categorization of populations according to racialized categories (not least their use in contemporary national censuses and health information systems), it seems unlikely that these categories will become redundant in the near future (Ellison and Jones 2002). The question has therefore shifted from whether using racialized categories is morally a good or bad thing to whether, on balance, the use of such categories can be justified by the genetic data or by the health benefits that accrue to racialized groups (and/or the population as a whole; Ellison 2005).

This chapter examines the various criticisms leveled at the continuing use of racialized categories within genetics and related biomedical research as (if they were) markers of genetic variation and aims to identify common themes emerging from a review of the literature on this topic. These themes are then analyzed with reference to previous qualitative research we (and our colleagues) have conducted with a range of geneticists and biomedical scientists (Outram and Ellison 2006a, 2006b; Ellison et al. 2007, 2008a). In this way, we hoped to establish how and why criticisms of this practice have been overlooked, ignored, rejected, or circumvented by contemporary geneticists and biomedical scientists. Our analyses suggest that they have adopted an approach characterized by selective engagement and the self-referential interpretation of criticisms against the use of racialized categories as (if they were) markers of genetic variation. The analyses also illuminate the interminable debate concerning the extent of genetic variation within and between racialized groups, which dates back to Richard Lewontin's work on protein polymorphisms in 1972 and has been reinvigorated by recent developments in genetic technology and genomewide analyses.

When comparing the themes emerging from articles criticizing the use of racialized categories as (if they were) markers of genetic variation against the explanations offered by geneticists and biomedical scientists for the continued use of these categories in this way, we were at pains to accept that geneticists are now able to correlate clinical patterns of genetic variation with a range of racialized categories. We also accepted that these correlations have been successfully used to generate credible predictions of the likely affiliation of individuals to racialized groups (albeit with varying degrees of accuracy, depending on the populations studied, the number and type of ancestry informative markers used, and related methodological constraints; Liu et al. 2006; Shriver et al. 1997; Risch et al. 2002; Rosenberg et al. 2002; Tang et al. 2005). For some commentators, such as Edwards (2003), these correlations and predictions seriously undermine Lewontin's (1972) conclusion (that racialized categories were of little use as genetic variables), and this interpretation is likely to play an important role in the continuing use of racialized categories within genetic research.[1] However, we have adopted a more skeptical interpretation of these correlations and predictions and conclude that the persistent use of such categories results, instead, from the choices made by geneticists and biomedical scientists about what to emphasize and what to ignore. This involves a narrow focus on what one might call the biogenetic correlates of racialized categories, as opposed to their sociopolitical origins and associated characteristics. In this we agree with those who argue that a new framework is required to fully understand what otherwise appear to be heritable and ostensibly innate disparities in health between racialized groups. This framework would recognize how the integral biological *and* social attributes of racialized categories contribute to disparities in health. It suggests that a more appropriate use of racialized categories as (if they were) markers of genetic variation would be one that recognizes these as, first and foremost, *social* categories that may only be usefully incorporated into biomedical research and practice in those instances (and these seem likely to be rare) when they are strongly associated with genetic differences responsible for disparities in health.

As such, an important limitation, or rather, an important *qualification* of the analyses that follow is that these focus on the ways in which racialized categories are used in genetics and related biomedical science; the arguments against their use therein; and why many geneticists and biomedical scientists have failed to engage with these.

Finally, it is important to note that this chapter does not attempt to enter into any discussions situated outside the study of racialized groups within genetics and biomedicine. As such, we have focused only on arguments *against* the use of racialized categories within genetics and biomedical research. And while the issues raised herein may resonate with, and may have potential implications for, identity politics and policy making, our chapter is an attempt to focus on the roots of the ongoing debate about the biogenetic nature of racialized categories—a debate that is frustrating (due to the failure of recent advances in genetic knowledge to deliver resolution or consensus; Weiss and Fullerton 2005), but also highly productive (in the way it illuminates the interpretative frameworks and methods used within genetics and the biomedical sciences). Thus our chapter does not seek to provide a comprehensive analysis of the various concerns raised about the use of racialized categories within other natural or social science disciplines, nor do we explore the social, political, and moral debates concerning the development or use of official racialized categories (such as those common in contemporary censuses) or unofficial racialized categories (such as those recognized more generally within contemporary society). Our chapter also makes no attempt to distinguish between the many different categories and labels used to classify racialized groups within science or society, not least because there is so little consensus on what these mean and because it seems clear to us that all have the potential to reify discredited notions of naturally occurring human populations with innate and heritable biogenetic (and/or sociocultural) characteristics. These issues have been discussed by Baum (2006), Jenkins (2001), and Woodward 2004), among others, and elsewhere in this volume.

Methods

To access articles debating the use and utility of racialized categories in genetics and related biomedical research, a citation-based (or snowball) literature search (Hart 1998, 2001) was conducted based on any articles that had cited McKenzie and Crowcroft's

(1996) editorial in the *British Medical Journal*—"Describing Race, Ethnicity, and Culture in Medical Research"—which accompanied the journal's "Guidelines for Research, Audit, and Publication" on ethnicity, race, and culture (the first such guidelines to be developed by a major biomedical journal; British Medical Journal 1996).

The ISI Web of Knowledge (http://isiwebofknowledge.com/) was used to identify any articles that had cited the editorial up until the end of 2007. These were selected for inclusion in our review on the basis of whether they had discussed in detail the use of racialized categories in genetics and/or biomedical research. This was determined by reading each article's abstract and, when this provided insufficient information on which to base a decision, by reading the main text of the article itself. Any articles selected for inclusion in the review were then forward- and back-referenced, to identify any relevant articles referenced within these and any relevant articles that had cited these, respectively.

All the articles selected for inclusion in the review were analyzed using thematic analysis, as described by Boyatsiz (1998) and Braun and Clarke (2006). More general guidance on the qualitative analysis of scientific literature was drawn from Silverman (2000, 2001). On the basis of these techniques, the first stage of the analyses involved identifying distinct criticisms and concerns raised within each of the selected articles and extracting verbatim quotes that illustrated the various forms in which these criticisms and concerns were presented. The second stage of the analysis involved assembling these quotes into common themes, which were continually reviewed and refined as additional data from subsequent articles were identified and extracted. This process aimed to develop a comprehensive yet coherent thematic overview of the criticisms and concerns raised, organized into thematic groupings to reflect the ontological and epistemological nature of the issues they contained. In this way, the number of themes fluctuated as subsequent articles were read, with new themes emerging and existing themes coalescing or separating out as the analysis proceeded.

Results

Articles Identified for Inclusion in the Review

Up until the end of 2007, McKenzie and Crowcroft's (1996) editorial had been cited by a total of seventy-one articles, thirty-two of which (45%) were judged to have discussed the use of racialized categories in genetics and/or biomedical research. These thirty-two articles contained a total of 1,327 references and had themselves been cited a total of 695 times. Of these references and citations, 303 were judged to have discussed the use and/or utility of racialized categories in genetics and/or biomedical research so that, together with the original 32 articles, 335 unique articles were included in the analyses that follow. This process of selection led to the following types of articles being excluded:

• Articles describing empirical studies of disparities in health among racialized groups that did not discuss the use of racialized categories as research variables, for example, an epidemiological study concerned with exploring variation in hypertension among racialized groups that did not question the use of the categories themselves.

• Articles exploring the formation of social identities that did not relate these processes to the use of racialized categories in genetic or biomedical research, for example, a study of identity among second- and third-generation migrants.

• Articles examining the historical and legal construction of racialized categories that did not relate these processes to genetics and biomedical research, for example, a study concerned with how the notion of a racial hierarchy became intertwined with the trans-Atlantic slave trade.

• Articles discussing appropriate methods for conducting studies in cross-cultural environments, for example, a study assessing whether the social identity of the interviewer might influence the conduct of interviews.

• Articles containing clinical advice concerning specific diseases, for example, studies that identified differences in disease risk or therapeutic efficacy among racialized groups and provided related clinical advice concerning the care of patients from different groups.

Issues Addressed by Articles Included in the Review

Seven types of articles were selected for inclusion in the review, although most of the articles took more than one of these forms:

• Articles describing studies of genotypic variation using racialized categories that discussed how such data might be applied elsewhere, for example, Liu et al. (2006) and Mountain and Risch (2004).

• Articles exploring how disparities in health among racialized groups are often interpreted as evidence of innate (i.e., genetic) differences by biomedical researchers, for example, Cooper (1984) and Osbourne and Feit (1992).

• Articles examining the methods and analytical assumptions used in epidemiological research to explore disparities in health between racialized groups, for example, Kaufman and Cooper (1999) and LaVeist (1994).

• Articles assessing available methods for classifying and categorizing racialized groups in biomedical research, for example, Hahn et al. (2002) and Sugarman (1996).

• Articles discussing the conceptual basis underlying the racialized categories used in biomedical research, for example, Aspinall (1997) and Cartmill (1999).

• Articles reviewing the use of racialized categories in studies published by biomedical journals, for example, Comstock, Castillo, and Lindsay (2004) and Ellison and de Wet (1997).

• Articles tackling the terminology and nomenclature used to identify racialized groups in biomedical research, for example, Bhopal (2004) and Gimenez (1989).

Thematic Analysis of Articles Selected for Inclusion in the Review
Thematic analysis of the 335 articles selected for inclusion in the review identified two broad groups of themes relating to criticisms and concerns about the use of racialized categories in genetics and biomedical research: the use of racialized categories as (if they were) markers for genetic variation per se and the use of racialized categories as (if they were) markers of genetic variation in biomedical research. These two groups of themes will be analyzed separately in the following sections.

The Use of Racialized Categories as (If They Were) Markers of Genetic Variation
There were five key themes relating to debates about the use of racialized categories as (if they were) genetic variables or markers of genetic variation. These themes included the following criticisms and concerns: (1) that most genetic variation is found within all racialized groups, (2) that a modest amount of genetic variation loosely clusters around racialized groups but does not reflect distinct packages of genetic traits that are unique to each racialized group, (3) that there are no genetically pure populations (and never have been), (4) that variation in phenotypic traits cannot be assumed to reflect variation in genotypic traits, and (5) that using racialized categories as (if they were) genetic variables or markers of genetic variation tends to reify these categories as innate and immutable entities, rather than recognizing these to be context-specific and fluid forms of sociocultural identity.

• **Most genetic variation is found within all racialized groups.** Perhaps the most powerful criticism leveled at the use of racialized categories as (if they were) markers of genetic variation stems from the observation that most genetic variation among human beings occurs *within*, rather than *between*, racialized groups. In Goodman's (1997, 24) exploration of racialized categories in forensic anthropology—*Bred in the Bone?*—he wrote, "Some thirty years ago the population geneticist Richard C. Lewontin of Harvard University conducted a statistical study of [genetically determined] blood groups with two of the more common forms. On average, he found about 94 percent of the variation in blood forms occurred within perceived races; fewer than 6 percent could be explained by variations among races." Such is the importance of Lewontin's analysis that the Race, Ethnicity, and Genetics Working Group (2005, 521), along with many others, cite Lewontin's (1972, 397) analysis, which found that only "5%–15% of genetic variation occurs between large groups living on different continents [i.e., groups commonly classified as different races], with the remaining majority of the variation occurring within such groups." Lewontin (1972, 397) concluded that given that genetic variation within groups was greater than that between them, "racial classification is now seen to be of virtually no genetic or taxonomic significance either [and, therefore] no justification can be offered for its continuance." Indeed, many of the concerns identified in the paragraphs that follow derive from Lewontin's (1972, 397) conclusion that race is of "virtually no genetic or taxonomic significance."

• **(Only) a modest amount of genetic variation loosely clusters around racialized groups.** Despite the observation that *most* genetic variation among humans occurs within racialized groups, a modest proportion is associated with racialized categories (i.e., varies between these). Nonetheless, because these associations are loose, there are no distinct or definitive genetic differences between racialized groups. To this end, Cooper (2005, 72) noted that "race, a quantitative distinction within a species, has no equivalent defining criterion—that is, genetic variability is not restricted to discrete packages," whereas Cartmill (1999, 654) has pointed out that "since there are thousands of separate, independently assorting variable loci in the human genome, it is highly unlikely *a priori* that variation at any particular locus will covary with any other." Turning specifically to one of the most commonly used racialized categories, Braun et al. (2007, 1423) argued that "assuming that 'African' origin can capture the complexity of migrations, artificial boundaries, and gene drift is scientifically unsupportable." Likewise, relating these clustering arguments to specific populations, the Race, Ethnicity, and Genetics Working Group (2005, 521) observed that "samples taken from India and Pakistan affiliate with Europeans or eastern Asians rather than separating into a distinct cluster . . . [whereas] samples from the Kalash, a small population living in northwestern Pakistan, form their own cluster on a level comparable with those of the major continental regions." Cooper (1984, 716) summed up the inadequacy of racialized categories under these circumstances: "historical efforts to use the race concept scientifically have ended in failure" because racialized categories do not "delineate important and consistent genetic differences [in the form of] . . . a 'package' of different genes . . . between groups." Thus, while a modest amount of genetic variation might cluster within geographical areas and sociocultural groups, such clustering does not fall within discrete racialized groups in such a way that these can be categorized as genetically distinct.

• **There are no genetically pure populations (and never have been).** Leading from arguments about the distribution of genetic variation between populations are concerns about the belief that racialized groups are genetically homogeneous—or at least, that they were before these groups started to move and mix. Two distinct criticisms of this belief were evident among the articles included in this review. The first, as summarized by Freeman (1998, 224), is simply that "races, in the sense of genetically homogeneous populations, do not exist in the human species today, nor is there any evidence that they have ever existed in the past." The second, as argued by Cartmill (1999, 653), is that although "it is true that human populations in some parts of the world were more uniform and distinctive a thousand years ago than they are at present . . . populations like those of modern North America, with high levels of phenotypic variability maintained partly by migration and gene flow from elsewhere, are not a new phenomenon." In essence, Cartmill's argument is that the idealized notion of genetically pure racialized groups is limited in both place ("some parts of the world") and time ("a thousand years ago"). Although these arguments seem to differ as to whether genetic homogeneity ever existed within (some, isolated and/or pure) racialized groups, both still draw the same conclusion regarding contemporary populations: that the notion of racialized groups as genetically homogeneous is limited and somewhat questionable, given that few of the world's populations have ever lived in sufficient isolation from one another to generate or maintain discrete genetic characteristics. As such, the *assumption* that racialized populations are genetically homogeneous (and, as we saw earlier, genetically distinct) is felt to be flawed or very limited in its applicability.

• **Variation in phenotypic traits cannot be assumed to reflect variation in genotypic traits.** While a range of phenotypic, sociocultural, and geographical markers are commonly used to classify racialized groups—that is, what you look like and where you or your family come from—it is widely accepted that the most salient historical and contemporary marker for classifying racialized groups is skin color. Indeed, the importance of skin color has led researchers to develop and test hypotheses based on skin color per se, and this is a practice that has been specifically addressed in several articles that question the utility of such phenotypic characteristics as markers of wholesale genotypic differences. For example, Garte (2002, 421) argued that "present definitions of race based on superficial characteristics, or on other phenotypes strongly influenced by natural selection, such as skin color, simply do not correlate with data from the whole genome." Likewise, Williams (1997, 323) pointed out that "skin and hair color, facial features, and other superficial external characteristics do not correlate well with biochemical or other genetic characteristics." As such, these writers conclude that focusing on observable phenotypic markers of racialized categories (especially, but not exclusively, skin color) to estimate genetic relatedness is a gross oversimplification and (mis)leads researchers to assume genetic homogeneity (erroneously) on the basis of shared phenotypic traits.

• **Using racialized categories as genetic variables reifies these categories as innate.** Finally, a number of arguments link critiques concerning the use of racialized categories as genetic variables to their (inappropriate) use in biomedical research. These arguments stress that assuming genetics to be an essential element of any disparities in health among racialized groups makes racialized categories appear inherently innate characteristics of the groups and individuals concerned (rather than fluid social/cultural/political forms of identity). For example, Williams, Lavizzo-Mourey, and Warren (1994, 27) argued that "research on racial variations in health has been dominated by a genetic model that views race as primarily reflecting biological homogeneity and black-white differences in health as largely genetically determined." This essentialization of racialized categories as genetic variables detracts from studies on nongenetic alternatives, as Muntaner, Nieto, and O'Campo (1996, 532) pointed out: "without any evidence from genetic studies, the observation that blacks tend to have lower leukocyte counts than whites for example, led scientists to the conclusion that neutropenia

is probably a normal genetically determined characteristic in people of African descent."
Likewise, Liu (1998, 1765) observed that "simple logic notes that races are different
physically and that these differences are determined by genes: some that are responsible for the pigmentation of the skin and others dictate hair color or the contour of
the nose. Because there are differences in cancer rates and mortality between the races,
specifically between blacks and whites, the same logic has led many to believe that
these distinctions must also be determined genetically." Liu goes on to say that "this
argument, however, is fundamentally flawed both on genetic and on social grounds."
Bradby (1995, 406) extended this critique of deterministic logic by pointing out that
"the existence of one disease-causing gene at a higher frequency in a population
defined by a particular physical appearance, say dark skin and tightly curled black
hair, does not mean that those so described have poor health in other respects." In
summary, these arguments focus on the way in which the essentialization of racialized
categories as genetic entities has led biomedical researchers to assume that differences
in health among racialized groups are predominantly genetically determined, and
thereby led them away from examining the structural, socioeconomic, political, and
cultural issues that many believe make a significant (if not larger) contribution to disparities in health.

The Use of Racialized Categories as Genetic Variables in Biomedical Research   In
addition to the five themes described in the preceding section, related to the use of
racialized categories (as if they were) markers of genetic variation, six additional
themes emerged from articles included in this review that referred more generally to
the use of racialized categories as (if they were) markers of genetic variation within
biomedical research. These included (1) a lack of consensus regarding the definition of
racialized categories, (2) the limited reliability and external validity of racialized categories, (3) the limited internal validity of racialized categories, (4) how using racialized
categories as markers of genetic variation can encourage their widespread use to infer
genetic causality for disparities in health among racialized groups, (5) how research
emphasizing differences in health risk and health care need between racialized groups
can lead to the development of inappropriately targeted interventions for different
racialized groups, and (6) how using racialized categories to explore disparities in
health (and particularly the genetic basis thereof) can lead to stigmatization and
stereotyping.

• **Lack of consensus regarding the definition of racialized categories.** A starting point
for many of the critiques leveled at the use of racialized categories in biomedical
research was the lack of consensus regarding how such groups and categories are
defined—something that is evident from any brief scan of biomedical dictionaries
(Ellison 1999). Indeed, within the literature included in this review, LaVeist (1994)
provided a detailed discussion of medical, biological, psychological, and epidemiologi-

cal definitions of race, which identified two significant features thereof: the first being a tendency to emphasize race as a genetically meaningful taxonomic category, and the second being a tendency toward uncertainty, ambiguity, and inconsistency. Sometimes both these are evident, as in the example LaVeist (1994, 5) quoted from Becker and Landav's *International Dictionary of Medicine and Biology*, which defined "race as a biological concept that defies discrete categorization: A subspecies or other division or subdivision of a species." These two features are also evident in the changing definitions of race offered in subsequent editions of some influential dictionaries, such as the *Dictionary of Epidemiology* (Last 2001, 150), the most recent edition of which emphasizes the use of race as a biological category but notes that the "biologic classification of human races is difficult because of significant genetic overlaps among population groups." In contrast, the previous version of this dictionary (Last 1995, 139) led with the sentence that races comprised "persons who are relatively homogeneous with respect to biological inheritance," but followed this with the sentence stating that "in a time of political correctness, classifying by race is done cautiously," with a footnote referenced to Cooper and David (1986) and Osbourne and Feit (1992). Such reviews of dictionary definitions suggest that race is an (increasingly) ambiguous, contentious, and politically sensitive term when defined as a biological and/or genetic entity.

The ongoing debate over the meaning (and utility) of race has led a number of writers to examine whether *ethnicity* might be a preferable term. As such, Wiencke (2004, 79) distinguished between the two by proposing that "race, as it is used in common discourse, is a subdivision of a species formed by a group of individuals that share common biological characteristics that distinguish them from other groups . . . [while the] concept of ethnicity emphasizes cultural, socioeconomic, religious and political qualities of human groups." This view, that race and ethnicity are conceptually distinct, is also evident in Huth's (1995, 620) review, in which he argued that "in contrast [to race], ethnicity represents a concept that makes no claims to biological precision and that reflects a broader view of factors that may influence the susceptibility of individuals to etiologic agents and the ways in which they may respond to those agents." Significantly, Huth's definition added another dimension to ethnicity—that of continuous contextual and temporal variation. This emphasis on the inherent flexibility of ethnicity is also evident in Nazroo's (1998, 723) argument that "ethnic identity cannot be considered as fixed, because culture is not an autonomous and static feature in an individual's life." As such, ethnicity has been distinguished from race by its fluid and predominantly social attributes, rather than the fixed biological and/or genetic attributes traditionally associated with the notion of race.

However, although racial and ethnic categories can be conceptualized very differently and are sometimes articulated as such, the two terms often overlap, not least when they refer to the same social groups or are classified using the same phenotypic, sociocultural, and geographical characteristics, and similar nomenclature. Moreover, as Karlsen (2004, 108) pointed out, there is "an assumption dominant in epidemiological research that the ethnic differentials found among various social and economic characteristics are a consequence of innate characteristics related to 'ethnic' or 'racial' difference: that ethnic differences are to some extent natural." Karlsen's argument is that within epidemiological research, there is a tendency to downplay the fluidity of ethnic (*as well as* racial) categories and to interpret these as markers for a set of fixed, and to some extent innate and naturalized, attributes. Indeed, as Pfeffer (1998, 1382) noted, "essentialism can be social as well as biological. Essentialist versions of ethnicity (defined as a belief in a shared destiny) see history as an unchanging truth. . . . Essentialist accounts of culture are found in 'factfiles,' information resources produced for health professionals. They present cultures as fixed products rather than dynamic processes." As such, there may be a tendency in health research to see ethnicity as a set of fixed social and cultural entities, rather than as fluid sociocultural concepts, just as race is routinely viewed as a fixed and natural biogenetic category, rather than a socially constructed identity in its own right. In the process, race and ethnicity tend to become conflated, however distinct they might be in the view of the researchers concerned.

• **The limited reliability and external validity of racialized categories.** Contextual variation in the meaning of race and ethnicity (and related racialized categories) is also at the root of concerns over the reliability and external validity of categories when operationalized within genetics and biomedical research. In particular, the contemporary practice of using self-identification to operationalize racialized categories (not least in the collection of data by contemporary censuses and health services information systems, which go on to be used by biomedical researchers) has been questioned in terms of both reliability (i.e., their repeatability) and external validity (i.e., their generalizability across contexts; see chapter 6). Changes to self-identification can be rapid and substantial. For example, Williams (1996, 487) reported that one "study of a large national population found that one-third of the U.S. population reported a different racial or ethnic status one year after their initial interview." Moreover, Jones (2001, 300) described how "I would have been counted as a slave [before the U.S. Civil War], in 1850 as either Black or 'mulatto,' in 1890 as one of Black, mulatto, 'quadroon,' or 'octoroon' ancestry, in 1950 as 'Negro,' and in 2000 as 'Black, African American, or Negro' plus 'White' and 'American Indian or Alaska Native' if I so chose." Jones's account provides a powerful example of how changing social structures and norms challenge the concept of racialized categories as fixed over time (and place). Elsewhere, LaVeist (1994, 3) described how Brazil, Japan, and the United States have each produced "five different policies for assigning racial status" in under ten years. As such, the populations and individuals included under each racialized category differ over time and place, making it difficult to assume that these categories are equivalent from one data set to the next.

An additional consequence of these variable and unstable categories is that researchers might overlook associated problems with external validity. Hammerschmidt (1999, 10) highlighted how little attention has been paid to this issue: "it is as though authors have considered racial assignment to be as unambiguous and straightforward as gender assignment, as though terms such as 'black' and 'white' will mean the same thing in one study (or study population) as they mean in another. Such is demonstrably not the case." Hahn, Truman, and Baker's (1995) discussion drew the issues of reliability and external validity together by pointing out the very different measurement systems then in use to allocate racialized categories within the United States, which included self-identification and classification by proxy, by interviewer, or by funeral director. These authors concluded that the classification of a person's racialized identity "varies over time and by method of ascertainment, relationship between person classifying and person classified, vital status of subject, and specific category of ancestry" (Hahn, Truman, and Baker 1995, 79). Unsurprisingly, different classification techniques tend to generate different numbers of people assigned to each category, making it difficult to identify the extent or possible causes of health disparities among racialized groups. This led McKenney and Bennett (1994, 19) to suggest that "different data collection methods, different content and format of the questions, and different definitions and classifications for race and ethnicity" were all "possible explanations for results to differ by race and ethnicity when data from the Bureau of the Census and the public health surveillance systems are used as the denominator and numerator." Taken together, the points these writers made all serve to highlight the problems that occur as a result of different data collection methods (over time and place) and the lack of standardized data collection techniques (even in the same place and at the same time) as well as the paucity of information provided by researchers regarding how they operationalized the racialized categories they used (as discussed previously). All these issues combine to severely curtail the reliability and comparability of studies exploring disparities in health among racialized groups.

• **The limited internal validity of racialized categories.** The use of racialized categories as if these reflected discrete and homogeneous groups drew criticism from many of the articles included in this review, including those that emphasized the limited validity of such categories as markers of wholesale genetic difference and those that questioned their ability to capture socioculturally distinct groups. Some, like Hammerschmidt (1999, 11), argued that using self-identification to apply "one of five broad [racialized] categories may be a useful tool in monitoring for evidence of discrimination, but it falls far short of scientific assignment to a group expected to have greater-than-chance homogeneity in some genetic or physiologic variable of interest." Others, like Caldwell and Popenoe (1995, 614), acknowledged that "single-word racial labels such as 'black' or 'white' are of occasional help to the clinician" but nonetheless recognized that, as a result of "their broad scope and lack of scientific clarity, these terms often poorly represent information—for example, about genetic risks and perceptions of disease—that they are supposed to convey." In his critique, Nazroo (1998, 713) argued that "many studies use 'ethnic' groupings with quite inappropriate boundaries, such as Black or South Asian. The data are then interpreted as though the individuals within them are ethnically (i.e. genetically and culturally) homogeneous, even though such categories are heterogeneous, containing ethnic groups with different cultures, religions, migration histories, and geographical and socio-economic locations." For these reasons, Caldwell and Popenoe (1995, 614) pointed out that "in many instances, [racialized categories] . . . are superficial and potentially misleading terms that fail to serve the patient's medical needs." As with the concerns over external validity described previously, the arguments presented here highlight another of the often hidden problems facing the use of racialized categories in biomedical research, particularly when this involves (or invokes) assumptions regarding the extent of genetic and/or socio-cultural homogeneity within, and heterogeneity between, racialized groups.

• **The use of racialized categories to infer genetic causality for disparities in health.** Relating concerns about internal validity to the contentious issue of causal inference, LaVeist (1994, 8) pointed out that "a statistically significant coefficient for the race binary variable without further analysis often leads to such illogical, yet commonly published conclusions as, 'race is a significant determinant of prenatal care utilization.' Such a conclusion eventually filters into medical and public health practice . . . [yet] Clearly, a person's skin color does not determine prenatal care utilization." LaVeist's argument, that racialized categories themselves should not be considered the specific or direct cause of disparities in health among racialized groups, was supported by many of the other articles included in this review. For example, Smaje (1996, 141) suggested that "on the one hand . . . [race] has been regarded as an explanatory principle *sui generis*, which can itself explain various dimensions of human action. On the other, it can be constituted as an object of analysis, something to be explained with reference to other modes of human action." The causal interpretation, whereby racialized categories are, of themselves, seen as sufficient to explain disparities in health—rather than as phenomena that need to be explained—has also been criticized by Buescher, Gizlice, and Jones-Vessey (2005, 397), who argued that "racial group is at best a crude marker for particular health problems, and certainly not a risk factor or cause."

Elsewhere, several authors of articles included in this review have criticized the tendency among biomedical scientists to use well-known and highly penetrative single-gene disorders, associated with racialized groups (particularly hemoglobinopathies), as models for understanding broader inequalities in health on three grounds: first, that the distribution of the alleles responsible for these single-gene disorders are not necessarily concordant with the distribution of other health-related alleles; second, that the impact of these highly penetrative single-gene disorders provide a poor model for understanding the impact of genetic variation on health-related phenotypes dependent on an interaction between more than one gene and more than one aspect of the environment; and third, that only a tiny proportion of disparities in health among racialized groups are the result of highly penetrative single-gene disorders. For example, Krieger et al. (1993, 85) argued that "the accumulated evidence indicates that for virtually every racial/ethnic group, a handful of genetic diseases seem specifically associated with geographic and biological heritage, yet these diseases nonetheless account for only a minute percentage of each group's overall morbidity and even less of their mortality." Similarly, Kaufman, Cooper, and McGee (1997, 621) pointed out that "single gene disorders such as hemoglobinopathies collectively make up less than 0.3% of the differential mortality burden [between blacks and whites in the United States]." Indeed, Krieger and Bassett (1986, 77) have suggested that "such uncommon genetic maladies have become important strictly because of their metaphorical value: they are used to support genetic explanations of racial differences in the 'big diseases' of the twentieth century—heart disease, stroke, and cancer. Yet no current evidence exists to justify such an extrapolation."

Meanwhile, a further concern regarding the analytical use of racialized categories in biomedicine is the incompleteness of statistical adjustment for differences in socioeconomic status among different racialized groups—an issue that Kaufman, Cooper, and McGee (1997, 621) felt was a major "threat to the validity" of such analyses. If residual confounding from incomplete adjustment is present, the assumption that any residual differences observed following adjustment are free from socioeconomic influences cannot be justified. The possibility of residual confounding was also highlighted by O'Loughlin (1999, 153), who pointed out that confounding will continue to "be a problem if measurement of socioeconomic status is incomplete," and by Karter (2003, 2193), who concluded that "one can safely assume that many [socioeconomic and social] factors are missing (not collected or not specified) from a statistical model that attempts to explain racial/ethnic differences." However, an important qualification of this concern, and one that questions the rationale for socioeconomic adjustment in the first place, was raised by Smaje (1996, 159), who pointed out that adjusting for socioeconomic status when exploring disparities in health among racialized groups "can have the unfortunate effect of directing attention away from a key analytical question, namely the nature of the relationship between ethnicity, socio-economic status and health." In essence, Smaje was concerned that socioeconomic status might lie on the causal pathway between racialized categories and disparities in health because socioeconomic status is likely to be the result of historical and contemporary discrimination. This is an issue that had previously been addressed by Cooper and David (1986, 111), who argued that "explaining racial differentials by education, income, etc. could in a causal sense be considered 'over-control'; race is not confounded by other variables, it is antecedent to them." Moreover, Kaufman and Cooper (2001) have since pointed out that it might not be possible to use racialized categories in multivariate analyses of this sort if, as they and others suggest, socioeconomic status is partly determined by the differential treatment of racialized groups, because these differences are largely inseparable from the racialized categories concerned. This important technical point hinges on the fact that racialized categories cannot be used in the sorts of multivariate analyses capable of generating plausible etiological insights because the categorical variables involved need to be amenable to counterfactual comparisons—that is, analyses capable of assessing what outcomes might have occurred had the study participants had different characteristics. Since it is often difficult to envisage how racialized categories might be reassigned—either hypothetically or empirically (Erasmus and Ellison 2005; 2008)—it is usually impossible to separate out those aspects of disparities in health that are associated with racialized groups from those associated with the socioeconomic differences such groups experience.

Taken together, these arguments present a strong critique of analyses that assume that disparities in health among racialized groups offer a definitive insight into their genetic, structural, and/or sociocultural determinants. Indeed, they suggest that alongside assumptions about the genetic (and sociocultural) homogeneity of racialized groups, which make them appear a self-evident explanation for disparities in health, the use of racialized categories in biomedical research is likely to detract from the more detailed, in-depth investigations required to explore the multifactoral issues responsible.

• **Research on racialized groups can lead to the development of inappropriately targeted interventions.** For the most part, the articles included in this review focused on conceptual and methodological issues related to the operationalization of racialized categories as markers of genetic (and, to some extent, sociocultural) differences in biomedical research (as outlined previously). However, some of the articles also voiced criticisms and concerns regarding the application of research using racialized categories to clinical practice. These manifested as concerns that the routine use of racialized categories in biomedical research might imply that specific health care services should be developed for different racialized groups and lead to the stigmatization and stereotyping of the least healthy groups. The first of these issues is discussed under this theme, while the second will be discussed in the theme that follows.

Commenting on how common it can be for racialized categories to be invoked in clinical contexts, Caldwell and Popenoe (1995, 614) highlighted how "in many institutions, medical students are routinely taught to begin their case presentations with a statement describing the age, sex, and 'race' of the patient." While such practices appear benign, they may inadvertently lead medical practice along diagnostic and therapeutic pathways that mistakenly assume that racialized groups are accurate markers of etiological risk. Witzig (1996, 676) referred to this as the medicalization of racialized categories—the process of transforming them into medical (rather than social) variables—and concluded that "unfortunately, the continued appearance of race taxons in the medical literature has legitimized them as acceptable descriptive labels for patients and has thus made them seem integral to the proper diagnosis and treatment of diseases." This reification of racialized categories as integral to (if not crucial for) clinical diagnosis and treatment, based as it is on common underlying assumptions that such categories are helpful markers of innate biological (i.e., genetic) causes, has been criticized for unduly narrowing the range of diagnoses and potential treatments applied to individual patients. In particular, Williams (1997, 324) described how "physicians can use assumptions about a patient's race to prematurely eliminate possible diseases or to inappropriately narrow the focus to one disease in the diagnosis of patients."

Given their common, if not routine, use in the clinical encounter, it is perhaps unsurprising that racialized categories have also provided a framework for pharmacogenomic research, in which assumptions about innate differences in the efficacy and safety of drugs among different racialized groups have made racialized categories key variables in the development, prescription, and monitoring of drugs. The most prominent example of this framework has been the heart failure drug BiDil (Lillquist and Sullivan 2004; Ellison 2006; Ellison et al. 2008b). Clearly the routine collection of data on racialized groups, together with common assumptions about genetic homogeneity within such groups, has resulted in practices whereby diagnostic and treatment regimes (including drugs) have been tailored to specific groups. While some such tailoring may be beneficial (i.e., when the assumptions involved turn out to be correct), given the concerns about the limited reliability and validity of racialized categories as useful markers of difference (be they genetic or sociocultural), it seems likely that translating such research into clinical practice would exclude some populations from gaining access to appropriate medical treatment and pharmaceutical products.

• **Using racialized categories to explore disparities in health can lead to stereotyping.** The last of the criticisms and concerns leveled at the use of racialized categories in biomedical research focused on their potential impact on the stigmatization and stereotyping of less healthy racialized groups. According to Williams, Lavizzo-Mourey, and Warren (1994, 34), assuming that racialized categories are in some way causal determinants of disparities in health, and thereby failing "to identify the specific factors that contribute to group differences, can reinforce racial prejudices and perpetuate racist stereotypes, diverting both public opinion and research dollars from the larger social factors that ultimately account for the patterns of disease variation." In Europe and North America, where much of this research takes place, a principal reason for such stereotyping is simply that the majority "white" population tends to be treated either as nonracialized or the norm, against which other populations are thereby racialized and appear deviant. This is evident in Drevdahl, Phillips, and Taylor's (2006, 56) assertion that "by classifying all forms of racial or ethnic diversity into 'non-white' or 'ethnic minority,' 'white' was the implied but often unstated norm against which all 'other' groups were compared." Because racialized deviance is commonly assumed to be genetic (or at least the product of heritable, innate, and immutable biosocial characteristics), it runs the risk of deflecting attention away from structural and related socioeconomic causes of disparities in health. Indeed, recent advances in genetic technology have elicited a shift in emphasis onto genetic explanations for a whole range of essentially social problems, as McCann-Mortimer, Augoustinos, and LeCouteur (2004, 412) explained: "entrenched social problems such as poverty, educational underachievement, mental illness, delinquency, alcoholism, violence, and criminal behaviour . . . [are] being increasingly attributed to 'deficient' or 'problematic' genes by experts, rather than to the social conditions in which people lived." Thus, while discrimination against racialized groups may not be an inevitable product of contemporary biomedical research using racialized categories, some of the articles included in this review have argued, as do Osbourne and Feit (1992, 275), that "it is naïve to believe that research methods can always compensate for racial bias." As a result, even health researchers who have explicitly set out to reduce health inequalities between racialized groups may inadvertently contribute to a circular argument, in which disparities in health among racialized groups are accepted as reflecting innate differences that are not amenable to intervention and thereby entrench and reproduce the disparities observed—disparities that may, directly and indirectly, perpetuate these inequalities by justifying inaction or discrimination. Whatever the actual impact of biomedical research using racialized categories as (if they were) accurate markers of innate difference, it seems clear that researchers and clinicians should recognize the *potential* impact of such research on future research and clinical practice as well as on lay perceptions of, and justifications for, persistent disparities in health among racialized groups.

Discussion

Limitations
Given the wealth of literature engaging critically with the use of racialized categories in genetics and biomedical research, this review was necessarily limited in scope. First, it focused exclusively on articles that had problematized the use of racialized categories as (if they were) markers of genetic variation in biomedical research and on the criticisms and concerns these articles contained. As such, the potential benefits of using racialized categories were not recorded or analyzed. This is an important qualification given that such benefits might, under some circumstances, outweigh any disadvantages of using racialized categories in genetics and biomedical research (Ellison 2005). Meanwhile, it is also important to point out that the literature review presented here will have been limited by the citation search strategy used (based on the McKenzie

and Crowcroft editorial of 1996), which excluded any unconnected articles (i.e., any outside this citation network). It is therefore possible that this approach might have generated a largely self-referential collection of articles that excluded alternative, minority, and/or controversial views. Certainly some of the most influential articles on this topic—such as Lewontin's (1972) assessment of genetic variation within and between racialized groups—were not included in the articles in this citation network and were therefore not included in this review. However, while it is possible that the citation search strategy reduced the diversity of opinions found, it is clear from the review's findings that the articles included expressed a wide range of different, and occasionally contradictory, views. It therefore seems unlikely that the search strategy used generated an assessment of the criticisms and concerns that was unduly biased or limited, except inasmuch as this drew exclusively on articles within a citation network emanating from an editorial in a medical journal (i.e., McKenzie and Crowcroft 1996).

Key Findings

Notwithstanding these limitations, the key unifying element in many of the arguments reviewed here is that their foundation lies in the unresolved interpretation of human genetic variation. More specifically, as Lewontin (1972, 397) put it, given that "less than 15% of all human genetic diversity is accounted for by differences between human groups," it can be argued that "racial classification is now seen to be of virtually no genetic or taxonomic significance either, [and, therefore] no justification can be offered for its continuance." While this may seem a very straightforward proposition, when the same genetic data are analyzed in terms of their correlation structure (i.e., when patterns among numerous genetic traits, rather than the presence or absence of individual genetic traits in different populations, are analyzed within populations), they can be used to argue that "the 'taxonomic significance' of genetic data in fact often arises from correlations amongst the different loci, for it is these that may contain the information which enables a stable classification to be uncovered" (Edwards 2003, 798). Indeed, from Edwards's perspective, Lewontin's often quoted figure of "less than 15%" is essentially an illusion (if not a fallacy) because Lewontin's "argument ignores the fact that most of the information that distinguishes populations is hidden in the correlation structure of the data and not simply in the variation of the individual factors" (Edwards 2003, 798). This very different interpretation of very similar data is partly what underlies contemporary disagreements about the genetic utility of racialized categories (Smart et al. 2006), and failure to resolve these disagreements has resulted in stalemate between those scientists who want to use racialized categories within genetics and biomedicine and those who criticize this practice. What is clear, however, is that technological improvements in our ability to measure and characterize genetic variation since Lewontin (1972) have not fundamentally changed the genetic arguments against the use of racialized categories as (if they were) markers of genetic variation. As Weiss and Fullerton (2005, 168) argue, "We already know the facts. In that sense, the endless cycling could stop, because we're already there. But people stubbornly continue to see what they want to see in the facts—either that or what they want to see determines which facts count." While the arguments identified in this review might justifiably be used to limit claims made with respect to the genetic basis of disparities in health among racialized groups, they do not mean that these claims will always be either incorrect (according to the genetic data) or *necessarily* counterproductive (in terms of subsequent biomedical analyses or applications). Instead, the use of racialized categories leaves genetics and biomedical science in something of a quandary—how should they deal with a fluid sociopolitical category that sometimes appears to be associated with what might turn out to be a useful amount of genetic variation?

Why have the criticisms leveled at racialized categories failed to curtail their use in genetics and biomedical research? Given the substantial volume and breadth of the criticisms and concerns included in this review, and the challenges these pose more broadly for science and clinical practice elsewhere, one might assume that geneticists and biomedical researchers would be only too pleased to abandon racialized categories. However, in the discussion that follows, we will argue that although arguments against the use of racialized categories appear well founded, they leave enough room for interpretation to make the use of such categories an attractive option for geneticists and biomedical researchers. During the course of the discussion, this process of interpretation is referred to as *selective engagement*—that is, the way in which the arguments themselves leave room for scientists to acknowledge the limitations of racialized categories and engage with these arguments, while, at the same time, continuing to emphasize the utility of racialized categories in their work.

This process of selective engagement can be broken down into three parts. The first is the process of selective engagement with definitional arguments and the methods employed to operationalize racialized categories. The second is selective engagement with the analysis and interpretation of observable health inequalities—particularly how selective engagement provides a framework through which epidemiological studies of disparities in health among racialized groups are interpreted as largely the product of genetic variation. Finally, it is argued that this genetic framework perspective has come to dominate clinical practice. This, arguably, produces a largely self-fulfilling frame of reference when setting research objectives and interpreting research findings—one that appears highly attractive to researchers wishing to find genetic answers to a variety of health questions, including the presumed genetic basis of disparities in health among racialized groups (Fine, Ibrahim, and Thomas 2005). However, we will argue that this process of selective engagement is only partially successful, leaving geneticists and biomedical researchers with the difficult task of justifying their work in the public sphere, while at the same time attempting to maintain the boundaries between science and society they have sought to create/reinforce.

While the lack of conceptual and definitional consensus surrounding racialized categories implies instability, which is, in turn, contrary to the requirements of scientific research (Rivara and Finberg 2001; Winker 2004), it is also indicative of the wide range of choices available to researchers with respect to the meanings applied to, and operationalization of, such categories. The failure to clarify these issues within biomedical dictionaries, and elsewhere, leaves researchers with an opportunity to view racialized categories as "relatively homogeneous with respect to biological inheritance" (Last 1995, 198). Although more recent definitions of some dictionaries appear to emphasize caution, this does not entirely discount the notion that such categories *can* be used as markers for genetic variation. Subsequently, researchers are relatively free to conceptualize and operationalize these categories in a variety of ways. For example, this is likely to manifest itself in moving from a conceptualization of racialized categories that assumes/implies that these are biogenetic entities but uses inherently nonbiological (and, to some extent, nonscientific) methods for collecting data thereon (such as those based on self-identification and official census categories; Smart et al. 2008). The ambiguity and variability in data collection methods, together with the absence of a specific conceptual rationale, is a common theme in articles critiquing the use of these categories in genetics and biomedical research (not least with respect to their internal and external validity), and these issues have also been highlighted in more recently published articles reviewing the use of such categories in human genetics and biomedical research (e.g., Hunt and Megyesi 2008; Sankar, Cho, and Mountain 2007; Shanawani et al. 2006). In this context, racialized categories become unexamined, commonsense entities, sustained without critical examination by their frequent appearance in the genetic and biomedical literature. As Epstein (2004, 1995) has argued, although "racial categories are culturally variable and change over time . . . [this] does little to disturb the common-sense understanding of racial difference." To summarize, *within the scientific* community, the popular conceptual basis underlying the social and scientific meaning of racialized categories escapes close scrutiny by a selective, partial engagement with both the data on genetic and sociocultural variation *and* the arguments against these (Outram and Ellison 2006a). And by routinely avoiding the explicit recognition of either the conceptual rationale or the methodological basis for using racialized categories, these scientists avoid close scrutiny of any glaring contradictions, not least those inherent in the collection of genetic markers using self-identification, and uncritical assumptions about the reliability and validity of such data.

With respect to the *analytical* and *interpretative* arguments against the use of racialized categories as (if they were appropriate) markers of genetic variation within genetics and biomedical research, a similar pattern of selective engagement occurs. Thus

genetic scientists are prone to argue, when questioned about their use of racial categories, that they are able to use race as a scientific category within their research as a
loose marker of genetic affiliation (and, by implication, as a useful biomedical marker
in clinical practice), while at the same time distancing themselves from the sociopolitical attributes of these categories (Outram and Ellison 2006b). Critics of this position
argue that such selective distancing leaves genetic science open to potential misinter-
pretation (or deliberate manipulation) to subscribe a genetic cause to inequalities in
health between populations and deflect attention away from the impact of discriminatory practices within society (and within the medical establishment) that continue to
impact on health. While many of the articles included in this review argued that the
separation of the biological from the social is untenable (due to residual confounding
and the absence of an appropriate counterfactual thesis; Kaufman and Cooper 2001),
geneticists and biomedical researchers act as if they have been able to achieve this
separation by framing the interpretation of racialized analyses in ways that appear to
make them immune from such critiques. As such, while these scientists might accept
some of the arguments against using racialized categories as interesting insights into
alternative (i.e., nongenetic) explanations for disparities in health among racialized
groups, they may still assume that the disparities in health they have studied are *primarily* the product of genetic variation. As Krieger (2005, 2156) has argued, this produces a largely self-referential body of analytical interpretation: "unobserved 'innate'
biological differences lead to observed biological differences—which in turn prove that
unobserved 'innate' biological differences exist." This a priori focus on genetic etiology
has taken hold of a considerable body of epidemiological analysis and is based on
what Kaufman (2008, 1668) calls an "apparent eagerness to embrace the message of
racial essentialism," which "seems to represent a very strong prior belief on the part
of many researchers." Kaufman (2008, 1668) concludes that "until this strong predilec-
tion for racial essentialism in biological thinking abates, there would seem to be little
hope that a more sensible and honest approach to statistical inference in observational
data will take hold more widely"—that is, one that questions the independence of
genetic, structural, and sociocultural factors and engages more fully with the challenges facing the analysis of the multifactoral causes for disparities in health among
racialized groups. In this context, the lack of a thoroughly examined theoretical or
conceptual basis for using racialized categories in genetics and biomedical research
appears to produce a largely unexamined and self-perpetuating analytical/interpreta-
tive framework (Weed 2000). Once racialized categories are used in this self-referential
manner, it becomes difficult to interpret disparities in health among racialized groups
(or, for that matter, differences in any other characteristics) as anything other than
genetically derived. Moreover, as Ahmad and Bradby (2007, 798) have argued, this
conceptual, analytical, and interpretive framework may not only distort the perception of *why* health disparities exist (i.e., their etiology), but may also extend to victim

blaming: "using culture and ethnicity as an explanation of inequality between groups [which] distorts perceptions of how ethnic relations, and the related inequities of power are produced. Defined by those in power, the disadvantage of minority ethnic groups too often continues to be seen as 'caused' by their diseased genetic and dysfunctional cultural inheritance." In attempting to rectify the tension between the potential utility and the potential dangers of using racialized categories, we have sought to steer a course whereby arguments against the use of racial groups within genetics and biomedical research have been identified and discussed; set against the context of what we know about genetics, health, and health care; and explored in relation to the sociopolitical and individual impact of racialization. Overall, we have argued that the analytical and interpretative framework that *assumes* racial identity to be strongly affiliated to genetic variation is neither scientifically defensible nor politically sustainable in the context of its potential social harms.

Finally, with respect to concerns about the *application* of racialized categories as genetic variables, it can be argued that both selective engagement and disengagement occur. First, with respect to the narrowing of diagnoses and treatment options, it can be seen that arguments against the use of racialized categories as (if they were appropriate) markers of genetic variation follow directly from the narrowing of analytical interpretations described previously. A preoccupation with genetic causes among researchers examining the etiology of health disparities among racialized groups can, and arguably has (Witzig 1996), led to a routine emphasis on racialized categories within medicine such that these categories increasingly influence the diagnostic and treatment pathways selected and are increasingly seen as an essential element of day-to-day clinical practice. Together with what Frank (2007, 1981) has referred to as the "head-long rush toward a genetic explanation for any race/ethnic difference in disease prevalence or etiology," it is easy to see how the triangular association between race, genes, and health has become such a robust and self-referential framework.

While most biomedical research is carried out with the explicit or implicit intention of improving clinical practice, a focus on racialized groups in such research is likely to have a number of (unanticipated and negative) social consequences. For example, efforts to target health services at specific racialized groups—such as the screening programs for sickle-cell anemia and Tay-Sachs disease that have been developed at various times in the past—are ostensibly attempts to use the findings of research on racialized groups to better direct limited health resources to groups at greater risk of disease (Aspinall, Dyson, and Anionwu 2003; Dyson et al. 2006). Yet they also provide mechanisms for stigmatizing and stereotyping the groups concerned as inherently unhealthy (Ahmad and Bradby 2007; Brandt-Rauf et al. 2006). Geneticists and biomedical researchers may find these bioethical implications difficult to engage with within the context of scientific work that is intended to be, and is often interpreted and presented as, objective and value-free. Indeed, it is not possible to deal with such concerns without either abandoning the distinctions between different scientific disciplines (and between science and society) that are so central to the culture of much scientific research (Gieryn 1995; Goodman and Leatherman 1998) or crossing over academic and contextual boundaries between the natural and social sciences and between pure and applied research. By focusing inward—on scientific methods and results that support the triangular framework of race, genes, and health—while largely ignoring the complexity and conceptual ambiguity of the tools used, it would seem that this form of scientific practice can present itself as being untainted by social values, pragmatic concerns, or unintended consequences. However, by embracing the racialized categories and labels that have become recognized as socioculturally meaningful (not least through their adoption by censuses as sociopolitical realities), genetics and biomedical science run the risk of entering a contentious social, political, and ethical arena in which scientific practice is subject to unprecedented scrutiny and control. In the process, scientific practice can become aligned to broader sociopolitical enterprises, as was the case with policies designed to tackle the underrepresentation of "minority" populations in biomedical research (which began in the United States and United Kingdom during the 1980s)—policies that have, somewhat paradoxically, resulted in an even greater emphasis on differences between racialized groups than had previously occurred (Epstein 2004).

Conclusion

Looking back over the criticisms and concerns identified during the course of this review, it is difficult to see how the routine use of racialized categories as (if they were) markers of genetic variation—one that is seldom accompanied by an explicit or adequate conceptual, methodological, or analytical rationale—might do anything other than undermine biomedical research and practice. Indeed, there appears to be a strong prima facie case for assuming that racialized categories are inappropriate approximations of medically important aspects of genetic variation. Likewise, there seems to be a strong case against assuming that disparities in health between racialized groups are usually or necessarily the result of genetic variation. Of course, in a few very specific contexts—that is, with very specific populations and for very specific genetic conditions—racialized categories might offer sufficiently precise markers of genetic variation to be etiologically or therapeutically useful (Ellison 2005). But such contexts appear to be far less common than is generally assumed, and even within these (very specific) contexts, it may still be more appropriate to appraise *all* potential determinants of disparities in health (i.e., structural, sociocultural, *and* genetic), rather than focusing on just one of these—not least whenever there is any etiological, diagnostic, or therapeutic uncertainty. This more holistic approach would have the benefit of establishing the precise relationship between race, genes, and health, including the role that structural and/or sociocultural factors might play in generating, exacerbating, or sustaining the impact of genetic variation on health.

Meanwhile, an ancillary conclusion that might be drawn from the articles examined in this review is that the use of racialized categories within genetics and biomedical research cannot be dissociated from their sociopolitical contexts or consequences—not least because both race and health are biosocial phenomena (i.e., with biological *and* sociocultural characteristics). In negotiating between the potential benefits of using racialized categories within scientific contexts and the potential structural and sociocultural ills this might cause, we have argued that conceptually distancing science from society when referring to racialized groups is likely to be counterproductive. Viewing the sociopolitical attributes of racialized categories as beyond the sphere of scientific enquiry may leave geneticists and biomedical scientists unable to understand the full meaning(s) of such categories and the ultimate consequences of using these as (if they were appropriate) markers of genetic variation. This self-imposed restriction on engaging with alternative meanings and interpretations of racialized categories denies geneticists and biomedical scientists the benefit of insight from the social sciences. In turn, it also limits the ability of the former to enter the clinical and political arenas whenever they see their work being inappropriately applied to health care policies and practices, or used to stigmatize, stereotype, and discriminate.

Thus, somewhat paradoxically, while a propensity among geneticists and biomedical scientists to selectively engage with arguments against the use of racialized categories as (if they were appropriate) markers of genetic variation seems to reify these categories as *scientifically* meaningful, the *ultimate* appeal of racialized categories remains their ability to capture the meld of genetic *and* social characteristics capable of generating persistent (and socially heritable) disparities in health between racialized groups. More specifically, these categories are likely to be crucial for any analyses of disparities in health within racialized societies simply because they are essential for identifying, exploring, and thereby addressing the consequences of injustice based on notions of racialized groups as genetically distinct. However, it is increasingly recognized that conceptualizing racialized categories as either sociopolitical *or* biogenetic constructs undermines the ability of genetics and biomedical research to identify their true biosocial character and how this character generates the circular arguments that sustain inequity (Dingwall, Nerlich, and Hillyard 2006; Duster 2003). By recognizing the biosocial (or what Goodman and Leatherman [1998] have called the biocultural) character of racialized categories, it may yet be possible to use these sensitively within the natural *and* social sciences as well as within scientific *and* sociopolitical arenas to address disparities in health (and related structural and sociocultural disparities), without generating the evidence needed to sustain the stigmatization, stereotyping, and unfair treatment of racialized groups.

Notes

1. We have previously conducted two quantitative reviews to examine the contemporary relevance of these issues. In the first of these, we surveyed the 102 journals categorized under "Medicine, General and Internal" within the ISI Web of Knowledge's Science Citation Index (SCI) Journal Citation Reports. This survey found that between 1995 and 2005, 90 of these 102 (88%) journals contained articles that referred to "race," "racial," "ethnic," and/or "ethnicity" in their titles and/or abstracts. A comparable survey of the 120 journals listed under the SCI category "Genetics and Heredity" found that 70 (58%) contained articles that referred to "race," "racial," "ethnic," and/or "ethnicity" in their titles and/or abstracts (Outram and Ellison 2006c). These figures appear to correspond reasonably well with other surveys of genetics journals (Sankar et al. 2007) and biomedical and public health journals (Ahdieh and Hahn 1996; Comstock, Castillo, and Lindsay 2004; Drevdahl, Taylor, and Phillips 2001; Ellison and de Wet 1997; Jones, LaVeist, and Lillie-Blanton 1991; Walsh and Ross 2003; Williams 1994), which have found that anything between 40% and 75% of articles referred to racialized categories in some form or another As such, the issue of racialized categories (i.e., their use and the criticisms associated with this use) cannot simply be seen as a side issue to much of the research published in these fields. Instead, concerns regarding the use of racialized categories in genetics and biomedical research raise fundamental questions about such research and, by implication, about the clinical services and public health programs based thereon, not least those seeking to address persistent disparities in health between racialized groups in a range of different countries; recent examples of such work include Jamieson, Armfield, and Roberts-Thomson (2007), Matijasevich et al. (2008), Goh et al. (2007), and Mann et al. (2008)—studies from Australia, Brazil, Malaysia, the United Kingdom, and the United States.

References

Ahdieh, L., and R. A. Hahn. 1996. Use of the terms "race," "ethnicity," and "national origins": A review of articles in the *American Journal of Public Health*, 1980–1989. *Ethnicity and Health* 1:95–98.

Ahmad, W. I. U., and H. Bradby. 2007. Locating ethnicity and health: Exploring concepts and contexts. *Sociology of Health and Illness* 29:795–810.

Aspinall, P. J. 1997. The conceptual basis of ethnic group terminology and classifications. *Social Science and Medicine* 45:689–698.

Aspinall, P. J., S. M. Dyson, and E. N. Anionwu. 2003. The feasibility of using ethnicity as a primary tool for antenatal selective screening for sickle cell disorders: Pointers from the research evidence. *Social Science and Medicine* 56:285–297.

Baum, B. 2006. *The rise and fall of the Caucasian race: A political history of identity*. New York: New York University Press.

Bhopal, R. 2004. Glossary of terms relating to ethnicity and race: For reflection and debate. *Journal of Community Health* 58:441–445.

Boyatsiz, R. E. 1998. *Transforming qualitative information: Thematic analysis and code development*. Thousand Oaks, CA: Sage.

Bradby, H. 1995. Ethnicity: Not a black and white issue. A research note. *Sociology of Health and Illness* 17:405–417.

Brandt-Rauf, S. I., V. H. Raveis, N. F. Drummond, J. A. Conte, and S. M. Rothman. 2006. Ashkenazi Jews and breast cancer: The consequences of linking ethnic identity to genetic disease. *American Journal of Public Health* 96:1979–1988.

Braun, L., A. Fausto-Sterling, D. Fullwiley, E. M. Hammonds, A. Nelson, W. Quivers, S. M. Reverby, and A. E. Shields. 2007. Racial categories in medical practice: How useful are they? *PLoS Medicine* 4:e271.

Braun, V., and V. Clarke. 2006. Using thematic analysis in psychology. *Qualitative Research in Psychology* 3:77–101.

British Medical Journal. 1996. Style matters: Ethnicity, race, and culture: Guidelines for research, audit, and publication. *British Medical Journal* 312:1094–1095.

Buescher, P. A., Z. Gizlice, and K. A. Jones-Vessey. 2005. Discrepancies between published data on racial classification and self-reported race: Evidence from the 2002 North Carolina live birth records. *Public Health Reports* 120:393–398.

Caldwell, S. H., and R. Popenoe. 1995. Perceptions and misperceptions of skin color. *Annals of Internal Medicine* 122:614–617.

Cartmill, M. 1999. The status of the race concept in physical anthropology. *American Anthropologist* 100:651–660.

Cavalli-Sforza, L. L., A. C. Wilson, C. R. Cantor, R. M. Cook-Deegan, and M. C. King. 1991. Call for a worldwide survey of human genetic diversity: A vanishing opportunity for the Human Genome Project. *Genomics* 11:490–491.

Comstock, R. D., E. M. Castillo, and S. P. Lindsay. 2004. Four-year review of the use of race and ethnicity in epidemiologic and public health research. *American Journal of Epidemiology* 159:611–619.

Cooper, R. S. 1984. A note on the biological concept of race and its application to epidemiologic research. *American Heart Journal* 8:715–723.

Cooper, R. S. 2005. Race and IQ—Molecular genetics as deus ex machina. *American Psychologist* 60:71–76.

Cooper, R. S., and R. David. 1986. The biological concept of race and its application to public health. *Journal of Public Health Politics, Policy, and Law* 11:97–116.

Dingwall, R., B. Nerlich, and S. Hillyard. 2006. Biological determinism and its critics: Some lessons from history. In *The nature of difference: Science, society, and human biology*, ed. G. T. H. Ellison and A. Goodman. Boca Raton, FL: Taylor and Francis, 17–34.

Drevdahl, D. J., D. A. Philips, and J. Y. Taylor. 2006. Uncontested categories: The use of race and ethnicity variables in nursing research. *Nursing Inquiry* 13:52–63.

Drevdahl, D., J. Y. Taylor, and D. A. Phillips. 2001. Race and ethnicity as variables in nursing research, 1952–2000. *Nursing Research* 50:305–313.

Duster, T. 2003. Buried alive: The concept of race in science. In *Genetic nature/culture: Anthropology and science beyond the two-culture divide,* ed. A. H. Goodman, D. Heath, and M. S. Lindee. Berkeley: University of California Press, 258–277.

Edwards, A. W. 2003. Human genetic diversity: Lewontin's fallacy. *BioEssays* 25:798–801.

Ellison, G. T. H. 1999. Contemporary definitions of "race" and "ethnicity" in medical dictionaries. *Annals of Human Biology* 27:104–105.

Ellison, G. T. H. 2005. "Population profiling" and public health risk: When and how should we use race/ethnicity? *Critical Public Health* 15:65–74.

Ellison, G. T. H. 2006. Medicine in black and white: BiDil®, race and the limits of evidence-based medicine. *Significance* 3:118–121.

Ellison, G. T. H., and T. de Wet. 1997. The use of "racial" categories in contemporary South African health research. *South African Medical Journal* 87:1671–1679.

Ellison, G. T. H., and I. R. Jones. 2002. Social identities and the "new genetics": Scientific and social consequences. *Critical Public Health* 12:265–282.

Ellison, G. T. H., J. Kaufman, R. F. Head, P. Martin, and J. Kahn. 2008b. Flaws in the US Food and Drug Administration's rationale for supporting the development and approval of BiDil® as a treatment for heart failure in black patients. *Journal of Law, Medicine, and Ethics* 36:449–457.

Ellison, G. T. H., A. Smart, R. Tutton, S. M. Outram, R. Ashcroft, and P. A. Martin. 2007. Racial categories in medicine: A failure of evidence-based practice? *PLoS Medicine* 4:e287.

Ellison, G. T. H., R. Tutton, S. M. Outram, P. A. Martin, R. Ashcroft, and A. Smart. 2008a. An interdisciplinary perspective on the impact of genomics on the meaning of "race" and the future role of racialized categories in biomedical research. *NTM Journal of the History of Science, Technology, and Medicine* 16:378–386.

Epstein, S. 2004. Bodily differences and collective identities: The politics of gender and race in biomedical research in the United States. *Body and Society* 10:183–203.

Erasmus, Y., and G. T. H. Ellison. 2005. Race reclassification and socio-political hierarchy in apartheid South Africa. *Annals of Human Biology* 32:792.

Erasmus, Y., and G. T. H. Ellison. 2008 What can we learn about the meaning of race from the classification of population groups during apartheid? *South African Journal of Science* 104: 450–452.

Fine, M. J., S. A. Ibrahim, and S. B. Thomas. 2005. The role of race and genetics in health disparities research. *American Journal of Public Health* 95:2125–2128.

Frank, R. 2007. What to make of it? The (re)emergence of a biological conceptualization of race in health disparities research. *Social Science and Medicine* 64:1977–1983.

Freeman, H. P. 1998. The meaning of race in science—considerations for cancer research. *Cancer* 82:219–225.

Garte, S. 2002. The racial genetics paradox in biomedical research and public health. *Public Health Reports* 117:421–425.

Gieryn, T. F. 1995. Boundaries of science. In *Handbook of science and technology studies*, ed. S. Jasinoff, G. E. Markle, J. C. Petersen, and T. Pinch. Thousand Oaks, CA: Sage, 145–167.

Gimenez, M. E. 1989. Latino/"Hispanic"—who needs a name? The case against a standardized terminology. *International Journal of Health Services* 19:557–571.

Goh, K. L., P. L. Cheah, M. D. Noorfaridah, K. F. Quek, and N. Parasakthi. 2007. Ethnicity and *H. pylori* as risk factors for gastric cancer in Malaysia: A prospective case control study. *American Journal of Gastroenterology* 102:40–45.

Goodman, A. H. 1997. Bred in the bone? *Sciences* 37:20–25.

Goodman, A. H., and A. H. Leatherman. 1998. Traversing the chasm between biology and culture. In *Building a new biocultural synthesis: Political-economic perspectives on human biology*, ed. A. H. Goodman and T. L. Leatherman. Ann Arbor: University of Michigan Press, 3–41.

Hahn, R. A., B. I. Truman, and N. D. Baker. 1995. Identifying ancestry: The reliability of ancestral identification in the United States by self, proxy, interviewer, and funeral director. *Epidemiology* 7:75–80.

Hahn, R. A., S. F. Wetterhall, C. A. Gay, D. S. Harshbarger, C. A. Burnett, R. G. Parrish, and R. J. Orend. 2002. The recording of demographic information on death certificates: A national survey of funeral directors. *Public Health Reports* 117:37–43.

Hammerschmidt, D. E. 1999. It's as simple as black and white! Race and ethnicity as categorical variables. *Journal of Laboratory and Clinical Medicine* 133:10–12.

Hart, C. 1998. *Doing a literature review: Releasing the social science research imagination*. London: Sage.

Hart, C. 2001. *Doing a literature search: A comprehensive guide for the social sciences*. London: Sage.

Hunt, L. M., and M. S. Megyesi. 2008. The ambiguous meanings of the racial/ethnic categories routinely used in human genetics research. *Social Science and Medicine* 66:349–361.

Huth, E. J. 1995. Identifying ethnicity in medical papers. *Annals of Internal Medicine* 122:619–621.

Jamieson, L. M., J. M. Armfield, and K. F. Roberts-Thomson. 2007. Indigenous and non-indigenous child oral health in three Australian states and territories. *Ethnicity and Health* 12:89–107.

Jenkins, R. P. 2001. *Rethinking ethnicity: Arguments and explorations*. London: Sage.

Jones, C. P. 2001. Invited commentary: "Race," racism, and the practice of epidemiology. *American Journal of Epidemiology* 154:299–304.

Jones, C. P., T. A. LaVeist, and M. Lillie-Blanton. 1991. "Race" in the epidemiologic literature: An examination of the *American Journal of Epidemiology*, 1921–1990. *American Journal of Epidemiology* 134:1079–1084.

Karlsen, S. 2004. "Black like Beckham"? Moving beyond definitions of ethnicity based on skin colour and ancestry. *Ethnicity and Health* 9:107–137.

Karter, A. J. 2003. Commentary: Race, genetics, and disease—in search of a middle ground. *International Journal of Epidemiology* 32:26–28.

Kaufman, J. S. 2008. Epidemiologic analysis of racial/ethnic disparities. *Social Science and Medicine* 66:1659–1669.

Kaufman, J. S., and R. S. Cooper. 1999. Seeking causal explanations in social epidemiology. *American Journal of Epidemiology* 150:113–120.

Kaufman, J. S., and R. S. Cooper. 2001. Commentary: Considerations for use of racial/ethnic classification in etiologic research. *American Journal of Epidemiology* 154:291–298.

Kaufman, J. S., R. S. Cooper, and D. L. McGee. 1997. Socioeconomic status and health in blacks and whites: The problem of residual confounding and the resiliency of race. *Epidemiology* 8:621–628.

Krieger, N. 2005. Stormy weather: Race, gene expression, and the science of health disparities. *American Journal of Public Health* 95:2155–2160.

Krieger, N., and M. Bassett. 1986. The health of black folk: Disease class, and ideology in science. *Monthly Review* 38:74–85.

Krieger, N., D. L. Rowley, A. A. Herman, B. Avery, and M. T. Phillips. 1993. Racism, sexism, and social class: Implications for studies of health, disease, and well-being. *American Journal of Preventive Medicine* 9:82–122.

Last, J. M., ed. 1995. *A dictionary of epidemiology*. 3rd ed. Oxford: Oxford University Press.

Last, J. M., ed. 2001. *A dictionary of epidemiology*. 4th ed. Oxford: Oxford University Press.

LaVeist, T. A. 1994. Beyond dummy variables and sample selection: What health services researchers ought to know about race as a variable. *Health Services Research* 29:1–15.

Lewontin, R. C. 1972. An apportionment of human diversity. In *Evolutionary biology 6*, ed. T. Dobzhansky, M. K. Hecht, and W. C. Steere. New York: Appleton-Century-Crofts, 381–398.

Lillquist, E., and C. A. Sullivan. 2004. The law and genetics of racial profiling in medicine. *Harvard Civil Rights–Civil Liberties Law Review* 39:391–483.

Liu, E. T. 1998. The uncoupling of race and cancer genetics. *Cancer* 83:1765–1769.

Liu, X. Q., A. D. Paterson, E. M. John, and J. A. Knight. 2006. The role of self-defined race/ethnicity in population structure control. *Annals of Human Genetics* 70:496–505.

Mann, A. G., C. L. Trotter, M. A. Balogun, and M. E. Ramsay. 2008. Hepatitis C in ethnic minority populations in England. *Journal of Viral Hepatitis* 15:421–426.

Matijasevich, A., C. G. Victora, A. J. D. Barros, I. S. Santos, P. L. Marco, E. P. Alernax, and F. C. Barros. 2008. Widening ethnic disparities in infant mortality in southern Brazil: Comparison of 3 birth cohorts. *American Journal of Public Health* 98:692–698.

McCann-Mortimer, P., M. Augoustinos, and A. LeCouteur. 2004. "Race" and the Human Genome Project: Constructions of scientific legitimacy. *Discourse and Society* 15:409–432.

McKenney, N. R., and C. E. Bennett. 1994. Issues regarding data on race and ethnicity: The Census Bureau experience. *Public Health Reports* 109:16–25.

McKenzie, K., and N. S. Crowcroft. 1996. Describing race, ethnicity, and culture in medical research—describing the groups studied is better than trying to find a catch all name. *British Medical Journal* 312:1054.

Mountain, J. L., and N. Risch. 2004. Assessing genetic contributions to phenotypic differences among "racial" and "ethnic" groups. *Nature Genetics* 36(11 Suppl. l):48–53.

Muntaner, C., F. J. Nieto, and P. O'Campo. 1996. *The Bell Curve*: On race, social class, and epidemiologic research. *American Journal of Epidemiology* 144:531–536.

Nazroo, J. Y. 1998. Genetic, culture or socio-economic vulnerability? Explaining ethnic inequalities in health. *Sociology of Health and Illness* 20:710–730.

O'Loughlin, J. 1999. Understanding the role of ethnicity in chronic disease: A challenge for the new millennium. *Canadian Medical Association Journal* 161:161–162.

Osbourne, N. G., and M. D. Feit. 1992. The use of race in medical research. *Journal of the American Medical Association* 267:275–279.

Outram, S. M., and G. T. H. Ellison. 2006a. The truth will out: Scientific pragmatism and the geneticisation of difference. In *The nature of difference: Science, society, and human biology*, ed. G. T. H. Ellison and A. H. Goodman. Boca Raton, FL: Taylor and Francis, 157–179.

Outram, S. M., and G. T. H. Ellison. 2006b. Anthropological insights into the use of race/ethnicity to explore genetic determinants of disparities in health. *Journal of Biosocial Science* 38:83–102.

Outram, S. M., and G. T. H. Ellison. 2006c. Improving the use of race and ethnicity in genetic research: A survey of instructions to authors in genetics journals. *Science Editor* 29:78–81.

Pfeffer, N. 1998. Theories in health care and research—theories of race, ethnicity and culture. *British Medical Journal* 14:1381–1384.

Race, Ethnicity, and Genetics Working Group. 2005. The use of racial, ethnic, and ancestral categories in human genetics research. *American Journal of Human Genetics* 77:519–532.

Risch, N., E. Burchard, E. Ziv, and H. Tang. 2002. Categorization of humans in biomedical research: Genes, race, and disease. *Genome Biology* 3:1–12.

Rivara, F. P., and L. Finberg. 2001. Use of the terms race and ethnicity. *Archives of Pediatrics and Adolescent Medicine* 155:119.

Rosenberg, N. A., J. K. Pritchard, J. L. Weber, H. M. Cann, K. K. Kidd, L. A. Zhivotovsky, and M. W. Feldman. 2002. Genetic structure of human populations. *Science* 298:2381–2385.

Sankar, P., M. K. Cho, and J. Mountain. 2007. Race and ethnicity in genetic research. *American Journal of Medical Genetics, Part A* 143:961–970.

Shanawani, H., L. Dame, D. A. Schwartz, and R. Cook-Deegan. 2006. Non-reporting and inconsistent reporting of race and ethnicity in articles that claim associations among genotype, outcome, and race or ethnicity. *Journal of Medical Ethics* 32:724–728.

Shriver, M. D., M. W. Smith, L. Jin, A. Marcini, J. M. Akey, R. Deka, and R. E. Ferrell. 1997. Ethnic-affiliation estimation by use of population-specific DNA markers. *American Journal of Human Genetics* 60:957–964.

Silverman, D. 2000. *Doing qualitative research: A practical handbook*. London: Sage.

Silverman, D. 2001. *Interpreting qualitative data*. London: Sage.

Smaje, C. 1996. The ethnic patterning of health: New directions for theory and research. *Sociology of Health and Illness* 18:139–171.

Smart, A., R. Tutton, R. Ashcroft, P. Martin, and G. T. H. Ellison. 2006. Can science alone improve the measurement and communication of race and ethnicity in genetic research? Exploring the strategies proposed by *Nature Genetics*. *Biosocieties* 1:307–318.

Smart, A., R. Tutton, P. Martin, G. T. H. Ellison, and R. Ashcroft. 2008. The standardization of race and ethnicity in biomedical science editorials and UK biobanks. *Social Studies of Science* 38:407–423.

Sugarman, J. R. 1996. Improving American Indian cancer data in the Washington State cancer registry using linkages with the Indian health service and tribal records. *Cancer* 78:1564–1568.

Tang, H., T. Quertermous, B. Rodriguez, S. L. R. Kardia, X. Zhu, A. Brown, J. S. Pankow, et al. 2005. Genetic structure, self-identified race/ethnicity, and confounding in case-control association studies. *American Journal of Human Genetics* 76:268–275.

Tutton, R., A. Smart, R. Ashcroft, P. Martin, and G. T. H. Ellison. 2010. From self-identity to genotype: The past, present and future of ethnic categories in post-genomic science. In *What's the use of race? Modern governance and the Biology of Difference*, ed. Ian Whitmarsh and David S. Jones. Cambridge, MA: MIT Press.

Walsh, C., and L. F. Ross. 2003. Whether and why pediatric researchers report race and ethnicity. *Archives of Pediatrics & and Adolescent Medicine* 157:671–675.

Weiss, K. M., and S. M. Fullerton. 2005. Racing around, getting nowhere. *Evolutionary Anthropology* 14:165–169.

Weed, D. L. 2001 Methods in epidemiology and public health: Does practice match theory? *Journal of Epidemiology and Community Health* 55: 104–110.

Wiencke, J. K. 2004. Impact of race/ethnicity on molecular pathways in human cancer. *Nature Reviews Cancer* 4:79–84.

Williams, D. R. 1994. The concept of race in health services research: 1966–1990. *Health Services Research* 29:1392–1393.

Williams, D. R. 1996. Race/ethnicity and socioeconomic status. *International Journal of Health Services* 26:483–505.

Williams, D. R. 1997. Race and health: Basic questions, emerging directions. *Annals of Epidemiology* 7:322–333.

Williams, D. R., R. Lavizzo-Mourey, and R. C. Warren. 1994. The concept of race and health status in America. *Public Health Reports* 109:26–41.

Winkler, M. A. 2004. Measuring race and ethnicity: Why and how? *Journal of the American Medical Association* 292 (13): 1612–1614.

Witzig, R. 1996. The medicalization of race: Scientific legitimization of a flawed social construct. *Annals of Internal Medicine* 125:675–679.

Woodward, K., ed. 2004. *Questioning identity: Gender, class, ethnicity.* 2nd ed. London: Routledge.

6 From Self-Identity to Genotype: The Past, Present, and Future of Ethnic Categories in Postgenomic Science

Richard Tutton, Andrew Smart, Richard Ashcroft, Paul Martin, and George T. H. Ellison

In 2004, we were funded by the Wellcome Trust—the world's largest medical charity—through its Biomedical Ethics Programme to conduct a three-year project to investigate how genetic scientists working in biomedical research understood and operationalized race and ethnicity as categories in their research.[1] There had been limited research on these questions in the U.K. context, so this was to be a significant undertaking. We focused on research studies examining genetic and environmental factors in the development of common, complex diseases and those exploring the genetic basis of differential drug response. These studies were chosen because both have engaged with well-documented disparities in health among racial and ethnic groups, and because there have been high expectations that the application of advances in genetic technology in both these areas will have a broad impact on future health care practice and policy (Bell 1998; Khoury, Burke, and Thomson 2000).

One of our interests was in the classificatory practices of scientists with respect to race and ethnicity. In British, American, and many other societies today, we have seen the institutionalization of the principle of racial and ethnic self-identification as an established (but not uncontested) practice in various domains of public life, including social statistics (Morning 2008). There have also been debates among geneticists and epidemiologists about the scientific merits of using self-identification for the purposes of studies into disease etiology (Bamshad et al. 2004; Burchard et al. 2003; "Census, Race, and Science" 2000; Royal and Dunston 2004; Risch et al. 2002). This debate takes place against the backdrop of the emergence of programs for genetic analysis, which aim to assign individuals to populations on the basis of their genotypes (e.g., Wilson et al. 2001).

At the policy level, legislation has been passed in the United States to mandate the greater inclusion of women and individuals from racial and ethnic minorities in clinical and biomedical studies (Epstein 2007; Friedman et al. 2000). While there is no similar regulatory requirement for U.K.-based studies to include specific numbers of subjects from ethnic, age, or other minority groups, there are informal expectations that research should be more inclusive of participants from minority ethnic groups

(Mehta 2006; Tutton 2008), and the 2000 Race Relations (Amendment) Act obliges researchers to ensure that they address the issue of diversity. Epstein's (2007, 91) analysis of policy developments in the United States suggests that there has been a "categorical alignment" whereby "the categories of identity politics, the biological categories of biomedical research, and the social classifications of state bureaucrats [became] one and the same system of categorization." In this way, the practices of self-identification have become a central part of the conduct and governance of biomedical and pharmaceutical science, becoming aligned with knowledge about biological and genetic variation and related characteristics.

Given these debates, we were interested in considering how the practices of self-identification are incorporated into the design and operationalization of biomedical research. How do scientists consider the uses and limitations of self-identification for scientific fields, such genetic epidemiology and pharmacogenetics, that are aiming to build on the Human Genome Project and to produce new or improved diagnostics and therapies for human diseases? How does this compare with new, emerging techniques for classification based on genotyping? This chapter draws on interviews that we conducted with a number of scientists working in the United Kingdom in the fields of genetic epidemiology and pharmacogenetics about their use of self-identification, to record the race and/or ethnicity of research subjects in their studies and to determine what this might reveal about both current practices and expectations of future practices. To preface this discussion of our research, we begin by considering the conceptual and practical basis of self-identification and its rise to dominance over observer-assigned approaches to racial and ethnic classification in the domain of social statistics. This will highlight a number of issues that we will pick up on in the discussion of our interviews.

The Rise of Self-Identification as a Classification Practice

It is possible to broadly delineate the social practices involved in classifying race and/or ethnicity as requiring one person to make judgments about another person (or people) or requiring a person to make judgments about himself or herself. Thus race and/or ethnicity can be ascribed by the person collecting the information (an *observer-assigned* classification), or it can be *self-identified*. At present, it is the latter approach that dominates in social science and public policy, to the extent that Peter Aspinall (2001, 839) notes that "observer-assigned ethnicity is no longer regarded as an acceptable method of assignment."[2] His phrase "no longer regarded as . . . acceptable" indicates that the practice in question has been subjected to pressures from norms and values that have changed over time. However, both observer-assigned and self-identification practices share many things in common. In both practices, the person doing the classifying uses either his or her own words (a free text response) and/or chooses from lists of predetermined responses to assign race and/or ethnicity or to respond to questions about specific criteria for classifying race and/or ethnicity.[3] The key facet of practices of self-identification is thus that the responsibility for classification rests with the person for whom the classification is being made. We might ask, therefore, why is this currently deemed the most acceptable practice?

The acceptability of self-identification reflects a mix of political, conceptual, and practical concerns that can (partially at least) be understood as a response to the scientific and political debates about the status of race as a category and the history of observer-assigned racial classifications.[4] For example, in the realm of state bureaucracy within the United States and United Kingdom, it has become widespread practice to ask people to self-identify from a prespecified classification scheme (e.g., in censuses and in a range of settings over which the state has oversight).[5] Importantly, the U.S. Office of Management and Budget (OMB) has, over time, moved to a position that explicitly states that the racial and ethnic categories that it prespecifies are "social-political" (rather than valid anthropological or scientific) constructs and, as such, seems to reject the idea that the state or scientific experts should classify individuals into different racial or ethnic groups. This position marks a departure from the assumption that races are natural types or can be derived on the basis of ostensibly objective, biological characteristics such as skull morphology or blood quanta (Kertzer and Arel 2001). Furthermore, once race and/or ethnicity are conceptualized as socio-political constructs, then self-identification becomes a practical approach for classifying people's experience of social identity that has face validity.[6] If race and ethnicity are viewed as social identities and not objective types, the person best placed to decide in what category a person belongs is clearly that person himself or herself. These developments in thinking can also be seen in the United Kingdom, where observer assignment continued to be used during the 1970s and 1980s in some administrative settings (Booth 1985). The U.K. Office for Populations Censuses and Surveys (the predecessor of the present U.K. Office of National Statistics, ONS), was, however, anxious that the introduction of the ethnic question in the national censuses should not lend credence to commonly held (but nonetheless discredited) ideas about racial types (Sillitoe and White 1992). Like the OMB, the ONS now favors self-identification using a range of what it calls "ethnic groups." This practice also reflects the dominance of ethnicity over race in the United Kingdom, at least in formal public discourse (where ethnicity is conceptualized as being primarily about self-association with sociocultural groupings).

Nevertheless, in some circumstances, observer assignment continues to be practiced by state agencies. For example, U.K. police categorize those suspected of, and arrested for, recordable crimes using a series of "ethnic appearance categories" (Hansard 2008).[7] This aberration from the self-identification norm aptly illustrates how the classification of race and ethnicity in any specific context depends not only on how they are conceptualized and operationalized, but also on the circumstances in which classification takes place. Questions about the appropriateness, reliability, validity, and implications of different classification practices and circumstances have been widely explored. In the context of health and biomedicine, questions have included, for example, issues such as the proper alignment of classificatory criteria with different conceptualizations, research questions, and research contexts, and the degree of correspondence between people's self-identification and observer assignment (e.g., Aspinall 2001; Bradby 2003; Nazroo 1998; Senior and Bhopal 1994; Smaje 1996). Without rehearsing these arguments in full here, a common lesson that has emerged from these debates is that the practices and decisions surrounding classification should aim to ensure that measurements correspond to the required uses of the measures (i.e., they should be fit for purpose).

If we accept this premise about fitness for purpose, it is necessary to recognize that the prevailing practice of self-identifying race and ethnicity suffers from a number of limitations. For example, data that are reliant on practices of self-identification might, in some instances, be problematic because self-assessment tends to be highly contingent, unstable, and out of the control of researchers (Senior and Bhopal 1994). And while self-identified race and ethnicity has face validity (as a measure of a person's experience of his or her social identity), it does not necessarily have content validity (i.e., it may not fully represent all of what a person perceives his or her race and/or ethnicity to be)[8] or external validity (i.e., it may not be generalizable to someone else in the same position). Moreover, in health research, self-identified ethnic identity might be of limited use if the research questions are focused on issues related to ancestry, descent, or ethnic origins (Bradby 2003). Self-identification is also a potentially poor marker of what other people think your race and/or ethnicity might be— something that can be important in questions about how people are perceived and treated by society, and how specific authorities (such as scientists and health care professionals) might enact conceptions about race and/or ethnicity in their routine practice. And of course, there are some circumstances in which people are unable or unwilling to self-identify (or ask other people to self-identify), which make a self-identified classification impossible, or very difficult, to attain.

At the same time, it is necessary to critically challenge an idealized notion that self-identification represents the triumph of self-determination over the authority of science and the state. It has, for example, been argued that the shift to self-identification is part of a tendency to count identities—to measure how people think about themselves in relation to a range of specified and socially meaningful categories (see Skerry 2007 Kertzer and Arel 2001). From this perspective, practices of self-identification are framed in terms of empowerment, freedom of choice, and respect for individual dignity (Skerry 2000). However, Ann Morning's (2008, 248) cross-national analysis of how different national censuses frame their questions about race, ethnicity, and nationality found that only twelve of the eighty-seven countries that include such questions "treat it as a subjective facet of identity by asking respondents what they 'think,' 'consider,' or otherwise believe themselves to be." In many other countries, Morning noted, race and ethnicity are treated almost as objective or essential features of an individual, which the individual, in turn, should know, recognize, and be able to assign to himself or herself for the purposes of a census return. Of course, the state is the final arbiter of both the range of categories (and their associated nomenclature) from which people are able to choose and the taxonomic relationship between them. As Yanow (2003, 94) argues, "within this seeming possibility of self-identification . . . the range of options is created and circumscribed by the state through its agencies." Moreover, it is clear that the labels, nomenclatures, and classification schemes from which people are asked to choose have tended to evolve from previous naturalized biogeographic group categories. Thus the U.S. and U.K. censuses both have categories rooted in skin color and geographical origins—two of the biogeographical characteristics used in traditional racial classifications.[9] This process of constructing predetermined categories from which people are then able to choose (or into which free-form self-identifications are subsequently reduced) is inevitably tainted by past conditioning of what *race* and *ethnicity* mean and how these terms have been used in discriminatory policies and practices. Similar conditioning will also affect the choices individuals make when using these categories (and related classification systems) to self-identify their race and/or ethnicity.

Nevertheless, it is widely recognized that state classification schemes for race and ethnicity are not straightforward political or scientific impositions. The emergence and acceptance of the categories has been, and continues to be, a matter of social and political debate and contest (see Cornell and Hartmann 2007, 176–178; Fenton 2003, 30–42, for examples from U.S. and U.K. contexts). Furthermore, as both Cornell and Hartmann (2007) and Fenton (2003) record, the categories that emerge for use by the state can also feed back into civic society. Even if the group categories sanctioned by state bureaucracies have little meaning to start with, their saliency is constituted by virtue of their being used in everyday social and sociopolitical practice. Therefore state-legitimized categorizations such as those used in censuses are sites at which individual and collective meanings are mutually constitutive, and individuals come to reconcile their own internal senses of self with the administrative categories available to them on census forms and the like (cf. Hacking 1981). These categories can also, however, be used to challenge hegemonic constructions of social reality (Urla 1993).

In summary, the ascendancy of racial and ethnic self-identification as a classification practice in state bureaucracy is framed by the history of the race concept and accompanying practices of observer assignment. This conceptual shift in classification practice accompanied the reorientation of "race" as a sociopolitical construct and, within the United Kingdom, its partial replacement by the notion of ethnicity (which is, in large part, an overtly sociocultural concept). Over time, observer assignment has become perceived as not only conceptually inappropriate, but also as not fit for purpose in relation to monitoring the social groups of which people perceived themselves to be a part. However, even self-identification of race and ethnicity does not easily overcome the long history of difficulties associated with the race concept and associated practices of observer assignment. It does not necessarily distinguish ethnicity from race, nor does it free either of these terms from their naturalistic, biogeographical conceptualizations or from the associated practices of oppression and discrimination that have tainted the authority of both science and the state. Practices of classification involving the self-identification of race and ethnicity are not free floating, but rather, operate within certain limits and relate to categories whose constitution and relevance are determined by a range of social actors with differential power to define, challenge, and reshape the boundaries of social groupings. The ascendancy and social acceptability of self-identification does not strictly rule out alternative approaches to classification, but it does cast them in a negative light as being potentially improper or reprehensible.

This analysis of the history and practice of self-identification has raised a number of issues that we develop now in relation to our research on the classificatory practices of U.K. scientists working in the fields of genetic epidemiology and pharmacogenetics.

Race, Ethnicity, and Genomics in the United Kingdom

Our first set of interviews were conducted with principal research staff of ten biobanks and cohort studies investigating the environmental and genetic factors involved in health and illness in a range of populations, including children and adult volunteers. These biobanks recruited volunteers at single or multiple sites, and four of them sought to exclude minority ethnic groups so that only "white" British volunteers were studied. The justification given for this exclusivity stemmed from the view that there was significant genetic variation between ethnic groups that might complicate the interpretation of any gene-disease associations identified among ethnically diverse study populations as a result of gene-gene interactions at ethnic-specific polymorphic loci. Therefore, to investigate the association between genetic polymorphisms and disease, these respondents felt that the greater the (perceived) genetic homogeneity of the cohort, the stronger the internal validity of any such association would be. Most of the remaining respondents worked either on studies that had adopted a race/ethnicity-blind approach to recruitment (which tended to result in the inclusion of only small numbers of nonwhite British participants) or on studies that actively sought to recruit disproportionate numbers of minority groups, ostensibly to specifically study the consequences of genetic variation in such groups on gene-disease associations.

The second set of interviewees comprised a group of academic researchers working on nine pharmacogenetic studies located in university research centers based in the United Kingdom. These researchers were predominantly investigating variation in drug-metabolizing enzymes (DMEs) across a range of pharmaceuticals developed to treat a variety of disease conditions. As before, many of these nine studies focused exclusively on "white" British participants (for very similar reasons to those described earlier for the four biobanks focusing on white British participants), although the remainder ($n = 4$) adopted what constituted a race/ethnicity-blind approach.

A key theme explored in the interviews concerned the classificatory practices followed by the scientists involved in the biobanks and pharmacogenetic projects examined. In particular, we investigated the extent to which contemporary practices of self-identification were incorporated into the design and operationalization of these studies. Fourteen of the nineteen studies explicitly used self-identification, and of that fourteen, twelve did so using the "standardized" ethnic group classification scheme produced by the ONS for the purposes of the national censuses.[10] For four of the other studies, we were unable to determine the exact procedure used for classifying race and/or ethnicity,[11] whereas for the remaining study, the scientific team involved had rejected self-identification altogether—an exception we discuss in more detail subsequently.

In what follows, we discuss the accounts provided by the scientists we interviewed concerning their studies' use of self-identification to record race and/or ethnicity. We focus on three interrelated strands in these accounts: the scientists' experiences of, and justifications for, adopting or rejecting self-identification in their research designs and practices; their views concerning the strengths and limitations of using self-identification in their scientific work; and their insights into future developments in which self-identification might be superseded by alternative approaches.

Self-Identification as a Practical Tool

Some of the scientists we interviewed considered self-identification in predominantly pragmatic terms. For example, the lead researcher on a regionally based biobank in England noted,

As far as I can understand in the literature in the area . . . people having gone round the houses looking at alternative ways to subclassify different racial groups or different ethnicities, they've come back to the understanding that, or the agreement that, this straightforward self-reported classification into one of these major groups is as good a tool as any in the context of genetic association studies.

This respondent justifies using self-reporting "into one of these major groups" on pragmatic grounds, this approach being "as good as any" within a context of long-standing, and seemingly intractable, debates about classifying racial groups or ethnicities. Furthermore, this view is grounded in practical issues and describes self-identification as straightforward and thereby uncomplicated. However, part of this argument concerning practicability relates to the fact that self-identification, as practiced here, is a structured process—one that is ordered by a predetermined set of categories that have some broader recognition and relevance elsewhere. Another scientist, this time working on a similar national study, broadly shared this view:

Asking people to assign themselves in ethnicity is not perfect but we can't—we don't have any better way of doing it at the moment.

Again, we can see that self-identification is justified on pragmatic grounds, and although this interviewee acknowledges that it is "not perfect," it is upheld as the best available approach compared with currently available alternatives.

Self-Identification as Standardization

When it came to putting self-identification into practice, most of the scientists we interviewed whose studies used self-identification to record race and/or ethnicity did so using the standardized ethnic group classificatory scheme developed by the ONS. These scientists justified their use of the ONS ethnic group categories on the basis that these were an accepted standard used by many other agencies and many other scientific studies. Using the ONS scheme, they argued, not only meant that they were adopting accepted classificatory practices, but also that they were generating data that would improve the comparability, generalizability, and applicability of their findings. For example, a pharmacogeneticist, reflecting on his team's choice of the census classification, said,

I feel that standardisation for certain things like ethnicity, within the terms of genetic testing in this way is probably very useful. Now that's not to say that, you know, people shouldn't feel comfortable to classify themselves however they want to—but to have a sense of when you're trying to develop a test that is useful at a sort of population level or over, you know, significant groupings of people, I think some form of standardisation probably is very useful to make sure that you are capturing the appropriate information and therefore offering testing that is useful and appropriate across the board.

While this scientist acknowledged the key benefits of standardized self-identification in terms of the comparability of research findings "across the board," the interviewee clearly perceived a tension between permitting people to freely self-identify (i.e., in any way they might choose) and the need to generate standardized data that could be generalized beyond the confines of a given study's sample population. As such, the ONS classificatory scheme was felt to offer a set of standardized categories that permitted the production of generalizable knowledge.

This rationale was further emphasized by a lead researcher on a large longitudinal study, which had previously classified its population cohort using researcher-assigned categories when it first began in the 1980s. The lead researcher discussed how the study had subsequently adopted the self-identification practices developed by the ONS to conform to perceived standards—what the researcher described as "the U.K. population reference method." However, the researcher also felt that this change in classificatory practice had scientific merit because the researcher considered that individual participants were a more reliable source of knowledge about their own ethnicity than researchers (who might otherwise identify and categorize people on the basis of potentially misleading criteria such as place of birth or appearance). Nevertheless, the use of classifications derived from the arena of public policy in biomedical science raised questions for this researcher about the validity of racial and ethnic categories from both a sociopolitical and scientific perspective:

How does one, how does one define the validity of an ethnicity classification? Well I mean there are formal definitions of validity, one is theoretical coherence, another one would be the word that you used which was reliability or reproducibility. But then I guess if you went outside the realms of the technical definition of validity then you know issues of eugenics or political classifications raise their head. And that's the thing . . . about the Pacific Islander classification in the States. . . . There was a political economic reason for creating a category of Pacific Islanders because it meant that resource would be available to that group . . . if it became officially accepted as a distinct category, distinct ethnic or race category. So I think validity is a very thorny subject in this context.

In short, the researcher recognized that racial and ethnic categories are the product of social, political, historical, *and* scientific discourses, and that the concept of what might constitute a valid classification (and, by implication, a valid classificatory scheme) would vary according to the context in which the classification was used. In particular, the researcher notes that political negotiations might generate new categories (such as Pacific Islander) in the context of social statistics, which has potential implications for the way in which scientists design and conduct studies to address related policy objectives or capitalize on the availability of new categories.

Elsewhere, there was substantive ambivalence concerning the nature of the racial and ethnic categories used in biomedical research. This was evident in an interview with another researcher, who talked about what the researcher perceived to be a gap between policy and practice regarding the use of self-identification in the researcher's study. This researcher worked at a biobank that aimed to study the development and incidence of disease in two ethnic populations it called "Asians" and "whites." This study had adopted the ONS classificatory scheme as part of its formal research protocol, but when commenting on what had actually happened in practice, this researcher described how the research nurses employed to recruit healthy volunteers into the study approached the task of classification in a very different way:

I know what they should do, which is they should give them a list of the [ONS] census definitions. I don't think they do; I think they ask them where they're from, I think they ask them their religion, I think they ask them where their grandparents are from and they classify them according to that. And actually it's more useful, in some ways I think what the nurses are doing; they're assigning in a way that we all understand and whilst I'm entirely sympathetic, I mean you know I could be in a bad mood and say I'm black, you know, West Indian and you'd have to accept that and that would be a nonsense, that's more, that's going to more, make my study much more problematic. So I don't think they're doing it along traditional or PC [politically correct] lines for the classification of ethnicity.

This account indicated that while a standardized approach to self-identified race and/ or ethnicity might be part of the formal procedure for this and other projects, in practice, those charged with conducting recruitment might adopt a range of different approaches such as asking volunteers about their religion or grandparental ancestry. Although this is essentially a departure from the stated protocol of the study, the scientist seemed content that the nurses were adopting a commonsense approach using criteria that "we all understand" and, as such, were able to address some of the potential pitfalls of self-identification (such as deliberate misidentification by grumpy volunteers). As such, they felt that these kinds of questions might actually elicit more useful information for the study. Nonetheless, they accepted that self-identification was the "politically correct" approach to the classification of ethnicity and, as such, implied that this was the approach that needed to be formally adopted when conducting ethnic classification.

Concerns about the scientific validity of self-identified ethnicity were underlined by one of the pharmacogeneticists we interviewed, who questioned whether the way people self-identified always matched what scientists thought they would find at the genetic level. In this context, ethnicity was interpreted as a proxy for ancestry and related to a widespread belief among the geneticists we interviewed that ethnic ancestry, even at the level of parental and grandparental geographical origins, captured a significant component of clinically relevant genetic variation:

So I suppose self-reporting of your ethnicity is presumably slightly inaccurate, maybe . . . , you know, at grand paternal level . . . but self-reported ethnicity is slightly inaccurate probably in large conurbations.

This brief quote encompasses two distinct points concerning the perceived limitations of self-identified ethnicity for genetic research. The first of these relates to the recognition that self-identified ethnicity might not accurately reflect the biogeographical origins or ancestry of individuals, where their knowledge of family history, beyond perhaps their parents or grandparents, is limited or incomplete. The second point concerns the impact of admixture within "large conurbations" on knowledge about, or clarity of, ancestry. This interviewee went on to illustrate these concerns by describing a previous study that had sought to exclude "non-Caucasians" in the belief that genetic variation between ethnic groups might complicate the interpretation of any gene-disease associations identified among ethnically diverse study populations as a result of gene-gene interactions at ethnic-specific polymorphic loci. Despite this study's focus on the recruitment of "Caucasians," the use of self-identification to select volunteers into the study failed to achieve the study's aims:

Interestingly enough we did a project where we wanted to just to have Caucasian, only South Londoners, just for ease of the genetic analysis, and found through stratification analysis that they weren't ethnically homogenous. So presumably, you know, the population of South Londoners has some mixed ethnicity, even though in the tick box way they are white Caucasians, but they obviously have some other influences coming into their ethnicity.

In this account, the scientist juxtaposed what he called the "tick box" approach to the self-identification of ethnicity (i.e., a system similar to that developed by the ONS classificatory scheme) with evidence from subsequent genetic analyses, which found higher than expected levels of genetic variation. In this instance, the researcher interpreted these findings as evidence of mixed ethnicity and thereby an example of the inherent limitations of self-identification for generating ethnically (and thereby genetically) homogeneous study populations. Similar genetic analyses had been used by a number of the other interviewees in their studies. These analyses helped to ascertain "whether their [the study participants'] report on ethnicity is similar to their genetic ethnicity" and indicate that geneticists view the "genetic identity" of groups and individuals as something that can be somewhat different to self-identified ethnicity. Ostensibly, the notion of genetic ethnicity conflicts with definitions of ethnicity that emphasize sociocultural practice, although it should be noted that shared ancestry and genealogy are prominent in sociological discussions of the concept (Fenton 2003). However, it seems clear that genetic ethnicity is not invoked by geneticists as a conceptual challenge to ethnicity as a sociocultural and political concept per se, but rather as a semantic sleight of hand, which reflects a shared belief among geneticists that some genetic polymorphisms are more commonly found in populations identified as ethnic groups in sociopolitical discourse.

Along similar lines to the approach adopted by the interviewee who described the study of Caucasian South Londoners, many of the pharmacogenetics studies sought to focus exclusively on participants described, variously, as white British, European, or Caucasian. These studies prioritized measures of ancestry over self-identification on the basis that ancestry provided a better marker of genetic heritage. To this end, researchers in these studies described how they would ask potential participants about their family histories when deciding whether to include or exclude them during the recruitment process. However, in practice, the use of these sorts of questions would only come into play if the physical appearance of volunteers led the researchers to conclude that, in terms of what one described as their "basic genetics," they were not of white British, European, or Caucasian descent.

One particular study went further by rejecting the use of ethnicity as a consideration when recruiting participants. This project was engaged in building a case-control panel of genetic samples to assist in the identification of genetic variants associated with common complex diseases. The lead researcher involved explained that they had decided to exclude ethnicity as a marker for genetic ancestry because they felt that people generally have little knowledge of their own ethnic origins:

If you . . . take people in this country, they have no idea what their ethnic origin is, I mean the people in Orkney think they're all Vikings. . . . There's no useful information that really is other than geographic and it's the geographic information that actually to a large extent does define the population. So, roughly speaking, you know . . . the Celtic precursors of people, who now would be considered the Celtic fringe, were the population of Britain before the agricultural revolution came, which was about five or six thousand years ago, and gradually invaders and others pushed them to the fringe and you get other communities, you've got invading communities around the coast. And those are largely geographic phenomena, so I think that's the only objective way to go about defining what the population of this country is.

Rather than relying on self-identification, which the researcher felt had little value as a marker of the genetic makeup of Britain's different populations, the study sought information on people's family history and, in particular, selected volunteers with four grandparents who had originated from a specific locality. Armed with this information, the study categorized samples on the basis of geographical location, using this as an alternative proxy for genetic ancestry.

However, this study was exceptional, and most of the scientists we interviewed described how their studies had practiced self-identification using the ONS classificatory scheme (or very similar classifications) for two principal reasons: it offered a standardized approach to the practice of ethnic classification that was socially and politically acceptable, and it could facilitate the comparability and generalizability of findings across different studies. For some, relying on self-identification using sociopolitical categories developed for implementing and monitoring social policy was potentially problematic within the context of science because the categories *available* could change in response to political imperatives, and the categories *chosen* were subject to the whims of potential participants. There was also a tension between the potential benefits of allowing people to freely self-identify and the need to generate reproducible scientific variables using predetermined categories (whether standardized or not). This was most apparent when concerns were expressed about whether self-identified ethnicity was an accurate measure of underlying ancestry-related genetic variation.

For most genetic analyses, the primary interest in ethnicity is as a proxy for ancestry and its presumed association with geographical or sociocultural patterns of genetic variation. Indeed, despite the fact that all the studies examined in our analyses shared an explicit interest in genetic *and* environmental contributions to disease and/or pharmacological efficacy, none of the researchers we interviewed emphasized the potential insights into environmental contributions that might be provided by data on self-identified race or ethnicity (and its related sociocultural and socioeconomic correlates). Instead, the studies we examined sought to ask volunteers questions about ethnicity, family background, place of birth, and so on, as an indication of their ancestry, or adopted post hoc genetic analyses to check whether these criteria had correctly identified populations believed to be genetically distinct and homogeneous. Indeed, given their concerns about the genetic validity of self-identified ethnicity (and related markers of ancestry), it is surprising that only one of the studies we examined had abandoned the use of self-identified ethnicity, although more had attempted to improve the utility of self-identification using specific questions about familial geographical origins and related criteria.

From Self-Assigned to Genotype Assigned?

Some of the scientists we talked to—especially in the pharmacogenetics field—anticipated that emergent technologies would transform practices of racial and ethnic classification (Tutton et al. 2008). Some enthusiastically imagined a future in which self-identification would ultimately be supplanted by the widespread use of genotyping samples. As one key scientist with a national biobank suggested,

Ultimately the reason for being concerned about ethnicity from the science perspective is because we think that the gene sets are going to be different and therefore if you can actually get the information at the genetic level, which we theoretically can ultimately, then that's obviously going to be more accurate and more useful for what we actually want to do. Now that wouldn't be true for example if you're doing an anthropological study then self-assignment is more important that genetic ethnicity but from the point of view of a genetic study then the genetic assignment would be better. But it is dependent on being able to do lots and lots of genotyping, which currently is still too expensive but will subsequently not be, and also that there will be available marker sets that we know define the different ethnicities, so there are things for the future.

This account explicitly articulates the principal rationale of geneticists for studying different racial and ethnic groups: the notion that these groups are genetically different. From this perspective, self-identified ethnicity offers a useful proxy for certain patterns of genetic variation and will, in the future, be superseded by more accurate categories derived from genomic data. However, if this respondent's vision of the future is to be realized, it is contingent on substantial investment to produce the genetic data required to determine and define the genetics of different racial and ethnic groups (including new groupings defined from genetic data, rather than sociopolitical categories). It is also dependent on the costs of genotyping falling so that the techniques involved become more widely available to researchers. This optimistic scenario was underscored by other interviewees. One, in particular, imagined a future in which not only would ethnic self-identification be superseded by genetic data, but the utility of ethnicity itself would be rendered irrelevant within biomedical research and practice by the advent of individualized medicine based on molecular characteristics:

I think ethnicity will eventually pale into insignificance because you'll know what the allelic variation there is across the whole population and you'll just test for a particular allele. It doesn't matter what the ethnic background is, which will tell you what the genotype or sensitivity or whatever of that person is to that drug.

In this scenario, ethnicity, as a biomedical variable, will be superseded by genetic information about allelic variations that will instead place people into somewhat different categories such as fast or slow metabolizers of certain classes of drugs (see Wilson et al. 2001). This interviewee did acknowledge that to achieve this future vision, scientists and science funders would need to invest heavily in what would be a complex and expensive process.

However, one of the scientists we interviewed did strike a more ambivalent tone:

I think when certain people go through, as people increasingly are doing, you know, their genealogies and finding out about their family trees, finding that they have origins that are different from their expectations is really quite profound for some people. And I think that genetic tests in that way could also have a similar sort of influence and might throw up things that might not necessarily be helpful. That needs to be counterbalanced, I think, by whether . . . getting that information would be truly of benefit as opposed to the self-reporting, whether you know that molecular level of classification of people's ethnicity, if there was some real benefit to that compared to self-reporting then it might be worth considering. But I can't really envisage that at the moment. I can see that technically it could happen but I can't, you know on the spot, think of an immediate application where I think that that would be particularly of benefit, you know, in a clinical setting or a day-to-day setting.

He conceded the technical possibility, but was less certain as to what benefits would arise from genotyping compared with the current use of self-identification. He also raised what might be seen as an ethical question regarding how the disclosure of findings of genomic analyses might conflict with people's own self-identifications. However, his was the lone dissenting voice in this (somewhat modest) sample of scientists interviewed.

In summary, given the doubts about the match between self-identified ethnicity and the underlying genetic variation that might be associated with ethnic origins, some of the scientists we interviewed saw the prospects of large-scale genotyping as offering the opportunity for ethnic group categories to become refashioned as genomic categories or superseded altogether in a new regime of individualized medicine.

Conclusions

In conclusion to this chapter, we reflect on the following question: what is the importance of self-identified race and ethnicity in social and political life, and to what extent do the perspectives and practices evident from our research threaten their continued use in the context of biomedicine? Earlier we argued that self-identification has emerged as a vital governmental practice in many contemporary societies in relation to how states and other agencies collect information about racial and ethnic groups. As Hacking (1981) has argued, social statistics largely defined biopolitics from the nineteenth century onward: as a technology of power, social statistics was the primary means by which the state intervened in the social body of the population. Alongside statistics related to morbidity, mortality, living conditions, and economic productivity, contemporary biopolitics also encompasses questions about who people think they are. As such, counting identities has become a notable feature of contemporary social statistics.

Crucially, self-identification is seen to mark a key departure from previous practices of racializing people and groups—in this instance, practices conducted by politically and economically privileged elites who claimed special scientific knowledge to classify others primarily on the basis of physical and behavioral traits and/or biogeographical origins. Self-identification, by contrast, conveys with it the idea that race and ethnicity are not objective, biologically derived categories that can, or should, be conferred on others, but instead, are a matter of self-perception and self-assertion. However, as we have argued, self-identification does not necessarily succeed in distinguishing race from ethnicity, nor does it free either of these concepts from naturalistic or essentialistic approaches to the framing differences. In any case, self-identification is now an established and even a taken-for-granted aspect of what Epstein (2007) calls "biopolitical citizenship." In this, through a burgeoning array of bureaucratic interactions with employers, health care providers, welfare agencies, educators, and so on, individuals are expected to self-identify (albeit using preselected categories, in most instances). When becoming a subject of, or participant in, biomedical research, people also find themselves asked to self-identify by the scientific investigators involved both for scientific reasons and to conform to policy requirements established to ensure that greater numbers of individuals from racial and ethnic minorities are included in biomedical research. Such polices have not, however, gone uncontested. Population geneticists, among others, have argued about the extent to which social categories of race and ethnicity might act as good proxies for identifying significant patterns of genetic variation among populations.

The perspectives and practices uncovered by our research in the United Kingdom indicate that, for some researchers, asking study participants to self-identify their ethnicity is a pragmatic solution for a practical task. They have sought recourse to what might be thought of as two standards: the principle of self-identification and the way in which (in most of the studies) this was standardized in practice using the ONS census ethnic group classification. As we noted earlier, using this ONS classification, researchers are able to realize the benefits of standardization, including comparability, generalizability, applicability, and social acceptance (see Smart et al. 2008). This approach would seem to reinforce the value of standardized self-identification practices because it both meets the social expectation (i.e., what is considered acceptable) that individuals should be the ones to assign themselves to racial or ethnic categories and serves the interests of the scientists concerned by supporting their aim to produce generalizable results from their studies. However, the principal interest of most scientists in these fields of study lies in capturing information on genetic ancestry. The worry, therefore, is that they have effectively adopted self-identified ethnicity as a proxy for genetic ancestry—an approach that has a number of scientific (classificatory and genetic) and social consequences (Ellison and Jones 2002, Foster and Sharp 2002; and Juengst 1998).

As we have documented here, some scientists expressed a concern that there would be a gap between people's perceptions and their self-reporting of ethnicity based on a set of categories that reflect political and social imperatives, as opposed to scientific ones (and the underlying biological reality of people's genetic ancestry). Given this, researchers adopted various strategies to reveal this reality such as using alternative (or additional) questions, inventing study designs that were deliberately exclusive, creating alternative conceptions of population groups, and/or conducting post hoc genetic tests on participants selected for inclusion on the basis of self-identified ethnicity. Some imagine a future in which genotyping techniques would supersede reliance on practices of self-identification and would, in turn, either redefine or supersede prevailing categories of (predominantly self-identified) race and/or ethnicity as used in biomedical research and practice. Self-identification, therefore, is a practice of what anthropologist Mike Fortun (2007) calls the "meantime"—the "making do" with present contingencies and compromises while the future takes shape—a future in which it is expected (by some) that genotyping will eventually supersede the use of self-identification in the design of biomedical studies and in the analysis of their results (thereby leading to new sets of standards). This future vision would seem to challenge the current status of self-identification and herald a shift from self-assigned to a form of observer-assigned categorization shaped and mediated by genetic technologies and the data these generate.

But there are two quite different future visions articulated in the interviews: one being that existing group categories might be defined and understood genetically, the other that existing group categories will become irrelevant and thus replaced by new types of categories based on genotypic information. The question of whether, or which of, these imagined futures will materialize cannot be answered here, but it is evident from our interviews that such expectations are shaping current practices associated with the use of self-identification. Indeed, the former tends to lend support to the continued use of the self-identified census categories, while the latter suggests that these categories are only of value to biomedical research and practice in the interim— that is, until they are replaced by other, yet to be determined categories with provenance in science, rather than politics.

In either case, it is evident that for most of the scientists we interviewed, genotypic information has greater authority than self-identity in research that focuses on the genetic determinants of health, presumably because the former is seen to be based on scientific fact, rather than on subjective and contextually contingent social and political factors. Many of the scientists we interviewed felt that either the redefinition of existing categories using genotypic data or the emergence of new categories using these data would introduce greater certainty to scientific practices focused on the genetic characteristics of individuals and groups. At present, the potential impacts of introducing new genotypic categories and their possible resonance and uptake within society remain uncertain.

In the meantime, however, as our research demonstrates, the process of racial and ethnic categorization is co-constructed from practices and resources drawn from social statistics and from the statistical and genomic techniques that have been developed to control for the uncertainties associated with self-identification. This strikes a balance between realizing the benefits of standardization and conforming to social and political classificatory norms, while preserving scientific interest in genetic ancestry, as opposed to ethnic group identity. This is then bracketed by expectations surrounding the potential for large-scale genotyping to play a more significant role in future scientific practices and to have a transformative effect on classificatory practices and, indeed, on scientific understandings of the genetics of disease.

In conclusion, analysts like Epstein (2007) and Nelson (2008) encourage us to think in terms of categorical alignments between the social and the biological ordering of categories (and how these are made in the arenas of new biomedical and genomic knowledge by various actors). The alignment of governmental and biomedical categories is, as Epstein has demonstrated, a central part of the current configuration of biopolitical citizenship in the United States and elsewhere, with significant traction in government policy as well as support among many important political actors. However, perhaps the futures envisaged by some of the scientists we interviewed suggest that *dis*-alignment might also be possible. The potential for such a disalignment exists where new socially meaningful genotypic categories are created or where genotypic information dynamically intersects with existing socially meaningful categories in ways that reshape or reform them. Furthermore, disalignment may also exist in terms of the practices that underlie the categories—the potential shift from self-identification to genotype that we have reported here. As we have documented, the practices of self-identification carry a significant normative load, and self-identified race and ethnicity using the census categories will continue to have relevance for health research. Nevertheless, there is an evolving relationship between different methods of categorization in genetics research, which is indicative of how tensions between the science and politics of racial and ethnic classification continue to be negotiated.

Notes

1. This project was called "Race/Ethnicity and Genetics in Science and Health" and was funded by the Wellcome Trust Biomedical Ethics Programme, 2004–2007. The project team comprised Paul Martin (principal investigator, University of Nottingham), Richard Ashcroft (Queen Mary's London), George Ellison (London Metropolitan University), Andrew Smart (Bath Spa University), and Richard Tutton (Lancaster University).

2. Aspinall's (2001) sole focus on ethnicity reflects the U.K. context, where, in many aspects of official public discourse, the language of ethnicity is often favored over that of race. However, as ethnicity is usually conceptualized as primarily being about self-association with sociocultural groupings, observer assignment of this kind of self-identity would raise methodological criticisms.

3. The labels, nomenclature, and classification schemes from which people are asked to choose are variable (although they are also subject to standardization, particularly within nation-states), and there are a wide variety of criteria that can be used for classifying individuals into racial and/or ethnic groups on the basis of "what you look like; what you do; and where you come from." A nonexhaustive list might include an individual's physical traits (such as skin color, hair texture, or facial features); his or her nationality; his or her birthplace and that of the individual's parents and/or grandparents; the individual's cultural or religious affiliations, beliefs, and/or practices (including lifestyle and diet); his or her name or what language the individual speaks; the individual's experiences of racism, stigmatization, discrimination, or exclusion; and his or her experiences of migration.

4. Pfeffer (1998) claims that political mobilizations played an instrumental role in this shift to self-identification.

5. Ostensibly, the purpose of collecting these data is to monitor the number and sizes of different racial and/or ethnic groups in a national population and support legislation designed to outlaw discrimination and variation in the need for, access to, and uptake of public services.

6. I.e., "where an indicator 'makes sense' as a measure of a construct" (Neuman 2006, 192): self-identification of race and/or ethnicity measures self-identification to a sociopolitical construct and/or sociocultural grouping.

7. A House of Commons written response to a question about the National DNA Database included the information that "ethnic appearance is based on the judgement of the police officer taking the sample as to which of six broad ethnic appearance categories the person is considered to belong. 'Unknown' means that no ethnic appearance information was recorded by the officer

taking the sample" (Hansard 2008). It is also notable that the six "categories" (black; Middle Eastern; Asian; white southern European; white northern European; and Chinese, Japanese, or Southeast Asian) do not directly match the ones developed for the 2001 censuses. This observer assignment process is markedly different to the one described by Delsol and Shiner (2006) in their account of the police protocols that are intended to govern stop-and-search practices.

8. What people self-identify on a census form may not be what they really think, or indeed what they might think at different moments in time. Nor is this necessarily as complex or as free formed as what they might, under other circumstances, report.

9. Indeed, in popular and political discourse within the United Kingdom, the term *ethnicity* sometimes appears to function as surrogate versions of race (Mason 2000, 14, citing Saggar), perhaps because it is seen as "politically correct."

10. This is standardized in the sense that it not only specifies the classification system, associated categories, and nomenclature used, but also the practices by which classification is conducted (i.e., by self-identification to a fixed number of predetermined categories).

11. In some cases, the interviewee did not know the processes involved in classifying study participants in his or her research study.

References

Aspinall, P. 2001. Operationalising the collection of ethnicity data in studies of the sociology of health and illness. *Sociology of Health and Illness* 23:830–862.

Ballard, R. 1996. Negotiating race and ethnicity: Exploring the implications of the 1991 census. *Patterns of Prejudice* 30:3–33.

Bamshad, M., S. Wooding, B. A. Salisbury, and J. C. Stephens. 2004. Deconstructing the relationship between genetics and race. *Nature Reviews Genetics* 5:598–609.

Bell, J. 1998. The new genetics in clinical practice. *British Medical Journal* 316:618–620.

Bhopal, R., J. Rankin, and T. Bennett. 2000. Editorial role in promoting valid use of concepts and terminology in race and ethnicity research. *Science Editor* 23:75–80.

Bonham, V. L., E. Warshauer-Baker, and F. S. Collins. 2005. Race and ethnicity in the genome era: The complexity of the constructs. *American Psychologist* 60:9–15.

Booth, H. 1985. Which "ethnic question"? The development of questions identifying ethnic origin in official statistics. *Sociological Review* 33:254–275.

Bradby, H. 1996. Genetics and racism. In *The Troubled Helix: Social and Psychological Implications of the New Human Genetics*. ed. T. Marteau and M. Richards. Cambridge: Cambridge University Press, 295–316.

Bulmer, M. 1980. On the feasibility of identifying "race" and "ethnicity" in censuses and surveys. *New Community* 8:3–16.

Burchard, E., E. Ziv, N. Coyle, S. L. Gomez, H. Tang, A. Karter, J. Mountain, E. Perez-Stable, D. Sheppard, and N. Risch. 2003. The importance of race and ethnic background in biomedical research and clinical practice. *New England Journal of Medicine* 348:1170–1175.

Census, race, and science. 2000. Editorial. *Nature Genetics* 24:97–98.

Cornell, S., and D. Hartmann. 2007. *Ethnicity and race. Making identities in a changing world*. 2nd ed. London: Pine Forge.

Delsol, R., and M. Shiner. 2006. Regulating stop and search: A challenge for police and community relations in England and Wales. *Critical Criminology* 14:241–263.

Ellison, G. T. H., and I. R. Jones. 2002. Social identities and the "new genetics": Scientific and social consequences. *Critical Public Health* 12:265–282.

Epstein, S. 2007. *Inclusion: The politics of difference in medical research*. Chicago: Chicago University Press.

Fenton, S. 2003. *Ethnicity*. Cambridge: Polity.

Fortun, M. 2007. Race in the meantime: The "care of the data" for complex conditions. Paper presented at the Business of Race, Massachusetts Institute of Technology, Cambridge.

Foster, M. W., and R. R. Sharp. 2002. Race, ethnicity, and genomics: Social classifications as proxies of biological heterogeneity. *Genome Research* 12:844–850.

Friedman, D. J., B. B. Cohen, A. R. Averbach, and J. M. Norton. 2000. Race/ethnicity and OMB Directive 15: Implications for state public health practice. *American Journal of Public Health* 90:1714–1719.

Hacking, I. 1981. How should we do the history of statistics? *Ideology and Consciousness* 8:15–26.

Hansard, H. C. 2008. Cols 798–802W. http://www.publications.parliament.uk/pa/cm200708/cmhansrd/cm081110/text/81110w0007.htm.

Juengst, E. T. 1998. Group identity and human diversity: Keeping biology straight from culture. *American Journal of Human Genetics* 63:673–677.

Kaufman, J. S., and R. S. Cooper. 2001. Commentary: Considerations for use of racial/ethnic classification in etiologic research. *American Journal of Epidemiology* 154:291–298.

Kertzer, D. I., and D. Arel. 2001. Censuses, identity formation, and the struggle for political power. In *Politics of race, ethnicity and language in national censuses*, ed. D. Kertzer. Cambridge: Cambridge University Press, 1–42.

Khoury, Muin J., Wylie Burke, and Elizabeth J. Thomson, eds. 2000. *Genetics and public health in the 21st century*. Oxford: Oxford University Press.

Mason, D. 2000. *Race and ethnicity in modern Britain*. 2nd ed. Oxford: Oxford University Press.

Mehta, P. 2006. Promoting equality and diversity in UK biomedical and clinical research. *Nature Reviews Genetics* 7:668.

Morning, A. 2008. Ethnic classification in global perspective: A cross-national survey of the 2000 census round. *Population Research and Policy Review* 27:239–272.

Nazroo, J. Y. 1998. Genetic, cultural or socio-economic vulnerability? explaining ethnic inequalities in health. *Sociology of Health & Illness* 20:710–730.

Nelson, A. 2008. Bio Science: Genetic Genealogy Testing and the Pursuit of African Ancestry. *Social Studies of Science* 38:809–833.

Neuman, W. L. 2006. *Social research methods: Qualitative and quantitative approaches*. 6th ed. London: Pearson.

Pfeffer, N. 1998. Theories of race, ethnicity, and culture. *British Medical Journal* 317:1381–1384.

Risch, N., E. Burchard, E. Ziv, and H. Tang. 2002. Categorization of humans in biomedical research: Genes, race, and disease. *Genome Biology* 3:1–12.

Royal, C. D. M., and G. M. Dunston. 2004. Changing the paradigm from "race" to human genome variation. *Nature Genetics* 36(11 Suppl.):5–7.

Senior, P. A., and R. Bhopal. 1994. Ethnicity as a variable in epidemiological research. *British Medical Journal* 309:327–330.

Sillitoe, K., and P. H. White. 1992. Ethnic group and the British census: The search for a question. *Journal of the Royal Statistical Society, Series A* 155:141–163.

Skerry, P. 2007. *Counting on the census: Race, group identity, and the evasion of politics*. Washington, DC: Brookings Institution Press.

Smaje, C. 1996. The ethnic patterning of health: New directions for theory and research. *Sociology of Health & Illness* 18:139–171.

Smart, A., R. Tutton, P. Martin, G. T. H. Ellison, and R. Ashcroft. 2008. The standardization of race and ethnicity in biomedical science: Editorials and UK biobanks. *Social Studies of Science* 38:407–423.

Tutton, R. 2008. Biobanks and the biopolitics of inclusion and representation. In *Monitoring bodies: The new politics of biobanks*, ed. H. Gottweis and A. Petersen. London: Routledge, 159–176.

Tutton, R., A. Smart, P. Martin, R. Ashcroft, and G. T. H. Ellison. 2008. Genotyping the future: Scientists expectations of race/ethnicity and genetics after BiDil®. *Journal of Law, Medicine, and Ethics* 36:464–470.

Urla, J. 1993. Cultural politics in an age of statistics: Numbers, nations, and the making of Basque identity. *American Ethnologist* 20:818–843.

Wilson, J. F., M. E. Weale, A. C. Smith, F. Gratrix, B. Fletcher, M. G. Thomas, N. Bradman, and D. B. Goldstein. 2001. Population genetic structure of variable drug response. *Nature Genetics* 29:265–269.

Yanow, D. 2003. *Constructing "race" and "ethnicity" in America: Category-making in public policy and administration.* Armonk, NY: M. E. Sharpe.

7   The Genomics of Difference and the Politics of Race in Canada

Amy Hinterberger

Developments in understanding and analyzing human genomic variation with regard to health and disease have reignited concerns, especially in the United States, about the rebiologization of race. As noted by Joan Fujimura et al. (2008, 644), "in the context of American race politics, folk-understandings of race, and the history of racist scientific investigations in the United States, it is not surprising that members of the media and other public groups have read the genetics of difference as the genetics of race." Yet what has been less discussed is whether the "genetics of difference," spawned from research on human genomic variation, have been read as the "genetics of race" in other contexts. In an article exploring the relationships between race, genomics, and identity in contemporary Brazil, Ricardo Ventura Santos (2004, 364) points out that although human genomic variation projects may be similar insofar as they address genomic difference, there may be significant distinctions between these projects from "the point of view of geography, the populations involved, the ethical clashes, the scope of the explanations (local, national and international) or reception by society." This chapter, then, seeks to push this point in relation to exploring how the categories of race, ethnicity, and population feature and are used in Canadian research projects addressing human genomic variation.

When considering the impacts and developments of human genomic variation studies outside of the United States, one needs to be attentive to any unmediated exportation of U.S. racial politics and technologies, which can sometimes pose categories and experiences as universal, rather than as part of specific historical or contextual developments. In other words, I am wary of the explanation or assumption that race is *the* primary category of concern in biomedical genomics research. The chapter thus seeks to make two interrelated points. First, sustained attention needs to be given toward how different nations draw on and reject, often simultaneously, aspects of their colonial histories in forming a contemporary approach to health and difference in the life sciences. While the race and genomics debate in the United States does indeed reflect where the majority of research on human genomic variation in relation to health and disease is occurring, it should not necessarily be cast as the dominant frame for understanding and evaluating human genomic diversity. Second, in drawing distinctions between the United States and Canada, the contrast I want to draw out is not one of biracial versus multicultural/ethnic pluralism; rather, I aim to demonstrate that both countries manage heterogeneity through selective discourses of mixing and homogeneity.

The overall goal of the essay is to bring sustained attention toward how different nations contend with the legacy and continuing aspects of their colonial histories as a condition of their transition to postcolonial or multicultural societies, in which governing is increasingly becoming linked to the life sciences. Specifically, the chapter traces how racialized histories have come to shape the politics of inclusion in contemporary population genomics projects in Canada. The main focus is on two areas of genomics practice: a Genome Canada–funded biobank announced in 2007, and a proposal for the inclusion of aboriginal communities as part of Canada's national genomics research strategy. Both examples emphasize how representations and narratives of founding populations, nation building, and genetic difference are explicitly rooted in the colonial histories of Canada. The outcome of Canada's national genomics strategy, as reflected in the establishment of Genome Canada and other related institutions, may have considerable impacts on population-specific health interventions in the realms of public policy, health care, and biomedical regulation. The chapter draws on interviews with Canadian scientists, bioethicists, and project managers, along with the analysis of recruitment documents and communication strategies. The two examples discussed in this chapter are part of a larger research project that explores the current manifestations of Canada's multiculturalism in light of the molecularization of biology.[1]

Placing Canada in a Postsequence World

With the mapping of the human genome, we have been given quite literally, the language of life itself. . . . In terms of genomics-based medicine, knowing who we are will cure us.
—Genome Canada (2008)

In 2000, the Canadian government launched a concerted funding effort to establish Genome Canada. Dedicated to developing and implementing a national strategy in genomics research "for the benefit of all Canadians," Genome Canada invests and manages large-scale genomics research projects relating to agriculture, fisheries, forestry, the environment, human health, and new technology development (Genome Canada 2007–2008, 12). In its relatively short history, Genome Canada has funded a wide range of diverse genomics- and proteomics-related research. As explained in its annual reports, Genome Canada seeks both to respond to the national interests of Canadians (helping Canadians "reap the benefits of genomic research") and to strengthen its international collaborations with other genomics-based research bodies (Genome Canada 2007–2008, 10). Genome Canada is not part of the formal state structure; however, the bulk of its funding comes from governmental sources, and it delivers devolved governmental responsibilities relating to Canada's research and development industry. It relies on fixed-term research grants from the Canadian government, but like other research organizations created through similar structures, it is not directly accountable to ministers or parliament (e.g., Genome Canada cannot be queried through any freedom of information legislation, unlike other public bodies in Canada).[2] The founding of Genome Canada was part of a broader governmental objective often referred to as Canada's national innovation strategy, which also led to the creation of the Canadian Institutes for Health Research and the Canadian Foundation for Innovation, among other research foundations.

The following provides a brief sketch of Genome Canada's institutional structures to highlight how Genome Canada fits into Canada's overall *biostrategy* as it relates to genomics-based biomedicine. Specifically, Genome Canada–funded projects in human genomic variation and health are highlighted as they relate to pharmaceutical development, medical research, commercial investment, and national politics in Canada. The recent merging of genomic technologies and health care networks in Canada has contributed to establishing population genomics projects as part of an integrated aspect of health policies and approaches. The outcomes of these various projects may significantly impact particular population groups, for example, by establishing health interventions for certain ethnic, regional, or cultural groups in Canada.

The recent establishment of Genome Canada reflects the changing priorities of Canada's overall national science and technology strategy. Indeed, Canada has not always been at the forefront of genomics research. In 1998, the Canadian Biotechnology Advisory Committee[3] reported back to the Canadian government on its genomics research programs (Government Canada 1998, 8) stating that

the reduction in Canada's genome program has not only hollowed out the country's existing capacity, but has jeopardized the chances of Canada leading the next wave of postgenomic studies. Canadians have major international strengths in areas that give them the potential to become world leaders. Yet, owing to the lack of resources, Canada stands to lose out on the commercialization of agricultural, medical, silvicultural and aquacultural discoveries of the 21st century.

Canada missed out on the Human Genome Project because the Canadian government did not put forward the fifty million U.S. dollars required to participate (Campbell 2002, 59). Thus, in 2000, not wanting to lose out on the promises of a postsequence world, the Canadian government announced new funding and a new strategy for genomics research. As reported at the time, the plan was to create an organization "unique to Canada, dubbed Genome Canada that will enable Canadian researchers to sequence the DNA of plants, animals and humans without having to do it abroad"

(Brown 2000, 1478). Initially, this investment in genomics was presented as part of catching up to the international community (Racine 2006, 1279). Genome Canada, then, emerged from the "culmination of three years' work by Canadian players in the biomedical research funding, biotechnology, genetics and resource industries" (Brown 2000, 1478).

Genome Canada's 2007–2008 corporate plan describes Genome Canada as a "not for profit corporation." The report goes on to describe Genome Canada's "innovative business model" as one that "is built on the premise of funding and managing large-scale and multidisciplinary research projects and platforms. . . . [It] brings together industry, governments, universities, research hospitals and the public in support of large-scale projects of strategic importance" (Genome Canada 2007–2008, 3). The president and CEO of Genome Canada suggests that Genome Canada is actually set up like a private-sector company, with its own fourteen-member board of directors, stating that "the lead investor is Industry Canada" (Campbell 2002, 59). The goal of Industry Canada is to promote conditions for investment in Canada and to increase Canada's share of global trade (Industry Canada 2007). As of 2007, Genome Canada has received 840 million dollars from the federal government (through Industry Canada). When combined with other sources of funding (both provincial and private), the investments total 1.4 billion dollars for 115 large-scale research programs and platforms (Genome Canada 2007–2008, 3). It should be noted that while Genome Canada funds genomics research, it argues that it does not necessarily initiate, foster, or encourage research activity in any one area. In other words, "Genome Canada does not do research, but funds research as recommended through a very stringent international peer review process" (interview, program manager, Genome Canada). Genome Canada funds an extremely heterogeneous group of researchers and scientists, all of which require cofunding from other sources to receive Genome Canada support.[4]

One major area of Genome Canada funding is dedicated to human health research. As the quote that opens this section states, "we have been given the language of life itself," and "in terms of genomics based medicine knowing who we are will cure us." One of the significant aspects of this quote is the ambiguity surrounding whether there is just one us, or whether there are many. The increasing emphasis on human genomic variation as the key to unlocking the promises of genomics-based biomedicine suggests that there may, in fact, be many. Indeed, Genome Canada funds a variety of projects that are seeking to harness these promises of a genomics-based biomedicine. These span studies that target complex and common diseases (such as diabetes), the analysis of structural and functional human genome variation, pharmacogenomic studies, and programs looking at rare or single-gene disorders.

Genomics-based biomedicine has been heralded as potentially able to deliver solutions to complex and common disorders and diseases. Yet, as noted by many genomic researchers and commentators, the "language of life itself" has been notoriously difficult to decipher and apply clinically. Beneath the assertion that knowing who we are will cure us, then, lies a range of tensions, anxieties, and hopes that are characteristic of emergent technologies such as genomics (Fortun 2005). More specifically, though, the assertion of knowing who we are to cure us points toward the continuing unification of human genomic variation and health as a focus for pharmaceutical development, medical research, and commercial investment in Canada. The advancements and developments relating to understandings of human genomic diversity in the field of population genomics are singled out in the 2007–2008 Genome Canada report. The introductory message from Genome Canada's CEO (Genome Canada 2007–2008, 3) exclaims,

Science magazine called it the "breakthrough of the year" in December 2007: the discovery of just how varied the human genome truly is, from population to population and person to person. It was a long time in the making, as most genomics discoveries are. . . . Canadians should be proud of the contributions their scientists made to this discovery—scientists such as those involved in the Canadian component of the HapMap Project.

Contributing to its recently established genomics strategy, Canada also has a universal health care system, which facilitates patient definition and identification, along with the existence of already well-established medical genetics research communities. These two aspects aid in both provincial and federal health-related projects that require the collection of clinical cohorts and the biobanking of tissue samples and cell lines. Furthermore, Genome Canada's network of regional centers is building expertise and specialties in population genomics (with recent initiatives such as CARTaGENE and Public Population Project in Genomics, P3G). The merging of genomic technologies and health care networks in Canada to establish population genomics projects as part of an integrated aspect of the health care system will no doubt impact the future of medical treatment and health policy implementation. The outcome of Canada's national genomics strategy may therefore have significant impacts for particular population groups, including health interventions for certain ethnic and cultural groups at the levels of public policy, the health care industry, and biomedical regulation.

The Use of Race in Canada

Though Canada shares geographical, economic, and political proximities with the United States, it also has distinct institutional structures, political categorizations, and rhetoric that contribute to shaping discourses of the genetics of difference. This is not to argue that Canada is exempt from the histories, processes, and politics of racialization; rather, I would propose that being attentive to the genetics of difference requires attention to specific national genealogies of citizenship and their racialized histories. These, of course, do not start and stop with the borders of the nation-state, but they often have particular local significance within the legal, institutional, and economic structures within the nation.

The word *race*, for example, cannot be found on a Canadian census form. The institutionalization of categories of difference in Canada, then, has been different from that of the United States. Census categories are important in the study of population genomics projects as these categories are often imported, or versions of them may be used in clinical recruitments (Epstein 2007), biobanking (Tutton 2007a; Smart et al. 2008), and other human genomic variation projects; however, as opposed to the only two ethnicities that the U.S. census records (Hispanic/not Hispanic), Canada recorded more than two hundred different ethnicities in its 2006 census (in contrast to the twenty-five different ethnic groups that were recorded in the 1901 census; Statistics Canada 2008a). This is not just an issue of semantics. What and who gets recorded in the Canadian census is the outcome of multiple political processes that are simultaneously a reflection of reprehensible racial histories but also a reflection of the demands of identity-based groups and the politics of recognition and inclusion.

Some interviewees, bioethicists particularly, argued that they did not see race as a problem in Canada, but that issues of cultural and ethnic pluralism were more significant. As one of my interviewees explained when we were discussing potential problems about the reinscription of racial categories in human health genomics,

I don't think race has become a big issue. Well, in Canada we don't use the word *race*, we would talk about ethnic communities. (interview, Canadian bioethicist 1)

Another interviewee thought that, as a result of its cultural pluralism, Canada may have an easier time integrating racial or ethnic categories into health-related genomics:

It's a very touchy subject, though it's a less touchy debate here than in the U.S. We have more of a pluralistic set of cultures and are not so dichotomous as the U.S. I think it will become easier as we move into more integrated health projects, which we really haven't had any of yet. (interview, Canadian bioethicist 2)

Canada is engaged in large-scale population genomics research projects, which rarely use the word *race*; rather, terms such as *ethnic communities, isolated populations, human diversity, cultural mosaic,* and *founder populations* are increasingly being relied on and expressed in discussions of human genomic difference. Debates about the use of *race* in genomics need to address, then, not only how the word *race* translates across national boundaries, intertwining itself with national histories, but also the ways in which ideas of difference and inclusion are rendered in Canadian discourses of multiculturalism. This point is also made by Steven Epstein (2007) in his consideration of how U.S.-style categories and policies of inclusion in biomedicine may be exported to other nations through transnational circuits, particularly Canada. To explore the competing interests at stake in the debates on race and genomics, attention needs to be given to how racial differences are being recodified through the molecular gaze of genomics, and also how ideas of racial difference have been supplanted and reworked in different national contexts.

Teasing out the intersections between Canada's genomics research strategy and categories of race, ethnicity, and population requires looking specifically at the nation-state and how national political struggles shape both biomedical and social policies in Canada. In this regard, contemporary national imaginaries in Canada may be seen to be characterized by a confrontation with American nationhood, the ambiguities of recognizing the distinctiveness of Quebec, and an emphasis on multiculturalism as an official policy since the early 1970s (Winter 2007). Awareness should also be paid to the contemporary politics of difference in Canada, which separate visible minorities, or ethnic communities, and aboriginal peoples.[5] Statistics Canada (2008b, 2), which conducts the Canadian census, defines the concept of visible minority as applying

to persons who are identified according to the *Employment Equity Act* as being non-Caucasian in race or non-white in colour. Under the Act, Aboriginal persons are not considered to be members of visible minority groups.[6]

Aboriginal politics occupy a distinct area of difference politics in Canada that emphasizes aspects of sovereignty, nationhood, and territory not found in political discourses of visible minorities. Created in 1995, the term *visible minority* has been called a Canadian invention, though it is infrequently applied in the United Kingdom (Kinsella 2007). The term is used in the Canadian census and as a marker to trace, for example, marginalized populations' access to health care. In this instance, the creation of this national classification (visible minority) was sought to function as a strategy of inclusion and equality. This cursory review of categories of difference outlined here cannot engage with the more substantive aspects they bring up (e.g., what the status of visible minority is in population genomics projects), and I review them here to highlight differences between Canada and other nations as well as the intricacies of racialized classification within Canada.

Attention to how categories of difference become institutionalized and their histories are significant for considering the transnational aspects of population genomics and how the findings of these projects may be applied to particular populations within different nations. Many nations, such as India, Mexico, and South Africa, along with Canada, are developing their own genomic variation initiatives to explore the relationship between population variance and disease predisposition, diagnosis, and drug response (Segiun et al. 2008). Similar to Canada's own national genomics strategy, these projects seek to harness genomics for the benefit of their populations, with the hope of developing diagnostics and therapeutics to address health and disease. Yet an integral part of these projects requires the mapping and recording of a nation's own local populations, bringing into question just what "local" means in human health genomics research—as it is hoped that both genomic diversity and homogeneity will provide some answers and clues to delivering the promises of genomics-based bio-medicine. Within national contexts, then, genomic approaches to race, ethnicity, and populations are increasingly informing and traversing social and political approaches to these categories. In light of these transnational circuits and the global aspects of major population genomic research projects, the task should not just be to consider how race may be used in these projects, but to connect these disparate biosocialtities (Rabinow 1996; Gibbon and Novas 2008), rooted in diverse histories, which employ multiple understandings of race, ethnicity, and populations.

Genetic Portraits

With increasing frequency, national imaginaries are harnessed as part of preparation for the era of genomics-based medicine (Pálsson and Rabinow 1999; Sunder Rajan 2006). Genome Canada recently announced its support of one of Canada's first major biobanks, CARTaGENE. Financed mainly by Genome Canada and Genome Quebec, CARTaGENE aims to produce a genetic portrait of the Quebec population (Langlois 2007). Described as a "large-scale, public resource genetic database conceived to improve our understandings of the role played by genetic health issues," the CARTa-GENE project collects sociodemographic and health assessment data, biological mate-rial, and DNA samples from citizens of Quebec, aged forty to sixty-nine, through a random sampling from four metropolitan census areas (Godard et al. 2007, 147). Like other current biobanks (such as the UK Biobank), emphasis is put on understanding the influence of genetic heritage as well as gene-environment interactions and the study of common complex diseases such as cancer and diabetes. In March 2008, CARTaGENE completed its first small-scale recruitment of 223 participants and is now embarking on the first major recruitment phase of the project (twenty thousand participants).[7]

The following discussion examines the politics of inclusion relating to the recruit-ment campaigns and communication strategies of the biobank. As CARTaGENE is a publicly funded project, there has been a significant amount of research addressing ethical aspects of the biobank on issues of public trust, consent, governance, and transparency (Godard et al. 2007; Wallace et al. 2008). My approach differs in that my interest is to attend to the wider political and historical contexts to explore how categories of race, ethnicity, and populations are mobilized by the project. This includes looking at wider racial and ethnic discourses in Quebec and how genomic diversity becomes mobilized on the grounds of health and deferred at the threat of perceived stigmatization.

CARTaGENE has been described as a mapping exercise integral to the health of the nation (Government Canada 2004, 4):

CARTaGENE is cartography of genetic diversity in the Quebec population. The project will map genetic variation in a large reference population of Quebec. This information will allow large-scale medical, pharmacogenomic and public health studies, including association studies of common diseases or "protective" phenotypes, and lead to the discovery of new susceptibility genes.

Media coverage of the CARTaGENE project has highlighted genomic diversity and the value of diverse populations as an important aspect of the biobank. One article (Cardwell 2003, 45) suggested, "Given the diversity of Quebec's population (there are about two dozen ethnic groups in Montreal alone), they say it could also be used to pinpoint the genetic origins of complex illnesses such as heart disease and mental health." However, in regard to concerns about perceived stigmatization on the basis of race, the organizers of CARTaGENE (Lévesque 2007b, 3–4) argue that the population database is not about race, or any form of difference, for that matter; rather, it is about health:

CARTaGENE will *not* be used for anthropological, ethno biological or other types of research dealing with ideologies and race. CARTaGENE is first, foremost and exclusively dedicated to health research. However CARTaGENE avoids the use of the negative form whenever possible in order to avoid the arousing of certain sensitive subjects.

Lévesque adds in a footnote, "This is also why CARTaGENE does not openly mention risks of stigmatization." Here genomic diversity becomes mobilized on the grounds of health and deferred at the threat of perceived stigmatization. The disclaimer itself (that the project will not deal with race) suggests that race is important insofar as it is kept separate from the project so as not to arouse "certain sensitive subjects" (though these are not explicitly articulated). Similar disclaimers have been made by previous population genomics projects such as the Human Genome Diversity Project and the International Haplotype Map (HapMap) Project (M'charek 2005; Reardon 2005, 2007).

The recruitment and communication strategy documents for CARTaGENE, from which the preceding quote is taken, offer insight into how institutions are reflexively engaging with the competing discourses of difference that population genomics projects elicit. For example, the first goal in the brainstorming session for the biobank's public theme was to put it in harmony with its recruitment campaign objective and offer the public "something catchy" (Lévesque 2007a, 1). This catchy teaser for the public is "CARTaGENE—The world within *you*" (Lévesque 2007a, 1). Drawing very much on a discourse of overcoming distance and difference, a report on developing a public theme for CARTaGENE explains the rationale for the slogan "the world within *you*" in four points:

1. Everyone has within oneself a part that is common to the rest of humanity: the genome. It is a complex part that is still to be discovered;
2. The theme opens up to the future and to others. It is directed toward what we have in common, not toward our differences. It is gathering and it awakens curiosity as well;

3. The theme reminds us that everyone can significantly contribute to a project like CARTaGENE;

4. Finally, "the world" reminds scientists of the "-omics" sciences, a Greek root they use to signify *totality*.

(Lévesque 2007a, 2)

There is particular emphasis here on how distances are transcended through the global genome (it is the *world* within *you*). Placed within the wider historical and political contexts of genetic research in Quebec, this emphasis on the "world within you" is significant. As was relayed to me by an interviewee, one of the things that makes Quebec unique is that it is possible to trace the founding populations of Quebec to the last detail (as opposed to creating a genetic map of Saskatchewan or British Columbia; interview, Canadian population geneticist 1). The descendants of about eighty-five hundred French settlers who arrived in Canada between 1608 and 1759 are said to have remained isolated and "reproduced wildly," which created a "genetic bottleneck" ideal for genomic research (Secko 2008). The migrations of these settlers and their descendents have led to a series of regional founder effects reflected in the geographical distribution of genetic diseases. In this explanation, the very fact that descendents of the Quebec founder population do *not* have the world within them makes them a desirable group with which to conduct genetic and genomic studies. However, the story of the French founder population is itself a very specific colonial story that effectively silences the complex set of both intimate and political relationships between the original inhabitants of Canada and colonial settlers. Nina Kohli-Laven's (2007–2008, 6) work in this area demonstrates that as a result, some Canadian researchers "have effectively overlooked the presence of non-Europeans in North American population histories, impacting the basic assumptions of subsequent genetic epidemiological studies."

Despite this, the homogenous genomes of the Quebec founder populations feature heavily within the wider population genomics-based research being carried out in Quebec. In 2007, a genomewide association study (GWAS), conducted by a private company that has been referred to as the "deCODE of Quebec" (Davies 2008), identified multiple genes underlying Crohn's disease in the Quebec founder populations (Raelson et al. 2007). GWAS are seen to offer a powerful method for identifying disease susceptibility for common diseases such as cancer and diabetes and are at the cutting edge of genomics-based biomedicine.[8] However, the value of the genetic homogeneity offered by French founder populations in Quebec for GWAS and the future commercial development of diagnostics and therapeutics is seen to be under threat. GWAS researchers in Quebec have suggested that the genetic uniqueness of these groups may "be lost in the next few generations" because "Quebec is becoming highly multiethnic, and intermarriage between different groups is becoming more and more common" (Secko 2008, 38). Citing Canadian census data, the same article goes on to explain that it is becoming difficult to find recruits for GWAS because "interracial marriages have increased more than 30% from 2001 to 2006" and "visible minorities (many of whom are new immigrants) also rose more than 30% during the same period" (Secko 2008, 38).

The political discourses of multiculturalism in a molecular era are drawn into sharp relief when the CARTaGENE project is located within broader debates about difference in Canada. The changing demographics of Quebec as an increasingly multicultural society have also been recognized by the CARTaGENE project. For example, the findings from its first community engagement projects to gauge public perception and response to the biobank contain a section dedicated to "The Impact of Cultural, Ethnic and Linguistic Groups on Receptivity to the CARTaGENE Project," which included "Arabic, English, French, Greek, Hispanic, Italian, Jewish" groups (Godard et al. 2007, 150). Yet there was little discussion of why consulting different cultural, linguistic and ethnic groups may matter, not only in terms of how they can contribute to the practical success of the biobank, but also in terms of how their inclusion in the biobank may alter or change a genetic portrait of Quebec. Though consulting different cultural and ethnic groups about how they perceive the biobank may reflect the increasing use of institutionalized multiculturalism as a strategy of bioethical expertise in the life sciences, what is less clear is how these groups' genomic inclusion (through biological samples and DNA) might impact the formation of genomic portraits and the kinds of genomic studies that may be performed from the data collected by the project.

Cultural Mosaics

In 2006, Genome Canada invited genomics and proteomics researchers to nominate strategic research themes by first submitting expressions of interest (EOIs), which, if supported, would develop into position papers and research streams. The EOIs would be commented on by the larger Canadian genomics community through interactive Web postings and would be adjudicated on by a committee of international experts. One EOI submitted for the adjudication process explicitly addressed aspects of cultural and ethnic diversity. Titled "Promising Practices and Emerging Culturally Appropriate Frameworks: Aboriginal Perspectives, Voice and Presence in Genomics in Canada," this EOI (Genome Canada 2006) argued that genomics research within Canada needed to recognize and consider aboriginal peoples. It stated the following:

Aboriginal peoples in Canada are a diverse entity within the Canadian mosaic. . . . As a people they offer unique perspectives, knowledge, experiences, and developments that will potentially inform and challenge conventional approaches to genomics and proteomics. . . . Aboriginal people constitute a significant population group . . . with consumer, collaborator and contributor potentials that cannot be ignored.

This EOI was not successful in Genome Canada's competition scheme, yet it raises the issue of how aboriginal communities are included within increasingly institutionalized genomics-based biomedical research. The EOI describes aboriginal groups as a "diverse entity" with "consumer, collaborator and contributor potentials" in genomics. This points to a tension where, on one hand, there is a need for a multicultural science, here translated as "culturally appropriate frameworks," and on the other, the ethnically and culturally distinct biological body seen as a site for increasing genomic knowledge. With regard to contributing to genomics, the EOI highlights two distinct yet interrelated ideas of inclusion. Aboriginal communities may contribute to genomics-based biomedical research through different epistemologies of science and different articulations of relationships to nature, according to the EOI, through challenging "conventional approaches to genomics." Yet they may also contribute (and collaborate) with genomic research through the knowledge produced from the tissue and other biological samples from aboriginal communities and individuals, which have been used to do genealogical, genetic, and epidemiological research.

These distinctions come into sharper relief when we look at the only independent source of support posted for the EOI, written by a Canadian genetic scientist, who made the following comment (Genome Canada 2006, 1):

Our studies in aboriginal health indicate clear differences in the genetics of the immune system between aboriginal and Caucasian populations. Attempting to interpret how these genetic differences translate into differences in actual immune function that might impact disease outcomes has been more challenging. We have found limitations in interpreting genetic data from aboriginal subjects according to SNP outcomes originally defined in Caucasian populations. Completing functional readouts in future genetic studies on aboriginals or any other population should be an important aspect in extrapolating meaning from genetic data.

Here the support for the multicultural scientific approach proposed by the EOI is based on genetic differences. The imperative is not only to take into account the cultural diversity of aboriginal peoples in Canada, but also to seriously consider the limitations of interpreting genetic data, which was originally done in, what the genetic scientist calls Caucasian populations. This does not necessarily imply that there are hard and fast distinctions between the population groups, but rather, that research needs to be done to assess extrapolating genetic data from Caucasian populations onto aboriginal population groups. However, in Canada, there has not been the same interest expressed through dedicated genomics projects targeting indigenous populations as there has been in other countries. Other nations, for example, have made concerted funding efforts to map indigenous populations, such as in Mexico, where the Mexican HapMap, sponsored by the Mexican National Institute of Genomic Medicine, mapped genomic variation in admixed and indigenous groups not included in the International HapMap Project (Schwartz-Marín 2008). While there has been no nationalized effort to genomically map aboriginal populations in Canada, increasing attention is being paid toward the distinctiveness of aboriginal communities in Canada and their inclusion in genomics-based biomedicine.

In 2007, Canada's main funding agency for health research, the Canadian Institutes of Health Research (CIHR), adopted new guidelines for health studies involving aboriginal peoples to "conduct ethical and culturally competent research that balances the pursuit of scientific excellence with Aboriginal values and traditions" (see Canadian Institutes of Health Research 2007b). These guidelines are not legally binding, but researchers who receive funds from the CIHR are required to follow them. The CIHR guidelines were drafted largely in response to the collection of biological samples that were used for research not consented to by aboriginal donors and communities.[9] To redress these cases, the CIHR, over many years of consultation with aboriginal groups and researchers, established these new guidelines. Perhaps one of the most significant aspects of the guidelines regards the concept of "DNA on loan," which suggests that "biological samples should be considered 'on loan' to the researcher unless otherwise specified in the research agreement" (Canadian Institutes of Health Research 2007b, 25). The guidelines further explain that the concept of DNA on loan "reflects Aboriginal philosophies regarding 'full embodiment,' in which it is held that every part and product of the body is sacred, and constitutes an essential part of the person" (Canadian Institutes of Health Research 2007b, 25).

Increasingly, aboriginal communities in Canada are establishing their own community-based review committees to establish biomedical research guidelines that incorporate versions of aboriginal philosophies on embodiment (such as DNA on loan). Clinical geneticist Laura Arbour notes that examples of successful approaches to biomedical and genetic research do exist between aboriginal communities and researchers "but do not get the same degree of attention as when research goes wrong" (Arbour and Cook 2006, 5). One of my interviewees, who conducted genetics research on diabetes in Canadian aboriginal communities, emphasized the positive research relationship he experienced:

Fortunately, the communities and subpopulations with whom I have worked with over the years have been extremely pro-active—to the point of actually initiating the research and mobilizing the assistance of university and academic research teams. There has to be an obvious benefit for the communities. Our experience with aboriginal communities has been similar: we have relied on their self-definition as a distinct community or population. (interview, Canadian population geneticist 2)

This emphasis on self-definition and being pro-active resonates with contemporary theorizations of what has been called *genetic citizenship* (Heath et al. 2004), *biological citizenship* (Rose and Novas 2005), and *biopolitical citizenship* (Epstein 2007). Rose and Novas (2005, 3) emphasize how biological citizenship helps to think through "the increasing importance of corporeality to practices of identity." The recent proposals and guidelines for the inclusion of aboriginal groups and individuals in genomics-based biomedicine explored in this section suggest that versions of inclusion rely on various levels of corporeal understanding (i.e., the body as sacred, the body as a source of genomic difference that needs to be accounted for). The contested and complex histories between aboriginal communities and the Canadian state with regard to citizenship (which cannot be fully addressed in this chapter) demonstrate, however, that the connection between corporeality and practices of identity is not straightforward, as who gets to count as part of a population or distinct community is far from self-evident. Emphasizing this point requires a brief but important historical detour.

The predefinition of (bio)political groups is a key issue of the regulation and recognition of aboriginal or "Indian" identity in Canada. Through regulatory systems such as Canada's Indian Act, if one is a "registered Indian" or "status Indian," one is accorded very different rights and resources than those deemed "nonstatus Indians." Until 1983, under the Indian Act, if an Indian woman married a white man, she was dispossessed of her Indian status under the act (as were her children); however, if a white woman married an Indian man, she gained state-recognized Indian status and the rights and resources that went with that. Despite the fact that these divisions and regulations were imposed and created in an artificial manner, these markers of identity and citizenship have become very real in experiences of nativeness (Lawrence 2003). These local aspects of exclusionary citizenship, which characterize settler colonies, such as Canada, need to be brought to bear on population genomics-based biomedical research. This is because they may not only have impacts, at the level of recruitment, on clinical and genetic studies that require certain familial genealogies, but they may also impact who gets to count as part of the aboriginal community in Canada.

Considering how race comes to matter in the politics of inclusion in Canada's genomics strategy with regard to aboriginal communities is further complicated by a distinct separation from discourses of race within aboriginal politics. The following quote from one of the seven commissioners from Canada's Royal Commission on Aboriginal Peoples (Chartrand 2002) explains why it may be wholly inappropriate to employ discourses of race in aboriginal politics:

One device to dismember the communities and to hide the true basis for Aboriginal group rights, has been the discredited notion of "race" which aims to describe all Aboriginal people as a single homogenous mass of individuals rather than as communities united by historical relations to place.

In this regard, many aboriginal groups in Canada argue that they do not want to be raced, and furthermore, that race has nothing to do with aboriginal claims to self-government and self-determination, which are rooted in national sovereignty, aboriginal nationhood, and territory. These distinctions are significant, particularly for building any analysis of the politics of race, ethnicity, and populations in Canadian genomics-based biomedical research. They are also significant in thinking about how researchers themselves should approach the politics of inclusion and recognition in the life sciences. If certain marginalized groups explicitly reject the term *race* in representational strategies, these differences should not be glossed over as merely local practice, but rather, should be seriously considered as part of the increasing complexity of biomedicalized governance in population genomics projects. The interrelationships between marginalized communities, strategies of representation and citizenship and practices of corporeality in the life sciences will continue to intersect and grow. Thus, as Steven Epstein (2007) argues, we need to emphasize the varying degrees to which different people or groups are able to lay claim to the prerogatives of citizenship, and other forms of identity, as well as consider how biomedical authority and institutions reproduce or transform social categories and exclusions.

Conclusion

In Canadian human genomics–based biomedicine, the term *race* has been neither solely recast within neutral terms nor catapulted into debates about the reemergence of a racist science; rather, it is one of the many terms, with specific histories and experiences, that needs to be accounted for within the broader politics of difference that characterizes Canadian genomics-based biomedical research. At the same time, discourses of multicultural difference appear to be far from dead or failing and, if anything, are finding renewed vigor in the molecular intersections between health, difference, and disease. Categories of race, ethnicity, and populations continue, then, to be defined in multiple ways, often strategically, in genomics-based biomedical research. The broad overview teased out in this chapter points toward an increasing interplay between categories of difference and classification at all levels of population genomics, from the historical demographers who contribute to shaping epidemiological studies, to the branding of Canadian genomics internationally through Genome Canada.

The nation-state and other related or adjacent institutions study, mobilize, and act on populations, but population groups may potentially mobilize resources and claims to act on the nation-state in the life science sectors. The value, then, of populations in the commercial, ethical, and molecular sense is at stake in national strategies of genomic research, regardless of whether groups are perceived as diverse or homogenous. As many nations, similar to Canada, are developing their own genomic variation initiatives to explore the relationship between population, disease, and diagnosis, attention to how categories of difference become institutionalized and their histories will be significant for considering the transnational aspects of population genomics and human genomic variation initiatives. In light of the growing number of nationalized genomics strategies and the global aspects of major population genomic research projects, the task should be not only to consider how race may be used in these projects, but to connect seemingly disparate biosocialities rooted in diverse histories and employing multiple understandings of race, ethnicity, and populations.

Notes

1. Many thanks to David Jones and Ian Whitmarsh for organizing the conference *What's the Use of Race?* at The Center for the Study of Diversity at MIT for which a version of this paper was originally written. I also want to thank them as editors for including my research in this volume and providing detailed feedback on an earlier draft. I would like to thank, as well, the following people for their careful readings of earlier versions: Suki Ali, Nina Kohli-Laven, Carolyn Pedwell, Hillary Rose, Nikolas Rose, and Andrew Smart. Finally, my sincere thanks to the scientists, project managers and bioethicists whom I interviewed. This research was funded by the Social Sciences and Humanities Research Council of Canada, the Harshman Scholarship Foundation, and the University of London Central Research Fund.

2. In this regard, Genome Canada is linked to an increasing governmental trend of creating independent autonomous organizations established by legislation or as not-for-profit corporations under the Canada Corporations Act or similar legislation. For more on the specific institutional structures of Genome Canada, see KPMG (2007). Also, for a discussion of intellectual property issues emanating from Genome Canada–funded research, see Power et al. (2008). There is not sufficient space in this chapter to explore the significant institutional and legislative aspects of Genome Canada as it relates to the scientific research and development industry and culture in Canada. Note that one of Genome Canada's mandates includes "the assumption of leadership in the area of ethical, environmental, economic, legal, social and other issues related to genomics research (GE^{3}LS) and, the communication of the relative risks, rewards and successes of genomics to the Canadian public." This is a remarkable development that not only has economic implications for researchers in the social sciences and humanities in Canada, but also reflects the rise of a bioethics expertise that has the authority to evaluate, critique, and authorize the legitimization of biomedical practices from the laboratory to commercialization.

3. The mandate of the Canadian Biotechnology Advisory Committee (CBAC), concluded on May 17, 2007, with the release of a new Government of Canada Science and Technology Strategy, "Mobilizing Science and Technology to Canada's Advantage" (http://www.ic.gc.ca/epublications/). CBAC is succeeded by the Science, Technology, and Innovation Council, which is described as providing evidence-based science and technology advice on issues, referred to it by government, which are critical to Canada's economic development and social well-being. The Council will also produce regular national reports benchmarking Canada's science and technology performance against international standards of excellence" (http://www.stic-csti.ca/). For an international response to these changes, see Nature (2008).

4. Much of Genome Canada funding is delivered through the six independent regional genomic centers in Canada. These regional centers seek to establish a life sciences cluster of genomics-related research institutions and companies working together within their respective regions. In tune with Genome Canada, the regional centers are called, from east to west, Genome Atlantic, Genome Quebec, Ontario Genomics Institute, Genome Prairie, Genome Alberta, and Genome British Columbia. The main aims and objectives for each regional center, broadly speaking, are to facilitate significant socioeconomic benefits for people within the region and secure invest-

ment and provide expertise to facilitate commercialization resulting from the research activities conducted in each region. The centers are distinct from each other and not necessarily connected to previously established research institutions or universities. Notably, the centers also have projects that reflect the traditional resource economies of the regions they represent: Genome British Columbia hosts a genomics program in conifer forest health, Genome Alberta a program on crop improvement, and Genome Atlantic a project on the cod-fishing industry. The centers are tied to the landscape and regions of Canada in terms of resources and traditional research areas.

5. The Canadian Constitution uses the term *aboriginal* to refer to three groups of indigenous peoples in Canada: Innu (northern Canada), Métis (French and aboriginal), and First Nations (who are under a separate set of legal structures called the Indian Act). These broad terms, along with the term *aboriginal*, do little to capture the geopolitical differences between the peoples who have been grouped in Canada's borders and identify with the terms *indigenous* or *aboriginal*. The employment and use of these terms are reflections of political contexts, aims, and positions as well as complex historical intersections of colonial law, national sovereignty, and identity; there is not space enough to address these issues adequately in this chapter. Here I use the term *aboriginal* because it is the term employed in the examples I explore.

6. This legislative definition links Caucasian to race, and whiteness to color. Richard Tutton (2007b) has written on the relationship between whiteness and the category Caucasian in the context of U.K. genetic studies identifying tensions between self-identification and genotyping practices. The term *Caucasian* finds its roots in eighteenth-century racial classification and continues to embody and reflect many historical vicissitudes: a recent article in *Nature* by researchers at the J. Craig Venter Institute (Ng et al. 2008, 307) reflects the term's continuous and illustrious career in population genomics: "Even the term 'Caucasian' can be deceptive. If a self-identified Caucasian originates from a founder population in which certain disease-specific alleles occur at higher frequencies (e.g., Quebec French Canadians or Ashkenazi Jews), his or her doctor may miss an important aspect of the patient's medical history. One's ethnicity/race is, at best, a probabilistic guess at one's true genetic make-up." Reflecting perhaps the assumption that Caucasian/whiteness is a readily knowable and obvious classification in relation to other categories (even it can be deceptive), the quote points to increasing tensions and contradictions between the corporeal/visible body and an emphasis on molecular difference/genotype within the categories white and Caucasian.

7. At the time of publication, I had conducted an interview with a CARTaGENE employee, who explained to me that was I not able to view the questionnaire because the project was still undergoing the approval process with research ethics committees, and hence the questionnaire was currently confidential.

8. GWAS involve scanning thousands of case-control cohorts, which use hundreds of thousands of SNP markers in the human genome. Algorithms are then applied that compare the frequencies of SNPs or haplotype markers between the disease and the control cohorts. Collecting consistent clinical phenotypes and, in addition, matching cases (and control groups) in relation to geographic origin and ethnicity is of critical importance for GWAS researchers. See chapter 8.

9. Perhaps the most well known example follows: between 1982 and 1985, Dr. Richard Ward (former head of the Institute of Biological Anthropology at Oxford) took 883 vials of blood from the Nuu-chah-nulth First Nations in British Columbia. Almost two-thirds of the population have arthritis, one of the highest rates of arthritis in the world. Unbeknownst to the donors, however, he kept the samples and used them in genetic anthropology studies, which identified "a substantial level of mitochondrial diversity for a small local population," and Ward et al. (1991, 8720) suggested "that their origin predates the entry of humans into the Americas." When this was revealed, the Nuu-chah-nulth argued that Ward should have returned the specimens and should not have shifted his research into an area not approved by the community.

References

Arbour, L., and D. Cook. 2006. DNA on loan: Issues to consider when carrying out genetic research with aboriginal families and communities. *Community Genetics* 9:153–160.

Brown, C. 2000. Canada hopes to climb the DNA ladder to success. *Canadian Medical Association Journal* 162:1478–1479.

Campbell, C. 2002. Genome gamble: Can Ottawa kick-start a new sector with $300 million? Or are the feds dreaming? *The Globe and Mail* (October): 59.

Canadian Institutes of Health Research. 2007a. Aboriginal peoples given stronger voice in health research. http://www.cihr-irsc.gc.ca/e/34214.html.

Canadian Institutes of Health Research. 2007b. CIHR guidelines for health research involving aboriginal people. http://www.cihr-irsc.gc.ca/e/29134.html.

Cardwell, M. 2003. Project aims to paint a genetic portrait of Quebec: funding problems have not stalled CARTaGENE's progress. *Medical Post* 39 (20): 45.

Chartrand, P. 2002. Debunking the "race" myth in debating BC treaties. Turtle Island Native Network News. http://www.turtleisland.org/news/news-chartrand1.htm.

Davies, K. 2008. The Galileo code. *BIO-IT World*. http://www.bio-itworld.com/archive/021105/galileo.com.

Epstein, S. 2007. *Inclusion: The politics of difference in medical research*. Chicago: University of Chicago Press.

Fortun, M. 2005. For an ethics of promising, or: a few kinds words about James Watson. *New Genetics and Society* 24:157–173.

Fujimura, J. H., T. Duster, and R. Rajagopalan. 2008. Race, genetics and disease: Questions of evidence, matters of consequence. *Social Studies of Science* 38:643–656.

Genome Canada. 2006. Expression of Interest (EOI #51) promising practices and emerging culturally appropriate GE3LS frameworks: Aboriginal perspectives, voice, and presence in geonomics in Canada. http://positionpapers.genomecanada.ca/en/expression-details.php?eoi=28.

Genome Canada. 2007–2008. Corporate plan. Ottawa, ON: Genome Canada.

Genome Canada. 2008. Genomics and our health. http://www.genomecanada.ca/xpublic/health/index.asp.

Gibbon, S., and C. Novas. 2008. *Biosocialities, genetics and the social sciences: Making biologies and identities.* New York: Routledge.

Godard, B., J. Marshall, and C. Laberge 2007. Community engagement in genetic research: Results of the first public consultation for the Quebec CARTaGENE project. *Community Genetics* 10:147–158.

Government Canada. 1998. *Biotechnology transforming society: Creating an innovative economy and a higher quality of life, report on biotechnology (1998–2003).* Ottawa, ON: Government of Canada.

Government Canada. 2004. Symposium report: Genomics, health and society—emerging issues for public policy. http://www.biobasics.gc.ca/english/view.asp?mid=396&x=671.

Heath, D., R. Rapp, and K. S .Tauisig. 2004. Genetic citizenship In *A companion to the anthropology of politics*, ed. D. Nugent and J. Vincent. Malden, MA: Blackwell, 152–167.

Industry Canada. 2007. About us. http://www.ic.gc.ca/epic/site/ic1.nsf/en/h_00007e.html.

Kinsella, N. A. 2007. Sober second thought: The United Nations and the phrase "visible minority." http://www.sen.parl.gc.ca/nkinsella/PDF/Speeches/SoberSecondThought-e.pdf.

Kohli-Laven, N. 2007–2008. Hidden history: Race and ethics at the peripheries of medical genetic research. *Genewatch* 20:5–7.

KPMG. 2007. Final report: Evaluation of foundations. Ottawa, ON: KPMG Advisory Services.

Langlois, S. 2007. Genome Canada, Genome Quebec and Universite De Montreal launch P3G Consortium and CARTaGENE project. *Medical News Today.* http://www.medicalnewstoday.com/articles/72178.php.

Lawrence, B. 2003. Gender, race and the regulation of Native identity in Canada and the United States: An overview. *Hypatia* 18:3–31.

Lévesque, L. 2007a. Executive summary of brainstorming session: A public theme for the CARTaGENE project. Report, CARTaGENE.

Lévesque, L. 2007b. Recruitment communications tools for a population and genomic resource. Version 1—consultation document. Report, CARTaGENE.

M'charek, A. 2005. *The Human Genome Diversity Project: An ethnography of scientific practice.* New York: Cambridge University Press.

Nature. 2008. Science in retreat. *Nature* 866:451.

Ng, P., Q. Zhao, S. Levy, R. L. Strausberg, and J. C. Venter. 2008. Individual genomes instead of race for personalized medicine. *Nature* 84:306–309.

Pálsson, G., and P. Rabinow. 1999. Iceland: The case of a national human genome project. *Anthropology Today* 15 (5): 14–18.

Power, C., E. Levy, E. Marden, and B. Warren. 2008. Alternative IP mechanisms in genomic research. *Studies in Ethnics, Law, and Technology* 2:1–11.

Rabinow, P. 1996. *Essays on the anthropology of reason.* Princeton, NJ: Princeton University Press.

Racine, E. 2006. Hyped biomedical science or uncritical reporting? Press coverage of genomics (1992–2001) in Quebec. *Social Science and Medicine* 62:1278–1290.

Raelson, J. V., R. D. Little, A. Ruether, H. Fournier, and B. Paquin. 2007. Genome-wide association study for Crohn's disease in the Quebec founder population identifies multiple validated disease loci. *Proceedings of the National Academy of Sciences of the United States of America* 104:14747–14752.

Reardon, J. 2005. *Race to the finish: Identity and governance in an age of genomics.* Princeton, NJ: Princeton University Press.

Reardon, J. 2007. Democratic mis-haps: The problem of democratization in a time of biopolitics. *BioSocieties* 2:239–256.

Rose, N., and C. Novas. 2005. Biological citizenship. In *Global assemblages: Technology, politics and ethics as anthropological problems*, ed. A. Ong and S. Collier. London: Blackwell, 439–463.

Santos, R. V. 2004. Race, genomics, identities and politics in contemporary Brazil. *Critique of Anthropology* 24:347–378.

Schwartz-Marín, E. 2008. *Genomic sovereignty and the creation of the INMEGEN: Governance, populations and territoriality.* Masters thesis, University of Exeter.

Secko, D. 2008. Rare history, common disease. *The Scientist* 22 (7): 38.

Segiun, B., et al. 2008. Human genomic variation initiatives in emerging economies and developing countries. *Nature Reviews Genetics* 9 (10): S3–S4.

Smart, A., R. Tutton, P. Martin, G. T. H. Ellison, and R. Ashcroft. 2008. The standardization of race and ethnicity in biomedical science: Editorials and UK biobanks. *Social Science and Medicine* 38:407–423.

Statistics Canada. 2008a. 2006 census: Ethnic origin, visible minorities, place of work and mode of transportation. *The Daily.* http://www.statcan.ca/Daily/English/080402/d080402a.htm.

Statistics Canada. 2008b. Visible minority population and population group reference guide, 2006 census. http://www12.statcan.ca/english/census06/reference/reportsandguides/visible-minorities.cfm.

Sunder Rajan, K. 2006. *Biocapital: The constitution of postgenomic life.* Durham, NC: Duke University Press.

Tutton, R. 2007a. Constructing participation in genetic databases: Citizenship, governance and ambivalence. *Science, Technology, and Human Values* 32:172–195.

Tutton, R. 2007b. Opening the white box: Exploring the study of whiteness in contemporary genetics research. *Ethnic and Racial Studies* 30:557–569.

Wallace, S., K. Bedard, A. Kent, B. M. Knoppers 2008. Governance mechanisms and population biobanks: Building a framework for trust. *GenEdit* 6:1–11.

Ward, R. H., B. L. Frazier, K. Dew-Jager, and S. Pääbo. 1991. Extensive mitochondrial diversity within a single Amerindian tribe. *Proceedings of the National Academy of Sciences of the United States of America* 88:8720–8724.

Winter, E. 2007. Neither "America" nor "Quebec": Constructing the Canadian multicultural nation. *Nations and Nationalism* 13:481–503.

8 Race and Ancestry: Operationalizing Populations in Human Genetic Variation Studies

Joan H. Fujimura, Ramya Rajagopalan, Pilar N. Ossorio, and Kjell A. Doksum

Across the social sciences, there has been broad acceptance that race and race categories are sociohistorical constructs that are relational, processual, and dynamic, changing over time and locale. Relatedly, some scholars have noted that there were attempts to move away from race categories as organizing principles in the biological sciences, particularly around the United Nations Educational, Scientific, and Cultural Organization statements in the middle of the twentieth century (Haraway 1989; Reardon 2005; Brattain 2007). In population genetics, some scholars argued that between-race differences are fewer than within-race differences (Lewontin 1974); others championed the mid-century idea of a single "family of man" as they simultaneously promoted efforts to construct and catalog genetic differences among humans (the Human Genome Diversity Project or HGDP; Cavalli-Sforza et al. 1991). Even so, biologists never abandoned the notion of races as biologically important categories (Mueller-Wille 2005; Gissis 2008), and the HGDP met with critiques of sanitizing and depoliticizing race concepts by using populationist terminology and frames (Reardon 2005).

At the end of the twentieth century, race appeared to have (re)gained prominence in the realms of medicine through, for example, transplantation research (Haraway 1997), although many physicians may never have stopped using race categories in their practice of medicine (Satel 2002). In the last fifteen years, new technologies have facilitated the investigation of genetic differences between individuals and groups, which have in turn fueled new debates about the role of race in the biomedical sciences (reviewed in Fujimura, Duster, and Rajagopalan 2008; Koenig, Lee, and Richardson 2008). Proponents of using race as an organizing concept for genetic studies argue that biological variation correlates well enough with race and ethnicity to be useful, and such variation can help account for differences in disease susceptibility, occurrence, etiology, and treatment response (e.g., Risch et al. 2002; Burchard et al. 2003). While some social scientists have discussed situations where there might be some propinquity between biological and race categories (e.g., Duster 2003; Rebbeck and Sankar 2005), they also point out that recent findings in genome variation science reveal that race is often a poor proxy for genetic ancestry, and they warn that the search for such genetic differences not only stigmatizes certain groups and reifies race as biological, but also diverts resources away from the investigation of much more significant factors in disease such as socioeconomic status and its related stratified access to quality healthcare, exercise, diet, and environments (e.g., Krieger and Fee 1994; Ossorio and Duster 2005; Kahn 2005; Montoya 2007; Fausto-Sterling 2008).

In this chapter, we focus on within-group differences among geneticists and the different concepts they devise to deal with "population differences." We examine the technologies that some geneticists have used to construct different populations for the purposes of finding genetic markers for disease. We especially focus on recent efforts by medical geneticists to conceptualize and measure population differences without using race or ethnic categories. In this process, medical and population geneticists emphasize that they are examining population differences due to different ancestries, rather than assessing differences among racial groups. We examine the relationships between the notions of *ancestry* and *race* by examining the theories and practices of medical geneticists and population geneticists who have joined forces to search for genetic markers for common complex diseases. A key point here is that these common complex diseases are thought to unite humans precisely because these diseases are not specific to any one group or groups.

Although the connections between *race* and *population* (and the use of either term in biomedical research) have been contested across the social sciences and the biological sciences, the notion of *ancestry* has received much less attention. Some have argued that assaying ancestry through genetics might be a more appropriate variable to use in biomedical research than race (Shields et al. 2005), but the production of ancestry concepts and its operationalization in scientific practice have been largely untreated.[1] Our point here is that just as race is a socially constructed set of categories, so ancestry is a constructed concept. In this chapter, we examine how ancestry is conceived and constructed as well as its connections to population or race concepts in biomedical research.

Our questions include the following: How do concepts of race and genetic ancestry operate in contemporary biomedical studies of human genetic variation? How do they interact to produce notions of population? To discuss these related notions, we will describe our ethnographic research[2] on two different kinds of biomedical genomic studies in which researchers seek disease-associated markers in human populations. The first are admixture mapping studies, and the second are genome-wide association studies (GWAS). In both approaches, the concept of population is key. We will examine how particular population constructs become entangled with research on disease, and we will analyze how scientists produce simultaneously different kinds of populations and population differences.

Populations and the Search for Genetic Contributions to Common Complex Diseases

Until this decade, medical geneticists focused largely on diseases with "simple" genotype-phenotype associations such as sickle-cell anemia, phenylketonuria (PKU), and so on. Many of these diseases are monogenic, meaning that almost all cases are caused by defects in a single gene, and many are quite penetrant, meaning that a person who has a defective copy of the gene will almost certainly show symptoms of the disease, though when and to what degree will vary. However, as a result of the development of genomics technologies, medical geneticists have increasingly turned to the challenges posed by common complex diseases such as diabetes, heart disease, and cancers. The etiology of these and other complex diseases is thought to involve combined contributions from environmental factors as well as from genetic factors distributed across the genome. Many factors and pathways, both outside and within bodies, are involved in the production of symptoms of these diseases. Some patients affected by a complex disease may have only a small contributing genetic component, while in other cases genetics may be more significant.

It is estimated that there are between twenty thousand and twenty-five thousand genes in a human genome, although many thousands of these genes remain a mystery in terms of their function. When searching for genetic associations to a complex disease, which may involve the action of tens or even hundreds of genes in several biological pathways, geneticists cannot use the same techniques that have worked in the past for monogenic diseases such as examining one gene at a time via candidate gene approaches. Instead, they conduct studies that examine many hundreds or thousands of regions of the genome simultaneously.

Since humans are estimated to be about 99.5 percent similar at the level of their DNA (Levy et al. 2007), it is believed that genetic contributions to disease are to be found in the 0.5 percent of DNA that varies across individuals.[3] In the wake of human genome sequencing, the International Haplotype Map (HapMap) project has attempted to catalog this genetic variation across several groups (four in the first stage of HapMap, with more groups added in HapMap2 and HapMap3). The HapMap project has focused on genetic markers known as single nucleotide polymorphisms, or SNPs. A SNP is a single base of DNA whose nucleotide identity (A, T, G, or C) varies among people. To hone in on disease-associated regions of the genome, medical geneticists who do genome-wide studies initially examine SNP markers for their association with disease. They rely heavily on statistical assessments of what counts as a "significant" association between a SNP and the disease being studied. Finding significant SNPs requires that geneticists genotype and examine hundreds or thousands of SNP markers in hundreds or thousands of people.

One of the big challenges in such studies is minimizing both the chance of finding an incorrect association (a false-positive association) and the chance of not finding a correct association (a false-negative association). Practitioners of admixture mapping and GWAS approaches have developed different techniques for dealing with these problems, and these techniques are at the heart of how they construct their populations for analysis. The concept of ancestry plays a central role in the design and deployment of these techniques.

Admixture Mapping Studies

Admixture mapping is a genome-wide approach that uses concepts of race and ethnicity to construct populations and analyze associations between genetics and disease. Racial and ethnic as well as geographical and historical descriptors and narratives inform how admixture mapping scientists conceive of ancestry. We examine the generation of the tools to do admixture mapping and the use of these tools to scan for disease associations by a research team that used admixture mapping to identify genetic variants for prostate cancer in African American men.

The theory underlying the admixture mapping approach interweaves ideas from population genetics, demographic data, and racial and cultural histories. Admixture mapping geneticists focus on the study of complex diseases in groups that they believe are *recently admixed. Admixed* means that their recent ancestors came from geographically distinct parts of the world, that these ancestral groups had distinguishable patterns of genetic variation, and that evidence of these distinctive patterns is still observable in the study population. The notion of a recently admixed population is connected to three main constraints that researchers use to construct study populations. First, the disease under study is chosen to be one for which epidemiological data suggest an elevated incidence in the admixed population, relative to the general population. (We note here that many epidemiological figures are calculated based on race and ethnicity.) Second, the admixed population should be recently admixed, which typically means fewer than twenty generations since admixture, for the statistical genetics to "work." Finally, the admixture should have involved at least two ancestral populations that were geographically separate from each other and had little interbreeding until the admixture occurred.

Admixture mapping researchers genotype DNA from individuals who have the disease under study and who self-identify as belonging to those groups researchers believe to be admixed. Unlike case-control studies of disease, there are typically no control groups in admixture mapping studies (which would include individuals who do not have the disease). Admixture scans aim to identify disease susceptibility loci by zeroing in on large chunks of DNA that have undergone little recombination over the small number of generations since the presumed admixture events. Researchers believe that such chunks are likely to be more significantly associated with one or the other of the two ancestries than the rest of the individuals' genomes. They analyze these chunks for markers that are statistically associated with the disease in the cases they are studying.

The acceptable definitions of study populations in admixture mapping are highly dependent on practices and assumptions in statistical genetics. Researchers view ancestral DNA chunks as belonging to one of the assumed ancestries that contributed to the admixture, and they have developed group definitions and statistical tools that they believe allow them to trace the inheritance of these chunks. For example, population geneticists have over time developed the restriction that the admixture event(s) should have occurred within the last twenty generations. They believe that this allows them to detect ancestral contributions even with the "scrambling" of DNA that occurs through recombination in every generation. As one respondent explained, twenty generations was an arbitrary cutoff established to facilitate the genetic analysis. Thus population geneticists view an admixed group to be a mix of the genetic material of the ancestral populations, while retaining discernible and separable traces of each of the ancestries—a mix that is, in some sense, a quantifiable sum of its imputed parts.

The restrictions that admixture mapping practitioners have built into their work, then, have direct implications for how populations are conceived and constructed in this research. Admixture mapping geneticists frequently seek out African Americans and Hispanic Americans as desirable populations to be studied in the U.S. context because they conceive of these groups, by way of history, evolutionary biology, and anthropology, to be the products of admixing.[4] For example, they assume that people who self-identify today as African Americans possess both African and European ancestry due to historical encounters with Europeans that brought people of African ancestry to the Americas. They assume that the genomes of people who self-identify as Latinos or Hispanic Americans are admixtures of DNA from native and indigenous groups living in what is now the Americas, and DNA from European colonizers. Thus practitioners of admixture mapping in the United States borrow heavily from stories of human isolation, migration, and mixing to determine groups they regard as suitable for this analysis.

The scientist respondents in our study described what they are doing as "tracking continental origin of lines of descent," under the belief that the ancestral populations were, according to one respondent, "very different . . . at a population level, genetically." Our respondents were able to conceive of admixture and admixed populations because they felt comfortable distinguishing ancestral populations from each other, along continental lines. As one respondent noted, "After all, the available admixed populations are fairly limited. . . . I mean, there are other possibilities, but by and large, right now, we're restricted to Hispanics or African Americans." This limitation may explain why admixture researchers are often interpreted as doing race-based science (Fullwiley 2008).

In admixture mapping, population geneticists draw boundaries between ancestral groups along continental lines. They differentiate two continental lines of descent by genotyping a predetermined set of a few thousand SNP markers that can, according to researchers, reliably distinguish between the two ancestral populations due to differences in variant frequencies in each ancestral group. These geneticists refer to such markers as ancestry-informative markers (AIMs), and refer to a set of AIMs designed for a particular group as an admixture map. The methods of making of admixture maps used by these scientists illuminates the contingent ways in which ancestral and admixed populations are conceived and operationalized. For example, the geneticists have to estimate marker frequencies in ancestral populations because no individuals from these ancestral groups from whom samples could be drawn exist today. Geneticists estimate these frequencies by assessing frequencies among purported contemporary representatives of these groups. For example, they often use European American samples such as the Centre d'Étude du Polymorphisme Humain samples of white Americans from Utah, or samples of white Americans from urban centers like Baltimore or Chicago, to stand in for the ancestral European population. They use marker frequencies measured in contemporary West African or sub-Saharan samples to stand in for frequency estimates for the African ancestors of African Americans.

In admixture studies, geneticists deploy particular genealogical stories in the ancestral origins labels they attach to chunks of DNA. They often conceptualize these ancestral origins in terms of the major continents, which they and others read as continental race categories (Fullwiley 2008). Admixture studies are therefore often viewed as using racial and ethnic categories, both in the collection of samples and in the analysis of data. Indeed, a few of our geneticist respondents who use admixture mapping approaches straightforwardly said that they do not find race to be a troubling concept in their research.

These geneticists view individuals as carrying in their genomes segments of DNA from their various ancestors. For individuals in groups they view as racially admixed, they believe that these ancestral contributions can be separated from each other. They base this belief on theories of genetic linkage and theories of human migration patterns, which themselves are based on historical records as well as physical anthropological, archeological, and linguistic research, which in turn are based on other theoretical and historical ideas and materials. We acknowledge the depth and breadth of their scientific work in the production of measurements of admixture; however, we also want to clarify that all these forms of evidence are both products of and productive of sociocultural frames and understandings. Furthermore, the inextricability of concepts of population, ancestry, race, and genetic difference that circulate in this science does the work of reinforcing and legitimating the collective, continued use in future studies of the very connections between genetic markers and sociocultural histories that we are problematizing here.

Genome-wide Association Studies: Genomics without Race?

In contrast to admixture mapping, the GWAS researchers we studied attempted to specify populations based on concepts of genetic ancestry. They argue that genetic ancestry produces a finer resolution of populations than would sociocultural categories of race. GWAS has been made possible by several recent advances in genomic technologies (particularly faster and cheaper genotyping technologies, the International HapMap, population genetics techniques, and new analytic tools). These infrastructures are critical tools in GWAS. GWAS have been widely touted by hopeful analysts in the genetics field and in the press; for example, the December 2007 issue of the journal *Science* named human genetic variation studies, especially GWAS, its "breakthrough of the year" (Pennisi 2007).

GWAS are large-scale, high-throughput studies, much more so than admixture mapping. Like admixture mapping researchers, GWAS researchers search for markers in genomes that may be causally linked to common complex diseases, such as heart disease, type II diabetes, and cancer, under the assumption that these diseases are likely to involve small, combinatorial influences from many genes distributed throughout the genome. They focus on the genetic elements of causation, although they acknowledge that many other social, environmental and behavioral factors and processes are involved in the etiology of common complex diseases.[5]

In contrast to admixture mapping, GWAS are typically case-control studies. They involve statistical analyses of differences in the frequencies of SNP markers between cases (those diagnosed with the disease) and controls (those who do not have the disease). Researchers genotype and evaluate hundreds of thousands of genetic markers per individual for association to disease, in thousands of individuals, all in a single study. With large numbers of cases, controls, and markers, GWAS researchers statistically examine potential relationships of certain markers to health outcomes.

Population Substructure: Genetic Similarity Scores Adjust for Population Differences

To find statistically significant SNPs that indicate disease risk, GWAS methods include efforts to avoid spurious associations due to systematic patterns of difference among the sampled genomes. To reduce the chance of false-positive associations, researchers need to account for genetic differences between cases and controls that may have nothing to do with the disease. They call this "adjusting for population substructure" or "adjusting for population stratification."

We describe our ethnographic research in a medical genetics lab where researchers were doing GWAS analysis of several common complex diseases. The researchers in this lab were very interested in avoiding the use of race groups as organizing categories for the design of their research. They were medical geneticists who stated that their projects were *not* about race—whether defined by ideas about phenotypic characteristics like skin color or by how people label themselves (called self-report). They believed that race does not refer to a genetic set of categories, and therefore it is the wrong concept to use in genomics research.

In making the adjustments for population stratification, the primary tool these medical geneticists used is a statistical software package, Eigensoft, designed by population geneticists. Software programs in Eigensoft have been designed to generate scores for the SNP variation in each individual DNA sample relative to the other samples. These SNP variation scores are generated through a modified version of a classical statistical approach called principal components analysis (PCA). The scores are subsequently used as input for a program called Eigenstrat (included in Eigensoft), which has been designed to carry out the statistical regression analysis to adjust for population stratification and compute potential associations to disease.

The researchers we interviewed were enthusiastic about the Eigenstrat program as their tool of choice because they regarded it as a method that allowed them to measure genetic similarities directly instead of using race as a proxy in their subsequent disease SNP searches.

Genetic Similarity and Ancestry

The researchers regarded the previously described process of correcting for population stratification as key to a proper GWAS analysis, often without a great deal of concern about any underlying population concept or definition.[6] When asked explicitly about what this process meant for definitions of population, some medical geneticists insisted that they use a *technical* definition of populations, and some of them emphasized that their software affords them a "genetic standpoint" from which to infer populations and population history. In making these assertions, they invoked the concept of *ancestry*. Some of the medical geneticists were comfortable using terms like *genetic history* and *ancestry*, in part because they have adopted the language and ideas used by the population geneticists who designed the statistical technologies they use to correct for population substructure. Many of the researchers called the process of adjusting for substructure using Eigenstrat "adjusting for ancestry." They viewed adjusting for ancestry as a required practice for reducing the chance that the results they obtain through genetic association studies are spurious because of differences between cases and controls due to ancestry and not to disease risk.

The practice of adjusting for ancestry depends critically on which markers in the genome get genotyped. In any GWAS study, a pre-determined set of SNPs are genotyped using SNP microarrays. Scientists who design the SNP genotyping microarrays for GWAS select which SNPs to include, relying heavily on data in the HapMap to select a set of SNPs with reasonable coverage of the genetic variation estimated in the HapMap sample groups. They take into account many population genetic considerations, such as the number and genomic distribution of selected SNPs, which tells them how useful the chips will be for assessing variation in different HapMap groups. They also include technical considerations, such as which SNPs will perform the best in the genotyping experiments. The building of the microarray, the selection of markers, and the genotyping itself are central to GWAS.

As one medical geneticist said, "Ancestry [is] shared allele frequencies due to shared ancestors." But this is an imprecise definition; like the notion of population, *ancestry* is a fluid term and has different interpretations and meanings in different contexts and usages. We focus on how the scientists we studied assessed or constructed ancestry. While the American Society for Human Genetics (ASHG), a leading human genetics association in the United States, notes that ancestry determination depends on "how underlying patterns of human genetic diversity are distributed among populations" (American Society for Human Genetics 2008, 4), we argue that these underlying patterns are known only through the data and data-producing technologies and practices of the geneticists.

For example, the precision of ancestry determinations depends on how far back in time or how many generations are considered by the assessment. Family histories can provide somewhat reliable information on very recent ancestors within a few generations. Anthropologists assess the earliest hominids from which modern humans evolved through archeological evidence. But intervening levels of ancestry, particularly during the early millennia of modern humans and their global migrations, are more difficult to define and interpret, and geneticists trying to assess these levels of ancestry resort to methods of inference with significant levels of uncertainty. It is precisely these levels of ancestry that are of interest to biomedical geneticists (American Society for Human Genetics 2008), particularly those studying common genetic variation. GWAS scientists believe that common variation may illuminate genetic factors involved in complex diseases. Such common variation is expected to occur in all groups, but at different frequencies, depending on the histories and migrations of ancestral peoples, who passed on their particular SNP variants to descendants in different parts of the world. Thus intervening levels of ancestry, if it were possible to assess them with greater certainty, would help illuminate the differential patterns of SNPs in different groups in which individuals share ancestors.

Translation of SNP Similarity to Relatedness

Some of the researchers took the notion of ancestry a step further. For example, one of the population geneticists interpreted individuals with similar SNP variation scores as having "shared ancestry," a belief based on established ideas about human genetic evolutionary relationships in his field of expertise. The population geneticists we interviewed worked under the theory that modern humans originated relatively recently in Africa and then spread, through different waves of migration, to other continents.[7] Although there are varying ideas about the degree of difference among populations that developed on separate continents, the general belief expressed by our respondents is that the differences are recent (in terms of human history) and useful for distinguishing portions of the genome from different continents.

This translation, or slippage, from SNP similarity to *genetic history*, to *ancestry*, to *shared ancestry* indicates a view that is shared by some researchers we interviewed, but not by all. That is, the software program can do the work of adjusting for population stratification "to genetically match cases and controls" without inferring shared ancestry for individuals with similar patterns of SNP variation and without assigning a *particular* ancestry label to such individuals. Nevertheless, some made the leap of reading shared ancestry and its implied relatedness onto individuals with similar SNP patterns.

Furthermore, some geneticists among the GWAS researchers attributed geographic meaning to differences in SNP frequencies, and they interpreted these geographic differences to mean different ancestries. This practice is a key point at which populations and population differences are produced.

In contrast, other geneticists we interviewed said that their GWAS research did not use race or ethnic categories in the genetic analysis because the Eigenstrat program automatically adjusted for population substructure or ancestry using PCA scores in the regression analysis. They said that there was no need to use descriptors of race, ancestry, or geographic origins when using Eigenstrat in biomedical applications of GWAS. Even when the samples are collected using self-reported racial or ethnic categories, as they are in some cohort collections, the analysts do not use that information for genetic analysis. And although they believe that adjusting for ancestry is necessary in these studies, they are looking at common variation and therefore do not believe that the alleles they find will be ancestry-specific; rather, they expect that SNP variants associated with disease will be present in all population or ancestry groups. Even the most cited "race-specific" genetic alleles, such as the Duffy null allele, which is much more common in people of African descent, are uncommon, but not absent, in other groups. Researchers are aware of this; still, their reporting of alleles that are prominent in certain groups and rare in others tends to elide the distinction between absent and rare.

Conclusion: Race versus Ancestry—Two Notions That Operationalize Human Populations

In this chapter, we have examined genetic epidemiological research conducted by medical geneticists; some use race explicitly, and others attempt to avoid the use of race categories in their research design and implementation. In admixture mapping studies searching for disease-related genetic markers, geneticists deploy particular genealogical stories in the ancestral origins labels they attach to chunks of DNA. These ancestral origins are often conceptualized in terms of the major continents. In contrast, some GWAS studies attempt to avoid race and ancestral origin labels and their attendant meanings[8] but, nevertheless, sometimes end up being interpreted as using notions of shared ancestry.

We show that in contrast to recent studies of the use of race in genetic, medical, and pharmaceutical research, there are researchers who view race as an incorrect categorization scheme for operationalizing their search for disease-associated genetic markers. These researchers have devised or adopted new tools, partly in response to critiques about the use of race in genomics. Their new methods thus allow them to distinguish themselves and their work from the generation of admixture mapping genetics, which explicitly uses race groups. These GWAS researchers have developed their alternative notions of population and their alternative technologies to produce what they call a "genetic standpoint" from which to assess and adjust for ancestry differences.

Still, there remains a complex interplay among ancestry and race concepts. Although many GWAS researchers attempt to sidestep the discourse of ancestral origins of the bits of DNA they study, they nevertheless sometimes invoke notions of shared ancestry, which often are interpreted as common geographic origin and, by others, as race categories. Because the medical geneticists deploy methods devised by population geneticists, they also sometimes inherit the notions of populations used by those population geneticists; that is, the designers of GWAS technologies that address population stratification interpret SNP variation groups as human groups that have related genetic histories or shared ancestry. While some geneticists specifically police their language and disavow notions of race or shared ancestry in their work, others do not.

Furthermore, policing their own language does not prevent audiences from reading race into the work of these practitioners. Although *ancestry*, as used in GWAS, is not equivalent to race, *shared ancestry* could be interpreted as race, especially when ancestry is traced back to the major continents of Africa, Asia, Europe, and the Americas. It is these continental geographies that lend GWAS analysis to racial interpretations. For example, *New York Times* science writer Nicholas Wade (2007) read race into the results of one of the first GWAS studies, conducted by the Wellcome Trust in 2007 on several thousand British patients. Thus, despite the fact that some of the researchers we studied who use the notion of ancestry believe that race categories are sociohistorical concepts and that race is an incorrect concept for use in genetics, the notion of shared ancestry is often read as race by the media, the public, or other researchers.

The relationship between race and ancestry, then, is intricate and difficult to disentangle, which also helps to explain the difficulties of separating the reading practices of consumers from the production practices of scientists. Although one could regard ancestry as a concept produced using population genetics tools and race as a socio-cultural set of understandings, the two are not so clearly separated in scientific or popular cultural deployments; that is, science and culture are not separate discourses.

Concepts of care and ancestry inform how populations are conceived and constructed in contemporary genomics methodologies, but in different ways. Admixture research uses race and ethnic categories to designate admixed and so-called ancestral populations. Both race and ethnicity are complex social concepts with blurry edges. Nevertheless, researchers use them to posit easily definable, isolated ancestral populations. For example, admixture researchers use race and ethnic categories to determine which individuals and groups are sampled and included in the study as well as to guide the analysis via the construction of ancestral frequencies and the inferred histories of groups. In contrast to this use of race and ethnicity, the notion of ancestry enters GWAS studies at the analysis stage, and while some GWAS geneticists infer shared ancestry and attach ancestry labels to individuals with similar SNP variation scores, others do not. Thus, with caution and care, GWAS technologies can provide alternative means to conduct research on genetic markers associated with disease, without using race or ethnic categories. The construction of populations in these two very different approaches illustrates that all human genomics research is not the same. It points to a diversity of methodologies and choices available to biomedical researchers, suggesting that genomics research into human genetic variation is varied and contingent. Indeed, there are even variations and differences of opinion among researchers at a single laboratory site, as we have described.

Notes

1. One exception here is Fullwiley's (2008) study of the use of a particular set of ancestry-informative markers in a laboratory using admixture mapping to study asthma. Others (Nelson 2008; Bolnick 2007) have examined the potential of consumer genetic ancestry testing to reinscribe race as biological.

2. Fieldwork described in this chapter (including interviews with researchers, observation in labs and other group meetings, and observation of some work practices) was conducted at three U.S. research sites between January 2007 and April 2009. The research sites consisted of large teams of researchers working on biomedical genetics projects. The research spanned many disciplines, including medical genetics, population genetics, epidemiology, statistics, bioinformatics, and medicine. Some of the projects also involved collaborations across laboratories, institutions, and even nations.

3. Researchers had earlier estimated that any two individuals were 99.9% similar in their DNA sequence, suggesting very little variability between human genomes. This most recent estimate

suggests much more variability than previously thought because it includes measurements of structural variation between genomes, including copy number variations.

4. Given that these groups overlap with traditionally disadvantaged groups in the United States, some practitioners of admixture mapping argue that such groups have received insufficient attention by the medical research establishment and view their work as potentially mitigating this gap (Risch et al. 2002; Burchard et al. 2003).

5. We point out that some geneticists have begun to caution that GWAS will not be able to unlock all the genetic contributions to common complex disease. Some are circumspect about the potential significance of any variants uncovered in the future by GWAS, arguing that the most highly significant variants should already have been identified for diseases that have been studied (Goldstein 2009), while others remind readers of the limited levels of risk that GWAS can explain (Kraft and Hunter 2009). A related critique is that too much infrastructural capital is being spent on finding genetic contributions to disease through GWAS, rather than examining and remediating the potentially far more significant contributions of diet, smoking, lack of exercise, stress, inadequate health care, racism, toxic waste or chemical exposure, living conditions, and various combinations of these that epidemiological studies can reveal (e.g., Duster 2003; Krieger and Fee 1994; Montoya 2007). In light of these cautions, the rise of direct-to-consumer genetic testing based on GWAS SNP findings raises concerns. Despite the uncertainties around SNP associations, whose causal relationships to disease remain unestablished, commercial genetic risk testing prematurely applies GWAS findings to individual diagnosis. "Home brew" tests produced by companies like 23andMe, Navigenics, and deCODEme fly under the radar of the Food and Drug Administration. Their availability, alongside media readings of race based on GWAS findings, makes it likely that certain groups or individuals will feel more vulnerable or at risk than others and may be overrepresented in the consumer base of these companies. What are the ramifications of using genetic findings to make broad claims about an individual's risk for certain diseases, when there are thus far only associations with almost no causal links to genetic markers, let alone to disease genes, and scant knowledge about the other factors outside of the genome, both inside the body and outside, involved in producing disease phenotypes?

6. Most medical geneticists we interviewed used stratification correction tools without thinking about their definitions of population concepts. However, some have thought and continue to think seriously about this issue and have adopted, at least in part, the social science view that races are socially constructed and have to do with much more than ancestry or phenotype.

7. This is the theory often mentioned by our respondents. The evolution of humans is a highly contentious topic, and we are not espousing any particular view here. We instead want to indicate that medical geneticists use some of the ideas and theories from population genetics, but they do not generate those ideas and theories.

8. Why do some researchers choose admixture mapping over GWAS? The rationale for this choice is that admixture mapping is much cheaper in terms of the technological tools required. Through admixture mapping techniques, researchers can achieve reasonable statistical power with fewer DNA samples and by genotyping about three thousand markers in each sample, rather

than hundreds of thousands. Thus some researchers believe that certain diseases may be studied more inexpensively using an admixture mapping approach. However, as one respondent noted, GWAS can be used to generate the same findings as admixture mapping without being restricted to admixed populations, and the admixture mapping approach is thus falling out of favor at some labs, even as it remains in use at others.

References

American Society of Human Genetics. 2008. The American Society of Human Genetics ancestry testing statement. http://www.ashg.org/pdf/ASHGAncestryTestingStatement_FINAL.pdf.

Bolnick, D. A. 2007. Individual ancestry inference and the reification of race as a biological phenomenon. In *Revisiting race in a genomic age*, ed. B. A. Koenig, S. S.-J. Lee, and S. S. Richardson. Piscataway, NJ: Rutgers University Press, 70–88.

Brattain, M. 2007. Race, racism and antiracism: UNESCO and the politics of presenting science to the postwar public. *American Historical Review* 112:1386–1413.

Burchard, E. G., E. Ziv, N. Coyle, S. L. Gomez, H. Tang, A. J. Karter, J. L. Mountain, E. J. Perez-Stable, D. Sheppard, and N. Risch. 2003. The importance of race and ethnic background in biomedical research and clinical practice. *New England Journal of Medicine* 348:1170–1175.

Cavalli-Sforza, L. L., A. C. Wilson, C. R. Cantor, R. M. Cook-Deegan, and M. C. King. 1991. Call for a worldwide survey of human genetic diversity: A vanishing opportunity for the Human Genome Project. *Genomics* 11:490–491.

Duster, T. 2003. Buried alive: The concept of race in science. In *Genetic nature/culture: Anthropology and science beyond the two culture divide*, ed. A. Goodman, D. Heath, and M. S. Lindee. Berkeley: University of California Press, 258–277.

Fausto-Sterling, A. 2008. The bare bones of race. *Social Studies of Science* 38:657–694.

Fujimura, J. H., T. Duster, and R. Rajagopalan. 2008. Race, genetics, and disease: Questions of evidence, matters of consequence. *Social Studies of Science* 38:643–656.

Fullwiley, D. 2008. The biologistical construction of race: "Admixture" technology and the new genetic medicine. *Social Studies of Science* 38:695–735.

Gissis, S. B. 2008. When is "race" a race? 1946–2003. *Studies in History and Philosophy of Biological and Biomedical Sciences* 39:437–450.

Goldstein, D. B. 2009. Common genetic variation and human traits. *New England Journal of Medicine* 360:1696–1698.

Haraway, D. 1989. *Primate visions: Gender, race, and nature in the world of modern science.* New York: Routledge.

Haraway, D. 1997. *Modest_Witness@Second-Millennium.FemaleMan©Meets_OncoMouse™.* New York: Routledge.

Kahn, J. 2005. From disparity to difference: How race-specific medicines may undermine policies to address inequalities in health care. *Southern California Interdisciplinary Law Journal* 15:105–130.

Koenig, B. A., S. Soo-Jin Lee, and S. S. Richardson, eds. 2008. *Revisiting race in a genomic age.* Piscataway, NJ: Rutgers University Press.

Kraft, P., and D. J. Hunter. 2009. Genetic risk prediction—are we there yet? *New England Journal of Medicine* 360:1701–1703.

Krieger, N., and E. Fee. 1994. Man-made medicine and women's health: The biopolitics of sex/gender and race/ethnicity. *International Journal of Health Services* 24:265–283.

Levy, S., G. Sutton, P. C. Ng, L. Feuk, A. L. Halpern, B. P. Walenz, N. Axelrod, et al. 2007. The diploid genome sequence of an individual human. *PLoS Biology* 5:2113–2144.

Lewontin, R. C. 1974. *The genetic basis of evolutionary change.* New York: Columbia University Press.

Montoya, M. 2007. Bioethnic conscription: Genes, race, and Mexicana/o ethnicity in diabetes research. *Cultural Anthropology* 22:94–128.

Mueller-Wille, S. 2005. Race and ethnicity: Human diversity and the UNESCO statement on race (1950–51). In *Sixty years of UNESCO's history: Proceedings of the International Symposium in Paris.* Paris: UNESCO, 211–220.

Nelson, A. 2008. Bio science: Genetic genealogy testing and the pursuit of African ancestry. *Social Studies of Science* 38:759–783.

Ossorio, P., and T. Duster. 2005. Race and genetics: Controversies in biomedical, behavioral and forensic sciences. *American Psychologist* 60:115–128.

Pennisi, E. 2007. Breakthrough of the year: Human genetic variation. *Science,* 318:1842–1843.

Reardon, J. 2005. *Race to the finish: Identity and governance in an age of genomics.* Princeton, NJ: Princeton University Press.

Rebbeck, T. R., and P. Sankar. 2005. Ethnicity, ancestry, and race in molecular epidemiologic research. *Cancer Epidemiology, Biomarkers and Prevention* 14:2467–2471.

Risch, N., E. Burchard, E. Ziv, and H. Tang. 2002. Categorization of humans in biomedical research: Genes, race and disease. *Genome Biology.* http://genomebiology.com/2002/3/7/comment/2007.

Satel, S. L. 2002. I am a racially profiling doctor. *New York Times Magazine,* May 5.

Shields, A., M. Fortun, E. M. Hammonds, P. A. King, C. Lerman, R. Rapp, and P. F. Sullivan. 2005. The use of race variables in genetic studies of complex traits and the goal of reducing health disparities. *American Psychologist* 60:77–103.

Wade, N. 2007. Researchers detect variations in DNA that underlie seven common diseases. *New York Times,* June 7.

Caring

9 Use of Racial and Ethnic Identity in Medical Evaluations and Treatments

Jay S. Kaufman and Richard S. Cooper

The "evidenced based medicine" movement is premised on the transformation of clinical practice from a loose collection of traditions and opaque judgments into a modern science. The defining notions of a science in this context are that it should be based on systematic observation and experiment and that it should be self-correcting in the sense that conventions and beliefs are open to scrutiny and revision. Whereas medicine was once comfortably thought of as a somewhat mysterious application of the healing arts, the last half of the twentieth century saw an energetic movement toward placing medical practice within the realm of rational assessment and quantitative evaluation. Under this paradigm, it is no longer enough to apply a diagnostic test or surgical technique because of habit, tradition, or opinion. The promise of evidence-based medicine is therefore one in which the tyranny of professional judgment is replaced by the transparent authority of the data. While this movement has not been without its critics and controversies, there is no doubt that scientific principles and quantitative techniques have revolutionized modern medicine in our lifetime and have exposed many outdated medical myths and irrational practices to the bright light of critical evaluation (Sox et al. 2007; Sackett et al. 2000).

Despite the successes of this ongoing revolution, many holdovers from the nineteenth-century world are still very much a part of contemporary medical thinking, and perhaps none has proven more difficult to exorcise than the tenacious habits of racialized medicine. Although race has been thoroughly discredited as a meaningful biologic subdivision of humanity (Collins 2004; Torres and Kittles 2007), it is still a recurring and common quantity in medical training and practice. Despite grandiose twenty-first-century pronouncements of the declining significance of race and the emergence of a postracial society, it is still unremarkable to hear clinical cases presented on the basis of age, race, and sex for conditions that have no presumed relationship to racial identity, even if it were a valid descriptor in some sociological, if not biological, sense (Finucane and Carrese 1990; Caldwell and Popenoe 1995; Garcia 2004). Moreover, the tradition of racialized medicine has been vigorously defended by some (Satel 2002), although many of the specific claims and assertions in these defenses have yet to be evaluated systematically or quantitatively. It is the purpose of this chapter, therefore, to outline a strategy for considering an evidentiary basis for when it would be rational and appropriate to include race as a consideration in medical evaluations and treatments.

Far from waning in the age of molecular genetics, race has been resurgent in biomedical discourse, especially in relation to a torrent of new interest in human biological variation and its quantification (Risch et al. 2002). There is little doubt that novel methodologies have ushered in a new era in our understanding of human evolution and variability, but the translation of this knowledge into sound clinical practice is what has gotten bogged down in a combination of old habits, reinvigorated superstitions, and outrageous promises. There are now not only race-specific guidelines for choice and dosage of existing therapies (Williams et al. 2004), for example, but even the advent of a wholly race-specific therapy (Sankar and Kahn 2005), with the promise of more on the way (Kahn 2007). The strange case of BiDil is exactly the kind of situation that clarifies why a methodically reasoned strategy is needed to assess such claims. Briefly, BiDil is a drug that was approved by the U.S. Food and Drug Administration (FDA) in June 2005 for treatment of heart failure in self-identified African Americans, on the basis of a successful randomized trial that recruited only self-identified African Americans (Taylor et al. 2004). Thus no formal claim of a race-specific effect was considered, and yet the therapy is labeled for use in only a single racial group. Clearly a systematic and sober approach to medical policy and practice regarding the use of race is, by now, long overdue. In this chapter, we attempt to outline what such an approach might look like, in broad terms, by working through a few simple examples and explaining the underlying logic employed.

Medical Decision Making

Medical decision making involves judgments under conditions of uncertainty and is therefore a naturally Bayesian exercise. To briefly explain the Bayesian paradigm, it is useful to contrast this with the frequentist paradigm that motivates much of the statistical analysis of data in contemporary biomedical sciences. The frequentist paradigm defines random variation as arising from the behavior of many repeated trials; for example, to say that a coin has a probability of landing on heads that is equal to 0.5 is a reference to the long-run proportion of heads over many repeated, identical flips. Frequentism is a natural paradigm for considering the behavior of a trial, such as a coin flipped many times, or the aggregate behavior of many electrons as they jump between energy shells around an atom. A weakness of frequentism, however, is that it cannot assign a probability to a single unrepeated event, such as the probability that average world average temperature will rise by five degrees within the next decade.

In the Bayesian statistical philosophy, however, probabilities are not proportions of repeated trials, but rather, statements of belief. A Bayesian begins with a prior probability distribution, which reflects some existing knowledge or belief. Then, in light of new data observed, the prior distribution is updated to form a new distribution, which is referred to as the posterior distribution. In this way, the Bayesian paradigm involves constantly changing one's degree of belief in light of new observations. This is exactly what should happen in the practice of clinical medicine (Weinstein and Fineberg 1980).

To make a diagnosis, prognosis, or decision regarding a potential medical intervention, a physician begins with prior knowledge. For example, when making a diagnosis, the prior probability distribution might be the frequency of the hypothesized disease in the source population. When seeing a patient with high fever in Africa, a physician might therefore assign a high prior probability to malaria as the underlying condition. The same encounter in the United States would instead assign a low prior probability to malaria, however, because the disease is rare in that setting. Next, the physician makes observations, for example, in the form of diagnostic tests, taking of history, and physical examination of signs and symptoms. These observed data serve to shift the clinician's prior beliefs, either toward confirmation or rejection of the original hypothesis. For example, observation of massive splenomegaly might move the physician much closer to certainty about the diagnosis of malaria. The goal of the exercise is to move close enough to certainty on either end of the belief spectrum that one can make a medical decision about the best course of action (figure 9.1).

It is not simple to state how close to one of the limits of certainty one must be to take some specific action, as this is a function of costs, risks, and patient's values. But the algebra for updating prior probabilities with the results of new observations can be quite straightforward, especially in the case of binary observations such as a positive or negative result for a diagnostic test. In that case, the basic formula is simply that posterior odds (O_2) is equal to prior odds (O_1) multiplied by the likelihood ratio of the test result (LR+ or LR–). The prior and posterior odds are simply $p/(1 - p)$, where p is the probability of the event of interest. For example, if prevalence of malaria is 20 percent, then $O_1 = 0.20/0.80 = 1/4$. For the result of a positive diagnostic test, the likelihood ratio positive LR+ is equal to the ratio of two conditional probabilities: the probability of a positive test result among those who truly have disease divided by the probability of a positive test result among those who truly do not have disease; that is, $\Pr(T+|D+)/\Pr(T+|D-)$, where the notation $\Pr(A|B)$ refers to the conditional probability of event A given event B. The definition of the likelihood ratio negative LR– is the similar ratio for that test result: $\Pr(T-|D+)/\Pr(T-|D-)$. This is all the algebra one needs to ask the simple question, how much does a given observed test result move us toward some degree of certainty? For example, if prevalence of malaria is 20 percent and splenomegaly has a LR+ = 5, then the observation of this symptom has the effect

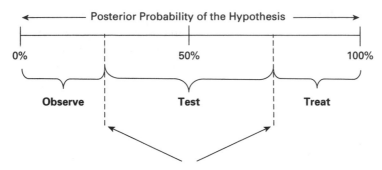

Figure 9.1

Posterior probability of the hypothesis. The posterior probability guides subsequent action. If the patient is nearly certain to have the disease, the clinician will initiate treatment. If the patient is nearly certain not to have the disease, the clinician will reevaluate at some future time. If the probability is somewhere in the middle of this range from 0 to 1, then the clinician must make further tests or observations until the posterior probability is pushed to one side or the other.

of changing one's rational assessment of the probability of malaria from $O_1 = 1/4$ to $O_1 \times$ LR+ $= 1/4 \times 5 = 1.25$. Therefore the posterior (i.e., updated) probability is now $1.25/2.25 = 0.56$. In light of the new evidence, the possibility of malaria is more likely than not, but the important feature to note is the role of the prior probability. If the same diagnostic test result were obtained in a low-prevalence setting, say, with prior probability of only 5 percent, then the posterior probability by the same calculation would be only 21 percent.

An Example: Screening for Sickle-Cell Trait

We now consider a simple example to show how this quantitative evaluation of evidence plays out when considering race as a possible determinant of medical diagnosis, prognosis, or treatment. The example revolves around screening newborn infants for sickle-cell trait, a condition that many would consider a paradigmatically racial trait (Wailoo 2001). Newborn children face a battery of screening tests, and so it is important to ask whether there are readily observable characteristics that might rule the newborn in or out for a particular screening test. For example, we do not routinely screen men for breast cancer, even though breast cancer does occasionally occur in men. Given the much lower occurrence of sickle-cell trait in nonblack infants, it was often proposed that screening be race-specific (Aspinall, Dyson, and Anionwu 2003).

We can therefore apply the logic outlined previously to evaluate such a proposal more formally.

The prior probability of sickle-cell trait for a black infant is more than tenfold higher than the corresponding probability for a white infant. Various surveys have estimated the prevalence of sickle-cell trait in the United States to be about 250 per 100,000 population in self-identified whites, and in the range of 6,500 to 7,000 per 100,000 population in self-identified blacks. Hispanics fall between these two values, with estimates around 500 per 100,000 population in the western United States and 3,000 per 100,000 population in the eastern United States. Asian and Native American populations have prevalences lower than whites, with estimates in the range of 100 to 200 per 100,000 population (Agency for Health Care Policy and Research 1993, Table 2). This might, at first, seem to favor the idea that race provides important information about the likelihood of uncovering a child with sickle-cell trait using a screening test, but it is instructive to subject the relevant numbers to the algebra described in the previous section before jumping to conclusions.

There were over 4 million children born in the United States in 2004, of which 2,304,181 were classified as "white, non-Hispanic" and 576,105 were classified as "black, non-Hispanic" (National Center for Health Statistics 2005). Using the sickle-cell trait proportions given earlier, this leads to 5,760 and 38,887 white and black births with sickle-cell trait in 2004, respectively. The calculation for the value of the likelihood ratio for white race is therefore $(5,760/44,648)/(2,298,421/2,835,638) = 0.16$. The corresponding likelihood ratio for black race is $(38,887/44,648)/(537,218/2,835,638) = 4.6$. We can now use these numbers to update the predictive probability of a newborn having sickle-cell trait, once we are able to observe and take account of the infant's race. The prior probability, before any race information is considered, is 0.0155 (i.e., between one and two cases per one hundred live births), so the prior odds is $0.0155/0.9845 = 0.0157$. Suppose that we observe that the birth certificate records a child's race as black, and we take account of this information to help decide if this child should be screened. The formula is $O_1 \times LR_B = O_2$, which, in this scenario, leads to $0.0157 \times 4.6 = 0.0722$. Converting back from odds to probability, we obtain the posterior probability as $0.0722/1.0722 = 0.0673$ (figure 9.2). To summarize, we began with an estimated probability for a newborn to have sickle-cell trait of about 1.5 percent, but taking into account that the child's race is categorized as black, we have updated that probability to 6.7 percent. While this increases the probability by over fourfold, it remains a relatively small probability. It would be difficult to specify costs and benefits of the screening program in such a way that it would be worthwhile to screen children with a 6.7 percent risk, but not children with a 1.5 percent risk.

What is more often considered, however, is ruling out the white infants. Similar calculations lead to a posterior odds of $0.0157 \times 0.16 = 0.0025$, which, converted to a probability, equals $0.0025/1.0025 = 0.0025$. Therefore, taking into account that the child's race is categorized as white, we have updated the probability from 1.5 percent to 0.25 percent. While this decreases the probability by about sixfold, the prior and posterior probabilities are both consistently small. If, under some cost and benefit structure, it is not worthwhile to screen children with an outcome probability of 0.25 percent, then it is probably not worth screening those with an outcome probability of 1.5 percent, either.

The overall conclusion here is that the use of racial information moves the initial probability a considerable distance in relative terms but a miniscule distance in absolute terms. For medical or public health treatment or policy decisions, therefore, the large prevalence difference in the population actually translates to a rather negligible quantity of information for making decisions about what to do with an individual. It is not surprising, therefore, that this conclusion was reached by an evidence review at the Agency for Health Care Policy and Research (AHCPR) in 1993. An expert panel reviewed similar information available at the time on prevalence of sickle-cell trait in the U.S. population by race and ethnic origin, to advise state screening programs (many of which had implemented race-specific targeting in their sickle-cell screening programs). In light of the limited information conveyed by race and ethnicity in this setting, however, and the high cost associated with missing a true case, the panel rec-

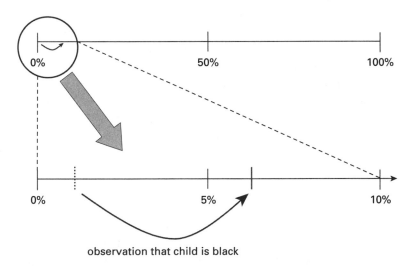

observation that child is black

Figure 9.2
Updating probability for a black child. When trying to decide whether to screen a child after observing that his or her race is black, the probability shifts in light of race only on the far left-hand side of the probability range. This is magnified in the lower panel to show more clearly that the prior probability is 0.0155 and the posterior probability is 0.0673. While considering race increases the probability by over fourfold, it remains close to zero with or without accounting for this factor.

ommended universal screening of all newborns, regardless of racial or ethnic background, a recommendation that has now been implemented in all U.S. states (Agency for Health Care Policy and Research 1993).

Another Example: Choice of Initial Antihypertensive Therapy

Angiotensin-converting enzyme (ACE) inhibitors are a common first- or second-line antihypertensive therapy and have been widely and successfully used for this purpose for several decades. These drugs act on the renin-angiotensin system, which is the body's natural mechanism for raising blood pressure, by preventing the conversion of angiotensin I into angiotensin II. It is widely believed that ACE inhibition (along with other antihypertensive therapies that target the renin-angiotensin system) is less effective for black patients than for white patients, and this disparity in therapeutic efficacy is now described in virtually every hypertension textbook and set of clinical guidelines. For example, the "Seventh Report of the Joint National Committee on Prevention, Detection, Evaluation, and Treatment of High Blood Pressure" (JNC 7) represents the state of clinical knowledge on hypertension treatment in the United States (Chobanian et al. 2003). Although the document recommends first-line treatment with thiazide-type diuretics for all demographic groups, it also notes, under the heading "Other Special Situations," that "monotherapy with BBs, ACEIs, or ARBs lowers BP to a somewhat lesser degree in African Americans than Whites" (National Heart Lung and Blood Institute 2004, 39).

British Hypertension Society guidelines take a more extreme position with respect to this racial distinction, however, stating that blacks and those older than fifty-five years of age should have first-line treatment with calcium-channel blockers or thiazide-type diuretics, whereas whites and those under fifty-five years of age should be treated first with ACE inhibitors, angiotensin receptor blockers, or beta-blockers (Williams et al. 2004). The authors explain this differentiation by noting that hypertension can be classified into etiologic subtypes that are high renin or low renin, and that antihypertensive drugs that inhibit the renin-angiotensin system, such as ACE inhibitors, are less effective in low-renin hypertensives. They note that studies measuring plasma renin levels have reported that younger people and Caucasians have higher renin levels than do older people or blacks (which they define as people "of African descent"). This logic seems curious because the cited studies on plasma renin concentrations also indicate that such measures are not effective at predicting subsequent blood pressure response to treatment (Sagnella 2001).

Nonetheless, the guidelines are consistent with common medical wisdom, and similar recommendations can be found in innumerable textbooks and review articles. Gibbs, Beevers, and Lip (1999, 187), for example, note that "diuretics and calcium antagonists are suitable first-line agents in black hypertensives, whilst beta-blockers and the ACE inhibitors tend to be less effective at lowering blood pressure, due to the low renin state in these patients." Likewise, a comprehensive review of treatment recommendations by Douglas et al. (2003, 534) noted that ACE inhibitors had "some evidence of less blood pressure lowering efficacy in African American versus white patients." Moreover, these treatment recommendations are also reflected in drug package insert information. The ACE inhibitor trandolapril, for example, is marketed under the brand name "Mavik," and its package insert states that "recommended initial dosage of MAVIK for patients not receiving a diuretic is 1 mg once daily in non-black patients and 2 mg in black patients" (Abbott Laboratories 2003). The FDA announced, in 2003, that it had begun to ask drug manufacturers to report the race and ethnicity of all trial participants. In justifying this new requirement, the FDA noted several examples of race effects on drug treatment response, including the statement that "black people . . . have a poorer response than white people to beta blockers and angiotensin converting enzyme inhibitors" (Josefson 2003, 244).

We sought to evaluate the quantitative basis for differential treatment of hypertension by race, using published studies of blood pressure treatment responses to ACE inhibitors. Relevant studies were sought through PubMed MeSH (Medical Subject Heading) searches, and additional articles were found by reviewing the reference lists of the articles identified. In searching for studies using electronic databases of published reports, the following MeSH terms were used: "Angiotensin-Converting Enzyme Inhibitors," "African Continental Ancestry Group," and "European Continental Ancestry Group." In addition to these terms, we asked PubMed to identify only those articles that were in English and published in 1990 and onward. Two hundred twenty-two articles were initially identified. The search was last updated December 31, 2007. Studies were excluded if they were not randomized, if they involved children, or if they did not provide race-specific changes in systolic or diastolic blood pressure or the standard deviations of these changes. Studies were also excluded if multiple antihypertensive drugs were given at the same time or if information was not available for both blacks and whites. Of the 222 articles found, 19 met the inclusion criteria, and a total of 12 groups were available with all data necessary for conducting a meta-analysis of blood pressure treatment responses (Cushman et al. 2000; Exner et al. 2001; Materson et al. 1993; Mokwe et al. 2004; Moran et al. 2007; Weir and Lavin 1992; Weir et al. 1995; Wright et al. 2005). Some articles provided more than one group for analysis by subsetting the analysis on a study characteristic (e.g., urban vs. rural).

A random-effects meta-analysis of the existing studies was conducted using the STATA 9.0 statistical software package (Stata Coporation, College Station, Texas) and examining systolic and diastolic blood pressure responses. For simplicity, only results for systolic blood pressure are reported here. The presence of heterogeneity was assessed by examining the p value of Cochran's Q statistic, and there was no substantial heterogeneity detected in these study effects beyond what would be expected by chance. The summary systolic blood pressure reduction difference between racial groups across these studies was estimated to be 4.14 mmHg, with a 95 percent confidence interval of 3.13 to 5.16 mmHg (figure 9.3). This value is largely consistent with the existing consensus in the literature, as described previously. Most large studies showed values that were very similar to this estimate, including the recently conducted ALLHAT trial (Wright et al. 2005).

Nonetheless, while the difference in population means was statistically significant in this summary over a large number of patients and studies, it was small compared to the within–racial group variability observed. Whites had a mean systolic decline in response to treatment of 10.7 mmHg (95% CI: 8.2, 13.3 mmHg), but the standard deviation of this value was 12.1 (95% CI: 8.9, 15.3 mmHg). Since these values have a roughly Gaussian (i.e., normal) probability distribution, this latter number indicates that about two-thirds of systolic blood pressure change values for whites obtained from a random sample would fall between –1.4 and 22.8 mmHg (i.e., ±1 standard deviation). For blacks, the mean systolic response was 6.8 mmHg (95% CI: 4.2, 9.4 mmHg), whereas the standard deviation for change in this group was estimated to be

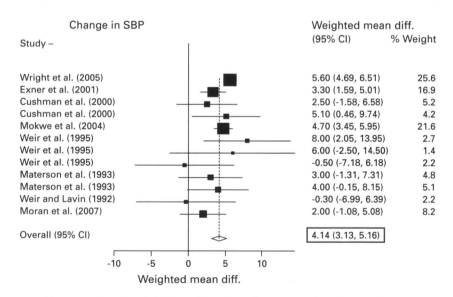

Heterogeneity χ^2 = 16.9 (df = 11); p = 0.11. Between-study variance τ^2 = 0.84

Figure 9.3
White-black systolic blood pressure reduction. In a formal meta-analysis of all available studies that met the stated inclusion criteria, the summary white-black difference in response to angiotensin-converting enzyme (ACE) inhibitor monotherapy was 4.14 mmHg (shown as a diamond at the bottom of the figure). Studies were judged to be sufficiently homogeneous to pool in this way.

14.5 mmHg (95% CI: 10.7, 18.4 mmHg). Thus racial differences are quite small compared with the variation within each racial group (figure 9.4). This implies that knowing to which group a patient belongs tells a clinician little about the patient's individual response to treatment (Sehgal 2004, Nguyen et al 2009). As an analogy, consider that the mean height of men is significantly greater than the mean height of women, yet knowing the gender of a person helps very little in trying to estimate his or her individual height.

We can now translate these numbers into their potential impact on rational clinical decision making. If a clinician wanted, for example, a 10-mmHg systolic blood pressure decline in a white patient, the probability of achieving this decline would be obtained by integrating the Gaussian probability distribution function in figure 9.4 from $-\infty$ to 10, which yields a cumulative probability of about 52 percent. The same calculation for a black patient yields about 41 percent, giving a relative probability of success at this cutoff point roughly equal to 1.27. Repeating this calculation at every possible desired blood pressure decrement shows that the ratio reaches its maximum for a desired decline of about 20 to 25 mmHg, with a relative likelihood of success (favoring whites) of around 1.35. One could also compare densities instead of cumulative probabilities at each point, but the conclusion is approximately the same: a rela-

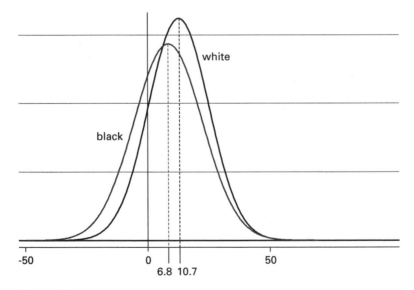

Figure 9.4
Systolic blood pressure reduction. Distributions of blood pressure response (in mmHg) for white and black adults receiving ACE inhibitor monotherapy are almost entirely overlapping. The means of the distributions may be "significantly" different, but knowing an individual's race tells one almost nothing about what that individual's blood pressure response will be.

tive benefit for whites in blood pressure reduction of as much as 30 percent to 40 percent. This relative benefit is also a likelihood ratio (i.e., the likelihood of successfully obtaining a desired systolic decline in whites relative to the likelihood in blacks). With a maximum value of less than 1.5, however, it is a very modest likelihood ratio in comparison with most clinical observations and diagnostic tests. A successful clinical indicator would separate the distributions of responders and nonresponders so that the clinician would have a high or low posterior probability that the patient would benefit from the treatment. It can be readily seen in figure 9.4, however, that at any desired blood pressure decline, there are many patients of each race group on either side of the cutoff point.

A substantial body of literature in medicine and epidemiology revolves around the large likelihood ratios necessary for individual inference in screening, diagnosis, or prognosis (Wald, Hackshaw, and Frost 1999; Pepe et al. 2004). For example, Pepe and colleagues note that if a potential marker (such as white race) misclassifies 10 percent of nonresponders as responders, the relative odds of successful response between whites and blacks is 3 (i.e., almost twice as large as the value in the case of ACE inhibition). This racial classifier can therefore identify only about 25 percent of the true responders; that is, 75 percent of the true responders are not going to be treated. Alternatively, if a marker of treatment susceptibility (such as white race) with a relative odds of 3 between whites and blacks can correctly classify 80 percent of the true responders, then it must mislabel almost 60 percent of the nonresponders as also being responders. Clearly this marker is not useful for individual-level prediction (Pepe et al. 2004).

Suppose a clinician had one hundred black and one hundred white patients and gave ACE inhibition only to the white patients. As shown previously, with respect to the values from our meta-analysis and a desired 10-mmHg decline in systolic blood pressure, the associated relative odds would be $(52 \times 59)/(41 \times 48) = 1.6$. So with respect to this 10-mmHg fall in systolic blood pressure, forty-eight of the white patients would fail to achieve the target blood pressure, and forty-one of the black patients would have achieved target blood pressure had they been given the drug, but instead, they were denied it. Therefore $(41 + 48)/200 = 89/200 = 45$ percent of the patients have been given the wrong treatment. From the point of view of any individual patient, this is not meaningfully better than being assigned by the flip of a coin.

Discussion

We have reviewed the basic notions of clinical decision making to assess how one would rationally decide when it might be appropriate to use racial identity as a clinical indicator. In a simple example involving screening for sickle-cell trait, we reviewed the logic that was used in recommending universal screening, which is now widely adopted. In a second example, we examined a setting in which therapy is generally assigned on the basis of racial group in contemporary medical practice, and we showed that this current consensus does not appear to be well justified as a rational strategy. A reasonable critique of this second example, however, is that we showed only that the benefit associated with considering racial group is very small. If there is no cost to considering race, then any benefit, even a tiny one, could be considered to be better. After all, why not have a 52 percent chance of success, instead of a 41 percent chance? If an expensive or invasive test provided this benefit, it would be easy to show that the cost outweighs the benefit, but in the case of observed racial identity, the classification is made at no expense of time or materials. So why not make this observation and use that information?

The answer lies in the true costs of racial classification that arise from stereotyping. Racial groups are defined in terms of social and cultural affiliations and therefore are naturally imbued with the associations gleaned from everyday life in American society. This makes them a poor choice for serving as biomedical quantities because they naturally suggest to the clinician the patterns of traits and characteristics that are linked in the popular imagination to the group, even when these are inaccurate. For example, a 2006 study published in the *American Journal of Cardiology* found that black patients admitted with congestive heart failure at Grady Memorial Hospital in Atlanta, Georgia, were undertreated with beta-blockers, the current standard of care. The authors recommended more careful attention to current treatment guidelines (Ilksoy et al. 2006). A letter published subsequently in the journal by a clinician at George Washington University Medical Center argued against this recommendation, however, on the grounds that black patients would not take these medications, even if they were prescribed (Cheng 2006, 568): "African-American patients seem to be far less compliant with β blockers than diuretics due to the side effects of the former causing sexual impotence and weakness," he wrote. "A medicine is only good if the patient takes it as prescribed." The letter contains several citations on other points but fails to identify any previous literature that might support this claim of differential noncompliance for beta-blockers because blacks have greater concern about sexual function than other groups. It appears that the author found this point so self-evident that no supporting documentation was necessary.

Another cost associated with the use of racial classifications in medicine is when real differences that exist between groups are exaggerated in the calculations because they are treated like categorical distinctions. An anecdote of this type is provided by pediatrician Richard Garcia concerning a childhood friend who failed repeatedly to receive a correct diagnosis of cystic fibrosis until she was eight years old (Garcia 2004). Despite constant medical attention for pneumonia and other telltale symptoms, clinicians were unable to make the diagnosis of cystic fibrosis because she was black, and this observation was considered to be a counterindication. Garcia asserts that had she been recognized as white, or even if she had been viewed as having no obvious racial identity of any kind, she would have been diagnosed immediately. Indeed, it was only when a radiologist, who had never seen her face-to-face, happened to see her chest X-ray that a correct diagnosis was made immediately. The problem in such circumstances is not that race can never be relevant for making diagnoses or other medical decisions—in fact, the prevalence of cystic fibrosis is indeed different in blacks and whites; rather, the potentially useful information conveyed by racial identity is simply much less than or much different than is commonly held, which puts many minority patients at a considerable disadvantage. The clinicians in Garcia's example, having learned that the prevalence of cystic fibrosis was lower in blacks, were acting as though the prevalence was therefore zero.

Moving beyond anecdotes like these, the overwhelming scientific evidence now suggests that these kinds of stereotypes and categorical elisions are commonplace in medical practice when it comes to clinicians trying to divine some information from patients' race (Smedley, Stith, and Nelson 2002). Various experimental trials have documented, under controlled conditions, the irrational and inappropriate use of racial identity in medical decision making. For example, Loring and Powell (1988) constructed dummy psychiatric case presentations that were intended to represent undifferentiated schizophrenia and labeled these with one of four race-sex combinations (black or white and male or female). The profiles were then assigned a diagnosis by psychiatrists, who returned questionnaires through the mail, with predictable results. Black patients, especially black men, were much more likely to be assigned the diagnosis of paranoid schizophrenia, indicating that clinicians perceived in these descriptions greater degrees of violence, suspiciousness, and dangerousness than for the identical white patients.

In a similar experimental design, Schulman and colleagues (1999) examined how often doctors recommended cardiac catheterization for hypothetical patients with chest pain. Physicians attending professional meetings were shown a videotaped interview with a "patient" (one of eight actors representing different combinations of race and gender) and were asked whether they would recommend catheterization. In addition to a significantly lower referral rate for black women, the authors reported significant differences by race and gender in the physicians' assessments of the patients' degree of hostility, negative affect, and socioeconomic status. Physicians also rated black patients as less likely to report symptoms, less likely to sue, and less likely to comply with treatment—all despite identical scripts read by the actors. The belief that minority patients are less likely to adhere to medication regimens or follow medical advice appears to be widely held, despite ambiguous evidence (Daniels, René, and Daniels 1994), and is used to justify undertreatment, as in the example of the heart failure treatment anecdote cited earlier. Beliefs that minority patients are less compliant or communicative leads to differential treatment that underserves these patients by treating them closer to the presumed mean for their group. If the physician holds irrational beliefs about the group, this mean value may additionally be misspecified. But even in the best-case scenario, that the physician uses valid information about the "typical" patient from the relevant group, treating the patient more on the basis of this mean value, instead of the values obtained from the individual patient, will still create a systematic disadvantage for minority patients (Balsa and McGuire 2003).

We have argued thus far that there are rational ways to consider the amount of useful information contained in racial identifiers, and that race is used in medicine in many instances when it offers no substantial benefit and, furthermore, risks substantial harm. Given the fact that most biologic traits are largely, if not entirely, overlapping, as in the example of blood pressure response to ACE inhibition in the example given previously, we would hypothesize that justifiable uses of race in medical decision making will be rare. This leads to the natural question, however, about the scenarios in which it is likely to be useful. Although most biological variability is within group, rather than between group, for any subclassification of human beings by race or ethnicity, this is not true of social variability. While there are, for example, many tall and short individuals in every population, one could not say the same about social traits such as speaking Mandarin or eating tortillas. When disease arises from social behaviors that are highly patterned by ethnic group, racial or ethnic identity can be highly informative. Dietary examples are obvious, but social affiliations also matter for a variety of other conditions for which the use of race could be informative, even if controversial.

An example would be sexually transmitted diseases (STDs), where risk is a function not only of unsafe behaviors, but also of one's contact group (Aral 2000). Race is a major determinant of sexual contact patterns because of its overarching social significance. Indeed, sexual contact across racial lines only recently became legal in sixteen of the U.S. states after the 1967 Supreme Court decision of *Loving v. Virginia* (Hollinger 2003), and interracial marriages still accounted for only about 5 percent of registered unions in the 2000 U.S. census (U.S. Bureau of the Census 2000).[1] Given this situation of highly assortative sexual contact, it is not surprising that rates of many sexually transmitted infections vary dramatically by racial group. Prevalence of chlamydia among U.S. blacks is roughly eight times higher than the rate among whites, for example, whereas for gonorrhea, the prevalence is roughly nineteen times higher. Syphilis is seven times higher in blacks, which marks a decline from 1999, when the prevalence was twenty-nine times higher (Centers for Disease Control and Prevention 2009).

The origins of this dramatic prevalence disparity are rooted in a wide variety of long-standing social inequalities, from differential access to medical care to enormously unequal rates of incarceration. Once this pattern was established, however, it was mostly endogamous partnership formation that operated to maintain such huge prevalence differences in STDs by race. Given such profound differences, reflecting the dominant role that race plays in U.S. society for social affiliations and residential patterns, it is not surprising that racial identity can play a legitimate (albeit uncomfortable) role in medical decision making around issues such as population screening for STDs.

For example, Stein et al. (2008) considered community-based testing for chlamydial infection in young adults under resource constraints. They found that using a small number of demographic characteristics as indications for screening, they could identify approximately 80 percent of infections, while testing less than half the population. However, the algorithm requires the use of racial identity because this variable is so highly predictive of infection. The reason that race turns out to be useful in this circumstance, but not in the earlier example of screening for sickle-cell trait, is also due, in part, to the higher absolute prevalence of chlamydia in the population when restricted by age and to the existence of other predictive covariates (e.g., number of sex partners in the last year), which led to even higher conditional probabilities. For ethical reasons, it may or may not be appropriate to use racial identity in this way. Nonetheless, with respect to the simple quantitative question of when race provides enough information to be of practical value, examples such as this one demonstrate that is more likely to occur when social recognition of race is a central etiologic factor.

Summary and Conclusion

It is well known that racial classification as practiced in Western society is only trivially correlated with genetic variability (Tishkoff and Kidd 2004). It is therefore unsurprising that biologic traits relevant for medical decision making tend to be largely overlapping across racial groups and that race is thus largely uninformative in diagnosis, prognosis, and treatment. Nonetheless, epidemiology and biostatistics provide a formal language for describing the quantity of information contained in a test or observation and a simple calculus for comparing a degree of belief before and after the introduction of this new information.

We have shown that even when the amount of information conveyed by race appears substantial, as in the case of sickle-cell trait, the use of this variable as a predictive tool may not be warranted. In a second example, involving antihypertensive treatment with ACE inhibition, we showed that although there is a reliably measurable difference in blood pressure response to the medication between racial groups, this difference is too small to be applied clinically to decisions involving an individual patient. Finally, after reviewing the limited benefits associated with use of race in medicine, we considered some of the costs in terms of stereotyping and the tendency to misapply quantitative differences between groups as though they were categorical differences.

These considerations do not necessarily rule out the possibility of a thoughtful and appropriate use of race in medical care. As we suggested, when the disease of interest is etiologically related to social affiliations and environments, then race can be recognized as a real and consequential part of a patient's history and circumstances, with important implications for a wide range of experiences and exposures (Bhopal 2007). The existing track record for appropriate consideration of race in medicine is not very encouraging thus far, and one may doubt whether a social variable with such profound historical connotations can ever be used dispassionately, without invoking all the irrational debris of its sordid use as an instrument of social oppression. Nonetheless, the standard for twenty-first-century medicine is clear. Medical uses of racial classification should be viewed suspiciously, until they are justified with appropriately compelling theory and data. The traditional practice of using racially descriptive labels for patients, for example, should be reconsidered and, if found irrelevant, abandoned. Just as race-specific screening for sickle-cell trait was examined carefully and abandoned as ultimately unwarranted, so, too, should racialized guidelines for hypertension treatment, such as those of the British Hypertension Society, be abandoned, unless or until it can be shown that such recommendations provide a real benefit for patients and clinicians. The very first step as regards the use of such classifications would simply be to do no harm.

Notes

This work was supported in part by a Robert Wood Johnson Foundation Investigator Award in Health Policy Research. The views expressed imply no endorsement by the Robert Wood Johnson Foundation. Additional support was received from the University of North Carolina Center for Genomics and Society through a grant from the National Human Genome Research Institute (P50-HG004488-01). We thank Thu Nguyen, MSPH, for research assistance in the meta-analysis of ACE inhibition studies.

1. Population genetic analyses demonstrate that although the African American population is approximately 20% admixed with European ancestry, this gene flow occurred almost entirely from male Europeans during the institution of slavery (Parra et al. 1998).

References

Abbott Laboratories. 2003. Patient information for MAVIK. Reference 03-5264-R2. http://www .rxabbott.com/pdf/mavik.pdf.

Agency for Health Care Policy and Research. 1993. Sickle cell disease screening, diagnosis, management, and counseling in newborns and infants: Clinical Practice Guideline number 6. AHCPR Publication 93-0562. http://www.ncbi.nlm.nih.gov/books/bv.fcgi?rid=hstat6.section.17018.

Aral, S. O. 2000. Behavioral aspects of sexually transmitted diseases: Core groups and bridge populations. *Sexually Transmitted Diseases* 27:327–328.

Aspinall, P. J., S. M. Dyson, and E. N. Anionwu. 2003. The feasibility of using ethnicity as a primary tool for antenatal selective screening for sickle cell disorders: Pointers from the research evidence. *Social Science and Medicine* 56:285–297.

Balsa, A. I., and T. G. McGuire. 2003. Prejudice, clinical uncertainty and stereotyping as sources of health disparities. *Journal of Health Economics* 22:89–116.

Bhopal, R. 2007. *Ethnicity, race, and health in multicultural societies: Foundations for better epidemiology, public health, and health care.* Oxford: Oxford University Press.

Caldwell, S. H., and R. Popenoe. 1995. Perceptions and misperceptions of skin color. *Annals of Internal Medicine* 122:614–617.

Centers for Disease Control and Prevention. 2009. Trends in reportable sexually transmitted diseases in the United States, 2007. National Surveillance Data for Chlamydia, Gonorrhea, and Syphilis. http://www.cdc.gov/STD/stats07/trends.pdf.

Cheng, T. O. 2006. Beta blockers versus diuretics for congestive heart failure in African-American patients. *American Journal of Cardiology* 98:568.

Chobanian, A. V., et al. 2003. The seventh report of the Joint National Committee on Prevention, Detection, Evaluation, and Treatment of High Blood Pressure: The JNC 7 report. *Journal of the American Medical Association* 289:2560–2572.

Collins, F. S. 2004. What we do and don't know about "race," "ethnicity," genetics and health at the dawn of the genome era. *Nature Genetics* 36:S13–S15.

Cushman, W. C., et al. 2000. Regional and racial differences in response to antihypertensive medication use in a randomized controlled trial of men with hypertension in the United States. Department of Veterans Affairs Cooperative Study Group on Antihypertensive Agents. *Archives of Internal Medicine* 160:825–831.

Daniels, D. E., A. A. René, and V. R. Daniels. 1994. Race: An explanation of patient compliance—fact or fiction? *Journal of the National Medical Association* 86:20–25.

Douglas, J. G., et al. 2003. Management of high blood pressure in African Americans: Consensus statement of the Hypertension in African Americans Working Group of the International Society on Hypertension in Blacks. *Archives of Internal Medicine* 163:525–541.

Exner, D. V., D. L. Dries, M. J. Domanski, and J. N. Cohn. 2001. Lesser response to angiotensin-converting-enzyme inhibitor therapy in black as compared with white patients with left ventricular dysfunction. *New England Journal of Medicine* 344:1351–1357.

Finucane, T. E., and J. A. Carrese. 1990. Racial bias in presentation of cases. *Journal of General Internal Medicine* 5:120–121.

Garcia, R. S. 2004. The misuse of race in medical diagnosis. *Pediatrics* 113:1394–1395.

Gibbs, C. R., D. G. Beevers, and G. Y. Lip. 1999. The management of hypertensive disease in black patients. *QJM* 92:187–192.

Hollinger, D. 2003. Amalgamation and hypodescent: The question of ethnoracial mixture in the history of the United States. *American Historical Review* 108:1363–1390.

Ilksoy, N., R. H. Moore, K. Easley, and T. A. Jacobson. 2006. Quality of care in African-American patients admitted for congestive heart failure at a university teaching hospital. *American Journal of Cardiology* 97:690–693.

Josefson, D. 2003. FDA calls for standardised racial and ethnic data. *British Medical Journal* 326:244.

Kahn, J. 2007. Race in a bottle. *Scientific American* 297:40–45.

Loring, M., and B. Powell. 1988. Gender, race, and DSM-III: A study of the objectivity of psychiatric diagnostic behavior. *Journal of Health and Social Behavior* 29:1–22.

Materson, B. J., D. J. Reda, W. C. Cushman, B. M. Massie, E. D. Freis, M. S. Kochar, R. J. Hamburger, et al. 1993. Single-drug therapy for hypertension in men. A comparison of six antihypertensive agents with placebo. The Department of Veterans Affairs Cooperative Study Group on Antihypertensive Agents. *New England Journal of Medicine* 328:914–921. Erratum, *New England Journal of Medicine* 330 (1994):1689.

Mokwe, E., S. E. Ohmit, S. A. Nasser, T. Shafi, E. Saunders, E. Crook, A. Dudley, and J. M. Flack. 2004. Determinants of blood pressure response to quinapril in black and white hypertensive patients: The Quinapril Titration Interval Management Evaluation trial. *Hypertension* 43: 1202–1207.

Moran, A., J. A. Simon, S. Shiboski, T. G. Pickering, D. Waters, J. I. Rotter, C. Lyon, and D. Nickerson, et al. 2007. Differential effects of ramipril on ambulatory blood pressure in African Americans and Caucasians. *American Journal of Hypertension* 20:884–891.

National Center for Health Statistics. 2005. Demographics and health characteristics of births. *National Vital Statistics Reports.* http://www.infoplease.com/ipa/A0763852.html.

National Heart Lung and Blood Institute. 2004. The seventh report of the Joint National Committee on Prevention, Detection, Evaluation, and Treatment of High Blood Pressure. NHLBI Report 04-5230. http://www.nhlbi.nih.gov/guidelines/hypertension/jnc7full.htm.

Nguyen, T. T., J. S. Kaufman, E.A. Whitsel, and R. S. Cooper. 2009. Racial differences in blood pressure response to calcium channel blocker monotherapy: A meta-analysis. *American Journal of Hypertension.* 22 (8): 911–917.

Parra, E. J., A. Marcini, J. Akey , J. Martinson, M. A. Batzer, R. Cooper, T. Forrester , D. B. Allison, R. Deka, R. E. Ferrell, M. D. Shriver.1998. Estimating African American admixture proportions by use of population-specific alleles. *American Journal of Human Genetics* 63:1839–1851.

Pepe, M. S., H. Janes, G. Longton, W. Leisenring, and P. Newcomb. 2004. Limitations of the odds ratio in gauging the performance of a diagnostic, prognostic, or screening marker. *American Journal of Epidemiology* 159:882–890.

Risch, N., E. Burchard, E. Ziv, and H. Tang. 2002. Categorization of humans in biomedical research: Genes, race and disease. *Genome Biology*. http://genomebiology.com/content/pdf/gb-2002-3-7-comment2007.pdf.

Sackett, D. L., S. E. Straus, W. S. Richardson, W. Rosenberg, and R. B. Haynes. 2000. *Evidence-based medicine: How to practice and teach EBM*. Edinburgh: Churchill Livingstone.

Sagnella, G. A. 2001. Why is plasma renin activity lower in populations of African origin? *Journal of Human Hypertension* 15:17–25.

Sankar, P., and J. Kahn. 2005. BiDil: Race medicine or race marketing? *Health Affairs* W5: 455–563.

Satel, S. 2002. I am a racially profiling doctor. *New York Times Magazine*, May 5.

Schulman, K. A., J. A. Berlin, W. Harless, J. F. Kerner, S. Sistrunk, B. J. Gersh, and R. Dubé, et al. 1999. The effect of race and sex on physicians' recommendations for cardiac catheterization. *New England Journal of Medicine* 340:618–626. Erratum, *New England Journal of Medicine* 340 (1999):1130.

Sehgal, A. R. 2004. Overlap between whites and blacks in response to antihypertensive drugs. *Hypertension* 43:566–572.

Smedley, B. D., A. Y. Stith, and A. R. Nelson, eds. 2002. Unequal treatment: Confronting racial and ethnic disparities in health care. Washington, DC: National Academy Press.

Sox, H. C., M. A. Blatt, M. C. Higgins, and K. I. Marton. 2007. *Medical decision making*. Philadelphia: American College of Physicians.

Stein, C. R., J. S. Kaufman, C. A. Ford, P. A. Leone, P. J. Feldblum, and W. C. Miller. 2008. Screening young adults for prevalent chlamydial infection in community settings. *Annals of Epidemiology* 18:560–571.

Taylor, A. L., S. Ziesche, C. Yancy, P. Carson, R. D'Agostino Jr., K. Ferdinand, M. Taylor, K. Adams, M. Sabolinski, M. Worcel, and J. N. Cohn; 2004. Combination of isosorbide dinitrate and hydralazine in blacks with heart failure. *New England Journal of Medicine* 351:2049–2057.

Tishkoff, S., and K. Kidd. 2004. Implications of biogeography of human populations for "race" and medicine. *Nature Genetics* 36:S21–S27.

Torres, J. B., and R. A. Kittles. 2007. The relationship between "race" and genetics in biomedical research. *Current Hypertension Reports* 9:196–201.

U.S. Bureau of the Census. 2000. U.S. census: PHC-T-19. Hispanic origin and race of coupled households: 2000. http://www.census.gov/population/cen2000/phc-t19/tab01.pdf.

Wailoo, K. 2001. *Dying in the City of the Blues: Sickle cell anemia and the politics of race and health*. Chapel Hill: University of North Carolina Press.

Wald, N. J., A. K. Hackshaw, and C. D. Frost. 1999. When can a risk factor be used as a worthwhile screening test? *British Medical Journal* 319:1562–1565.

Weinstein, M. C., and H. V. Fineberg. 1980. *Clinical decision analysis.* Philadelphia: Saunders.

Weir, M. R., J. M. Gray, R. Paster, and E. Saunders. 1995. Differing mechanisms of action of angiotensin-converting enzyme inhibition in black and white hypertensive patients. The Trandolapril Multicenter Study Group. *Hypertension* 26:124–130.

Weir, M. R., and P. T. Lavin. 1992. Comparison of the efficacy and tolerability of Prinivil and Procardia XL in black and white hypertensive patients. *Clinical Therapeutics* 14:730–739.

Williams, B., N. R. Poulter, M. J. Brown, M. Davis, G. T. McInnes, J. F. Potter, P. S. Sever, S. McG. Thom. 2004. Guidelines for management of hypertension: Report of the Fourth Working Party of the British Hypertension Society, 2004-BHS IV. *Journal of Human Hypertension* 18:139–185.

Wright, J. T. Jr., J. K. Dunn, J. A. Cutler, B. R. Davis, W. C. Cushman, C. E. Ford, and L. J. Haywood, et al. 2005. Outcomes in hypertensive black and nonblack patients treated with chlorthalidone, amlodipine, and lisinopril. *Journal of the American Medical Association* 293:1595–1608.

10   What's the Use of Culture?: Health Disparities and the Development of Culturally Competent Health Care

Angela C. Jenks

In March 2005, the governor of New Jersey signed Senate Bill 144. At the announcement ceremony, the bill's sponsor, Senator Wayne Bryant, declared that "the practice of denying critical care to patients is both immoral and unfair, and it is time to end the discrimination. This new law shows that the State is concerned with ending health care disparities, and is working to solve the issues plaguing minority patients" (Heck 2005). S144 requires that physicians receive cultural competency training as a condition for medical licensure. It is designed to ensure that New Jersey physicians learn about conditions that are prevalent among minority groups and become aware of the cultural beliefs that might affect the health care decisions their patients make.

Over the last several decades, the incorporation of culture into biomedicine has become a central aspect of the struggle against health disparities. Patient advocacy groups are demanding that greater attention be paid to the needs of culturally specific populations, and legal organizations are beginning to see the development of culturally appropriate care as essential to meeting the requirements of civil rights legislation. Most prominently, as S144 exemplifies, medical schools, clinics, and HMOs are instituting cultural competency training requirements for clinicians and other health workers.

Far from being a marginal trend in biomedicine, the push for cultural competency is becoming increasingly institutionalized. In 2000, the U.S. Department of Health and Human Services' Office of Minority Health released what have become known as the CLAS standards—a list of fourteen requirements and recommendations for the development of "Culturally and Linguistically Appropriate Services" (for the full report and discussion of the standards, see Office of Minority Health 2001). With the passage of S144, New Jersey became the first state to require some form of cultural competency training in physician education, and several other states have since passed similar legislation or have bills pending (for an overview of cultural competency legislation throughout the United States, see Graves et al. 2007). The American Medical Association and other professional organizations have issued statements of support for cultural competency, and agencies like the Joint Commission and the National Committee for Quality Assurance have included cultural competency criteria in their accreditation programs.

At the same time it is institutionalized, however, cultural competency remains an emerging field. Advocates lament the fact that there are no "best practices" that have been defined, no clear agreement on the goals of training, and little statistical evidence that cultural competency efforts actually have any effect on medical care or health disparities. What *cultural competency* even means is often unclear, and the phrase is defined in multiple and ever-shifting ways.[1] In everyday practice, cultural competency can include activities that range from the use of medical interpreters for communication with Limited English Proficient (LEP) patients to the recruitment of minority providers, the implementation of diversity education and sensitivity training programs, or the creation of ethnically specialized clinics.

The argument for cultural competency is based on the notion that contemporary biomedicine is not available to or able to meet the needs of patients who differ from the so-called mainstream of American society—particularly racial and ethnic minorities; women; lesbian, gay, bisexual, or transgendered individuals; and recent immigrants. Refusing the idea that one size fits all, advocates emphasize that to provide equal health care for everyone, distinct cultural groups must be treated differently. Culturally competent health care, they say, will improve communication between patients and providers, increase patient trust and satisfaction, and will ultimately increase the likelihood of compliance with provider recommendations (Bentacourt et al. 2003, 2005; Brach and Fraserirector 2000).

The development of cultural competency in health care raises several questions that are central to the politics of difference in the United States. What does it mean for marginalized groups to base their struggle for equal access to care on the assertion of a fundamental difference (Stepan 1998; Santiago-Irizarry 2001)? What is the culture that cultural competency refers to, and how does it intersect with other understandings of difference, including race, ethnicity, and nationality? What are the implications of identifying culture as both a problem behind, and a solution to, health disparities? This chapter draws on two years of fieldwork among cultural competency advocates to ask the question, what's the use of culture?

The culture concept has a long and complex history in both health science and anthropology and is intricately intertwined with understandings of race (Trouillot 2002; Hartigan 2005). In American anthropology, an elaboration of the culture concept was central to Boasian critiques of both race and racism (Armelagos and Van Gerven 2003; Caspari 2003; Boas 1962, 1974; Baker 1998). Culture shifted attention away from the supposedly unchangeable traits of biology toward an understanding of human differences as learned, socially patterned, and historically contingent. For many, the culturalist movement offered a "liberating alternative to racial formalism" (Tapper

1997, 268), highlighting the socially produced, rather than biologically innate, nature of racial inequality.

But, as many anthropologists have pointed out, the culture concept can also be used to subordinate and can become an instrument of social control (Dominguez 1992; Visweswaran 1998; Abu-Lughod 1991). Common sense understandings of race as a biological category have often led to the bounding and biologizing of culture in a way that can essentialize difference (Harrison 1995; Visweswaran 1998; Trouillot 2002). Culture becomes reified, "conceived as a compact, bounded, localized, and historically rooted set of traditions and values transmitted through the generations" (Stolcke 1995, 4), much as race was before it. Colonial projects have depended on the construction of a cultural Other, leading some anthropologists to "write against" the culture concept (Abu-Lughod 1991), while others seek to abandon it altogether (Trouillot 2002).

This chapter offers a critical exploration of the use of the culture concept in cultural competency work. I am not focused on identifying a "correct" approach to culture; rather, I follow Dominguez (1992, 21), who argues that "we need to move away from asking *about* culture . . . and toward asking *what is being accomplished* socially, politically, discursively when the concept of culture is invoked to describe, analyze, argue, justify, and theorize." I suggest that the use of culture in cultural competency work can decontextualize difference, drawing attention away from the power dynamics involved in health disparities and focusing it on individual personality traits. This use of culture not only blames inequality on those who differ from the norm, but runs the risk of naturalizing and reinforcing the social order, making disparities seem inevitable and masking the conditions that produce them.

Making Sense of Health Disparities

Nearly all arguments for cultural competency begin by citing the increasing diversity of the U.S. population and the significant health disparities that persist among racial and ethnic groups. Studies have demonstrated that minority groups are more likely than whites to suffer from a wide variety of diseases but are less likely to receive necessary care and less likely to have successful treatment outcomes. Disparities have been noted in cardiovascular care, cancer diagnosis and treatment, HIV infection rates and access to antiretrovirals, diabetes, mental health, and rehabilitative services (for extensive reviews of this research, see Smedley, Stith, and Nelson 2003; LaVeist 2005; Satcher and Pamies 2006).

While there has been a relative consensus on the *existence* of differential health outcomes among minority groups, the *meaning* of these data has been more controversial. Health disparities, as David S. Jones (2004, 7) has pointed out, are "never objective scientific facts. Instead, they [are] produced by social forces, interpreted through social biases, and used to perpetuate social advantage." To some observers, health disparities have proven the biological distinctiveness of racial groups and reaffirmed their "natural" hierarchy (e.g., Krieger [1987], Jones [2004], Wailoo [2001], and Byrd and Clayton [2001] give important overviews of these approaches). To others, they have reflected social, economic, and political injustices (LaVeist 2005; Smedley, Stith, and Nelson 2003; Dressler 1993). Still others have seen disparities as evidence of misbehavior and poor lifestyle choices (e.g., Satel 2000). More recently, disparities within the health care system have been understood to reflect a cultural disconnect between physicians and their patients.

This debate over the meaning of health disparities revolves around a central question: when do our measures of disparities reflect inequity, and when do they reflect other dimensions of difference? The question is significant, for, as Carter-Pokras and Baquet (2002) have pointed out, there is a moral judgment behind definitions of disparity that divide the unavoidable from the unfair, or so-called acceptable inequality from unacceptable inequity. While *disparity* is a politicized term implying unacceptable social injustice, *difference* is more neutral and is often acceptable because it is understood to be natural and unavoidable (Kahn 2005; Rathore and Krumholz 2004; Geiger 2006; Epstein 2007).

Much of the concern about this shift from *disparity* to *difference* has emerged from critiques challenging assumptions about the relationship between biology and health disparities. Notions of innate biological racial difference have historically been closely linked to understandings of health disparities in the United States. Not only have minority groups been seen as "reservoirs of disease" threatening white populations (Jones 2004), but nineteenth-century debates over slavery and the removal of Native Americans were closely tied to understandings of the relationship between race and disease (Krieger 1987; Jones 2004; Wailoo 2001; Byrd and Clayton 2001).

These ideas about biological racial difference continue to have a profound influence on how health disparities are understood. Jonathan Kahn (2005, 125), for example, in his examination of BiDil, the first ethnic drug proposed for use in the treatment of heart disease among African Americans, argues that the "appropriation of race . . . serve[s] larger political agendas aimed at transmuting health disparities rooted in social and economic inequality into mere health 'differences' rooted in biology and genetics." Steven Epstein (2007), as well, examines the use of health disparities as a rationale for the inclusion of minorities in research funded by the National Institutes of Health, arguing that his inclusion-and-difference paradigm reaffirms the biomedical significance of racial categories (see also chapter 4). The appeal and the danger of this story linking race to medical science "lies in the way in which it naturalizes the social order in a racially stratified society such as ours" (Hammonds 2006).

Asserted in opposition to race, the notion of culture is central to critiques of this naturalization of disparities. The push for cultural competency seeks to direct attention toward the social and cultural factors that prevent some populations from accessing quality medical care. Studies have documented differential treatment for African Americans, Hispanics, Native Americans, and Asian/Pacific Islanders, even after controlling for insurance status, income, education, age, gender, state and severity of disease, and the presence or absence of comorbid illness (Smedley, Stith, and Nelson 2003; Geiger 2006). Women and blacks are less likely to be referred for cardiac catheterization than men and whites (Schulman et al. 1999), and African Americans are anywhere from 41 percent to 73 percent less likely than whites to receive particular HIV/AIDS drug therapies (Mayberry et al. 1999). In a presentation on cultural competency for medical students that I attended, one physician pointed to similar data on health care disparities and asked, "If we all are giving care equally across the board as clinicians, why is it that these exist?" The persistence of disparities among even those who have health insurance and financial access to the health care system, cultural competency advocates argue, reflects very serious issues within the practice of medicine itself.

In 2003, the Institute of Medicine's (IOM) report *Unequal Treatment* (Smedley, Stith, and Nelson 2003) created a great deal of controversy when it concluded that bias, prejudice, and stereotyping on the part of health care providers may contribute to these disparities in care and outcomes. The report proposed a number of interventions, most of which can be included under definitions of cultural competency. In addition to suggesting interpretation services, patient education programs, and racial concordance between patients and physicians, the authors emphasized the importance of providing cross-cultural education to health professionals. "When sociocultural differences between patient and provider," they said, "aren't appreciated, explored, understood, or communicated in the medical encounter, the result is patient dissatisfaction, poor adherence, poorer health outcomes, and racial/ethnic disparities in care" (Smedley, Stith, and Nelson 2003, 200).

In these arguments, the deployment of the culture concept becomes a way of challenging notions of innate difference that naturalize social and political disparities and is designed to draw attention specifically to issues of racism and discrimination. The rest of this chapter, however, argues that in practice, the use of culture can have a similar effect as the use of biological race, shifting attention from politicized disparities to a more neutral understanding of difference.

From Race to Culture?

While the culture of cultural competency is not simply used as a substitution for race, ideas about race do continue to inform how culture is thought about and invoked. Racial categories are not only central to how difference is understood in the United States, but also to how we measure health disparities and other social inequities.

Partially underlying the link between health disparities and cultural competency is an assumption that the classic racial and ethnic groups outlined by the Office of Management and Budget's Directive 15 must also reflect some kind of cultural difference. Epstein (2007, 91) refers to the production of such an association as "categorical alignment work" and emphasizes the danger of taking it as "self-evident that the mobilization categories of identity politics, the biological categories of medical research, and the social classifications of state bureaucrats were all one and the same system of categorization." When culture, too, is mapped onto these categories, it can often be conceptualized as a set of natural character traits—individual beliefs and practices that are timeless, rather than produced within certain relations of power.

Critiques of cultural competency, like many critiques of the culture concept within anthropology, have tended to center around the danger of stereotyping, of reifying culture as an objective, one-dimensional entity attached to particular groups. Many anthropologists working in the health care field express their frustration with being asked to "tell me what I need to know about my Latino patients" or to provide lists of dos and don'ts for various racial or ethnic groups. The early days of cultural competency gave rise to a number of cultural handbooks and "tip sheets," which are available for health care professionals. One cultural competence handbook for nurses (Lipson et al. 1996), for example, is set up as a pocket guide, with an alphabetized list of racial and ethnic groups, each containing a collection of important information. Presumably, a practitioner can keep the guide available and, on encountering a culturally different patient, is able to flip to the appropriate section and learn pertinent information.

While ideas about cultural difference often overlap not just with race, but with ethnicity, nationality, language, and religion as well, there has been a tendency to define cultural groups primarily in racial terms. Kaiser Permanente's early efforts at cultural competency, for example, involved the production of three provider's handbooks on culturally competent care, focused on African American, Latino, and Asian and Pacific Island American populations. Each of the handbooks gives an overview of demographic data, health beliefs and behaviors, risk factors, and major diseases affecting these groups. While the handbooks emphasize that these groups should not be thought of as homogeneous, they still reflect commonsense assumptions that African Americans, Latinos, and Asian Americans are separate groups, unified at least in part by cultural similarities, and made distinct from each other because of cultural differences.

Racialized aspects of cultural difference are often considered to be more important than other aspects. One area of cultural competency work, for example, focuses on the importance of racial concordance between patients and physicians. Such concordance has been associated with increased utilization of health services (LaVeist, Nuru-Jeter, and Jones 2003), higher patient satisfaction (Saha et al. 1999), and a greater intention to adhere to physician recommendations (Street et al. 2008). These associations are a major part of why the effort to increase the numbers of racial minorities entering the health professions has been seen as a way to improve the cultural competency of the field overall.

The emphasis on race in measures of concordance, however, often leads to a neglect of other areas of identity or experience. Early in this project, I conducted fieldwork on a "black unit," one of a series of ethnically specialized psychiatric units designed to provide culturally competent care for African American patients. The units are intended to bring together what the current director of the program calls "scarce human resources" to provide better care to minority groups. Most of the black staff in the hospital's psychiatry department work on this unit, and during my time there, the unit chief, one of two head psychiatrists, both social workers, the head nurse, and several other nurses were black. The unit chief, however, was black South African, whereas the unit was designed to address the cultural needs of African Americans. The unit was not based on the assumption that all black individuals are the same, but rather, that racial similarity is the most important aspect of cultural identity. Being black trumped national difference as well as the significant economic and educational differences that existed between the unit physicians and staff and their mostly indigent patients.

As a result of this association of race with culture, the racially marked are nearly always also culturally marked. They are identified as different from an assumed normal patient and are often portrayed as the possessors of timeless, standardized, and mutually exclusive collections of traits. Recently, however, the danger of racialized, essentialized notions of culture has become well recognized, and cultural competency advocates and educators are currently struggling with the question of how to teach about culture without lists of traits or oversimplified distinctions among racial groups.

The Collision of Cultures

Cultural competency advocates and educators walk what they describe as a fine line between essentializing culture and giving information their audience of physicians and medical students will find useful. Recent approaches have emphasized that being culturally competent should not be about knowing the beliefs and practices of every cultural group, but about identifying the central issues that culture can affect. The focus shifts, then, from specific cultural traits to the effects of a more generalized cultural difference.

Bringing the culturally different into the health system is a major focus of cultural competency work. For example, the following excerpts from a news article (Hernandez 2005) reflect many of the issues frequently raised in public discussions of the need for cultural competency:

For one Latina resident of East L.A., trudging through the day with a plastic smile became an exhausting routine that was unbearably difficult. The recent loss of her son to a violent beating by gang members shattered her façade of complacency. She lost interest in day-to-day activities, withdrew from social interaction and curled into a cocoon of sadness and guilt.

Realizing that she needed help, this Spanish-speaking Angelena crossed the cultural divide and sought professional counsel from a local physician. The doctor soon diagnosed her with clinical depression and she was referred to a La Puente clinician named Alfred Sanchez who treated her for three months. Sanchez noted marked improvement in her emotional and psychological well-being and her depressive symptoms began to wane. (Hernandez 2005)

The article continues with a discussion of the disparities in mental health care for Latinos and then seeks to identify the cause of these disparities (Hernandez 2005):

Where does this problem stem from? Ironically, the answer lies in some of the richest facets of Latino culture, including its beautiful language, deep family ties and close-knit communities.

According to Lopez, members of the Latino community often misunderstand the gravity of mental health and label the mentally ill as "crazy" or "loca." Applying these labels marginalizes and discourages people from seeking treatment. Other Latinos are encouraged by family members to practice spiritual rituals or to try traditional treatment methods in lieu of seeking costly medical care.

Ana Lazu, founder of Latinos Unidos Siempre, encountered cultural barriers to obtaining the mental health services she needed while suffering from depression. Lazu was made to feel as though her "depression was a result of witchcraft," according to a statement released by Join Together Online. "As a Latina, I didn't believe in mental illness," Lazu said. "I faced a double stigma—the stigma of mental illness and the shame that I felt from my culture" (Hernandez 2005).

The problem of disparities in mental health care, in this case, is that Latinos are not seeking biomedical care often enough. The cultural factors emphasized are those that are most exotic and seen to be most different from the "normal" population—spiritual rituals, traditional treatments, and ideas about witchcraft prevent Latinos from getting care. The emphasis is placed on recognizing the value of these aspects of Latino culture, while also demonstrating that they are now maladaptive in the conditions of the United States.

This approach to culture glosses over other aspects of the social world that might affect both the development of mental illness and the decision to seek biomedical treatment: the woman's loss of her son to a gang beating or the need to seek treatments that are less costly are mentioned, but are not included as cultural issues; rather than addressing these issues directly, the solution is to try to bridge the gap between the Latino patients' culture and the physicians by educating both of them (Hernandez 2005):

Lopez lauds the efforts made by a slew of organizations to heighten linguistic and cultural sensitivity as well as outreach to members of the Latino community. The National Alliance on Mental Illness offers Hispanics a family-to-family self-help group program to support family members caring for their ill relatives. The Los Angeles Department of Mental Health's Training and Cultural Competency Bureau actively reaches out to communities, while the Latino Behavior Health Institute hosts an annual conference to educate mental health practitioners about the latest advances in care for Latinos.

Within this framework, differential access to care is not a result of the social position of Latinos in the United States, but rather, of their inherent cultural difference.

This focus on cultural difference itself as a factor behind health disparities has become common. Anne Fadiman's (1997) book *The Spirit Catches You and You Fall Down* offers one of the clearest and best known examples of the way cultural difference can affect the practice of medicine. Fadiman tells the story of Lia Lee, the child of Hmong immigrants to California, who began having seizures when she was three months old. She was diagnosed with epilepsy at the Merced County hospital and sent home with a complicated and varying regimen of medications that her parents administered irregularly. Her parents attributed her condition, in which "the spirit catches you and you fall down," to soul loss and treated it with a variety of remedies, including amulets, animal sacrifices, and a visit to a *txiv neeb*, or shaman. When she was four, Lia suffered from the "big one" and was left comatose and brain-dead. Fadiman tells this story as a "collision of two cultures," arguing that Lia's "life was ruined not by septic shock or noncompliant parents but by cross-cultural misunderstanding" (Fadiman 1997, 262).

Lia's case, and others like it, became rallying points for advocates of cross-cultural medicine in the 1990s, and Fadiman's book continues to be one of the primary texts of the cultural competency movement. In a critique of the book, however, Taylor (2003, 160) points to the troubling way in which culture is presented as a "reified, essential, static thing." While Fadiman does not present a simple list of "Hmong beliefs," Taylor argues that the book, rather, suggests that "it is 'culture' in a billiard-ball mode, manifested in the main protagonists' very different understandings of illness and their very similar inability to compromise, that caused the 'collision' that left Lia brain-dead" (Taylor 2003, 170).

This notion of cultural difference manifested in conflicting understandings arose often throughout my fieldwork. One striking example occurred at a training session that was designed to teach health care interpreters to be "cultural clarifiers"—to identify "cultural bumps" between patients and providers, and to intervene, when necessary. I joined one group of students and facilitators as we role-played two scenes.

In the first scene, I played the physician's role, reading from a script with another student, who played the patient. Leila practiced interpreting our conversation into

Arabic. The scene involved a discussion of treatments for thyroid cancer. The doctor recommends surgery, and the patient says she needs to talk to her husband, who makes medical decisions. The doctor asks, "Why do you need to talk to your husband?" and tells her that if she waits too long, the cancer could get worse. The patient does not answer directly, but wants to know if she can take some pills. The doctor explains that no, the cancer needs to be surgically removed before it spreads to other parts of the body, and the scene ends.

As we concluded, Eri, the session's facilitator, reminded Leila that the topic of the day was cultural issues and asked what the doctor said that may not have been culturally sensitive.

Leila: Oh, about her husband!

Eri: Yeah, she needs to consult with her husband, right? Then she [the doctor] said, "Why do you have to wait for your husband?" So that was culturally, what, not quite—

Leila: —acceptable. But the patient did not seem to be bothered. We do have to clarify cultures, but only based on certain issues if the patient is bothered.

Eri: In your own culture, that was not a problem?

Leila: No. Even if I'm interpreting in Arabic, a lot of people who speak Arabic come from different cultures, so I don't know what their perception of cancer is. In this situation, she wants to ask her husband if this procedure would really cure her, so it was not a cultural competency issue.

Eri: But it wasn't an issue of the cancer itself, it was the decision making.

Leila: Right, the decision making. But I don't think that was a cultural obstacle itself. I've been living here [in the United States] for fifteen years and sometimes I like to check with my husband for his opinion.

Eri: OK. Even if I didn't know her culture, I know the difference between the provider and the patient, because the patient is saying, "I'm going to have to talk with my husband." That is her culture, right?

Leila: But I was interpreting everything she said. So if she didn't want me to clarify the culture, why should I clarify the culture if she's just saying she wants to ask her husband?

Eri: Because you want to be culturally competent.

In this case, Leila argues that a woman discussing surgery with her husband is not a cultural issue—it seems reasonable, and the patient was not confused or outwardly affected by the doctor's question. But, Eri tries to make her see, the cultural issue comes from the fact that the doctor was confused by the patient. The issue is not the specific cultural beliefs, but rather, the difference between them. "The point is," Eri said later, "we've been talking about the cultural issue, and if you see the difference between the cultural background, the values, ultimately were different between what she [the patient] was saying and what the provider was saying."

In the next role-play scene, we were given a new script and a different student interpreted the conversation into Korean. The patient complained of skin lesions and fatigue, and the doctor suggested a number of tests, including an HIV test. The patient refused, saying he would do anything else, but did not want to know if he had HIV. At the end of the scene, Eri again asked what cultural issues the scene raised.

Leila: There's lots. He doesn't want to take a blood test.

Eri: That's a cultural issue?

Leila: He doesn't want to know if he has AIDS. The fear of people rejecting him in his family and community. It's like a taboo.

Eri: So [the patient] has the fear of taking the test because the community may reject him. . . . I don't see the cultural difference between the patient and the doctor. The fear is rampant among people at risk.

Leila: Yeah, the fear of getting it and the fear of people rejecting you for who you are.

Eri: And the doctor would know that.

Leila: Not necessarily. Don't you think it's a cultural clarification issue? It's like invading your privacy when people know you have HIV. He probably doesn't want his family or his wife or his kids to know he has HIV. That's a cultural clarification issue for me.

Eri: I still don't see the cultural difference. When you want to do the cultural clarification is when the situation presents itself that the provider's cultural values and the patient's cultural values are so different that you need to have an explanation. But in this community, the provider has been asking patients to take the HIV test many times, and the patients are always telling the doctor, "I don't want to take that test, I don't want to know." That's a very typical, typical response. So I don't see any cultural difference there.

Leila: OK, so why, when she [the first patient] wants to talk to her husband is that a cultural clarification issue?

Eri: Because she wants to consult her husband.

Leila: He [the second patient] is scared of people knowing.

Eri and Leila never reached complete agreement, and these two cases highlight some of the complexities of determining what counts as a cultural issue and what exactly should be done about it. In the first case, for Leila, the idea of a woman discussing the possibility of surgery with her husband was not significant—"that's something normal," she said later. But from Eri's perspective, it was not normal. The doctor's question indicated that she, too, saw it as different, and the fact of that difference itself is what necessitated an intervention. In the second case, the opposite was true. Eri did not see the stigma around HIV as a significant cultural issue because he saw it as common and something the physician would recognize. Culture, in these cases, was identified as the strange and unfamiliar, as that which was decidedly *not* normal.

The need to clarify culture once it was identified further added to the confusion. As he argued with Leila about the first case, another facilitator asked Eri what he would do. He answered,

What would I do? Because I see the cultural difference between these two parties. So I need to clarify this. OK. [I would say] "The reason she is saying this, she needs to consult with her husband, is probably from what I understand, the culture that she has been in has been telling her that the decision making for the treatment or whatever it is has to be done familywise, not on a personal level, because the culture says the wife is the property of the family, rather than an individual."

"OK," Leila responded, "but we don't believe in that. As a culture, we don't believe that." Although Eri had earlier emphasized that the specific cultural beliefs of the patient and physician were not important—it was the difference between them that was central—acting as a cultural clarifier requires that one give a specific explanation.

The approach used in this training session is designed to move beyond oversimplified understandings of culture. The goal is not to teach health providers or interpreters a list of traits for various cultural groups, but to help them recognize that there are different ways of thinking and approaching issues—what seems normal to one might not be to another. In practice, however, it becomes very difficult to move beyond essentialized notions of culture because more fundamental ideas about the clinical encounter remain unchallenged.

The idea that the doctor-patient relationship—and thus health outcomes—would be improved if the doctor understood the patient better has the effect of identifying the patient's difference itself as a problem that is ultimately behind health disparities. It places part of the blame for health disparities on the patient's culture and implies that if only "they" (the culturally different, blacks, Latinos, immigrants, etc.) acted more like "us" (the so-called mainstream, normal population), inequalities would disappear.

Importantly, cultural clarification also worked in only one direction. The interpreter was supposed to interrupt the session and explain the patient to the doctor, but not explain the doctor to the patient. This reaffirms understandings that it is the patient's culture that matters and that is causing problems, and the ultimate goal of providing culturally competent health care is to get the patient to do what the doctor says. In a follow-up conversation, Eri emphasized this goal:

I don't think they [health providers] can really know every single different attitude, different approach to things. They just need to know that there are different ways of thinking, different cultures out there, and when the patient's culture is different in a specific situation, you know, when the patient responds with an unexpected answer to a question, the provider really needs to acknowledge what the patient is saying, and then, once the patient is acknowledged about what they believe, it's much easier to persuade the patient to the direction the provider wants him to go in.

The recognition of cultural difference, then, is not designed to challenge the culture of biomedicine or the social norms that have produced it, but to overcome the obstacles created by the patient's culture.

We Don't Want to be *Too* Sensitive

The movement away from specific cultural traits and toward the emphasis on difference itself has also led to a further individualization of the notion of culture. When asked, "What is culture?" many people told me that culture should be thought of as what makes you unique: my culture is what makes me an individual, different from anyone else. Cultural competency, then, becomes about treating every patient as an individual, about being open to difference. With this approach, not only does culture become increasingly ahistorical and apolitical, but the fundamental aspect of culture taught in every introductory anthropology course—that culture exists in groups—is removed.

Just as the culture of patients is reduced to a set of individual personality traits, the bias, racism, and discrimination identified by the IOM report also come to be seen not as structurally or socially produced, but as individual character flaws among medical practitioners—attitudes that can be corrected with knowledge and education. Examples of such culturally *in*competent care were cited by several people to whom I spoke. A medical interpreter, for example, expressed her frustration with physicians, who, she said, "lack understanding when it comes to culture":

I remember a particular issue when [I] went with a [Latina] patient that had five kids—this was a worker's compensation claim. And the doctor said to me, "Is she here for a tubal ligation?" And we're here for a work injury! And I said, "Excuse me? I don't understand." And he says, "Five kids, isn't that about enough? She should stop now." And I'm going "what is it to you?" And the lady's there, and I said, "Doctor, don't forget that I am bound to interpret anything you say, would you like me to interpret that?" And no, no, we're just going to let it slide. And it makes you angry inside.

The cultural competency movement runs the risk of suggesting that physicians such as the one in this example cannot help their cultural beliefs and simply are not educated enough. As culture is seen to affect health care primarily when physicians and patients do not understand each other, issues of racism can also be recast as individual traits. Culture becomes not about social position, or the relationship between groups, but about the differences between individuals—little more than personality traits.

At the same time, this individualized notion of cultural difference can become a way of avoiding discussions of more fraught topics like race and racism. Many of the cultural competency trainers with whom I spoke specifically avoid discussing race in their courses. One cultural and linguistic specialist at an HMO said she always starts discussions of the dangers of stereotyping by using examples of age groups: "all teenagers are on drugs" or "all seniors are frail." After all, she said, "we don't want to be *too* sensitive." Similarly, the director of the cultural competency curriculum at a major medical school said she also tries not to get into race and ethnicity when teaching about stereotyping. "I didn't want to be inflammatory," she said. "I wanted to be instructive. So we use homeless patients, because you'd think homeless patients would be alcoholic bums, but they're you and me with bad luck."

A medical student said she thought talking about cultural competency "hurts a little less" than talking about race. The discrimination cited by the IOM report then becomes, she says, "a little more palatable" when it is recast as an issue of cultural competency. As cultural competency comes to stand in for more intractable issues in the doctor-patient relationship—like trust, racism, or power—culture becomes a way to avoid talking about the inequalities that race can so often highlight.

Conclusion

Shortly after completing my fieldwork, I was discussing this project with an African American colleague and professor of history. "At least," he said after I described my concerns with the use of the culture concept, "they're talking about culture and not about race." I understand this sentiment. The focus on biological racial difference as an explanation for health disparities has a long legacy of drawing attention away from the effects of racism, from class inequality, and from social marginalization. I am not convinced, however, that focusing on cultural difference as a cause of health disparities necessarily offers a better alternative.

Cultural competency offers an important critique of biomedicine. It argues against the mechanistic conception of the patient that medical anthropologists have identified in biomedicine (Lupton 1994; Scheper-Hughes and Lock 1987; Gordon 1988) and emphasizes that patients are not simply bodies. The push for cultural competency has arisen out of a strongly antiracist agenda that seeks to counteract the differential access to quality care that many believe has led to extreme health disparities in the United States. The people I met throughout my fieldwork were committed to social justice and to addressing the legacies of racism and inequality in the United States.

Few anthropologists would object to the assertion that *culture matters* in the clinical encounter. What exactly that culture is, however, remains difficult to define, and the notions employed by cultural competency work can have unintended, and potentially dangerous, consequences. The cultural competency movement ultimately accepts the idea that discreet, definable cultures exist; that culture is an apolitical, ahistorical object that can be separated from institutions and possessed by particular individuals; and that communication between cultural groups is inherently unproductive. As cultural competency advocates work to move away from simplistic, stereotypical understandings of culture as a list of traits, they often individualize the issue of health disparities, locating the problem ultimately in the patient and his or her inability to adapt to the current system. This use of culture shifts attention from the inequity in health care to the more natural, and unavoidable, difference of cross-cultural communication and can become a way to avoid difficult conversations about racism.

So what, then, is the use of culture? It is useful to remember that before culture was a theoretical construct in anthropology, it referred not to static conditions or to groups, but rather, to process (Williams 1983, 87). The power of the culture concept lies in its ability to highlight the contingent, socially produced nature of human difference. We must refocus attention away from the notion of culture as a bounded object or a set of characteristics located within individuals, and toward a recognition of culture as a dynamic set of relationships that are always connected to historical circumstances, political conditions, and relations of power.

Notes

1. The Office of Minority Health uses one of the more widely accepted and cited versions, stating that "cultural and linguistic competence is a set of congruent behaviors, attitudes, and policies that come together in a system, agency, or among professionals that enables effective work in cross-cultural situations. 'Culture' refers to integrated patterns of human behavior that include the language, thoughts, communications, actions, customs, beliefs, values, and institutions of racial, ethnic, religious, or social groups. 'Competence' implies having the capacity to function effectively as an individual and an organization within the context of the cultural beliefs, behaviors, and needs presented by consumers and their communities" (adapted from Cross et al. 1989, quoted in Office of Minority Health 2001, 28).

References

Abu-Lughod, L. 1991. Writing against culture. In *Recapturing anthropology*, ed. R. Fox. Santa Fe, NM: School of American Research Press, 137–162.

Armelagos, George J., and Dennis P. Van Gerven. 2003. A century of skeletal biology and paleopathology: Contrasts, contradictions, and conflicts. *American Anthropologist* 105:53–64.

Baker, Lee D. 1998. *From savage to Negro: Anthropology and the construction of race, 1896–1954.* Berkeley: University of California Press.

Bentacourt, Joseph R., Alexander R. Green, J. Emilio Carrillo, and Owusu Ananeh-Firempong II. 2003. Defining cultural competence: A practical framework for addressing racial/ethnic disparities in health and health care. *Public Health Reports* 118:293–302.

Bentacourt, Joseph R., Alexander R. Green, J. Emilio Carrillo, and Elyse R. Park. 2005. Cultural competence and health care disparities: key perspectives and trends. *Health Affairs* 24 (2): 499–505.

Boas, Franz. 1962. *Anthropology and modern life*. New York: Dover.

Boas, Franz, and George W. Stocking Jr., eds. 1974. *The shaping of American anthropology, 1883–1911: A Franz Boas reader*. New York: Basic Books.

Brach, Cindy, and Irene Fraserirector. 2000. Can cultural competency reduce racial and ethnic health disparities? A review and conceptual model. *Medical Care Research and Review* 57(Suppl 1):181–217.

Byrd, W. Michael, and Linda A. Clayton. 2001. Race, medicine, and health care in the United States: A historical survey. *Journal of the National Medical Association* 93:11S–34S.

Carter-Pokras, Olivia, and Claudia Baquet. 2002. What is a "health disparity"? *Public Health Reports* 117:426–434.

Caspari, Rachel. 2003. From types to populations: A century of race, physical anthropology, and the American Anthropological Association. *American Anthropologist* 105:65–76.

Cross, Terry L., Barbara J. Bazron, Karl W. Dennis, and Mareasa R. Isaacs. 1989. *Towards a culturally competent system of care: A monograph on effective services for minority children who are severely emotionally disturbed*. Vol. I. Washington, DC: Georgetown University Child Development Center.

Dominguez, Virginia. 1992. Invoking culture: The messy side of "cultural politics." *South Atlantic Quarterly* 91:19–42.

Dressler, William W. 1993. Health in the African-American community: Accounting for health inequalities. *Medical Anthropology Quarterly* 7:325–345.

Epstein, Steven. 2007. *Inclusion: The politics of difference in medical research*. Chicago: University of Chicago Press.

Fadiman, Anne. 1997. *The spirit catches you and you fall down: A Hmong child, her American doctors, and the collision of two cultures*. New York: Noonday Press.

Geiger, H. Jack. 2006. Health disparities: What do we know? What do we need to know? What should we do? In *Gender, race, class, and health: Intersectional approaches*, ed. Amy J. Schulz and Leith Mullings. San Francisco: Jossey-Bass, 261–288.

Gordon, Deborah R. 1988. Tenacious assumptions in Western medicine. In *Biomedicine examined*, ed. Margaret Lock and Deborah R. Gordon. Boston: Kluwer, 19–56.

Graves, Darci L., Robert C. Like, Nataly Kelly, and Alexa Hohensee. 2007. Legislation as intervention: A survey of cultural competence policy in health care. *Journal of Health Care Law and Policy* 10:339–361.

Hammonds, Evelynn M. 2006. Straw men and their followers: The return of biological race. Is Race "Real"? Web forum, June 7; http://raceandgenomics.ssrc.org/Hammonds.

Harrison, Faye V. 1995. The persistent power of "race" in the cultural and political economy of racism. *Annual Review of Anthropology* 24:27–74.

Hartigan, John. 2005. Culture against race: Reworking the basis for racial analysis. *South Atlantic Quarterly* 104:543–560.

Heck, Kelley. 2005. Codey signs bill to improve medical care for minorities. Press release, March 23. http://www.state.nj.us/cgi-bin/governor/njnewsline/view_article.pl?id=2429.

Hernandez, Joaquin. 2005. The elephant in the room: Latinos and mental health. Eastern Group Publications, October 4. http://news.newamericamedia.org/news/mobile.html?view=article&article_id=5b1385599f72d12bb3f4c2ce9f24191c.

Jones, David S. 2004. *Rationalizing epidemics: Meanings and uses of American Indian mortality since 1600*. Cambridge, MA: Harvard University Press.

Kahn, Jonathan. 2005. From disparity to difference: How race-specific medicines may undermine politics to address inequalities in health care. *Southern California Interdisciplinary Law Journal* 15:105–130.

Krieger, Nancy. 1987. Shades of difference: Theoretical underpinnings of the medical controversy on black/white differences in the US 1830–1870. *International Journal of Health Services* 17:250–278.

LaVeist, Thomas A. 2005. *Minority populations and health: An introduction to health disparities in the United States*. San Francisco: Jossey-Bass.

LaVeist, Thomas A., Amani Nuru-Jeter, and Kiesha E. Jones. 2003. The association of doctor-patient race concordance with health services utilization. *Journal of Public Health Policy* 24:312–323.

Lipson, Juliene G., Suzanne L. Dibble, and Pamela A. Minarik, eds. 1996. Culture and Nursing Care: A Pocket Guide. San Francisco: UCSF Nursing Press.

Lupton, Deborah. 1994. *Medicine as culture: Illness, disease and the body in Western societies*. Thousand Oaks, CA: Sage.

Mayberry, Robert M., Fatima Mili, Isam G. M. Vaid, Aziz Samadi, Elizabeth Ofili, Meryl S. McNeal, Patrick A. Griffith, and Ghania LaBrie. 1999. *Racial and ethnic differences in access to medical care: A synthesis of the literature*. Menlo Park, CA: Henry J. Kaiser Family Foundation.

Office of Minority Health. 2001. *National standards for culturally and linguistically appropriate services in health care: Final report*. Washington, DC: U.S. Department of Health and Human Services.

Rathore, Saif S., and Harlan M. Krumholz. 2004. Differences, disparities, and biases: Clarifying racial variations in health care use. *Annals of Internal Medicine* 141:635–638.

Saha, Somnath, Miriam Komaromy, Thomas D. Koepsell, and Andrew B. Bindman. 1999. Patient-physician racial concordance and the perceived quality and use of health care. *Archives of Internal Medicine* 159:997–1004.

Santiago-Irizarry, Vilma. 2001. *Medicalizing ethnicity: The construction of Latino identity in a psychiatric setting.* Ithaca, NY: Cornell University Press.

Satcher, David, and Rubens J. Pamies, eds. 2006. *Multicultural medicine and health disparities.* New York: McGraw-Hill.

Satel, Sally. 2000. *PC, M.D.: How political correctness is corrupting medicine.* New York: Basic Books.

Scheper-Hughes, Nancy, and Margaret M. Lock. 1987. The mindful body: A prolegomenon to future work in medical anthropology. *Medical Anthropology Quarterly* 1:6–41.

Schulman, Kevin A., Jesse A. Berlin, William Harless, Jon F. Kerner, Shyrl Sisturnk, Bernard J. Gersh, Ross Dube, et al. 1999. The effect of race and sex on physicians' recommendations for cardiac catheterization. *New England Journal of Medicine* 340:618–626.

Smedley, Brian D., Adrienne Y. Stith, and Alan R. Nelson, eds. 2003. *Unequal treatment: Confronting racial and ethnic disparities in health care.* Washington, DC: National Academies Press.

Stepan, Nancy. 1998. Race, gender, science and citizenship. *Gender and History* 10:26–52.

Stolcke, Verena. 1995. Talking culture: New boundaries, new rhetorics of exclusion in Europe. *Current Anthropology* 36:1–13.

Street, Richard L., Kimberly J. O'Malley, Lisa A. Cooper, and Paul Haidet. 2008. Understanding concordance in patient-physician relationships: Personal and ethnic dimensions of shared identity. *Annals of Family Medicine* 6:198–205.

Tapper, Melbourne. 1997. An "anthropathology" of the "American Negro": Anthropology, genetics, and the new racial science, 1940–1952. *Social History of Medicine* 10:263–289.

Taylor, Janelle S. 2003. The story catches you and you fall down: Tragedy, ethnography, and "cultural competence." *Medical Anthropology Quarterly* 17:159–181.

Trouillot, Michel-Rolph. 2002. Adieu, culture: A new duty arises. In *Anthropology beyond culture*, ed. Richard G. Fox and Barbara J. King. New York: Berg, 37–60.

Visweswaran, Kamala. 1998. Race and the culture of anthropology. *American Anthropologist* 100:70–83.

Wailoo, Keith. 2001. *Dying in the City of the Blues: Sickle cell anemia and the politics of race and health.* Chapel Hill: University of North Carolina Press.

Williams, Raymond. 1983. *Keywords: A vocabulary of culture and society.* New York: Oxford University Press.

11   The Science and Epidemiology of Racism and Health: Racial/Ethnic Categories, Biological Expressions of Racism, and the Embodiment of Inequality—an Ecosocial Perspective

Nancy Krieger

What's the use of race? The question posed by the title of this book, and the conference that gave rise to it, is deceptively simple. Its use of the singular for both *use* and *race* implies that there is only one use of—and only one entity captured by—the notion of race.

The reality, however, is far more complex, as made amply clear by the other chapters in this volume. The framing of and answer to this question—what's the use of race?—has everything to do with who is asking it, who is answering, and why.

In this chapter, I approach the question, what's the use of race? from the standpoint of a social epidemiologist who is concerned with the impact of racism on health and whose conceptual and empirical research focuses on the societal determinants of the population distribution of health, disease, and well-being (Krieger et al. 1993; Krieger 1994, 2000a, 2001, 2003, 2005a, 2008). The answer I offer is straightforward: to determine how racism harms health, it is necessary to employ the socially created categories of race/ethnicity, to distinguish between and compare the health status of the populations that are likely to be harmed by—or benefit from—racial injustice.

Three arguments that support the use of racial/ethnic categories in epidemiologic studies of racism and health are as follows:

1. Racism harms health.
2. Racism creates the very categories of race, which, in turn, demarcates groups differentially harmed and benefited by inequitable race relations.
3. Racial/ethnic health inequities are a biological expression of racism; their origins lie in injustice, not biology.

Although there may well be other questions that health researchers seek to answer about the relationship of what they define to be race to the health outcomes they find to be of interest, my twofold purpose in this chapter is to focus attention on racism and its health and to provide evidence that these health inequities are not immutable and can be changed. When categories of race/ethnicity are no longer linked to inequity, we will see it in the epidemiological data. Until then, we cannot afford to be blind to the realities and impact of racism on health.

Bean Counting, Gene Counting, and Health Inequities: On Race, Scientific Racism, and the Countervailing Claims of Antiracist Science

The legacy of scientific racism runs long and deep and is beyond the purview of this chapter (Chase 1977; Krieger et al. 1993; Gould 1996; Ernst and Harris 1999; Ewen and Ewen 2008). Its essential claims are that (1) race equals genetics; (2) "races" are natural populations, meaning that they are defined by innate genetic differences, rather than socially created demarcations; and (3) observed differences in the social standing and health status of racial groups are due to inherent, inborn factors. A recent prominent example of this orientation was provided in October 2007, when Dr. James Watson, one of the codiscoverers of the double helix structure of DNA and first director of the U.S. National Institute of Health's Human Genome Project, publicly asserted that blacks are inherently less intelligent than whites (see box 11.1; Milmo 2007).

The good news is that Watson was widely excoriated by leading scientific institutions and scientists for what he said (box 11.1; AFP 2007; Zerhouni 2007; Gumbel 2007). The criticisms impaled him for speaking scientific garbage and for attempting to use his scientific laurels as a substitute for scientific evidence. In no short order, Watson was suspended from the Cold Spring Harbor labs, where he served as chancellor, and he resigned in ignominy a few days later (BBC News 2007). As Henry Kelley, the president of the Federation of American Scientists, said, it was one "sad and revolting way to end a remarkable career" (AFP 2007).

The bad news is that the views Watson expressed are all too common, deeply ingrained, and legitimized by centuries of scientific racism (Chase 1977; Krieger et al. 1993; Gould 1996; Ernst and Harris 1999; Ewen and Ewen 2008). Hence, as part of the work required to debunk this heavy legacy, we need to counter with the science of investigating the health consequences of racism.

What are some of the testable claims of this alternative science? The first claim, also discussed in other chapters in this book, is that the long-standing simplistic equation that race equals genetics is wrong (Goodman 2000; Feldman, Lewontin, and King 2003; Krieger 2005a; Braun et al. 2007). This allegedly scientific view, articulated so baldly by Watson, racializes both biology and ancestry. Premised on the view that genes-R-us (i.e., gene counting) and that genetic differences explain why racial/ethnic groups can be differentiated and counted (i.e., bean counting), it proffers genetics as the reason why different racial/ethnic groups have different health statuses. Strong evidence shows, however, that not only can a given phenotypic trait, for example, skin color, be compatible with many different genotypes for other traits (Parra et al. 2003; Parra et al. 2004), but also that genetic variation within groups demarcated by conventional, "racial" categories is far greater than between them (Goodman 2000; Feldman, Lewontin, and King 2003). The alternative is to posit that race/ethnicity, like social class, is a historically contingent social category that imposes biological

Box 11.1

October 2007 comments by James Watson on the innate biological inferiority of black persons and the response of the scientific establishment

October 14, 2007 (not 1607, or 1707, or 1807, or 1907): *Dr. James Watson* (1962 Nobel Prize recipient for codiscovering the DNA double helix and genetic code) "told *The Sunday Times* that he was 'inherently gloomy about the prospect of Africa' because 'all our social policies are based on the fact that their intelligence is the same as ours whereas all the testing says not really.' He said there was a natural desire that all human beings should be equal but 'people who have to deal with black employees find this not true.'" (Milmo 2007)

October 18, 2007: Federation of American Scientists (FAS) president Henry Kelly: "Dr. Watson chose to use his unique stature to promote personal prejudices that are racist, vicious and unsupported by science . . . a sad and revolting way to end a remarkable career." (AFP 2007)

October 19, 2007: Watson is suspended from chancellor position at Cold Spring Harbor. (Gumbel 2007)

October 19, 2007: National Institutes of Health director Elias Zerhouni: "The comments, which were attributed to Dr. James Watson earlier this week in the London Times, are wrong, from every point of view—not the least of which is that they are completely inconsistent with the body of research literature in this area. Scientific prestige is never a substitute for knowledge. As scientists, we are outraged and saddened when science is used to perpetuate prejudice." (Zerhouni 2007)

October 25, 2007: Watson resigns from Cold Spring Harbor. (BBC News 2007)

consequences (Krieger et al. 1993; Krieger 2000a, 2001, 2003). One corollary is that gene expression, and not gene frequency, is key to generating and explaining health inequities (Krieger 2005). Another is that even in those cases where groups differ in gene frequency due to histories of geographical ancestry and migration (both forced and voluntary), the existence of such differences in no way contradicts the more general thesis that racism can harm health—no matter what the genotype at issue. Differences and inequity are not the same (Braveman and Gruskin 2003), and my concern here pertains to the excess burden of disease and death due to racial injustice.

A second claim, turning racist notions of racial categories on their head, is that there can be meaningful social categories of race/ethnicity that can be used thoughtfully to document, monitor, and analyze the impact of racial injustice on people's lives, including their health (Krieger 2000a, 2000b, 2003, 2004a; Kington and Nickens 2001; Mays et al. 2003; Smedley, Stith, and Nelson 2003; Blank, Dabady, and Citro 2004). What this statement recognizes is a profound change in the use of racial/ethnic data: from an initial purpose of discriminating adversely to, instead, providing evidence of discrimination that must be countered. Consider, for example, the case of the U.S. census, the population data of which are used for many reasons, including providing denominators to calculate population rates of disease, essential for quantifying the magnitude of racial/ethnic health disparities (Anderson 1988; Krieger 2000b). In the mid-nineteenth century, scientists lobbied for inclusion of racial categories to confirm their ideas about racial inequality (Anderson 1988; Nobles 2000). The current reason why the U.S. census obtains data on age and race/ethnicity in the 100 percent population count, however, is the recently renewed Voting Rights Act, combined with the 1990 Census Redistricting Act, whereby the collection of racial/ethnic data for the voting-age population is mandated to create fair voting districts and prevent racial gerrymandering that would dilute the vote of racial/ethnic minorities (U.S. Commission on Civil Rights 1981; U.S. Bureau of the Census 2009a). Although there still are problems, at least there are data to document the problems and contest illegitimate boundaries in court.

In other words, we cannot escape history—or pretend that it has not happened. The seemingly same categories of race have been used, at different times, and by different groups, for very different reasons: either (1) to argue for inherent racial difference and inequality, or, conversely, (2) to argue against assumptions of innate racial difference and for racial justice. Making clear that these are not simply academic points is the example of California's recently defeated Proposition 54, which, in 2003, sought to prohibit the state government from collecting or using any racial/ethnic data, including census data, allegedly on the grounds that because race is not real, biologically, data on race should not be collected (see figure 11.1; Racial Privacy Initiative 2003; Krieger 2004a). Funded by conservative groups, the actual intent of Proposition 54 was to end statistical documentation of discrimination, following a time-honored, or perhaps I should say time-disgraced, practice of getting rid of problems by removing them from view, otherwise known as "no data, no problem" (Krieger 1992). To counter, opponents argued that the social realities of race and ongoing racism require collecting the data to monitor racial/ethnic inequalities in health and other outcomes—and, indeed, the public health arguments about the need for data to document and address racial/ethnic health disparities proved decisive in helping defeat the measure (Coalition for an Informed California 2003; Schevitz 2003; Krieger 2004a).

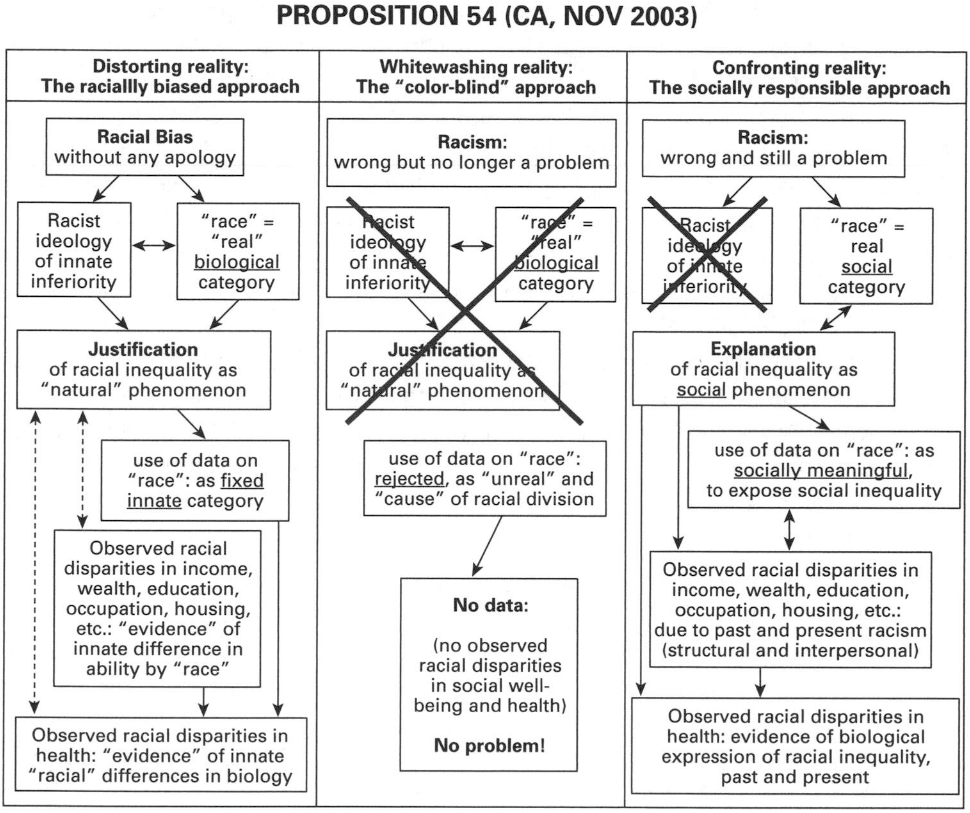

PROPOSITION 54 (CA, NOV 2003)

Distorting reality: The raciallly biased approach	Whitewashing reality: The "color-blind" approach	Confronting reality: The socially responsible approach

Racial Bias
without any apology

Racist ideology of innate inferiority ⟷ "race" = "real" biological category

Justification
of racial inequality as "natural" phenomenon

use of data on "race": as fixed innate category

Observed racial disparities in income, wealth, education, occupation, housing, etc.: "evidence" of innate difference in ability by "race"

Observed racial disparities in health: "evidence" of innate "racial" differences in biology

---

Racism:
wrong but no longer a problem

Racist ideology of innate inferiority ⟷ "race" = "real" biological category

Justification
of racial inequality as "natural" phenomenon

use of data on "race": rejected, as "unreal" and "cause" of racial division

No data:
(no observed racial disparities in social well-being and health)

No problem!

Racism:
wrong and still a problem

Racist ideology of innate inferiority

"race" = real social category

Explanation
of racial inequality as social phenomenon

use of data on "race": as socially meaningful, to expose social inequality

Observed racial disparities in income, wealth, education, occupation, housing, etc.: due to past and present racism (structural and interpersonal)

Observed racial disparities in health: evidence of biological expression of racial inequality, past and present

Figure 11.1
Three approaches to conceptualizing and collecting data on race/ethnicity and racial inequality, as revealed by the Proposition 54 campaign in California, 2003.
Source: Krieger (2004).

Analyzing the Impact of Racism on Health: Conceptual Issues

How, then, to conduct scientific research to test the hypothesis that racism harms health? One useful place to start is with definitions of key concepts relevant to formulating research questions and study design on through data collection, analysis, and interpretation.

Briefly stated, racism refers to institutional and individual practices that create and reinforce oppressive systems of *race relations* and their contingent *racial definitions*, whereby dominant groups define themselves and others through the possession of arbitrary physical characteristics, such as skin color, and adversely restrict, by judgment and action, the lives of those against whom they discriminate, and benefit from so doing (Krieger 2000a). Health consequences can thus be conceptualized as biologic expressions of race relations, referring to how harmful physical, biological, and social exposures, plus people's responses to these exposures, are ultimately embodied and manifested in racial/ethnic disparities in somatic and mental health (Krieger 2000a, 2000c). The recognition that race/ethnicity is a *social*, and not a *biological*, construct in turn helps clarify that the arbitrary phenotypic characteristics invoked as so-called markers of race are more accurately understood as racialized expressions of biology (Krieger 2000a, 2000c). The fact that we know what race we are—and that racial/ethnic disparities in health exist—says more about our society than it does our biology (Krieger and Bassett 1986).

Consequently, the task becomes that of understanding the myriad ways racial inequality becomes biologically embodied, over the life course and across generations, thereby creating racial/ethnic health inequities. One theory useful for systematically approaching this question is *ecosocial theory*, a theory of disease distribution concerned with health inequities that I have been developing since 1994 (Krieger 1994, 2001, 2004b, 2005b, 2008). Its four core constructs are as follows:

1. embodiment, referring to how we literally embody, biologically, our lived experience, thereby creating population patterns of health and disease
2. pathways of embodiment, referring to how there are often multiple pathways to a given outcome, via diverse physical, chemical, biological, and social exposures, and involving gene expression, not just gene frequency
3. cumulative interplay of both biological and social exposure, susceptibility, and resistance across the life course, because all these matter
4. accountability and agency, both for social inequalities in health and for ways they are—or are not—monitored, analyzed, and addressed

As emphasized by ecosocial theory, we must pay heed to context; to life course; to historical generation; to levels of analysis; to the interrelationships between diverse forms of social inequality, including racism, class, and gender, among others—and also to people's relationship to the rest of the ecosystem.

Informed by ecosocial theory, figure 11.2 accordingly lists broad categories of inequitable exposures by which racism is posited to shape population distributions of disease, taking into account domains, levels, and spatiotemporal scale (from individual life course to historical generation, and from current geographical location to histories of territorial dispossession and migration). These exposures include economic and social deprivation; toxic substances, pathogens, and hazardous conditions; social trauma; targeted marketing of harmful commodities; and inadequate and degrading medical care (Krieger 2000a). The net implication is that there can be many different ways of studying how racism harms health, depending on the type of exposure and outcome considered. No one study can ever investigate all the pathways, but any given study can at least specify which pathways it is addressing, and why (Krieger 2006).

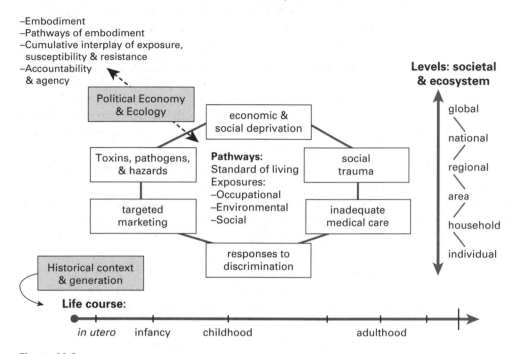

Figure 11.2

An ecosocial approach to conceptualizing racism as a societal determinant of population health.

Source: Krieger (2000a, 2008).

Moreover, once a study opts to investigate the impact of racism on health, it necessarily must use categories of race/ethnicity to demarcate the groups at risk of being harmed by racial injustice. Otherwise, there would be no exposed groups and no comparison groups and, in the case of both research studies and public health surveillance systems and medical records, no ability to document, monitor, or analyze racial/ethnic health inequities. The caveat is that the use of the racial/ethnic categories must be clearly justified and defined, in relation to both (1) how race/ethnicity is being conceptualized (e.g., as a social category reflecting societal race relations) and (2) the specified study hypotheses regarding the impact of racism on health (Krieger 2000a; Kaplan and Bennett 2003; Mays et al. 2003; Braun et al. 2007). Race/ethnicity, consequently, is an obligate, not optional, construct for research on racism and health.

As I have reviewed previously (Krieger 2000a), two kinds of studies are needed to investigate, empirically, the impact of racism on health, *direct* and *indirect*, each of which can employ quantitative or qualitative methods. First, by *direct*, I mean health studies explicitly obtaining information on people's self-reported experiences of—and observing people's physiological and psychological responses to—real-life or experimental situations involving racial discrimination, as both an acute and, also, perhaps especially, chronic exposure. The caveat, as well recognized in the enormous body of literature on stress and health (Cohen, Kessler, and Gordon 1995), is that such research must reckon with not only exposures, but also perceptions of these exposures as well as cognitive issues pertaining to memory and disclosure (Stone et al. 2000; Blank, Dabady, and Citro 2004; Krieger et al. 2005b). Second, by *indirect*, I mean studies that investigate racial/ethnic disparities in distributions of deleterious exposures and/or health outcomes and explicitly infer that racism underlies these disparities—even as they do not, per se, document discriminatory acts or people's interpretation of these acts. Taken singly, each approach has its flaws, yet both are necessary as each addresses questions the other cannot.

Specifically, only the direct approach can be used to study the health consequences of social trauma; there is no substitute. By contrast, for most of the other pathways, the indirect approach is required precisely because these pathways involve distributions of exposures that go beyond an individual's perception. For example, knowledge of discrimination in wages, or in occupational or environmental hazards, or in medical care can be obtained only if one has information on what others experience (Krieger 2000a; Smedley, Stith, and Nelson 2003; Blank, Dabady, and Citro 2004).

Empirical Research on Racism and Health: Selected Examples

The number of studies explicitly testing hypotheses about the impact of racial discrimination on health is burgeoning (Krieger 2000a; Williams, Neighbors, and Jackson 2003; Paradies 2006; Mays, Cochran, and Barnes 2007; Kressin, Raymond, and Manze 2008; Williams and Mohammed 2009). In 1999, when I wrote the first epidemiologic review article on the topic, I could identify only fifteen relevant studies in the broader public health literature (Krieger 2000a). By contrast, an epidemiologic review article published in 2006, which focused on articles published between 2000 and 2004, was able to include 138 articles (Paradies 2006), and a new 2009 review article has identified 115 articles, listed in the PubMed database and published solely between 2005 and 2007, that investigated associations between self-reported experiences of racial discrimination and either health status or health care utilization (Williams and Mohammed 2009). Thus my purpose in this section is not to review this large and growing literature, but instead, to illustrate some of the approaches being used, using examples of my own research.

Indirect Approach: Racism, Class, and Health Inequities

I start with two studies that employed the indirect approach; each was concerned with links between racial/ethnic inequality, socioeconomic deprivation, and health. The first example draws on data from my Public Health Disparities Geocoding Project (Krieger et al. 2003, 2004, 2005a), which we developed to address the absence of socioeconomic data in most U.S. public health surveillance systems. Two problematic consequences of this gap are that it precludes both (1) monitoring the magnitude of socioeconomic health inequities, both overall and within diverse racial/ethnic groups, and (2) documenting the impact of racial/ethnic economic inequalities on racial/ethnic health inequities.

To address the problem of nonexistent socioeconomic data in public health data systems, our project accordingly systematically investigated a possible solution, drawing on an approach used eclectically in U.S. health research for over seventy-five years: that of using geocoding and area-based socioeconomic measures (ABSMs). In brief, the basic method is to characterize both cases and the population from which they arise by the socioeconomic characteristics of their residential areas, using U.S. census data. This, in turn, permits calculating rates stratified by the ABSMs—which, because they are census derived, can be used in any region in the United States. Our central finding was that U.S. socioeconomic inequalities in health can suitably be monitored with the common metric of the census tract poverty measure—and we further note that one advantage of this approach is that, unlike individual-level education and occupation, this measure can be applied to all persons, regardless of age and gender, and whether in or out of school, or in or out of the paid labor force (Krieger et al. 2003, 2004, 2005a).

Table 11.1 presents the impact of adjusting for census tract poverty on black-white and Hispanic-white age-adjusted health disparities for a variety of outcomes, using data from my home state of Massachusetts, centered around the U.S. 1990 census (Krieger et al. 2004, 2005a). The first point to note is that the magnitude of racial/ethnic health inequities varied by race/ethnicity, by outcome, and by gender. African Americans, for example, generally were at excess risk compared to white Americans across the board, with relative risks ranging from around 2 (e.g., premature mortality) to upward of 20 (gonorrhea and tuberculosis). By contrast, for Hispanics, the picture was more variable; Hispanics were often at higher risk than whites for the childhood and infectious disease outcomes, but at lower risk for premature mortality (possibly a reflection of immigrants returning to their home countries to die). In both groups, the racial/ethnic disparity for deaths due to HIV/AIDS was far greater for women compared to men.

Nevertheless, the second major point is that even with this heterogeneity of risk, what table 11.1 reveals is that adjusting for census tract poverty, in virtually every case, reduced the observed racial/ethnic disparities, as shown by the shaded cells. In some cases, the reduction was quite dramatic, as shown by the outcomes in boldface, for example, nearly a halving of the excess risk, if not more, for childhood lead poisoning, gonorrhea, tuberculosis, and for mortality due to HIV/AIDS and to homicide

Table 11.1

Effect of adjusting for socioeconomic position on racial/ethnic health inequities: Results of the Public Health Disparities Geocoding Project for Massachusetts and Rhode Island, circa 1990

| | | Black-white | | | | Hispanic-white | | | |
| | | Women | | Men | | Women | | Men | |
Outcome	Adjusted for	RR	(95% CI)	RR	(95% CI)	RR	(95% CI)	RR	(95% CI)
% Low birth weight	Age	2.8	(2.6, 3.0)	2.5	(2.3, 2.7)	1.5	(1.4, 1.6)	1.5	(1.4, 1.7)
	Age + census tract poverty	2.3	(2.1, 2.5)	2.0	(1.8, 2.2)	1.2	(1.1, 1.3)	1.2	(1.1, 1.3)
Childhood lead poisoning	Age	6.5	(5.6, 7.6)	5.4	(4.7, 6.3)	4.0	(3.5, 4.5)	3.4	(3.0, 3.8)
	Age + census tract poverty	2.4	(2.0, 2.9)	2.1	(1.8, 2.6)	1.3	(1.1, 1.6)	1.2	(1.1, 1.4)
Gonorrhea	Age	22.0	(19.9, 24.2)	21.3	(19.6, 23.2)	10.7	(9.5, 12.0)	10.5	(9.4, 11.6)
	Age + census tract poverty	14.0	(12.6, 15.7)	13.0	(11.8, 14.3)	6.2	(5.4, 7.1)	5.9	(5.2, 6.6)
Tuberculosis	Age	20.4	(16.5, 25.3)	13.9	(11.8, 16.4)	19.8	(14.6, 26.9)	15.1	(12.1, 18.7)
	Age + census tract poverty	13.8	(10.7, 17.8)	6.9	(5.7, 8.3)	15.1	(10.5, 21.7)	8.0	(6.3, 10.3)
Premature mortality	Age	1.9	(1.8, 2.0)	2.0	(1.9, 2.1)	0.9	(0.9, 1.0)	1.2	(1.1, 1.3)
	Age + census tract poverty	1.5	(1.4, 1.6)	1.4	(1.3, 1.5)	0.7	(0.7, 0.8)	0.9	(0.8, 0.9)
Diabetes mortality	Age	2.0	(1.6, 2.4)	1.5	(1.2, 1.9)	1.0	(0.7, 1.5)	0.9	(0.6, 1.4)
	Age + census tract poverty	1.7	(1.3, 2.0)	1.4	(1.1, 1.8)	0.9	(0.6, 1.3)	0.8	(0.5, 1.3)
HIV/AIDS mortality	Age	17.3	(12.6, 23.6)	4.3	(3.7, 5.0)	8.9	(5.9, 13.2)	2.9	(2.4, 3.5)
	Age + census tract poverty	9.3	(6.4, 13.5)	2.2	(1.9, 2.6)	4.4	(2.7, 7.0)	1.5	(1.2, 1.8)
Homicide and legal intervention	Age	9.3	(6.5, 13.2)	19.6	(16.2, 23.7)	3.9	(2.3, 6.5)	9.4	(7.4, 12.0)
	Age + census tract poverty	5.6	(3.7, 8.4)	10.8	(8.7, 13.4)	2.3	(1.3, 4.0)	5.1	(3.9, 6.7)

Note: Shaded rows show outcomes for which adjusting for census tract poverty reduced the magnitude of racial/ethnic health inequities; data in boldface are for outcomes for which there was effectively a halving or more of risk. CI = confidence interval. RR = relative risk.

Source: Krieger et al. (2004, 2005a).

and legal intervention. If these are the results we obtained with just this one admittedly crude measure of socioeconomic position, measured at the time of the health outcome, it is highly likely that the magnitude of racial/ethnic health inequities would have been further reduced had we been able to use more comprehensive measures of socioeconomic position, across domains and across the life course (Krieger, Williams, and Moss 1997; Shaw et al. 2007).

A third major point is that our results are complex, which is likewise the message of the extant literature on the impact of adjusting for or stratifying by socioeconomic position when analyzing racial/ethnic disparities in health (Krieger et al. 1993; Krieger 2000a; Kington and Nickens 2001; Williams and Jackson 2005). In other words, there is no one-size-fits-all scenario. That said, it is safe to say that more often than not, racial/ethnic socioeconomic inequities do play a major role in racial/ethnic health inequities, both in the onset of the event and once disease is diagnosed. Moreover, within the U.S. context, the continued salience of poverty for racial/ethnic health inequities remains large. Data from the U.S. Current Population Survey (U.S. Bureau of the Census and U.S. Bureau of Labor Statistics 2007), for example, documented that in 2006, fully 12.3 percent of the U.S. population, including 20.7 percent of children under age five—that is, one in every five children—lived under the notoriously stingy U.S. poverty line (O'Connor 2001). This is a very high level of poverty, and especially childhood poverty, compared to other industrialized nations (UNICEF 2005). Only then consider the magnitude of the racial/ethnic inequities in poverty identified in this survey, which translated to fully four in ten black children and three in ten Hispanic children, versus less than one in ten white children, growing up impoverished. At a time when ever more research shows the profoundly devastating effects of childhood poverty not only on children, but also on their later health status as adults (Krieger 2006; Shaw et al. 2007), it is obvious that research on health inequities must reckon with huge socioeconomic disparities between U.S. racial/ethnic groups. Equally obvious, it is only through the use of racial/ethnic categories that it becomes possible to see the patterning of racial/ethnic socioeconomic inequities and their implications for racial/ethnic health inequities.

The second example concerns long-term trends in U.S. racial/ethnic and socioeconomic health inequities. Motivating our study (Krieger et al. 2008b) were articles in the current literature arguing that racial/ethnic and socioeconomic health disparities are, in effect, inevitable and likely to increase because the more educated and wealthier will always be most able to take advantage of the latest health knowledge and medical innovations (Phelan and Link 2005; Mechanic 2005; Cutler, Deaton, and Lleras-Muney 2006). But is this necessarily the case? Or might the magnitude of these health inequities be historically contingent and reflect, in part, societal priorities—and hence be amenable to social change?

To address this question, we decided to examine, empirically, long-term trends in socioeconomic inequities in U.S. premature mortality and infant death rates, overall and by race/ethnicity (Krieger 2008b). Prior to our study, research on this topic had been hampered by the absence of socioeconomic data in U.S. death and birth certificates until 1989 and 1968, respectively—and also because the public access version of the U.S. Compressed Mortality Files only goes back to 1968 (National Center for Health Statistics 2009a). Arguably, however, from a policy and public health perspective, the period directly preceding 1968 is crucial. Critical changes included the 1964 Civil Rights Act, the 1965 establishment of Medicare and Medicaid and the consequent desegregation of U.S. medical facilities, the accompanying expansion of community health centers and maternal and child health programs, and the many other federal policies comprising what was then called the "War on Poverty" (Davis and Schoen 1978; O'Connor 2001; Fairclough 2001; Quadagno and McDonald 2003; Almond, Chay, and Greenstone 2006; Lefkowitz 2007). These policies, intended to counter structural racism, could plausibly be conceptualized as societal determinants of health, whose embodied consequences would be manifest in trends in U.S. health inequities.

We accordingly sought out data to analyze rates of premature mortality and infant death among U.S. counties, ranked by income level, for the period 1960–2002, for both the total population and also stratified by what W. E. B. Du Bois (1904/2004) famously termed the U.S. "colorline," which divides the racially dominant U.S. white population and U.S. populations of color. We decided that this dichotomy—between whites and people of color—was the best way to handle the limitations of the available racial/ethnic mortality data that extended back to 1960, which used only the categories of white, black, and other. We chose age sixty-five as the cutoff point for premature mortality because this age determines eligibility for Social Security and Medicare and also because an average life expectancy of at least sixty-five years was consistently attained by U.S. black men only in 1995—compared to 1944 for the total U.S. and white population and 1973 for the black population overall (National Center for Health Statistics 2009b).

To create our study database, we extracted the 1968–2002 mortality data from the public-use U.S. Compressed Mortality Files, and then we also obtained U.S. county 1960–1967 mortality data, which additionally required manually locating and identifying the correct county code for each of the 3,073 counties. Denominators consisted of U.S. census decennial counts and intercensal estimates. With regard to socioeconomic data, because of the loss of the computerized 1960 census "100 percent detail" file, the economic measure we employed was county median family income, chosen because we were able to locate this for the 1960 as well as the 1970–2000 census. We assigned counties to quintiles of median family income weighted by county population size and then calculated, for each calendar year, each quintile's aggregated age-standardized premature mortality rate (deaths before age sixty-five, using the year 2000 standard million) and infant death rate (deaths among persons under age one).

We then tested our hypotheses about trends in the socioeconomic inequities in premature mortality and infant death in several ways, using measures of relative risk, absolute difference, changes in slope, and excess fraction of premature deaths. Our a priori hypothesis was that inflection points—that is, changes in the rate of decline (slope) of the premature mortality and infant death rates—would occur in 1965 and 1980, given major federal policy changes during the Kennedy/Johnson and Reagan administrations.

As we reported in our study findings, and as shown in tables 11.2a and 11.2b and figure 11.3, the key results were that between 1960 and 2002, in the United States overall, even as premature mortality (table 11.2a) and infant death (table 11.2b) rates declined in all county income quintiles, the gap between the lowest- and highest-income quintiles persisted and was relatively greatest for premature mortality in 2000, and barely changed for infant deaths. The greatest progress in reducing these income gaps occurred between 1965 and 1980; thereafter the health inequities widened. Lending further support to our a priori hypothesis, additional analyses showed that the average annual percentage change in premature mortality rates dropped to less than half that of the preceding period for all socioeconomic-racial/ethnic strata—except for the white population living in the two highest county income quintiles, whose rate of decline stayed the same or increased. The population impact of these trends is highlighted by our finding that between 1960 and 2000, 18 percent of premature deaths would have been averted had the populations in the bottom four quintiles experienced the same yearly, age-specific, premature mortality rates as the highest quintile. This excess fraction translates to an estimated 4.9 million lives cut short.

The overall picture, however, obscures stark racial/ethnic disparities within and across income quintiles. As additionally revealed by tables 11.2a and 11.2b, the steep decline in rates in the 1965–1980 period was especially notable in the populations of color, and especially in the two lowest income quintiles. The combined impact of class and color is further underscored by our results showing that between 1960 and 2002, had everyone experienced the same yearly age-specific mortality rates as whites in the highest-income county quintile, then 14 percent of white premature deaths, yet fully 30 percent of the premature deaths among populations of color, would have been averted.

At one level, our finding that risk of premature mortality increased with economic deprivation and racial inequality obviously is not new; research documenting these social facts easily extends back to the late eighteenth century (Rosen 1958/1993; Krieger 2000d). That said, what our results newly underscore is that contemporary U.S. inequities are not immutable: they shrunk considerably between 1965 and 1980, and increased or stagnated thereafter. The early trends give grounds for hope; the latter augur poorly for the Healthy People 2010 objective of eliminating U.S. socioeconomic and racial/ethnic health disparities.

Table 11.2a
U.S. premature mortality rates (death before age sixty-five) per one hundred thousand, 1960–2002

Race/ethnicity	Income quintile	Premature mortality rate by year (95% CI)					Average change in rate per year		
		1960	1970	1980	1990	2000	1960–1965	1966–1980	1981–2002
Total	Q1	377 (375, 380)	417 (414, 419)	335 (333, 337)	291 (289, 292)	268 (267, 270)	**12.6**	**-6.2**	**-3.0**
	Q2	426 (423, 428)	398 (396, 400)	310 (308, 312)	265 (263, 267)	224 (222, 225)	**3.0**	**-8.4**	**-4.0**
	Q3	404 (401, 406)	368 (365, 370)	284 (283, 286)	271 (270, 273)	225 (223, 226)	-0.7	**-7.6**	**-2.5**
	Q4	384 (381, 386)	371 (369, 373)	296 (294, 298)	252 (250, 253)	200 (199, 202)	**3.1**	**-6.2**	**-4.7**
	Q5	342 (340, 344)	311 (309, 313)	250 (249, 252)	204 (203, 206)	163 (162, 164)	-1.8	**-5.1**	**-4.3**
White	Q1	318 (316, 320)	367 (364, 369)	297 (295, 299)	261 (259, 263)	244 (243, 246)	**13.0**	**-4.9**	**-2.6**
	Q2	379 (376, 381)	356 (353, 358)	279 (277, 281)	239 (237, 241)	210 (208, 211)	**2.7**	**-7.3**	**-3.2**
	Q3	377 (375, 380)	341 (339, 344)	268 (266, 270)	239 (238, 241)	204 (203, 206)	-0.7	**-7.0**	**-2.8**
	Q4	366 (363, 368)	338 (336, 340)	271 (269, 273)	230 (228, 231)	182 (181, 184)	0.6	**-6.1**	**-4.4**
	Q5	322 (319, 324)	298 (296, 300)	241 (239, 243)	195 (194, 197)	157 (155, 158)	-1.3	**-4.4**	**-4.3**
Of color	Q1	672 (664, 680)	691 (683, 699)	518 (512, 524)	460 (454, 466)	371 (366, 375)	**15.9**	**-14.1**	**-6.3**
	Q2	774 (764, 784)	699 (690, 708)	530 (523, 538)	431 (425, 437)	298 (294, 303)	-0.3	**-15.6**	**-10.6**
	Q3	701 (689, 713)	637 (627, 647)	450 (442, 458)	441 (435, 447)	318 (314, 322)	0.3	**-15.6**	**-6.2**
	Q4	592 (581, 603)	611 (603, 620)	437 (431, 444)	360 (355, 365)	294 (289, 298)	**16.0**	**-13.8**	**-6.5**
	Q5	579 (568, 590)	476 (466, 487)	336 (329, 343)	262 (257, 267)	194 (191, 198)	-4.4	**-15.1**	**-6.3**

Note: Premature mortality rates were age-standardized to the year 2000 standard million. Changes in rate per year in boldface are statistically significant at the $p < 0.05$ level. Q1 = lowest county family income quintile; Q5 = highest county family income quintile.
Source: Krieger et al. (2008b).

Table 11.2b

U.S. infant death rates (per one thousand persons under age one), 1960–2002

Race/ethnicity	Income quintile	Premature mortality rate by year (95% CI)					Average change in rate per year		
		1960	1970	1980	1990	2000	1960–1965	1966–1980	1981–2002
Total	Q1	29 (29, 30)	26 (25, 26)	15 (15, 16)	10 (10, 11)	9 (8, 9)	**-0.2**	**-1.0**	**-0.3**
	Q2	30 (29, 30)	23 (23, 24)	14 (14, 15)	10 (10, 10)	7 (7, 8)	**-0.9**	**-0.9**	**-0.3**
	Q3	28 (27, 28)	21 (21, 21)	13 (13, 14)	10 (10, 11)	8 (7, 8)	**-1.1**	**-0.7**	**-0.2**
	Q4	26 (25, 26)	21 (21, 22)	14 (14, 15)	10 (10, 10)	7 (7, 8)	**-0.8**	**-0.6**	**-0.3**
	Q5	22 (22, 22)	17 (17, 17)	12 (11, 12)	8 (7, 8)	6 (5, 6)	**-0.9**	**-0.5**	**-0.3**
White	Q1	23 (23, 23)	22 (21, 22)	13 (12, 13)	9 (8, 9)	7 (7, 7)	**0.0**	**-0.8**	**-0.2**
	Q2	26 (25, 26)	20 (20, 21)	12 (12, 13)	8 (8, 9)	6 (6, 6)	**-0.7**	**-0.8**	**-0.2**
	Q3	25 (25, 26)	19 (19, 19)	12 (12, 12)	8 (8, 8)	6 (6, 6)	**-1.0**	**-0.7**	**-0.2**
	Q4	24 (24, 24)	19 (18, 19)	12 (12, 12)	8 (8, 8)	6 (6, 6)	**-1.0**	**-0.6**	**-0.3**
	Q5	20 (20, 20)	15 (15, 16)	10 (10, 11)	7 (6, 7)	5 (5, 5)	**-0.8**	**-0.4**	**-0.3**
Of color	Q1	49 (48, 50)	39 (38, 40)	24 (23, 25)	16 (16, 17)	13 (12, 13)	**-0.5**	**-1.6**	**-0.5**
	Q2	51 (50, 52)	37 (35, 38)	24 (23, 25)	17 (17, 18)	12 (12, 13)	**-2.3**	**-1.3**	**-0.5**
	Q3	45 (44, 47)	36 (35, 37)	23 (22, 24)	18 (17, 19)	12 (12, 13)	**-1.2**	**-1.2**	**-0.5**
	Q4	40 (39, 41)	36 (35, 37)	25 (24, 25)	16 (16, 17)	13 (12, 13)	**-0.3**	**-1.0**	**-0.5**
	Q5	40 (38, 41)	31 (30, 33)	19 (18, 20)	13 (12, 14)	9 (8, 9)	**-1.0**	**-1.2**	**-0.4**

Note: Changes in rate per year in boldface are statistically significant at the p < 0.05 level. Q1 = lowest county family income quintile; Q5 = highest county family income quintile.

Source: Krieger et al. (2008b).

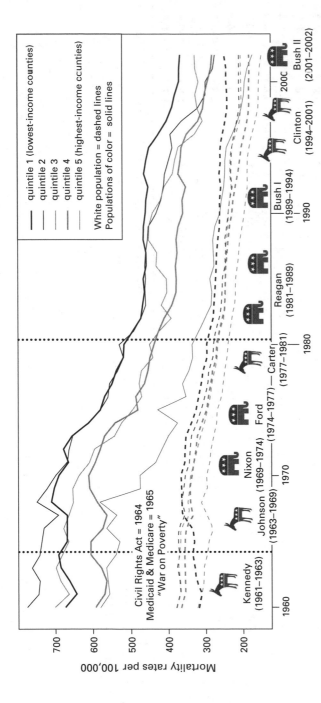

Figure 11.3

U.S. trends in racial/ethnic and socioeconomic inequities in premature mortality, 1960–2002: Data and interpretation.

Source: Krieger et al. (2008b; political events and symbols added).

In our published study, we exhaustively consider competing hypotheses that might explain our findings (Krieger et al. 2008b). Here, I summarize them, and I start by noting that the finding of a declining—then increasing—gap is unlikely to be an artifact of inaccurate numerator or denominator data. Since 1960, 99 percent of all U.S. deaths and births have been registered (Hetzel 1997). The U.S. census undercount (disproportionately affecting lower-income populations and populations of color) has declined considerably (e.g., for blacks, from 6.6% in 1960 to 2.8% in 2000), a trend that would increasingly reduce, not inflate, estimates of social disparities in mortality (Clark and Moul 2004). Results are also unlikely to be affected by racial/ethnic misclassification, given the broad groupings employed; rather, demographic trends should have lowered risk of premature mortality among U.S. populations of color, given the increase in foreign-born U.S. populations of color and their associated "healthy immigrant" effect, and the corresponding proportional decline in the U.S. African American population (from 92% of U.S. populations of color in 1960 to 72% in 2000; Singh and Siapush 2001; U.S. Bureau of the Census 2009b).

What, then, might explain the observed trends? First, the rising U.S. per capita gross domestic product (GDP) likely contributed to the overall decline in premature mortality rates (e.g., GDP grew by 32% during 1961–1970, 23% during 1970–1980, 25% during 1980–1990, and 22% during 1990–2000; Centre for the Study of Living Standards 2009). But this rising GDP cannot explain the observed pattern of a diminishment and then increase in the socioeconomic gradient. Nor can the observed trends be explained simply by relative positioning in a social hierarchy, a hypothesis some have proposed to explain social gradients in health (Phelan and Link 2005; Wilkinson 2005; Adler and Rehkopf 2008), because such an explanation would not account for either the overall falling rates of premature mortality or the shrinking and then widening of the gap. It is also unlikely that purely individual-level behavioral factors can explain the faster and then slower decline in premature mortality among persons in the lower income quintiles, unless an argument can be made that health promotion efforts in this group were more successful in the earlier, rather than later, time period, which is unlikely.

As an alternative explanation, the most plausible one involves two likely major societal determinants of health: economic priorities and civil rights (Krieger et al. 2008b). Likely contributing to the 1965–1980 improvements are the positive impact of the "War on Poverty" and the civil rights legislation that expanded economic opportunity and resources, and also availability of health services, for both the poor and populations of color, especially African Americans (Davis and Schoen 1978; O'Connor 2001; Fairclough 2001; Quadagno and McDonald 2003; Almond, Chay, and Greenstone 2006; Lefkowitz 2007). Conversely, the subsequent slowdown likely reflects the adverse impact of post-1980 neoliberal and neoconservative policies to roll back the welfare state (O'Connor 2001; Auerbach, Card, and Quigley 2006; Navarro

2007). Here, I mean cutting federal responsibility and funds for public health and antipoverty programs, opposing affirmative action, blocking rises in the minimum wage, and selectively decreasing taxes on the wealthy, coupled with rising medical uninsurance and persistent racial/ethnic disparities in quality of care (O'Connor 2001; Smedley, Stith, and Nelson 2003; Auerbach, Card, and Quigley 2006; Navarro 2007).

To summarize, our results refute the view that widening health disparities necessarily accompany improvements in population health. Death is inevitable; premature mortality is not. One potentially hopeful hypothesis accordingly prompted by our findings is that if addressing social injustice and its embodied health consequences becomes a priority, we can make progress. Another implication is that we need to understand not only how class inequalities harm health within each and every racial/ethnic group, but also how racial inequality harms health, including within and across class strata. As our data illustrate, the point is not race versus class—both matter, and we need data on both. The implication is that we need more than simply indirect studies to investigate how racism harms health: it is also necessary to consider the direct impact of racial discrimination on health, including within and across socioeconomic strata.

Direct Approach: Self-Reported Experiences of Racial Discrimination and Health

The next set of examples accordingly focuses on the inclusion of data on self-reported experiences of racial discrimination in public health research. I begin with a description of an instrument to measure exposure to racial discrimination and then discuss its application in two studies.

The Experiences of Discrimination (EOD) instrument (see table 11.3), which we validated (in both English and Spanish) in 2005 (Krieger et al. 2005b), is based on an instrument I first developed in 1990 (Krieger 1990; Krieger and Sidney 1996) and have used with slight modification since. It is among the two most widely used self-report measures in empirical studies on self-reported experiences of racial discrimination and health (Krieger 2000a; Paradies 2006). The approach of the EOD is to ask participants, explicitly, about whether they have "experienced discrimination, been prevented from doing something, or made to feel inferior in any of the following situations because of your race, ethnicity or color." The nine situations then listed each pertain to commonly identified domains in which people report having experienced racial discrimination, that is, involving education, work, housing, health care, public settings, and the police. Respondents who answer yes to any given item are then asked a follow-up question about frequency. Additional questions ask about response to unfair treatment. As shown in the validation study, which was conducted among a cohort of low-income workers in the greater Boston area, the EOD has a high Cronbach's alpha (0.8 or higher among black Americans and Latinos), high test-retest reliability (over 0.7), and no response item bias; moreover, confirmatory factor analysis indicated that there was an acceptable fit to the data for a single underlying factor (Krieger et al. 2005b). Also of note, we included several single-item measures of experiences of discrimination in the validation study, all of which we found had very low test-retest reliability (correlations of 0.4 or less), a result that cautions against using single-item questions about exposure to racial discrimination, as currently used, for example, in the U.S. Behavioral Risk Factor Surveillance Survey (National Center for Chronic Disease Prevention and Health Promotion 2009).

Relevant to the question, what's the use of race? in the validation study, all three racial/ethnic groups reported having experienced racial discrimination, albeit at different frequencies. Thus 38 percent and 24 percent of the black and Latino participants reported having experienced discrimination in three or more of the nine situations, versus only 12 percent of the white participants; a similar difference in magnitude was evident for the frequency score (Krieger et al. 2005b). Moreover, self-reports of racial discrimination were associated with the odds of having smoked cigarettes only among the black and Latino workers, but not among the white workers; self-reports also tended to be associated with the risk of being psychologically distressed among the black workers and, to a lesser extent, the Latino workers, but once again, not the white workers. These findings, along with the literature on "reverse discrimination"(Pincus 2003; Bonilla-Silva 2003; Crosby 2004), underscores a key problem with the suggestions offered by some researchers to "abandon" (Fullilove 1998) race as a variable in health research and to instead use only measures pertaining to racial discrimination (Fullilove 1998) or other social measures (e.g., socioeconomic position; Bhopal and Donaldson 1998; Stolley 1999): without data on race/ethnicity, it becomes impossible to offer meaningful interpretation of the self-report data on racial discrimination or to analyze if it is similarly or differentially associated with health status across all racial/ethnic groups. Thus, as increasingly recognized in the literature distinguishing between the use of race/ethnicity as a descriptive versus ascriptive category (Kaplan and Bennett 2003; Braun et al. 2007), studies that ask about self-reported experiences of discrimination for the purpose of testing causal hypotheses necessarily must also employ appropriate descriptive racial/ethnic categories.

Also important to note is evidence indicating that people with fewer resources tend to report less racial discrimination compared to those with more resources. In the case of the EOD, for example, self-reports of having ever experienced racial discrimination were notably higher, compared to self-reports by the low-income, working-class participants in the EOD validation study (Krieger et al. 2005b), in three investigations with more affluent populations: the proportion was nearly one and a half times higher in the CARDIA study (52%), a multicity, population-based, longitudinal investigation concerned with black-white differences in risk of cardiovascular disease (Krieger and Sidney 1996), and over two times higher (80%) in both a study of pregnant women with health insurance (Dominguez et al., 2009) and a Web-based study in which 60

Table 11.3

Experiences of Discrimination instrument

Measure	Question	Stem
English version		
Experience of discrimination	Introduction: "This next section is going to ask about how you and others like you are treated, and how you typically respond."	
Response to unfair treatment	If you feel you have been treated unfairly, do you usually: (please select the best response)	1. Accept it as a fact of life 2. Try to do something about it
	If you have been treated unfairly, do you usually: (please select the best response)	1. Talk to other people about it 2. Keep it to yourself
Discrimination	Have you ever experienced discrimination, been prevented from doing something, or been hassled or made to feel inferior in any of the following situations because of your race, ethnicity, or color? 1. At school? 2. Getting hired or getting a job? 3. At work? 4. Getting housing? 5. Getting medical care? 6. Getting service in a store or restaurant? 7. Getting credit, bank loans, or a mortgage? 8. On the street or in a public setting? 9. From the police or in the courts?	For each situation to which the participant replied yes (vs. no), the follow-up question was, How many times did this happen? 1. Once 2. Two or three times 3. Four or more times
Spanish version		
Experience of discrimination	Introduction: "En esta sección se le preguntará acerca de cómo usted, y otros como usted, son tratados, y cómo usted responde típicamente."	
Response to unfair treatment	En caso de sentir que ha sido tratado de manera injusta, usted normalmente: (por favor elija la mejor respuesta)	1. Lo toma como un hecho de su vida 2. Trata de hacer algo al respecto
	Si usted ha sido tratado injustamente, usted normalmente: (por favor elija la mejor respuesta)	1. Habla acerca de esto con otras personas 2. Se lo guarda para sí mismo

Table 11.3

(continued)

Measure	Question	Stem
Discrimination	¿Alguna vez ha experimentado discriminación, no se le ha permitido hacer algo, se le ha molestado o hecho sentir inferior en alguna de las siguientes situaciones debido a su raza, etnia o color? 1. ¿En la escuela? 2. ¿Al ser contratado u obtener un empleo? 3. ¿En el trabajo? 4. ¿Al obtener una casa? 5. ¿Al obtener asistencia médica? 6. ¿El requerir servicio en una tienda o restaurante? 7. ¿Al obtener crédito, préstamos bancarios o hipotecarios? 8. ¿En la calle, en un lugar público? 9. ¿De la policía o en las cortes?	For each situation to which the participant replied *sí* (vs. *no*), the follow-up question was, ¿Cuántas veces ocurrió esto? 1. Una vez 2. Dos o tres veces 3. Cuatro o más veces

Note: The Experiences of Discrimination instrument and instructions for its use are freely available online (http://www.hsph.harvard.edu/faculty/nancy-krieger/).

Source: Krieger et al. (2005b).

percent of the respondents had a bachelor's degree or higher (Krieger et al., in press). The positive association between socioeconomic resources and self-reports of racial discrimination is a robust finding (Krieger 2000a; Paradies 2006; Williams and Mohammed 2009). One possible explanation is that people with more power and resources may be more able and willing to identify experiences of racial discrimination (Krieger 1990; Krieger and Sidney 1996; Krieger 2000a; Blank, Dabady, and Citro 2004). An important implication is that research on racial discrimination cannot be concerned only about race/ethnicity, but must also take into account socioeconomic position.

Demonstrating that it does make a difference, empirically, to include data on self-reported experiences of racial discrimination in epidemiologic research are results of a CARDIA study on racial discrimination and risk of preterm delivery, in which I was a coinvestigator (Mustillo et al. 2004). Motivated by the unanswered question of what accounts for higher rates among U.S. black women, as compared to white women, of preterm delivery—a major determinant of low birth weight and infant mortality (Krieger et al. 1993; Schempf et al. 2007)—in this study, we sought to assess whether including data on self-reported experiences of racial discrimination, in addition to major known conventional risk factors, would affect the magnitude of the observed black-white disparities.

The study population consisted of 367 women who gave birth between the year 7 and year 10 CARDIA exams (Mustillo et al. 2004). From the year 7 exam, we obtained prospective data on self reported experiences of racial discrimination (using a prior version of the EOD), socioeconomic position, and other relevant baseline characteristics; from the year 10 exam, we obtained data on birth outcomes. The four key results were as follows (see table 11.4):

1. As shown in model 1, overall, the odds of black women having a preterm delivery were two and a half times higher as compared to white women.

2. When we additionally added data on self-reported experiences of racial discrimination, we found that the black excess risk was reduced to 1.7, and also that increased exposure to racial discrimination was associated with a twofold higher odds of risk of preterm delivery (model 2).

3. In analyses that controlled for other major risk factors for preterm delivery, such as income, education, smoking, alcohol, and depression (model 3), we found that adjusting for these risk factors somewhat reduced the initially observed black-white difference (model 1), but the odds of black women having a preterm delivery were still about two times more than compared to white women.

4. Last, when we additionally included the data on self-reported experiences of racial discrimination (model 4), we found that there was no longer any racial/ethnic difference in risk: the odds of black women and white women having a preterm delivery *were the same* (model 4). We also found that, as compared to women reporting no racial discrimination, the odds of having a preterm delivery were two times higher among women who reported experiencing moderate racial discrimination (in one or two situations) and three times higher among those reporting high exposure (in three or more situations).

Table 11.4

Self-reported experiences of racial discrimination and risk of preterm delivery: The CARDIA study (1992–1995)

Characteristic	Model: Odds ratio (95% CI)			
	1	2	3[a]	4[a]
Black vs. white	2.5 (1.3, 4.8)	1.7 (0.8, 3.5)	1.9 (0.8, 4.1)	1.1 (0.5, 2.4)
Racial discrimination				
1–2 vs. 0 domains		2.0 (0.9, 4.4)		2.0 (0.9, 4.5)
3+ vs. 0 domains		2.4 (1.0, 5.7)		3.0 (1.3, 7.3)

[a]Controlling for income, education, smoking, alcohol, and depression.

Note: Study population comprised 152 black and 200 white women who gave birth between the year 7 exam (1992) and the year 10 exam (1995).

Source: Mustillo et al. (2004).

Thus what our results showed—for the first time—was that experiences of racial discrimination not only predicted risk of preterm delivery, but also explained the excess black-white risk that the other conventional risk factors could not.

Prior to our investigation, however, most studies had included only conventional risk factors, like those we included in model 3, thereby concluding that the remaining unexplained black excess risk of premature delivery must be due to some innate biological difference between black and white women (Krieger et al. 1993; Giscombé and Lobel 2005). But we show that this interpretation is wrong because our study clearly demonstrated that by including information on experiences of racial discrimination, we could explain the observed black-white disparities. This is a very powerful finding— and it adds further evidence to the claim that the source of racial/ethnic disparities is the injustice in our society, not innate biology.

The last empirical example serves as a reminder that racial discrimination, however important it may be as a determinant of racial/ethnic health inequities, is not the only adverse type of social hazard to which people of color are exposed. Thus, drawing on the full cohort of 1,202 low-income employed workers that served as the population with which we validated the EOD, we found that participants reported not only racial discrimination, but also workplace abuse and sexual harassment (Krieger et al. 2006, 2008a). More specifically, among the black workers, the two most common combinations, together reported by over half the women and men, were, first, racial discrimination combined with workplace abuse, followed by all three types combined, with the latter most common among the black women. Among the Latino workers, a different set of combinations were the two most common, again reported by over half the women and men: first, racial discrimination plus workplace abuse, followed by workplace abuse alone. Last, among the white workers, the most common category by far was workplace abuse alone, reported by slightly over 40 percent of the women and men. Additional analyses showed that, in the case of sexual harassment, one additional social category was relevant: that of sexuality, with the lesbian, gay, bisexual, and transgender (LGBT) workers reporting twice as much sexual harassment as their heterosexual counterparts.

The net implication is that racial discrimination matters—and does not occur in isolation. This, too, is the point of the ecosocial construct of embodiment and its recognition that each and every day, our bodies daily integrate our experiences. Hence, to analyze the determinants of health inequities, including racial/ethnic health disparities, we have to remember that we are not one day a woman or a man, another day white or a person of color, another day working class or a professional, another day straight or LGBT, and still another day U.S. born or foreign born: we are all of these at once, with the implication being that our research must reckon with diverse, yet combined and embodied, aspects of social position (Krieger 1994, 2005b, 2006).

Conclusion: From "What's the Use of Race" to the Need for Research and Action on Racism and Health

As the arguments and examples of this chapter make clear, in the case of population health and racial/ethnic health inequities, the meaningful question becomes, what's the use of race in research on racism and health? This is because (1) racism and the social categories of race/ethnicity that it creates are socially real and (2) racism harms health, and does so differentially by race/ethnicity, thereby producing racial/ethnic health inequities. Consequently, to measure the impact of racism on health, we need to employ (1) appropriate racial/ethnic categories to distinguish its targets—and perpetrators—and (2) relevant measures of exposure to structural, institutional, and interpersonal racism. These same considerations pertain to research regarding the links between class and health, gender and health, and any other social construct implicated in health inequities: we need categories to identify the populations defined by these social relations, and we need data to quantify the relevant measures of exposure to adverse conditions. The corollary is that calls for being color-blind in data collection are not color neutral; rather, they are an expression of denial and bias about the seriousness of how racism harms individuals and societies.

One final question, then, ought be asked: what's the use of research on racism and health? The clear-cut answer is that this research is necessary to understand and provide evidence relevant to addressing racial/ethnic health inequities. Although scientific knowledge, like any knowledge, can by itself change nothing, when people organize to apply it, change can happen. The example I have provided regarding the shrinking of U.S. socioeconomic and racial/ethnic health inequities between the mid-1960s and 1980 is a case in point: descriptive and analytic knowledge about the existence of these inequities and their causes was critical to spurring and guiding action to rectify them.

Consider, too, the recent the Public Broadcasting Service series *Unnatural Causes . . . Is Inequality Making Us Sick?* (California Newsreel 2009), aired nationally in spring 2008 (and for which I served, by way of disclosure, as one of the scientific advisors and participants). The series's clear message is that racism and economic deprivation harm health and can be challenged and countered. Widely acclaimed, it was bestowed the prestigious 2009 Alfred I. duPont–Columbia University Award, broadcast journalism's equivalent of the Pulitzer Prize (California Newsreel 2009). Its power derived in part from its ability to link the findings of extant research about racism, economic deprivation, and health to individual stories that simultaneously illuminated and gave credence to the experiences of those now suffering the brunt of health inequities. The series likewise succeeded in breaking through the individualism so rampant in our society, by making clear that—in the old-fashioned language of the day—the personal is, in fact, political. By this I mean that the series revealed how people's health woes—including those involving racial/ethnic health inequities—are at once individual and societal: we experience them as the unique individuals we are, within a context of societally structured options and constraints. Already shown at over twelve thousand community and organizational meetings by the end of 2008 (California Newsreel 2009), the series is being used by health professionals and health advocates, nationally and locally, to educate the broader public and affected communities about how social injustice harms health—and what can be done to change this. As should be obvious, the series's insights, evidence, and recommendations for action are premised on meaningful use of data about race/ethnicity, racism, and health; without using categories of race/ethnicity, the series would not have been possible.

In conclusion, the use of "race"—that is, racial/ethnic categories—is essential for the science and epidemiology of racism and health. The rationale for this work is to generate knowledge that, if put into action, can inform current efforts to eliminate health inequities and improve population health. To do this work, it is not an option either to ignore categories of race/ethnicity or to analyze them without reference to their societal context and the impact of racism on health. Only by grappling with the paradox of using categories of race/ethnicity to vanquish racial injustice, rather than attempting to proscribe their use, do we stand a chance in furthering our goals of racial justice and social equity in health.

References

Adler, N. E., and D. H. Rehkopf. 2008. U.S. disparities in health: Descriptions, causes, and mechanisms. *Annual Review of Public Health* 29:235–252.

AFP. 2007. Science group condemns Nobel laureate's "racist" remarks. Google News, October 18, 2007. http://afp.google.com/article/ALeqM5hiTnxQI4Errj7nB1JqhN8cJOgajw.

Almond, D. V., K. Y. Chay, and M. Greenstone. 2006. Civil rights, the War on Poverty, and black-white convergence in infant mortality in the rural South and Mississippi. MIT Economics Working Paper 07–04, Massachusetts Institute of Technology. http://ssrn.com/abstract=961021.

Anderson, M. 1988. *The American census: A social history*. New Haven, CT: Yale University Press.

Auerbach, A. J., D. Card, and J. M. Quigley, eds. 2006. *Public policy and income distribution*. New York: Russell Sage Foundation.

BBC News. 2007. Lab suspends DNA pioneer Watson. http://news.bbc.co.uk/go/pr/fr/-/2/hi/science/nature/7052416.stm.

Bhopal, R., and L. Donaldson. 1998. White, European, Western, Caucasian, or what? Inappropriate labeling in research on race, ethnicity, and health. *American Journal of Public Health* 88:1303–1307.

Blank, R. M., M. Dabady, and C. F. Citro, eds. 2004. *Measuring racial discrimination: Panel on Methods for Assessing Discrimination, National Research Council*. Washington, DC: National Academies Press.

Bonilla-Silva, E. 2003. *Racism without racists: Color-blind racism and the persistence of racial inequality in the United States*. Lanham, MD: Rowman and Littlefield.

Braun, L., A. Fausto-Sterling, D. Fullwiley, E. M. Hammonds, A. Nelson, W. Quivers, S. M. Reverby, and A. E. Shields. 2007. Racial categories in medical practice: How useful are they? *PLoS Medicine* 4:e271.

Braveman, P., and S. Gruskin. 2003. Defining equity in health. *Journal of Epidemiology and Community Health* 57:254–258.

California Newsreel. 2009. Unnatural causes . . . is inequality making us sick? http://www .unnaturalcauses.org/.

Centre for the Study of Living Standards. 2009. Aggregate income and productivity trends, Canada vs United States. http://www.csls.ca/data/ipt2006.pdf.

Chase, A. 1977. *The legacy of Malthus: The social costs of the new scientific racism*. New York: Knopf.

Clark, J. R., and D. A. Moul. 2004. Census 2000 testing, experimentation, and evaluation program topic report no. 10, TR-10, coverage and improvement in census 2000 enumeration. Washington, DC: U.S. Bureau of the Census.

Coalition for an Informed California. 2003. Vote no on Prop 54. http://www.defeat54.org/ (accessed November 25, 2003).

Cohen, S., R. C. Kessler, and L. U. Gordon. 1995. *Measuring stress: A guide for health and social scientists*. Oxford: Oxford University Press.

Crosby, F. J. 2004. *Affirmative action is dead: Long live affirmative action*. New Haven, CT: Yale University Press.

Cutler, D., A. Deaton, and A. Lleras-Muney. 2006. The determinants of mortality. *Journal of Economic Perspectives* 20:97–120.

Davis, K., and C. Schoen. 1978. *Health and the war on poverty: A ten-year appraisal*. Washington, DC: The Brookings Institute.

Dominguez, T. P., E. F. Strong, N. Krieger, M. W. Gillman, and J. W. Rich-Edwards. 2009. Differences in the self-reported racism experiences of US-born and foreign-born black pregnant women. *Social Science and Medicine* 69:258–265.

Du Bois, W. E. B. 1904/2004. *The souls of black folk*. 100th Anniversary ed. Boulder, CO: Paradigm.

Ernst, W., and B. Harris, eds. 1999. *Race, science and medicine, 1700–1960*. London: Routledge.

Ewen, S., and E. Ewen. 2008. *Typecasting: On the arts and sciences of human inequality*. New York: Seven Stories Press.

Fairclough, A. 2001. *Better day coming: Blacks and equality, 1890–2000*. New York: Viking.

Feldman, M. W., R. C. Lewontin, and M. C. King. 2003. Race: A genetic melting-pot. *Nature* 424:374.

Fullilove, M. T. 1998. Comment: Abandoning "race" as a variable in public health research—an idea whose time has come. *American Journal of Public Health* 88:1297–1298.

Giscombé, C. L., and M. Lobel. 2005. Explaining disproportionately high rates of adverse birth outcomes among African Americans: The impact of stress, racism, and related factors in pregnancy. *Psychological Bulletin* 131:662–683.

Goodman, A. H. 2000. Why genes don't count (for racial differences in health). *American Journal of Public Health* 90:1699–1702.

Gould, S. J. 1996. *The mismeasure of man*. Rev. and exp. ed. New York: W. W. Norton.

Gumbel, A. 2007. Watson's words disowned by own institute. Los Angeles Times, October 19. http://www.independent.co.uk/news/science/watsons-words-disowned-by-own-institute-397259.html.

Hetzel, A. M. 1997. *History and organization of the vital statistics system*. Bethesda, MD: National Center for Health Statistics.

Kaplan, J. B., and T. Bennett. 2003. Use of race and ethnicity in biomedical publication. *Journal of the American Medical Association* 289:2709–2716.

Kington, R. S., and H. W. Nickens. 2001. Racial and ethnic differences in health: Recent trends, current patterns, future directions. In *America becoming: Racial trends and their consequences*, vol. 2, ed. N. J. Smelser, W. J. Wilson, and F. Mitchell. Washington, DC: National Academies Press, 253–310.

Kressin, N. R., N. L. Raymond, and M. Manze. 2008. Perceptions of race/ethnicity-based discrimination: A review of measures and evaluation of their usefulness for the health care setting. *Journal of Health Care for the Poor and Underserved* 19:697–730.

Krieger, N. 1990. Racial and gender discrimination: Risk factors for high blood pressure? *Social Science and Medicine* 30:1273–1281.

Krieger, N. 1992. The making of public health data: Paradigms, politics, and policy. *Journal of Public Health Policy* 13:412–427.

Krieger, N. 1994. Epidemiology and the web of causation: Has anyone seen the spider? *Social Science and Medicine* 39:887–903.

Krieger, N. 2000a. Discrimination and health. In *Social epidemiology*, ed. L. Berkman and I. Kawachi. Oxford: Oxford University Press, 36–75.

Krieger, N. 2000b. Counting accountably: Public health implications of new approaches to classifying race/ethnicity in the United States 2000 census—US and global perspectives. *American Journal of Public Health* 90:1687 1689.

Krieger, N. 2000c. Refiguring "race": Epidemiology, racialized biology, and biological expressions of race relations. *International Journal of Health Services* 30:211–216.

Krieger, N. 2000d. Epidemiology and social sciences: Towards a critical re-engagement in the 21st century. *Epidemiologic Reviews* 11:155–163.

Krieger, N. 2001. Theories for social epidemiology in the 21st century: An ecosocial perspective. *International Journal of Epidemiology* 30:668–677.

Krieger, N. 2003. Does racism harm health? Did child abuse exist before 1962?—On explicit questions, critical science, and current controversies: An ecosocial perspective. *American Journal of Public Health* 93:194–199.

Krieger, N. 2004a. Data, "race," and politics: A commentary on the epidemiologic significance of California's Proposition 54. *Journal of Epidemiology and Community Health* 58:632–633.

Krieger, N. 2004b. Ecosocial theory. In *Encyclopedia of health and behavior*, ed. N. Anderson. Thousand Oaks, CA: Sage, 292–294.

Krieger, N. 2005a. Stormy weather: "Race," gene expression, and the science of health disparities. *American Journal of Public Health* 95:2155–2160.

Krieger, N. 2005b. Embodiment: A conceptual glossary for epidemiology. *Journal of Epidemiology and Community Health* 59:350–355.

Krieger, N. 2006. Researching critical questions on social justice and public health: An ecosocial perspective. In *Social injustice and public health*, ed. B. S. Levy and V. W. Sidel. New York: Oxford University Press, 460–479.

Krieger, N. 2008. What's level got to do with it?—Proximal, distal, and the politics of causation. *American Journal of Public Health* 98:221–230.

Krieger, N., and M. Bassett. 1986. The health of black folk: Disease, class and ideology in science. *Monthly Review* 38:74–85.

Krieger, N., J. T. Chen, P. D. Waterman, C. Hartman, A. M. Stoddard, M. M. Quinn, G. Sorensen, and E. Barbeau. 2008a. The inverse hazard law: Blood pressure, sexual harassment, racial discrimination, workplace abuse and occupational exposures in the United for Health study of US low-income black, white, and Latino workers (greater Boston area, Massachusetts, United States, 2003–2004). *Social Science and Medicine* 67:1970–1981.

Krieger, N., J. T. Chen, P. D. Waterman, D. H. Rehkopf, and S. V. Subramanian. 2005a. Painting a truer picture of US socioeconomic and racial/ethnic health inequalities: The Public Health Disparities Geocoding Project. *American Journal of Public Health* 95:312–323.

Krieger, N., J. T. Chen, P. D. Waterman, D. H. Rehkopf, and S. V. Subramanian. 2003. Race/ethnicity, gender, and monitoring socioeconomic gradients in health: A comparison of area-based socioeconomic measures—the Public Health Disparities Geocoding Project. *American Journal of Public Health* 93:1655–1671.

Krieger, N., D. H. Rehkopf, J. T. Chen, P. D. Waterman, E. Marcelli, and M. Kennedy. 2008b. The fall and rise of US inequities in premature mortality: 1960–2002. *PLoS Medicine* 5:e46.

Krieger, N., D. L. Rowley, A. A. Herman, B. Avery, and M. T. Phillips. 1993. Racism, sexism, and social class: Implications for studies of health, disease, and well-being. *American Journal of Preventive Medicine* 9(Suppl):82–122.

Krieger, N., and S. Sidney. 1996. Racial discrimination and blood pressure: The CARDIA study of young black and white adults. *American Journal of Public Health* 86:1370–1378.

Krieger, N., K. Smith, D. Naishadham, C. Hartman, and E. M. Barbeau. 2005b. Experiences of discrimination: Validity and reliability of a self-report measure for population health research on racism and health. *Social Science and Medicine* 61:1576–1596.

Krieger, N., P. D. Waterman, C. Hartman, L. M. Bates, A. M. Stoddard, M. M. Quinn, G. Sorensen, and E. M. Barbeau. 2006. Social hazards on the job: Workplace abuse, sexual harassment, and racial discrimination—a study of black, Latino, and white low-income women and men workers (US). *International Journal of Health Services* 36:51–85.

Krieger, N., P. D. Waterman, J. T. Chen, D. H. Rehkopf, and S. V. Subramanian. 2004. The Public Health Disparities Geocoding Project monograph. http://www.hsph.harvard.edu/thegeocodingproject.

Krieger, N., D. Carney, P. D. Waterman, A. Kosheleva, M. Banaji. Forthcoming. A novel method for measuring racial discrimination for health research: combining implicit and explicit measures. *American Journal of Public Health*.

Krieger, N., D. Williams, and N. Moss. 1997. Measuring social class in US public health research: Concepts, methodologies and guidelines. *Annual Review of Public Health* 18:341–378.

Lefkowitz, B. 2007. *Community health centers: A movement and the people who made it happen.* Piscataway, NJ: Rutgers University Press.

Mays, V. M., S. D. Cochran, and N. W. Barnes. 2007. Race, race-based discrimination, and health outcomes among African Americans. *Annual Review of Psychology* 58:201–225.

Mays, V. M., N. A. Ponce, D. L. Washington, and S. D. Cochran. 2003. Classification of race and ethnicity: Implications for public health. *Annual Review of Public Health* 24:83–110.

Mechanic, D. 2005. Policy challenges in addressing racial disparities and improving population health. *Health Affairs* 24:335–338.

Milmo, C. 2007. Fury at DNA pioneer's theory: Africans are less intelligent than Westerners. The Independent, October 17. http://www.independent.co.uk/news/science/fury-at-dna-pioneers-theory-africans-are-less-intelligent-than-westerners-394898.html.

Mustillo, S. A., N. Krieger, E. P. Gunderson, S. Sidney, H. McCreath, and C. I. Kiefe. 2004. The association of self-reported experiences of racial discrimination with black/white differences in preterm delivery and low birth weight: The CARDIA study. *American Journal of Public Health* 94:2125–2131.

National Center for Chronic Disease Prevention and Health Promotion. 2009. Behavioral Risk Factor Surveillance System: Survey questions (Module 20: Reactions to race). http://www.cdc .gov/BRfss/questionnaires/pdf-ques/2009brfss.pdf.

National Center for Health Statistics. 2009a. Compressed mortality files. http://www.cdc.gov/ nchs/products/elec_prods/subject/mcompres.htm.

National Center for Health Statistics. 2009b. Life expectancy. http://www.cdc.gov/nchs/fastats/ lifexpec.htm.

Navarro, V., ed. 2007. *Neoliberalism, globalization, and inequalities: Consequences for health and quality of life*. Amityville, NY: Baywood.

Nobles, M. 2000. *Shades of citizenship: Race and the census in modern politics*. Stanford, CA: Stanford University Press.

O'Connor, A. 2001. *Poverty knowledge: Social science, social policy, and the poor in twentieth-century U.S. history*. Princeton, NJ: Princeton University Press.

Paradies, Y. 2006. A systematic review of empirical research on self-reported racism and health. *International Journal of Epidemiology* 35:888–901.

Parra, F. C., R. C. Amado, J. R. Lambertucci, J. Rocha, C. M. Antunes, and S. D. J. Pena. 2003. Color and genomic ancestry in Brazilians. *Proceedings of the National Academy of Sciences of the United States of America* 100:177–182.

Parra, E. J., R. A. Kittles, and M. D. Shriver. 2004. Implications of correlations between skin color and genetic ancestry for biomedical research. *Nature Genetics* 36(Suppl):54–60.

Phelan, J. C., and B. G. Link. 2005. Controlling disease and creating disparities: A fundamental cause perspective. *Journals of Gerontology, Series B*, 60:27–33.

Pincus, F. L. 2003. *Reverse discrimination: Dismantling the myth*. Boulder, CO: Lynne Rienner.

Quadagno, J., and S. McDonald. 2003. Racial segregation in southern hospitals: How Medicare "broke the back of segregated health services." In *The New Deal and beyond: Social welfare in the south since 1930*, ed. E. C. Green. Athens: University of Georgia Press, 120–137.

Racial Privacy Initiative. 2003. Proposition 54. http://www.racialprivacy.org/.

Rosen, G. 1958/1993. *A history of public health*. Exp. ed. Baltimore: Johns Hopkins University Press.

Schempf, A. H., A. M. Branum, S. L. Lukacs, and K. C. Schoendorf. 2007. The contribution of preterm birth to the black-white infant mortality gap, 1990 and 2000. *American Journal of Public Health* 97:1255–1260.

Schevitz, T. 2003. Prop. 54 defeated soundly—State initiative on racial privacy raised issues about health, education. San Francisco Chronicle, October 8. http://www.sfgate.com/cgi-bin/article .cgi?f=/c/a/2003/10/08/MN215579.DTL&hw=prop+54+soundly+defeated&sn=001&sc=1000.

Shaw, M., B. Galobardes, D. A. Lawlor, J. Lynch, B. Wheeler, and G. Davey Smith. 2007. *The handbook of inequality and socioeconomic position: Concepts and measures*. Bristol, UK: Policy Press.

Singh, G. K., and M. Siapush. 2001. All-cause and cause-specific mortality of immigrants and natives born in the United States. *American Journal of Public Health* 91:392–399.

Smedley, B. D., A. Y. Stith, and A. R. Nelson, eds. 2003. *Unequal treatment: Confronting racial and ethnic disparities in health care. Committee on Understanding and Eliminating Racial and Ethnic Disparities in Health Care, Board on Health Sciences Policy, Institute of Medicine*. Washington, DC: National Academies Press.

Stolley, P. D. 1999. Race in epidemiology. *International Journal of Health Services* 29:905–909.

Stone, A. A., J. S. Turkann, C. A. Bachrach, J. B. Jobe, H. S. Kurtzmann, and V. S. Cain, eds. 2000. *The science of self-report: Implications for research and practice*. Mahwah, NJ: Lawrence Erlbaum Associates.

UNICEF. 2005. *Child poverty in rich countries, 2005*. Innocenti Report Card 6. Florence, Italy: UNICEF Innocenti Research Centre.

U.S. Bureau of the Census. 2009a. Strength in numbers: Your guide to the 2000 redistricting data from the U.S. Census Bureau. http://www.census.gov/rdo/pdf/strenghth2.pdf.

U.S. Bureau of the Census. 2009b. US decennial census data: 1960–2000. http://www.census .gov/.

U.S. Bureau of the Census and U.S. Bureau of Labor Statistics. 2007. Current Population Survey (CSP) 2007 annual social and economic supplement. http://pubdb3.census.gov/macro/032007/pov/new01_000.htm.

U.S. Commission on Civil Rights. 1981. *The Voting Rights Act: Unfulfilled goals. A Report of the United States Commission on Civil Rights*. Washington, DC: U.S. Commission on Civil Rights.

Wilkinson, R. 2005. *The impact of inequality: How to make sick societies healthier*. New York: New Press.

Williams, D. R., and P. B. Jackson. 2005. Social sources of racial disparities in health. *Health Affairs* 24:325–334.

Williams, D. R., and S. A. Mohammed. 2009. Discrimination and racial disparities in health: Evidence and needed research. *Journal of Behavioral Medicine* 32:20–47.

Williams, D. R., J. W. Neighbors, and J. S. Jackson. 2003. Racial/ethnic discrimination and health: Findings from community studies. *American Journal of Public Health* 93:200–208.

Zerhouni, F. A. 2007. Statement by Elias A. Zerhouni, M.D., Director, NIH, regarding comments attributed to Dr. James Watson. http://www.nih.gov/about/director/10192007statement.htm.

Looking Forward

12 Race and the New Biocitizen

Dorothy Roberts

Amy Harmon of the *New York Times* won a 2008 Pulitzer Prize for a prominent series of articles called "The DNA Age," about the many ways genetic discoveries are influencing our lives. One of these articles, titled "Gene Map Becomes a Luxury Item," quoted a millionaire, saying, "I'd rather spend my money on my genome than a Bentley" (Harmon 2008a, F1). Sequencing your genome can be quite pricey. Knome, in Cambridge, Massachusetts, charged private clients $350,000 to read their entire genome and provide a face-to-face, customized analysis of what it tells about them. Scientists predict that, in the near future, they will be able to map everyone's personal genetic code at a more reasonable cost, allowing doctors to make more accurate predictions about our health and prescribe medications designed specifically to match each person's individual DNA profile.

In fact, several biotech companies already offer to genotype DNA sent to them by customers and provide personalized reports about their ancestry and risk for various conditions. Using the tag line "genetics just got personal," the Silicon Valley company 23andMe is an online service that sends customers an at-home kit to collect a saliva sample and, based on a genetic scan, gives them quantitative estimates of their risk for certain diseases and traits based on research that has found genetic associations. The company also uses genotyping to "compare your genetic information to that of people from around the globe."[1]

23andMe markets itself as a tool not only for gathering personal information, but also for creating social connections. Its Web site prominently displays "sharing and community" as a chief service, noting, "Seeing your own genetics is just the beginning of the 23andMe experience. Our features also give you the ability to share and compare yourself to family, friends and people around the world."[2] In September 2008, the *New York Times* style section carried a colorful splash about the celebrity "spit party," hosted by Barry Diller, Rupert Murdoch, and Harvey Weinstein, at which the glitterati spit into test tubes so their DNA could be analyzed (Salkin 2008). Cofounder of 23andMe Anne Wojcicki explained that the company helps people use their genomes as a platform for social networking: "If you want to have a community around psoriasis, we'd like to be able to allow you to form a psoriasis-specific community" (Salkin 2008, ST1). But her vision of this new citizenship based on DNA is even grander: "We envision a new type of community where people will come together around specific genotypes, and these artificial barriers of country and race will start to break down" (Weiss 2008, A1).

Sharing one's DNA is becoming a civic duty as well as a basis for civil engagement. In October 2008, Harvard genetics professor George Church launched the Personal Genome Project (PGP), which will build the only public DNA database that links genes to diseases, physical traits, and abilities (Harmon 2008b). In exchange for having their genomes inventoried, PGP participants agree to make it all public, along with personal information about their health, ancestries, and habits. Ten people, called the PGP-10, initially volunteered, and Church appealed to 99,990 more of his fellow citizens to join him in donating their genetic material as part of the new civic responsibility to aid scientists in their mission to advance personal genomics. "We're all at risk for everything to some extent," Church said, "and so we need to have a rich set of data and we need to be sharing that data until we get a much deeper understanding of what all the risk factors are, environmental and genetic" (Nakashima 2008, A1). A key component of 23andMe's services is similarly to put customers' genetic information in a database for research. As the company explains on its Web site, "Because we believe 23andMe's mission extends to the advancement of science, we intend to give you the opportunity to participate in research that could improve understanding of how genetics influences our lives."[3]

The expansion of genetic research and technologies has helped us cross a threshold into a new type of biopolitics concerned with our capacity to control and manipulate human life. As British sociologist Nicholas Rose (2007) has shown, so-called biological citizenship is grounded in the unprecedented authority wielded by individuals over their well-being at the molecular level. According to Rose (2007, 40), "our very biological life itself has entered the domain of decision and choice." Biological citizenship entails both individuals' autonomy over personal welfare and a biosociality that links people together around their common genetic traits (Rabinow 1996). Genetic information enables individuals not only to manage their own health, but also to unite with others around their common health conditions, as revealed by DNA testing. Rose (2007, 4) and others celebrate biocitizenship because it enhances human agency, as patients "become active and responsible consumers of medical services and products ranging from pharmaceuticals to reproductive technologies and genetic tests," and as they are empowered to form alliances with physicians, scientists, and clinicians to advocate for their interests (Franklin and Roberts 2006).

The relationship between citizenship and biology entails far more than organizing around shared health concerns. Genetics becomes the basis for political relationships that extend beyond the family and that include a broad range of ties among citizens and with the state. Genetics provides novel means for reinterpreting existing political identities and creating new ones, for forming communities, for participating in civic life, and for imposing civic duties.

We could describe the emerging category of biological citizenship without regard to race. Indeed, biological citizenship is supposed to transcend race. But I have been struck by the way race is fundamental to the new biocitizen. Race is treated as a key—even essential—classification in the genetic research and testing that informs biocitizens. Race is at the cutting edge of technologies that empower biocitizens. Race is integral to the public discourse about genetics that promotes biocitizenship. Why? Why is race, a category invented in premodern times, so central to the most modern scientific advances? What is the use of race in constructing the biocitizen and in promoting biocitizenship as the prevailing relationship among individuals, the market, and the state?

I want to take up Rose's (2007, 167) admonition to "locate the current debates over race and genomics firmly within the transformed biopolitics of the 21st century." But just as we cannot apply the same old sociocritiques or paste the same label of eugenics on contemporary biopolitics, nor can we uncritically assume that the new biocitizenship necessarily fosters individual life and choice and necessarily intervenes on the consequences of inequality, rather than legitimizing inequality.

By placing race at the foundation of biocitizenship, race appears more significant at the molecular level, precisely as it appears less significant in society. On one hand, scientists have recently claimed genetic confirmation of classical racial categories; pharmacogenomic researchers use race as a proxy for genetic difference in studies of disparities in health and drug response; and biotech companies market a variety of products that treat race as a biological grouping. On the other hand, the U.S. Supreme Court has affirmed a color-blind approach to social policy that rejects race consciousness as a tool for addressing inequality, while many pundits have declared the Obama presidency to be evidence of a postracial America. Scientists, politicians, and corporations are constructing biocitizenship in a way that not only obscures the continuing social significance of race, but helps to promote post–civil rights mechanisms for preserving the racial inequality.

The Expansion of Race-Based Biotechnology

The emergence of biocitizenship is occurring at the same time as we are witnessing a resurgence in scientific and commercial interest in genetic differences among "races." (Duster 2005). After World War II, the rejection of eugenics, which had supported sterilization laws and other destructive programs in the United States, generated a compelling critique of the biological basis of race. The classification of human beings into distinct biological races is a system of governance that arose out of European conquest, enslavement, and colonization of people in Africa and Asia. Biocitizenship did not really originate in the twenty-first century. Race has always been a form of biocitizenship: its function is to include or exclude residents from full citizenship according to their assignment to a political hierarchy based on invented biological demarcations and justifications.

Social scientists' conclusion that race is socially, politically, and legally constructed was confirmed by genomic studies of human variation, including the Human Genome Project. These studies showed high levels of genetic similarity within the human species. Genetic differences among human beings are "clinally distributed"—they appear gradually across geographic space; they do not fall into sharply demarcated groupings (Bolnick 2008, 72). On June 26, 2000, when President Bill Clinton unveiled the results of the Human Genome Project, he proclaimed that "human beings, regardless of race, are 99.9 percent the same." Most genetic variation occurs within populations, not between them. Some scholars believed that the science of human genetic diversity would replace race as the preeminent means of grouping people for scientific purposes.

In his manifesto against racial thinking, *Against Race*, sociologist Paul Gilroy (2000, 37) predicted that advances in genomic research would eventually discredit the idea of "specifically *racial* differences" by rendering race a useless way of classifying people. Similarly, Aravinda Chakravarti (2009, 380) wrote, in a recent issue of *Nature*, that "each of us has around 6.7 billion relatives. . . . The global picture of relatedness that is emerging from DNA studies stands to shatter many of our beliefs about ourselves." Chakravarti is hopeful that by shifting the focus of genomewide studies from populations to individuals, "we could test once and for all whether genetic race is a credible concept" (Chakravarti 2009, 381).

Reports of the demise of race as biological fact were premature. Attention quickly shifted from the 99.9 percent genetic similarity to the 0.1 percent genetic difference, and that difference was presumed to encompass race. One of the first sites for resuscitating race was also an important aspect of biological citizenship: personalized medicine. By prescribing therapeutics that match each individual's genetic predisposition to disease and response to drugs, scientists will enable people to manage and advocate for their own health more effectively. Key to the National Institutes of Health Pharmacogenetics Research Network, which studies how genes affect people's response to drugs, is the belief that "it is important to understand the 0.1 percent difference because it can help explain why one person is more susceptible to a disease or responds differently to a drug or an environmental factor than another person" (National Human Genome Resource Institute 2005). Some researchers see race as a critical first step to producing personalized medicine because it can serve as a proxy for individual genetic difference (Tate and Goldstein 2004).

The Raw Materials of Pharmacogenomic Research

In her ethnographic study of two biopharmaceutical labs, medical anthropologist Duana Fullwiley (2008) discovered that race served as an unquestioned organizing principle for the collection, analysis, and reporting of genetic data. During a six-month fieldwork stay at the University of California, San Francisco, Department of Biopharmaceutical Sciences, Fullwiley interviewed researchers investigating the pharmacogenetics of cell membrane transporters, molecules that are vital to drug delivery. The human genomic DNA that provided the raw material for their research entered the lab already classified by race. The researchers purchased DNA from the Coriell Institutes for Medical Research Cell Repository, which identified samples according to self-reported race. Unsatisfied, they also sought a grant to build a genetic database specifically for their project that collected more "racially pure" DNA by "excluding anyone who reported racial mixing in their genealogies for the past three generations" (Fullwiley 2008, 159).

The researchers not only assumed that African American and Caucasian DNA samples would have significantly different haplotype frequencies, but they also perceived each as the other's *"opposite* race" (Fullwiley 2008, 162). When researchers found results that were inconsistent with their perception of racial categorization, instead of rethinking their presumptions about racial sameness and difference, they usually reacted against the data. So when African American genetic frequencies were too similar to Caucasian ones, the scientist concluded that the racially labeled samples must have been contaminated. The organizing principle of race has marked the very raw materials that go into creating the new biocitizen and shape the scientific conclusions researchers draw from them.

Race at the Frontier of Personalized Medicine

The promise of personalized medicine, matching drugs to each individual's unique genome, hinges on race. Until pharmacogenomics can live up to this promise, race stands in as a surrogate for individual genetic variation. In June 2005, the Food and Drug Administration (FDA) approved the first race-based pharmaceutical, BiDil, to treat heart failure specifically in African American patients. BiDil was not designed only for black people. Jay Cohn, the University of Minnesota cardiologist who patented BiDil, combined two generic drugs that have been prescribed to patients regardless of race for decades and originally intended to market it to all suitable patients. Cohn and the biotech start-up firm Nitromed repackaged BiDil as a race-specific drug as a way to get marketing approval from the FDA and to extend the patent (Kahn 2004). What is more, the clinical trial that tested BiDil involved only African Americans. Because there was no comparison group, the researchers never showed that BiDil functions only or even better in black patients than in others. Yet the FDA permitted Nitromed to market BiDil as a drug for black people.

Why do heart patients need a race-specific therapy? One theory supporting this need is that the reason for higher mortality rates among black heart patients lies in their genetic difference, either in the reason for getting heart disease or the reason for responding differently to medications for it. In its March 2001 press releases, Nitromed explained that BiDil's efficacy stemmed from "a pathophysiology found primarily in black patients." "Observed racial disparities in mortality and therapeutic response rates in black patients may be due in part to ethnic differences in the underlying pathophysiology of heart failure," the company asserted (Kahn 2003, 474). The FDA similarly explained its decision to approve BiDil specifically for African American patients in a January 2007 article in *Annals of Internal Medicine*. "We hope that further research elucidates the genetic or other factors that predict the usefulness of hydralazine hydrochloride-isosorbide dinitrate [the ingredients in BiDil]," the authors wrote. "Until then, we are pleased that one defined group has access to a dramatically life-prolonging therapy" (Temple and Stockbridge 2007, 61).

In the past, the FDA has had no problem generalizing clinical trials involving white people to approve drugs for everyone. White bodies function like human bodies. But with BiDil, a clinical trial involving all African Americans could only serve as proof of how the drug works in blacks. By approving BiDil only for use in black patients, the FDA emphasized the supposed distinctive—and substandard—quality of black bodies (Bowser 2004).

BiDil is only one example of the growing trend toward what law professor Jonathan Kahn (2006, 1349) calls "the strategic use of race as a genetic category to obtain patent protection and drug approval." The emergence of race-based biomedicine means that the pharmaceutical and biotech industries see blacks and other racialized groups as profitable markets and test populations, as companies are searching for new money-making drugs and as the expansion of biotechnologies increases demand for human subjects and sources of human tissue. Race is a key channel through which scientists and corporations convert biomedical research into biocapital. In this way, powerful market forces help to construct the new biocitizen along racial lines.

Extending Reprogenetics to Women of Color

Genetic science is empowering biocitizens to manage and manipulate their own health through another form of personalized medicine. At the turn of the twenty-first century, advanced reproductive technologies that combine assisted conception with genetic selection, or *reprogenetics*, increasingly allow individuals to reduce genetic risk itself by determining some parts of their children's genetic makeup (Parens and Knowles 2007; Spar 2006). With preimplantation genetic diagnosis (PGD), clinicians can biopsy a single cell from an early embryo, diagnose it for the chance of having hundreds of genetic conditions, and select for implantation only those embryos at low risk of having these conditions. As Reprogenetics, LLC, a New Jersey–based genetics laboratory that specializes in PGD, puts it, this technique allows for the "replacement to the patient of those embryos classified by genetic diagnosis as normal."[4]

In my prior work, I used to place white, affluent women who had access to high-tech reproduction and women of color who were targets of population control policies at opposite ends of a reproductive hierarchy (Roberts 1997). But the recent expansion of both reproductive genetic screening and race-based biomedicine signals a dramatic change in the racial politics of reproductive technologies. First, the important role of genetic screening in the new biopolitics that gives individual citizens the responsibility for ensuring good health by reducing genetic risk may support the wider incorporation of certain reprogenetic technologies into the health care system. Second, companies that market race-based biotechnologies now promise to extend the benefits of genetic research to people of color, and reproductive technologies are no exception.

Media promoting genetic technologies prominently feature people of color in images representing the new genetic age, in contrast to prior portrayals, which emphasized whiteness as the exclusive standard of genetic fitness. Moreover, some clinics that offer high-tech reproductive services, including PGD, explicitly appeal to clients of color.[5] Women of color are now part of the market and cultural imaginary of the new reprogenetics. As with personalized medicine, race is an essential component of reprogenetics, as clients who buy and sell eggs are grouped according to race (Fogg-Davis 2001). The price of eggs is determined by a racial supply and demand system, and customer satisfaction hinges on racial results. A Dominican woman and her white husband sued a New York fertility clinic when their daughter came out too dark (Williams 2007).

Numerous advertisements on craigslist explicitly solicit egg donors of color. For example, a posting by Beverly Hills Egg Donation notes, "ALL ETHNICITIES WELCOME!"[6] F. Williams Donor Services's listing states, "Ethnic Diverse Egg Donors Needed," and includes a photo of an Asian, a white, and a black woman.[7] Happy Beginnings, LLC, advertises, "EGG DONORS WANTED ALL ETHNIC BACKGROUNDS," specifying, "WE HAVE A VERY HIGH DEMAND FOR JEWISH, EAST INDIAN, MIDDLE EASTERN, ASIAN, ITALIAN, AND BLONDE DONORS."[8] Similarly, Pacific Fertility Center boasts that it "maintains a diverse egg donor database including Jewish egg donors, Asian egg donors, and a variety of backgrounds and ethnicities."[9]

Although Reproductive Health Specialists, Ltd., in Illinois, displays a photograph of a large group of white couples holding white babies, captioned "Baby Picnic," its Web site contains a photograph of a smiling black man and woman and a drawing of a pregnant black woman attended to by a black male partner and a female physician.[10] Likewise, Houston IVF's Web site shows a beaming black couple holding a black baby.[11] The Illinois-based Karande and Associates, S.C., takes a very multicultural approach, using a photo of a pregnant East Asian woman for scheduling an appointment, a black woman and child for its link to donor egg information, and a South Asian man and child for the insurance information link.[12]

Some fertility clinic Web sites not only market their reprogenetic services to people of color; they also perform race-based genetic testing as part of those services. Pacific Fertility Center's Web site includes the statement, "Genetic screening is also recommended, based on ethnic background."[13] Reproductive Genetics Institute, in Chicago, similarly includes race in the factors it takes into account in its genetic testing: "Screening Results and Accuracy: By combining the results of the ultrasound and blood test along with the age, race and weight of the mother, a number can be generated by computer which represents the risk of the pregnancy being affected by Down syndrome or another chromosome problem."[14] Granted there are some rare genetic problems that are so highly concentrated in an ethnic group that is arguably defensible to segregate testing for these conditions, but most genetic mutations are not linked to race. This race-based testing reinforces the myth that races are genetically distinct from one another and that our genetic profile is determined by our race (chapter 9). It also reinforces the importance of race to the genetic technologies that empower biocitizens.

Genetic Ancestry Testing and Racialized Identity

African Americans have joined the growing ranks of Americans who use commercially available technologies to determine their ancestry and genealogy, one of the most popular hobbies in the United States. A cottage industry of online businesses employ techniques developed in forensic genetics and human genomic research to provide customers information about their genetic lineage. An increasing segment of this business is devoted to identifying not only genetic ancestry, but also *racial* identity. By submitting a sample of DNA and paying a fee, customers of these companies can trace their roots to particular racialized population groups (Nelson 2008).

AncestryByDNA, for example, promises to determine customers' genetic heritage by assigning percentages of ancestry from the "four anthropological groups": Native American, East Asian, sub-Saharan African, and European, described in contemporary terms as "anthropological lineages that extend back in time tens of thousands of years." Other companies attempt to restore the genealogical histories irreparably broken by the slave trade. African Ancestry, established by University of Chicago geneticist Rick Kittles, offers DNA testing to African Americans to trace their ancestry to more than 160 ethnic groups in Africa. Riding the popularity of his PBS specials, *African American Lives*, parts 1 and 2, and his book, *Finding Oprah's Roots*, Henry Louis Gates launched his own ancestry testing service, African DNA.

While the interest of many people in tracking their genetic lineage stems from curiosity about their *family* tree, African Americans are using genetic technologies to learn more about and to reconfigure their *group* identity. The companies that specialize in recovering black people's African roots cannot possibly identify customers' individual ancestors who lived in regions of Africa prior to their capture by slave traders; rather, these companies match black customers with groups of people living in Africa today based on their shared genetic traits. Ancestry testing will not reveal the identity of a black customer's great, great, great, great grandmother, but it may tell a black customer that "her mt-DNA traces to the current Mende people of Sierra Leone" (Nelson 2008, 254). Alondra Nelson (2008, 254) describes these genetic tools as "ethnic lineage instruments through which undifferentiated racial identity is translated into African ethnicity and kinship." Distinct from family-focused genealogical projects, these provide the sources for "constituting new forms of diasporic affiliation and identification" (Nelson 2008, 254).

Not only does ancestry testing help to fortify black Americans' identification with ethnic groups on the African continent; it is also a way to cement black community ties here in the United States, as it becomes incorporated into traditional black institutions and customs. For example, African Ancestry partnered with Mt. Ennon Baptist Church, a large Black church outside Washington, D.C., for a whole series of genetic events during the month of February 2008.[15] The pastor and his wife launched the program by revealing their ancestral roots during church service. Then "Where Are You From?" workshops were held during Bible study and in the chapel following each service during the month. The campaign culminated with a "Community Testing Day," when the entire congregation was offered ancestry testing at a special price and were provided a room to get their cheeks swabbed in the church building. The following Sunday, African Ancestry invited them to "receive your ancestry results and connect with your friends and family in a whole new way during the Church Anniversary Celebration."

For his part, Gates is developing an ancestry-based curriculum for public school children that centers on studying their own DNA: "My plan," he announced, "is to revolutionize the way we teach history and science to inner-city black and minority kids" (Horowitz 2007). Gates envisions a six-week unit focused on tracing students' ancestry that will be incorporated in history class. Students will initially collect family stories and records, but would turn to genetic testing when historical archives are exhausted. "We'll swab their cheeks, and this is where the science class comes in. We'll teach them how DNA works, how ancestry tracing is possible through the analysis of their DNA" (von Zastrow 2008). Gates sees students' fascination with their own genealogies as a hook for getting black children more involved in learning, to reverse their alarming high school dropout rates. He also relates the ancestry curriculum to blacks' citizenship: "I think that any time you get kids interested in the history of the country—in this case, through the history of themselves or their extended selves, their families—it is performing a civic function" (von Zastrow 2008).

Black Americans are at the cutting edge of using genetic technologies to map not only their individual genomes, but their biosociality—and their citizenship. This is not a separate citizenship that revolves around health issues, but rather, one that incorporates new genomic research into racial identities and everyday institutions. Nelson (2008, 258–259) emphasizes that blacks use ancestry testing as part of a cultural project that seeks to reconcile the destructive legacy of slavery; rather than base their identity solely on genetic data, they treat test results as a resource that they incorporate into a more complicated process of "affiliative self-fashioning." The role genetic gene-alogy plays in identity making depends on black people's desire to be affiliated with Africa and on cultural understandings of kinship. The work of constructing an identity rooted in African ethnicity starts with the "Certificate of Ancestry"; it is not deter-mined by it. Yet despite its extragenetic dimensions, treating genetic genealogy as the linchpin of identification and affiliation helps to reinforce the emerging understand-ing of citizenship rooted in biological sameness and difference.

There are also companies that market DNA testing specifically to Native American tribes to decide questions of enrollment (TallBear 2008). These companies use genetics either to trace an individual's recent ancestry to tribal members or to determine an individual's percentage of Native American "biogeographical ancestry." Kimberly TallBear (2008, 238) notes that DNA testing to confirm tribal membership reflects "a linear-descendency understanding of kinship and race that is focused on relationships between individuals," rather than on traditional notions of belonging based on social relationships with other tribal members. "The molecular knowledge produced by DNA tests does not account well for group kinship that is central to tribes," writes TallBear (2008, 238). Kinship is a social, legal, and cultural concept of relatedness that need not entail genetics at all; yet some ancestry testing companies reduce kinship exclu-sively to a genetic determination (Nash 2004).

Moreover, some ancestry testing services that claim to confirm unique Native American genetic patterns replace notions of community based on tribal relatedness with race as the source of Native American identity. These companies assume that there is a pure Native American biogeographical ancestry reflected in the genome and that genetic testing can therefore reveal whether someone is authentically Native American. Thus, these technologies promote a kind of racial identification that depends more on common genetic makeup than on common sociopolitical experiences and solidarity around the struggle against racial oppression.

The New Biopolitics of Race

As Steve Epstein (2007) chronicles in his book *Inclusion*, claims about justice in scien-tific research have shifted from protecting socially disadvantaged subjects from unethi-cal practices toward promoting access to clinical trials and biotech products. There is strong support for racial therapeutics among some black advocates, researchers, and physicians precisely to redress past discrimination and fulfill long-standing demands for science to attend to the health needs of African Americans.

Representative Donna Christian-Christensen of the Black Congressional Caucus advocated FDA approval for BiDil as a remedy for medical wrongs against African Americans, "for whom treatment has been denied and deferred for 400 years" (Reverby 2008, 479). While Keith Ferdinand (2008, 458), chief science officer of the Association of Black Cardiologists, concedes that "race lacks any true biologic definition," he calls BiDil a "life-saving drug" that addresses "evidence of racial and ethnic differences in cardiac care in the United States which may significantly affect health outcomes." Gary Puckrein (2006, W372), executive director of National Minority Health Month Foundation, similarly writes that "concern about the medical and scientific validity of the concept of race . . . is valid, but, under present circumstances, impractical." According to this view, the urgent crisis of African American heart disease must take precedence over political objections to the use of race as a biological category.

When I stated, at a Massachusetts Institute of Technology conference on race-based medicine, that not all black people thought it was good for us, Juan Cofield, president of the National Association for the Advancement of Colored People (NAACP) New England branch, stood up in the audience and emotionally castigated me for jeopardizing black lives by raising any criticism of the drug. He claimed that there was a consensus among African Americans because the NAACP, the Association of Black Cardiologists, and members of the Black Congressional Caucus supported BiDil. According to Cofield, I had no right to suggest that blacks are not united behind promoting racial therapeutics. Besides, why wouldn't we want to be the focus of technologies that are ushering in the new biocitizenship? Don't we want to stake our claim in this new biopolitics? These black advocates not only state a view of black interests that is tied to the racialized concept of biological citizenship, but also assert an exclusive authority to make claims about black citizenship.

As citizenship claims center on race at the molecular level, there is a corresponding retreat from race consciousness at the social level (Bonilla-Silva 2003). In June 2007, the U.S. Supreme Court did just that in its 5–4 decision striking down race-conscious plans to desegregate elementary schools in Seattle and Jefferson County, Kentucky.[16] The Court adopted the position that the Constitution requires the government to be color-blind by paying no explicit attention to race in policy making. As Chief Justice John Roberts concluded, "the way to stop discrimination on the basis of race is to stop discriminating on the basis of race." This is just a recent example of court decisions and ballot initiatives implementing a color-blind approach to social policy. So race consciousness is decreasing in government social policy at the very moment it is increasing in biomedicine and biotechnology.

In addition, conservative pundits like Jon Entine and Sally Satel of the American Enterprise Institute have developed an analysis of race and genetics that explicitly defends this trend. "We talk a lot about diversity in the United States, as long as we wink and smile that this diversity is not real, just superficial, a cultural patina," Entine

(2007) writes. "But in some aspects of our humanity, it is very real, and such differences can have huge consequences in everything from sports performance to success in the classroom." Thus, Entine views race as superficial and inconsequential in our culture, but real and significant in our genomes.

Similarly, Sally Satel (2002, sec.6, 56), author of the article "I Am a Racially Profiling Doctor," approves race consciousness in medical practice: "In practicing medicine, I am not color-blind. I always take account of my patient's race. So do many of my colleagues. . . . When it comes to practicing medicine, stereotyping often works. . . . It is evident that disease is not color-blind, and therefore doctors should not be either." She distinguishes, however, between the proper use of race as a biological category in medicine and the improper use of race as a social category in policy: "Social race is the phenomenon constructionists have in mind. . . . Biological race, however, is what BiDil's developers are concerned with—that is, race as ancestry" (Satel 2005).

In other words, racial differences are real at the molecular level, but merely constructed in society; so doctors and researchers cannot be color-blind, but social policy should be. Genetic race is scientific truth; social race is politically correct ideology. It is as wrong for medicine to ignore race as it would be for social institutions to consider it.

Duana Fullwiley (2008) found a similar dichotomy between the reality of genetic race and the fuzziness of social race in the minds of the scientists she studied. One postdoc defended the racial categories she used in the lab because she believed "there are ethnic specific SNPs." But then she conceded that she could not apply those categories to herself because her father was Indian and her mother was part Czechoslovakian. She concluded that she approached race in two extreme ways: "When I'm doing my genetic type research, I want things very well defined, and in a social setting I don't even want to think about it" (Fullwiley 2008, 165). This is a key aspect of the new biopolitics: citizens should attend to scientists' efforts to define, identify, and apply race in genetics, but we should stop thinking about race in society.

Biological citizenship reflects the shift of responsibility for public welfare from the state to the private realms of market and family (Harvey 2005). Selling genetic testing products directly to consumers is big business for private fertility clinics and biotechnology companies. Biomedical research and technology have correspondingly become major sources of capital accumulation, aided by federal patents on genetic information, FDA approval of pharmaceuticals, and public funding of lucrative private research ventures such as California's stem cell research initiative.

In this neoliberal context, genetic testing serves as a form of privatization that some interpret as empowering individuals to manage their own health but that also makes the individual the site of governance through the self-regulation of genetic risk. In addition to the deregulation that typically occurs in the service of big business, the new responsibilities imposed on individuals constitute a re-regulation that supports capital investment in market-based approaches to health care and other social needs, while state investment in public resources shrinks (Mykitiuk 2000). The view of biocitizenship as all choice and freedom ignores how state policies and corporate power make individuals responsible for managing their own health because of lack of public support.

Moreover, while biocitizens may join with business for increased access to genetic services, this new mode of activism sharply contrasts with social justice struggles aimed at overturning the structural inequities of race, sex, and class that numerous researchers have powerfully shown are mainly responsible for health disparities (Barr 2008; see also chap. 11 of this volume). In April 2008, Congress passed a law that bans discrimination by employers and health insurers on the basis of genetic tests: the Genetic Information Nondiscrimination Act, or GINA. Its Senate sponsor, Republican Olympia Snowe, calls it "the first civil rights act of the 21st century" (Pollack 2008, C1). A true reflection of neoliberal biocitizenship, GINA was backed by an alliance of drug companies, scientists, and patient groups that see the legislation as ushering in a new age of genetic medicine. As Edward Abrahams, the executive director of the Personalized Medicine Coalition, put it, "This bill removes a significant barrier to the advancement of personalized medicine"—people's fear that their genetic information would be used against them (Pollack 2008, C1). But though the law furthers the business of diagnosing genetic risk, it does not guarantee medical care for people who are sick or address the social determinants of health inequities.

At the same time that the government has reduced support for citizens' welfare, there has been a parallel increase in state intervention in poor people's lives. Over the last two decades, the welfare, prison, foster care, and deportation systems have clamped down on poor communities of color, increasing many families' experience of insecurity and surveillance (Collins, diLeonardo, and Williams 2008). In other words, economic insecurity is increasing among the most disadvantaged communities not only because of state inaction, but also because of policies that affirmatively sustain, replicate, and intensify systemic inequities. And these two trends—private remedies for systemic inequality and punitive state regulation of the most disadvantaged communities—are mutually reinforcing.

The contraction of the U.S. welfare state paralleled the astronomical expansion of prisons. The United States has the highest incarceration rate of any country in the world, and those confined in U.S. prisons are disproportionately black and brown (Liptak 2008; Davis 2003; The Sentencing Project 2005; Garland 2001). The sheer scale and acceleration of U.S. prison growth is unprecedented in the history of Western democracy. Most people sentenced to prison today are black. On any given day, nearly one-third of black men in their twenties are under the supervision of the criminal justice system—either behind bars, on probation, or on parole. Black men are seven times more likely than white men to be incarcerated (Wagner 2005). As a result, a black male child has a one in three chance of going to prison during his lifetime, and the likelihood is even higher in some cities. The *New York Times*, which tends to be so quick to see the importance of race to genetics, said only this about race in a recent front page story about the astronomical inmate count: "Many specialists dismissed race as an important distinguishing factor in the American prison rate" (Liptak 2008).

It is as if straining their eyes to see race at the molecular level blinds people to the continuing impact of race in society. More specifically, it seems to obscure the glaring contradiction of barbaric state practices and gaping social inequities that perpetuate the racial order in our advanced, liberal democracy. Nikolas Rose (2007) rejects critical intellectuals' use of eugenics rhetoric to contest preimplantation genetic diagnosis and other aspects of contemporary biological politics. He argues that eugenics practiced in the first half of the twentieth century was a particular biopolitical strategy that sought to improve the population as a whole through deliberate state action. This effort "to control the biological makeup of the population" as a whole, Rose (2007, 56) claims, distinguishes eugenics from the new biopolitics' concern with the genetic health of individuals. Rose (2007, 177) writes, "In advanced liberal democracies at least, the biopolitics of identity is very different from that which characterized eugenics . . . [because it involves] choice, enterprise, self-actualization, and prudence in relation to one's genetic makeup." I think the use of race in the new biopolitics is precisely that it allows many people to believe this fairy tale about liberal democracy in the United States.

Conclusion

Race is central to the way the new biocitizen is being constructed by the state, consumers, and business—a way that helps to promote the neoliberal move toward privatization as well as post–civil rights mechanisms for preserving the racial order. The prominence of race in the new biocitizenship supports neoliberalism by making racial inequities seem like molecular, rather than social, problems. As the state and market jointly offer individualized technological solutions for social inequities, race remains relevant to social policy even as citizens are admonished to be more color-blind. It is not that stark racial inequities in health, welfare, and opportunity no longer exist in this postracial America, but rather, their roots in racial bias and systemic inequality are obscured by an intensified attention to race at the molecular level. The pivotal role of race in creating biocitizens ensures that they will support the interests of bio-corporations and make no demands for social change.

We can also envision an alternative approach to race in the biopolitics of the twenty-first century. There is a tradition within black politics of skepticism about the claim of inerrant scientific progress in America, of basing our solidarity on common struggle and not common biology, and of using race as a political tactic to document and contest racism. Recognizing the relationship between neoliberalism and a new biopolitics of race creates the potential for alliances between antiracist; disability rights; and economic, reproductive, and environmental justice movements for social change. I see the new era of biocitizenship as a critical opportunity for people dedicated to social justice to intervene collectively in biopolitics—not just to gain greater access to products of biomedical research, but also to change the relationship between biotechnology and power to create a more humane world.

Notes

Support for this chapter was provided by an RWJF Investigator Award in Health Policy Research from the Robert Wood Johnson Foundation, Princeton, New Jersey, and by the Kirkland & Ellis Fund.

1. See the 23andMe Web site at https://www.23andme.com/health/all and https://www.23andme.com/ancestry/techniques.

2. See the 23andMe Web site at https://www.23andme.com/community/.

3. See the 23andMe Web site at https://www.23andme.com/about/values.

4. See the Reprogenetics Web site at http://reprogenetics.com/.

5. See the Pacific Fertility Center's appeal to prospective donors at http://www.donateyoureggs.com and information about egg donation at http://www.pacificfertilitycenter.com/treat/agency_donation.php.

6. See Beverly Hills Egg Donation, advertisement, Los Angeles craigslist, SF Valley, etcetera jobs, November 22, 2008.

7. See F. Williams Donor Services, advertisement, Inland Empire craigslist, etcetera jobs, November 24, 2008.

8. See Happy Beginnings, LLC, advertisement, Reno craigslist, etcetera jobs, November 13, 2008.

9. See the Pacific Fertility Center's appeal to prospective donors at http://www.donateyoureggs.com.

10. See the Reproductive Health Specialists Web site at http://ivfplus.com/baby_party.htm; http://ivfplus.com/treatments.htm; http://ivfplus.com/patients_only.htm.

11. See the Houston IVF Web site at http://www.houstonivf.net/houstonivf/OurServices/OurServices.asp.

12. For images from the Karande and Associates Web site, see http://www.karandeivf.com.

13. See the Pacific Fertility Center's Web site at http://www.pacificfertilitycenter.com/treat/agency_donation.php.

14. See the Reproductive Genetics Institute's Web page on first-trimester screening at http://www.reproductivegenetics.com/first_trimester.html.

15. African Ancestry advertised the "Community Testing Day" during February 2008 on its Web site at http://www.AfricanAncestry.com.

16. *Parents Involved in Community Schools v. Seattle School District No. 1*, 127 S. Ct. 2738 (2007).

References

Barr, Donald A. 2008. *Health disparities in the United States: Social class, race, ethnicity and health.* Baltimore: Johns Hopkins University Press.

Bolnick, Deborah A. 2008. Individual ancestry inference and the reification of race as a biological phenomenon. In *Revisiting race in a genomic age*, ed. Barbara A. Keonig, Sandra Soo-Jin Lee, and Sarah S. Richardson. Piscataway, NJ: Rutgers University Press, 70–85.

Bonilla-Silva, Eduardo. 2003. *Racism without racists: Color-blind racism and the persistence of racial inequality in the United States.* Lanham, MD: Rowman and Littlefield.

Bowser, Renee. 2004. Race as a proxy for drug response: The dangers and challenges of ethnic drugs. *De Paul Law Review* 53:1111–1126.

Chakravarti, Aravinda. 2009. Kinship: Race relations. *Nature* 457:380–381.

Collins, Jane, Micaela diLeonardo, and Brett Williams. 2008. *New landscapes of inequality.* Santa Fe, NM: School of American Research Press.

Davis, Angela Y. 2003. *Are prisons obsolete?* New York: Seven Stories Press.

Duster, Troy. 2005. Race and reification in science. *Science* 307:1050–1051.

Entine, Jon. 2007. 10 questions for Jon Entine, Gene Expression Web log. http://www.gnxp.com/blog/2007/10/10-questions-for-jon-entine.php.

Epstein, Steven. 2007. *Inclusion: The politics of difference in medical research.* Chicago: University of Chicago Press.

Ferdinand, Keith. 2008. Fixed-dose isosorbide dinitrate-hydralazine: Race-based cardiovascular medicine benefit or mirage? *Journal of Law, Medicine, and Ethics* 36:458–463.

Fogg-Davis, Hawley. 2001. Navigating race in the market for human gametes. *Hastings Center Report* 31:13–21.

Franklin, Sarah, and Celia Roberts. 2006. *Born and made: An ethnography of preimplantation genetic diagnosis.* Princeton, NJ: Princeton University Press.

Fullwiley, Duana. 2008. The molecularization of race: U.S. health institutions, pharmacogenetics practice, and public science after the genome. In *Revisiting race in a genomic age*, ed. Barbara A. Keonig, Sandra Soo-Jin Lee, and Sarah S. Richardson. Piscataway, NJ: Rutgers University Press, 149–171.

Garland, David. 2001. Introduction: The meaning of mass imprisonment. In *Mass imprisonment: Social causes and consequences*, ed. David Garland. Thousand Oaks, CA: Sage, 1–3.

Gilroy, Paul. 2000. *Against race: Imagining political culture beyond the color line*. Cambridge, MA: Harvard University Press.

Harmon, Amy. 2008a. Gene map becomes a luxury item. *New York Times*, March 4.

Harmon, Amy. 2008b. Taking a peek at the experts' genetic secrets. *New York Times*, October 19.

Harvey, David. 2005. *A brief history of neoliberalism*. New York: Oxford University Press.

Horowitz, Mark. 2007. The 2007 Rave Awards: Henry Louis Gates Jr./ancestry-based curriculum. http://www.wired.com/culture/lifestyle/multimedia/2007/04/ss_raves?slide=3.

Kahn, Jonathan. 2003. Getting the numbers right: Statistical mischief and racial profiling in heart failure research. *Perspectives in Biology and Medicine* 46:473-483.

Kahn, Jonathan. 2004. How a drug becomes "ethnic": Law, commerce, and the production of racial categories in medicine. *Yale Journal of Health Policy, Law, and Ethics* 4:1–46.

Kahn, Jonathan. 2006. Patenting race. *Nature Biotechnology* 24:1349-1351.

Liptak, Adam. 2008. Inmate count in U.S. dwarfs other nations. *New York Times*, April 23.

Mykitiuk, Roxanne. 2000. The new genetics in the post-Keynesian state. Unpublished paper. http://www.cwhn.ca/groups/biotech/availdocs/15-mykitiuk.pdf.

Nakashima, Ellen. 2008. Genome database will link genes, traits in public view. *Washington Post*, October 18.

Nash, Catherine. 2004. Genetic kinship. *Cultural Studies* 18:1–33.

National Human Genome Resource Institute. 2005. International consortium completes map of human genetic variation. National Institutes of Health News. October. http://www/genome.gov/17015412.

Nelson, Alondra. 2008. The factness of diaspora: The social sources of genetic genealogy. In *Revisiting race in a genomic age*, ed. Barbara A. Keonig, Sandra Soo-Jin Lee, and Sarah S. Richardson. Piscataway, NJ: Rutgers University Press, 253–268.

Parens, Erik, and Lori P. Knowles. 2007. Reprogenetics and public policy: reflections and recommendations. In *Reprogenetics: Law, policy, and ethical issues*, ed. Lori P. Knowles and Gregory E. Kaebnick. Baltimore: Johns Hopkins University Press, 253–294.

Pollack, Andrew. 2008. Congress near deal on genetic test bias bill. *New York Times*, April 23.

Puckrein, Gary. 2006. BiDil: From another vantage point. *Health Affairs* 25:w368–w374.

Rabinow, Paul. 1996. *Essays on the anthropology of reason*. Princeton, NJ: Princeton University Press.

Reverby, Susan. 2008. "Special treatment": BiDil, Tuskegee, and the logic of race. *Journal of Law, Medicine, and Ethics* 36:478–484.

Roberts, Dorothy. 1997. *Killing the black body: Race, reproduction and the meaning of liberty*. New York: Pantheon.

Rose, Nikolas. 2007. *The politics of life itself: Biomedicine, power, and subjectivity in the twenty-first century*. Princeton, NJ: Princeton University Press.

Salkin, Allen. 2008. When in doubt, spit it out. *New York Times*, September 12.

Satel, Sally. 2002. I am a racially profiling doctor. *New York Times*, May 5.

Satel, Sally. 2005. Race and medicine can mix without prejudice: How the story of BiDil illuminates the future of medicine. http://www.medicalprogresstoday.com/spotlight/spotlight _indarchive.php?id=449.

Spar, Debora L. 2006. *The baby business: How money, science and politics drive the commerce of conception*. Boston: Harvard Business School Press.

TallBear, Kimberly. 2008. Native-American-DNA.com: In search of Native American race and tribe. In *Revisiting race in a genomic age*, ed. Barbara A. Keonig, Sandra Soo-Jin Lee, and Sarah S. Richardson. Piscataway, NJ: Rutgers University Press, 235–252.

Tate, Sarah K., and David B. Goldstein. 2004. Will tomorrow's medicines work for everyone? *Nature Genetics* 36:S34–S42.

Temple, Robert, and Norman L. Stockbridge. 2007. BiDil for heart failure in black patients: The U.S. Food and Drug Administration perspective. *Annals of Internal Medicine* 146:57–62.

Von Zastrow, Claus. 2008. Mounting a curricular revolution: An interview with Henry Louis Gates, Jr. Public School Insights Weblog. http://www.publicschoolinsights.org/node/2144.

Wagner, Peter. 2005. Incarceration is not an equal opportunity punishment. Prison Policy Initiative. http://www.prisonpolicy.org/articles/notequal.html.

Weiss, Rick. 2008. Genetic testing gets personal. *Washington Post*, March 25.

Williams, Patricia J. 2007. Colorstruck. *The Nation*, April 23.

About the Contributors

Richard Ashcroft is professor of bioethics in the School of Law at Queen Mary, University of London. His research interests include social and ethical issues in public health and the evaluation of new medical technologies. He is editor in chief of *Principles of Health Care Ethics* (second edition; Wiley, 2007) and coeditor of *Case Analysis in Clinical Ethics* (Cambridge University Press, 2005).

Richard S. Cooper is Anthony B. Traub Professor and chairman of the Department of Preventive Medicine and Epidemiology at Loyola University Stritch School of Medicine, Chicago. He is a cardiovascular epidemiologist with a long-term interest in hypertension and related conditions in populations of African origin. He has active research interests in the significance of molecular genetics for variation in common disease among racial groups and the clinical significance of genetics for medical decision making based on race.

Kjell A. Doksum is professor in the Department of Statistics at the University of Wisconsin, Madison. He is a fellow of the Institute of Mathematical Statistics and of the American Statistical Association. He is joint author, with Peter Bickel, of *Mathematical Statistics: Basic Ideas and Selected Topics* (second edition; Pearson Prentice Hall, 2007).

George T. H. Ellison is professor of interdisciplinary studies and director of the Research & Graduate School at London Metropolitan University. His research spans medical anthropology, social epidemiology, and evidence-based policy and practice. He is coeditor, with Cathy Campbell and Melissa Parker, of *Learning from HIV and AIDS* (Cambridge University Press, 2002) and, with Alan Goodman, of *The Nature of Difference: Science, Society, and Human Biology* (Taylor and Francis, 2006). His Web site can be viewed at http://www.gthellison.info/.

Steven Epstein is the John C. Shaffer Professor in the Humanities and professor of sociology at Northwestern University, Evanston, Illinois. His book *Impure Science: AIDS, Activism, and the Politics of Knowledge* (University of California Press, 1996) won awards from three professional societies. His more recent book, *Inclusion: The Politics of Difference in Medical Research* (University of Chicago Press, 2007), has also received multiple awards, including the American Sociological Association's Distinguished Book Award and the Ludwig Fleck Prize from the Society for Social Studies of Science.

Joan H. Fujimura is professor of sociology and founding director of the Holtz Center for Science and Technology Studies at the University of Wisconsin, Madison. Fujimura's recent publications include "Postgenomic Futures," *New Genetics and Society* 24, no. 2 (2005); "Sex Genes," *Signs* 32, no. 1 (2006); "The Science and Business of Genetic Ancestry Testing," *Science* 318 (October 19, 2007) (coauthored); a special issue on race, genomics, and medicine in *Social Studies of Science* 38, no. 5 (2008) (coauthored); and "Calculating Life," *EMBO Reports* 10, special issue (2009) (coauthored).

Amy Hinterberger is a doctoral candidate in the Department of Sociology and the BIOS Centre for the Study of Bioscience, Biomedicine, Biotechnology, and Society at the London School of Economics. Her doctoral research addresses the intersections between new technologies and categories of race and ethnicity, along with other articulations of difference.

Angela C. Jenks is a medical anthropologist and anthropology instructor at Los Angeles Southwest College. Her research examines the ways in which concerns over health disparities, racial and ethnic demographic shifts, and the need for cultural competency affect health institutions and medical care in the United States.

David S. Jones is associate professor of the history and culture of science and technology, in the Program in Science, Technology, and Society, at the Massachusetts Institute of Technology, Cambridge, where he also directed the Center for the Study of Diversity in Science, Technology, and Medicine. His past research explored health inequalities, focusing on epidemics of American Indians. This was published as *Rationalizing Epidemics: Meanings and Uses of American Indian Mortality since 1600* (Harvard University Press, 2004). He is now working on two projects: a history of pharmacogenetics and racial therapeutics and a history of cardiac revascularization. In addition, he teaches social medicine and global health at Harvard Medical School.

Jonathan Kahn is professor of law at Hamline University School of Law, St. Paul, Minnesota. He is the author of numerous articles on law, genetics, and identity, including "How a Drug Becomes 'Ethnic': Law, Commerce, and the Production of Racial Categories in Medicine," *Yale Journal of Health Policy, Law, and Ethics* 4, no. 1, and "Race-ing Patents/Patenting Race: An Emerging Political Geography of Intellectual Property in Biotechnology," *Iowa Law Review* 92, no. 2 (2007).

Jay S. Kaufman is an associate professor of epidemiology at the Department of Epidemiology, Biostatistics, and Occupational Health, McGill University, Montreal, Quebec, Canada. His research examines the use of race in clinical decision making, the epidemiology of reproductive health, and the relation between social factors and health.

Nancy Krieger is a social epidemiologist and professor of society, human development, and health at the Harvard School of Public Health, Boston. Her work focuses on three aspects of social inequalities in health: (1) etiologic studies on the determinants of health inequities, including the impact of racism on health; (2) methods for improving the monitoring of social inequalities in health; and (3) development of theoretical frameworks, including ecosocial theory, to guide work on understanding and addressing health inequities, as informed by analysis of the history and politics of epidemiology and public health.

Paul Martin is reader in science and technology studies and deputy director of the Institute for Science and Society at the University of Nottingham, United Kingdom. His research interests cover innovation in the biotechnology industry, the social and ethical issues raised by genetics, and the regulation of new medical technologies. He is principal investigator on a Wellcome Trust–funded project titled "The Use of Race/Ethnicity in Applied Population Genetics Research."

Pilar N. Ossorio is associate professor of law and bioethics at the University of Wisconsin, Madison. She has published widely in genetics and bioethics, particularly on issues pertaining to race. She is a member of numerous federal advisory committees that address questions of science policy.

Simon M. Outram was recently awarded a two-year postdoctoral fellowship in neuroethics at Dalhousie University in Halifax, Nova Scotia, Canada. This follows a successful British Council–funded postdoctoral fellowship at the Open University's Centre for Social and Economic Research on Innovation in Genomics (Innogen), in which he explored the intersection between biotechnology, social science, and the media in sub-Saharan Africa. He holds master's degrees in social anthropology and environmental epidemiology and received his doctoral degree in 2007 from St. George's, University of London, for a thesis exploring the use of racial and ethnic categories in genetics and biomedical research.

Ramya Rajagopalan is currently postdoctoral research associate at the Department of Sociology and the Holtz Center for Science and Technology Studies at the University of Wisconsin, Madison. Rajagopalan received her doctoral degree in genomics and molecular biology from the Massachusetts Institute of Technology in 2007. She has coauthored (with editors Joan H. Fujimura and Troy Duster) the introduction to a special issue on race, genomics, and medicine in *Social Studies of Science* 38, no. 5 (2008).

Dorothy Roberts is the Kirkland & Ellis Professor at Northwestern University School of Law, Chicago, with joint appointments in the departments of African American Studies and Sociology (courtesy), and a faculty fellow of the Institute for Policy Research. She is the author of the award-winning *Killing the Black Body: Race, Reproduc-*

tion, and the Meaning of Liberty (Pantheon Books, 1997) and *Shattered Bonds: The Color of Child Welfare* (Basic Books, 2002) as well as the coauthor of casebooks on constitutional law and women and the law. She has published more than seventy articles and essays in books and scholarly journals, including *Harvard Law Review*, *Yale Law Journal*, and *Stanford Law Review*. Her current book project is on the politics of race-based biotechnologies.

Pamela Sankar is associate professor of bioethics in the Department of Medical Ethics and a fellow at the Center for Bioethics at the University of Pennsylvania, Philadelphia. Her current research project, "Beyond Stigma: Interpreting Genetic Difference," examines the relationship between genetic conditions, racial and ethnic identities, and stigma.

Andrew Smart is senior lecturer in sociology at Bath Spa University, United Kingdom. His research is focused on the impacts of genetic science and technologies in health care, in particular, the challenges faced by practitioners, patients, and policy makers. He has published work in journals including *Sociology of Health and Illness*, *Bioethics*, *Critical Public Health*, *Biosocieties*, and the *International Journal for Quality in Health Care*.

Richard Tutton is senior lecturer at the Centre for Economic and Social Aspects of Genomics (Cesagen) at Lancaster University, United Kingdom. His research interests are in the sociotechnical issues of biobanking for biomedical research and the implications of developments in science, technology, and medicine for cultural and social identities. He edited (with Oonagh Corrigan) *Genetic Databases: Socio-ethical Issues in the Collection and Use of DNA* (Routledge, 2004).

Ian Whitmarsh is assistant professor of anthropology at the University of California, San Francisco. His research explores tensions in the uses of biomedical categories linking race and disease among researchers, medical practitioners, government officials, and patients. He is the author of *Biomedical Ambiguity: Race, Asthma, and the Contested Meaning of Genetic Research in the Caribbean* (Cornell University Press, 2008).

Index